THE

AFRICAN FOOD SYSTEM AND

ITS INTERACTION

WITH

HUMAN HEALTH AND NUTRITION

~~~~~~~

THE

AFRICAN FOOD SYSTEM AND

ITS INTERACTION

WITH

HUMAN HEALTH AND NUTRITION

edited by

PER PINSTRUP-ANDERSEN

PUBLISHED IN COOPERATION

WITH THE

UNITED NATIONS UNIVERSITY

CORNELL UNIVERSITY PRESS   ITHACA AND LONDON

First published 2010 by Cornell University Press in cooperation
with the United Nations University
Printed in the United States of America

Library of Congress Cataloging-in-Publication Data

The African food system and its interaction with human health and
nutrition / edited by Per Pinstrup-Andersen.
          p.   cm.
"Published in cooperation with the United Nations University."
Includes bibliographical references.
ISBN 978-0-8014-7692-1 (pbk. : alk. paper)
1. Food supply—Africa, Sub-Saharan. 2. Nutrition—Africa,
Sub-Saharan. 3. Agricultural systems—Health aspects—Africa,
Sub-Saharan. 4. Food industry and trade—Health aspects—Africa,
Sub-Saharan. 5. Food security—Africa, Sub-Saharan. 6. Public
Health—Africa, Sub-Saharan. I. Pinstrup-Andersen, Per.
II. United Nations University. HD9017.A3572A35 2010
338.1´967—dc22   2010033393

CONTENTS

~~~~~~~

FIGURES

~~~~~~

TABLES

~~~~~~~~

FOREWORD

~~~~~~~~~~

This volume is the first in a planned series focused on the continent of Africa. The intent of the Africa Series is to bring together leading scholars from Africa and around the globe to deepen our understanding and provide new insights into the gaps in knowledge and policy that hinder the progress of Sub-Saharan governments in achieving the Millennium Development Goals. The series also aims to inform the development and implementation of future policies and practices in the region and provide a forum for sharing best practices in the unique African context. This effort brings together two academic institutions, the United Nations University and Cornell University, which share a commitment to global scholarship focused on poverty alleviation and to global public engagement focused on enhancing the capacity of people, governments, and institutions.

It is both appropriate and timely that this inaugural volume focuses on the interactions and causal relationships among agriculture, health, and nutrition. Advances in the health sciences, including genomics and stem cell biology, continue to reinforce the principle that nutritious food is essential for the achievement of full physical and cognitive potential for all individuals and populations and for sustaining health through the aging process. Likewise, advances in the social and behavioral sciences are revealing the many dimensions of health, the behaviors that promote health, and the value of health in the development of agricultural systems and the many capacities required for sustainable development. Health is now considered a primary goal and quantifiable endpoint of food systems. It is also an emerging force in agricultural policy, driven in part by the emergence of the "double burden" of malnutrition that has resulted in part from a lack of harmony between food systems and the promotion of human health. As this volume emphasizes, improving food quality in ways that support human health will require an integrated approach that encompasses both the agriculture and health sectors and will open new avenues of agriculture research. It will require coordinated efforts in the study of soil quality, plant varieties, crop and food engineering, food safety, climate change, agricultural economics, plant and animal health, and food processing, among others. And because such an approach will require more diversity in the types of crops grown, with implications for all aspects of farming, it will raise new challenges for efforts to achieve sustainable agriculture. Harmonizing food systems and human health in Sub-Saharan Africa would represent a remarkable achievement, especially considering the imbalance between natural resources and human resources that has persisted for generations.

Many individuals share responsibility for the success of this volume and the related symposia held in Ithaca, New York, and at the United Nations in New York City. I am grateful for the individual contributions by the authors and symposium speakers, each internationally renowned in his or her area of expertise. The organization and content of the volume directly reflect the inspiration and vision of Per Pinstrup-Andersen, and I am grateful for his tireless commitment to this project. The Africa Series was conceived by Jean-Marc Coicaud of the United Nations University, New York, who has played an essential role in developing this project. I thank Muna Ndulo and the Institute for African Development for planning and organizing the Ithaca symposium. The funding for this volume and the symposia was generously provided by the United Nations Children's Fund (UNICEF), the United Nations University, and Cornell University through the Division of Nutritional Sciences, the University Lectures Committee, the Einaudi Center, and the Institute for African Development. I would also like to extend my appreciation to the devoted staff of the United Nations University, including Sara Shapiro of the Food and Nutrition Programme and Jin Zhang in the New York City office.

Patrick J. Stover

Director, Division of Nutritional Sciences, Cornell University
Director, United Nations University Food and Nutrition Programme
for Human and Social Development

PREFACE

~~~~~~~~

Early in my professional career I became aware that agricultural project proposals submitted for funding frequently justified the proposed agricultural research and development on the basis of widespread malnutrition. However, most of the proposals I reviewed never mentioned how the project would reduce malnutrition. Was alleviating malnutrition not a goal, but merely a useful argument to support fundraising? Or did the originators of the proposals assume it was obvious that their proposed projects would reduce malnutrition even if the projects were not tailored to nutritional goals? To satisfy my curiosity about whether such agricultural projects would have a greater nutritional impact if nutrition goals were explicitly integrated into their design and implementation, I undertook a set of analyses to explore how agricultural research priorities would change if improved nutrition (I actually used food security as a proxy for nutrition) were an explicit goal of the research and whether nutrition goals would conflict with traditional agricultural research goals (Pinstrup-Andersen 1980, 1981a, 1983; Pinstrup-Andersen and Franklin 1977; Pinstrup-Andersen, Berg, and Forman 1984; Pinstrup-Andersen, Ruiz de Londoño, and Hoover 1976). The results of these analyses and subsequent research, including analyses of the nutrition effects of cash cropping and food subsidies, convinced me that the interaction between agriculture and nutrition should be explicitly considered in designing and implementing research and policies for either sector. An integrated approach to agricultural development and nutrition improvements would yield more effective and efficient solutions to both.

But why only nutrition? Would you not expect similarly strong interactions and opportunities for synergies between agriculture and human health? And why stop with agriculture? Would not strong relationships and synergies also be likely between human health and other parts of the food system? And should we not include the natural environment as well? As I began to review the literature on health–food system interactions, I sensed an invisible firewall that, I believe, reflects how we organize university-level training and research. Health training, research, and projects reside in one part of the university, and agricultural training, research, and projects reside in another. Rarely did I find evidence of a focus on the relationships between health and agriculture and the opportunities embodied in integrated research and projects across the two.[1]

In this book, experts from various disciplines review the existing knowledge about these relationships, recommend research to fill knowledge gaps, and point to policy action that can be taken now. This effort began when some of the chapter authors and others gathered in two symposia to discuss various aspects of the interaction between the food system and human health and nutrition in Africa and to suggest action that would improve health and nutrition. The idea to invite a group of experts to come together for such discussions came alive in conversations with Rebecca Stoltzfus, the leader of Cornell's International Nutrition Program; Patrick Stover, the director of Cornell's Nutrition Division and chair of the United Nations University (UNU) Food and Nutrition Program; Muna Ndulo, the director of Cornell's Institute of African Development; and Jean-Marc Coicaud, the director of UNU's New York Office. It was decided to proceed with two symposia, one at the UNU in New York City and another at Cornell University. A small number of individuals were invited to present papers on specific topics at the symposia, and many more participated in the discussions.

Following the symposia, I agreed to serve as editor of a volume that would include the papers presented as well as other papers commissioned specifically for the volume. In commissioning the additional papers, I attempted to make this volume even more comprehensive than the symposia. I would like to have added two additional chapters, one on water-borne diseases and the links to the food system and another on obesity and the food system, but I was not able to do so.

The work on this volume has further strengthened my belief that closer collaboration between researchers, policy makers, and program implementers in the food system and those in human health and nutrition is critically important. This volume provides ample evidence of the potential health and nutrition gains from such collaboration and the gains forgone by maintaining existing firewalls between the two sectors. Food systems are means to an end rather than ends in themselves. They exist to serve people. Their relations to human health and nutrition are many and strong, and they offer tremendous opportunities for improving or harming people's well-being, opportunities that need to be fully understood and acted upon. Food systems also interact closely with natural resources and the climate, and the sustainability of food systems and improved health and nutrition depend on the health of the natural environment.

The evidence provided in this volume strongly supports the notion of a comprehensive, multidisciplinary approach to research, policy making, and action that explicitly accounts for the interactions between the food system, human health and nutrition, and the health of the natural environment. Nowhere is such a comprehensive approach more important than in Africa, where the majority of the people suffering from poor health and nutrition are closely linked to agriculture and other parts of the food system and where land degradation, increasing water scarcity, and climate change challenge the health of the natural environment and sustainability.

The book is divided into 14 chapters. The first provides a conceptual overview of the linkages between the African food system and human health and nutrition and a brief summary of the evidence and recommendations for research and policy presented in the chapters that follow. The next two chapters, by Derrill D. Watson, Per Pinstrup-Andersen, and Onesmo K. ole-MoiYoi, present information about the current health and nutrition situation and related trends, with particular attention to the World Food Summit goals and the Millennium Development Goals. As discussed in chapter 4 by E. Fuller Torrey, the majority of illnesses affecting humans originated in animals. The chapter suggests how closer research and policy attention to the transmission of disease from animals to humans could help reduce health risks. As discussed by Stuart Gillespie in chapter 5, there are strong two-way causal links between HIV/AIDS and the food system in Africa and underutilized opportunities to reduce negative and enhance positive links. The next three chapters deal with environmental issues as they interact with the food system and human health and nutrition. First, Rebecca Nelson discusses the health and productivity effects of pesticide use in African agriculture and suggests alternative approaches that might reduce health risks, increase productivity in the food system, and protect the natural environment. Then follows a comprehensive treatment by Anna Herforth of the interactions between human and environmental health. In the last of the three chapters, Dorothy Nakimbugwe and Kathryn J. Boor discuss food safety as a bridge between the food system and human health.

Efforts to achieve sustainable food systems in Africa must take population growth into account. Can future food security goals be met? This question is addressed by Barbara Boyle Torrey in chapter 9. Meeting food security and nutrition goals may require transfers to those households that, because of poverty, are unable to express their food needs in terms of economic demand. Food-based transfers are discussed by Harold Alderman in chapter 10. Poor health and nutrition are not just personal problems, but also public health and economic problems. As discussed by David E. Sahn in chapter 11, sick and undernourished people have low productivity and earn less income. Poverty is undoubtedly the most serious hindrance to good health and nutrition and a well-functioning food system in Africa. In chapter 12, Christopher B. Barrett discusses the interaction between the food system and poverty/hunger/ill-health traps in Africa and how to escape from such traps. Much of the book's content has a gender-specific dimension. Laura K. Cramer and Speciosa Wandira in chapter 13 note that effective action to achieve health, nutrition, and food-related goals must consider such gender dimensions. Last but not least, Joachim von Braun, Marie T. Ruel, and Stuart Gillespie discuss synergies between the food system, health, and nutrition and how research and policy may foster positive synergies to achieve the Millennium Development Goals in Sub-Saharan Africa.

Per Pinstrup-Andersen
February 2010

Notes

1. Efforts by the World Health Organization to promote an integrated systems perspective (WHO Commission on Health and Environment 1992; WHO 1993) and World Bank efforts to promote an integrated agriculture–nutrition approach (Berg 1987; Berg and Muscat 1973; Pinstrup-Andersen 1981b; Reutlinger and Selowsky 1976) were important rays of sunshine in the murky environment of sector-specific approaches, which unfortunately still predominate.

ACKNOWLEDGMENTS

〜〜〜〜〜

This book has benefited from the support and contributions of many individuals. The unwavering support of Patrick Stover, the director of Cornell University's Division of Nutritional Sciences and chair of the United Nations University (UNU) Food and Nutrition Program, from the birth of the idea through the symposia to the final publication, was of critical importance. I am also grateful to Jean-Marc Coicaud, the director of the UNU office in New York City, for hosting one of the symposia where some of the papers that became chapters were presented and discussed and to Muna Ndulo, the director of the Institute for African Development at Cornell University, for hosting the symposium at Cornell University. I warmly acknowledge the cosponsorship of the symposia by the Institute for African Development; the UNU; the Cornell Institute for Public Affairs; the Africana Studies and Research Center; the Einaudi Center for International Studies; the Cornell International Institute for Food, Agriculture, and Development; the Cornell Division of Nutritional Sciences; and the H. E. Babcock Chair at Cornell University. Anna Herforth and Emily Jackson Levitt, both graduate students at Cornell at the time, prepared excellent reports that captured the content of the symposia discussions.

Thanks to the chapter authors, this book makes an outstanding contribution to knowledge about the interface between the African food system and human health and nutrition. In addition to state-of-the-art knowledge, the chapter authors provide important policy-relevant suggestions about how to improve the African food system for the benefit of African people's health and nutrition. They exhibited much patience and great professionalism in response to my many requests and the reviewers' and editor's suggestions. It was truly a pleasure to work with them, and I am in their debt. Without them, there would be no book. The anonymous reviewers were instrumental in assisting the chapter authors and me, and the effective and professional editing by Heidi Fritschel is greatly appreciated. So too are the great contributions made by my assistants Mary-Catherine French and Coleen Boland, who facilitated project coordination and communication throughout the process.

CHAPTER 1

~~~~~~~~

The African Food System and Human Health and Nutrition:
A Conceptual and Empirical Overview

Per Pinstrup-Andersen

Abstract

This chapter presents a brief conceptual overview of the relationships between the African food systems and human health and nutrition. It then proceeds to summarize the empirical evidence presented in the chapters to follow and the recommendations for research and policy interventions made by the chapter authors. Emphasis is on the two-way causal relationships between food systems and health and nutrition and how policy interventions may have a greater impact if these relationships are explicitly considered.

A Brief Conceptual Overview

A food system may be described simply as a process that turns natural and human-made resources and inputs into food. As illustrated in Figure 1.1, such a system may consist of the resources (such as land, water, and sunshine); inputs (such as plant nutrients, pest control measures, and knowledge); primary or agricultural production; secondary production or processing; and transport, storage, and exchange activities to make the food available at the time and place desired by consumers. Food systems need not be stagnant. In fact, if the goal is to improve them, it is useful to visualize food systems as dynamic behavioral systems that can change in response to changes in the behavior of the various decision makers and agents in the system, such as consumers, producers, market agents, resource owners, nongovernmental organizations, and governments. Three sets of tools are available for governments to influence the behavior of the agents in the system: incentives, regulations, and creation and dissemination of knowledge.

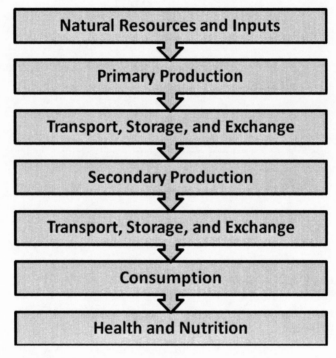

Figure 1.1   A food system
SOURCE: Author.

Food systems operate within biophysical, socioeconomic, political, and demographic environments. Of particular interest in this book is the human health and nutrition context. Energy and nutritional deficiencies, infectious diseases, obesity, and chronic diseases may influence food systems by lowering the labor productivity of food system workers, by reducing the adoption of improved technology and the use of inputs and credit, and by leading to suboptimal use of land, water, and other resources. Labor productivity may also be influenced by infectious diseases, such as malaria and bacterial and virus contamination, associated with water management in the food system (Pinstrup-Andersen 2006a).

Each of the food-system activities may interact with health and nutrition. The most obvious interaction is the way in which the food system makes food available to meet people's needs for dietary energy and nutrients. Yet availability of food is necessary but not sufficient to assure the food security of individuals. To achieve food security, individuals must have access to the food available, and their access is influenced by their purchasing power, their own production, and other factors. The food system may increase people's access through lower food prices brought about by lower unit costs of production, higher incomes among farmers and farm workers, and higher incomes outside the agricultural sector resulting from income multiplier effects generated by higher farm incomes. Thus, changes in food systems may improve or worsen the nutrition situation, with repercussions for other health factors. It is estimated, for example, that more than half of developing countries' child mortality is associated with malnutrition and hunger. Children who suffer from hunger or malnutrition are less resistant to several infectious diseases and more likely to die from such illnesses. The food system may also contribute to increasing or decreasing the prevalence of chronic diseases by influencing changes in the prevalence in overweight and obesity.

Figure 1.2 illustrates several other interactions between the food system and human health. These interactions may take place in various parts of the food system. Although much past research and debate have focused on the impact of agriculture on nutrition, it is important to recognize that there is a two-way causal relationship. Moreover, in examining this relationship, it is important to amplify the concept from agriculture to the food systems as a whole and from nutrition to health aspects other than nutrition. This amplification is attempted in the chapters that follow.

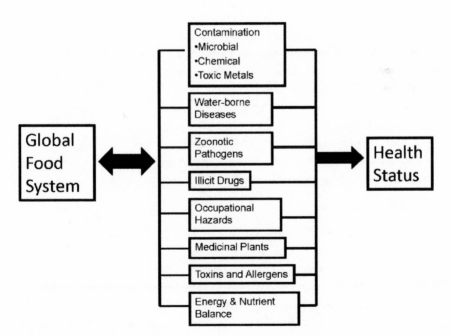

Figure 1.2   Interactions between food systems and human health
SOURCE: Author.

The Current Health and Nutrition Situation

As detailed by Watson, Pinstrup-Andersen, and ole-MoiYoi in chapters 2 and 3, the prevalence of hunger, malnutrition and a variety of health problems is high in Africa. A large share of the African population suffers from infectious diseases and one or more elements in the triple burden of malnutrition: dietary deficiencies or hunger; micronutrient deficiencies; and overweight, obesity, and chronic diseases (Pinstrup-Andersen 2006b, 2007). Every third preschool child is malnourished, and the rates of low birth weight and child mortality are high. According to the Food and Agriculture Organization of the United Nations (FAO), the number of people suffering from hunger in Sub-Saharan Africa has doubled during the past 40 years. The subcontinent now accounts for 20 percent of the world's hungry people. If current trends continue, that share will increase to 30 percent by 2015, the deadline for meeting the World Food Summit goal and the Millennium Development Goal for hunger alleviation. With business as usual, neither of these goals will be met and the number of hungry people in Sub-Saharan Africa will continue to increase. It does not have to be so. One country—the Democratic Republic of the Congo—is responsible for a large share of the increase in hunger, whereas most countries in the subcontinent experienced no rise in hunger. Thus, efforts to improve the situation in the DRC are critical (Watson and Pinstrup-Andersen, chapter 2). In addition to hunger, widespread nutrient deficiencies contribute to poor health in the region.

Poverty, poor sanitation, and unclean water are the key factors underlying the spread of infectious diseases caused by viruses, bacteria, protozoa, and intestinal worms. These diseases interact with hunger and malnutrition to cause serious health problems—malaria, helminthic infections, African trypanosomiasis, and others—exacerbated by the high prevalence of AIDS (ole-MoiYoi, chapter 3, and Gillespie, chapter 5). In chapter 3, ole-MoiYoi presents current knowledge about the causes of and possible solutions to these health problems and suggests specific approaches to alleviating each of them, with an emphasis on a comprehensive approach that takes into account the synergistic aspects.

Linking Food Systems and Human Health: Zoonotic Diseases

Most of the health problems affecting humans, whether in Africa or elsewhere, originated with animals, and the transmission of diseases from animals to humans continues, according to Torrey (chapter 4). Measles, tuberculosis, AIDS, avian influenza, and mad cow disease are but a few of the zoonotic diseases affecting Africans. Transmission of these illnesses in Africa is facilitated by a large number of disease-transmitting arthropods, contaminated water supplies, and malnutrition. Reducing transmission will require better understanding of disease transmission mechanisms and the development of an extensive surveillance system for early detection of new and recurrent infectious disease outbreaks. Torrey suggests four other factors that will also require attention: (1) changes in the relationship between animals and humans and reconsideration of the sharing of living space; (2) changes in modes of transportation that facilitate transmission of infectious diseases; (3) changes in the process of animal slaughter and other food-processing activities; and (4) changes in the ecology and the environment such as urbanization, climate change, and deforestation.

HIV/AIDS and Its Interaction with the Food System in Africa

In chapter 5 Gillespie points out that food insecurity and AIDS coexist and interact in potentially vicious circles in many parts of Africa. Based on a review of existing knowledge on the subject, he concludes that food security for the African population will not be achieved unless the agricultural sector proactively takes HIV/AIDS into account. African agriculture and international agricultural organizations must mainstream AIDS considerations, or the Millennium Development Goal to halve poverty and hunger "will remain a hopeless dream" (Gillespie, chapter 5). Gillespie proposes what he calls HIV-responsive agricultural policies and programs and concludes that there is significant scope for agricultural policy to further both AIDS-related goals and agricultural productivity goals. He calls for collaboration among nutritionists, agricultural economists, and program managers "to investigate the broader issue of household and community-level nutrition security, policy, and programming in the context of AIDS." Building bridges between the agriculture and health sectors is urgent and critically important.

Crop Protection and Health: Pesticides and Alternatives

As discussed by Nelson in chapter 6, such bridges are also important to reduce health risks from pest control while pursuing productivity increases in agriculture. Heavy crop losses in African agriculture due to insects and other pests contribute to low yields, rural poverty, hunger, and poor health and nutrition. Although the use of chemical pesticides is an effective means of controlling most pests, it may lead to loses of natural biological control mechanisms. It also increases the health risks for farmers from exposure during application, and it may increase food safety risks by introducing toxins in the food supply. Nelson (chapter 6) proposes an integrated crop management approach that includes agroecological intensification based on a context-specific, integrated analysis of agroecosystems and human health. Such an approach should consider crop diversity and crop resiliency and incorporate host-plant tolerance and resistance, where such crop varieties are available. Chemical pesticides should be used only when no other acceptable protection is available. Nelson suggests that research is needed to move toward better agroecological pest management. This research should use agroecological principles and a participatory approach. Researchers should work to breed pest resistance into locally adapted germplasm. Nelson states that the potential role of genetic engineering is an "open question," but she concludes that "transgenetic technologies are available for viruses and insects and could be valuable for protection of crops that lack adequate levels of native resistance."

Health, the Natural Environment, and the Food System

With a focus on the nutrition-related aspects of health, Herforth (chapter 7) agrees with Nelson that an integrated systems approach to food production and human nutrition is critically important to achieve sustainable nutrition improvements and stresses that much more must be done to consider the food system's interaction with the natural environment. She demonstrates that the linkages among agriculture, the natural environment, food security, and nutrition are particularly important in Sub-Saharan Africa, where most people live in rural areas and depend directly on land, water, and other natural resources for their livelihood. Unsustainable management of these resources leading to soil erosion, siltation in watersheds, and seasonal water scarcities may have direct negative effects on people's health and nutrition through reductions in yields and incomes. Inappropriate water management may lead to exposure to waterborne and insect vector–transmitted diseases. Adverse weather conditions leading to drought, floods, and temperature changes, whether caused by climate change or not, lead to volatile production and associated transitory food insecurity and nutritional deficiencies.

Changes in biodiversity may affect the diversity of foods available to people from their own production, gathering, and the local market. Herforth reports findings from recent research showing that the dietary diversity of farm households in East Africa is influenced by the diversity of their production. Given the importance of dietary diversity in meeting nutritional needs and the income opportunities associated with a shift to high-value fruits and vegetables on smallholdings, these findings send an important message that agricultural research and development should focus on a portfolio of food crops rather than just a few—a message that is supported by Nelson (chapter 6), Herforth (chapter 7), and von Braun, Ruel, and Gillespie (chapter 14). This message calls for a more comprehensive systems approach in which the principal goal is improved health and nutrition rather than maximum production of a particular food commodity. Both

Herforth (chapter 7) and Nakimbugwe and Boor (chapter 8) call for expanded production and consumption of fruits and vegetables to improve health and nutrition, but Nakimbugwe and Boor point out that such foods are highly perishable, frequently contaminated with pathogens, and often carriers of food-borne diseases. Street foods, which may provide another source of dietary diversity, are also exposed to microbial contamination caused by factors like poor sanitation and unclean water. Efforts to reduce food safety risks must include sanitary improvements and access to clean water.

Given the prevalence of nutrient deficiencies and the importance of dietary diversity in eliminating them, Herforth criticizes the single-minded focus on measuring what the FAO calls "undernourishment" by using data on intake of dietary energy to stand in for nutrition or food security. A sufficient intake of calories does not assure that a person is well nourished. According to available global statistics, twice as many people suffer from micronutrient deficiencies as from calorie deficiencies. Limiting the statistics to energy deficiencies does a disservice by framing the problem and solution in terms of dietary energy alone. This approach also conflicts with the FAO's own definition of food security, which states that a person is food secure if he or she has access to sufficient, safe, and nutritious food to meet dietary needs for a healthy life.

Food Safety, Health, and the Food System

The African population suffers from a high burden of food-borne diseases, and the health consequences are severe (Nakimbugwe and Boor, chapter 8). The authors of the chapter refer to food- and water-borne diseases as "silent killers" because they are frequently overlooked, unreported, or ignored by governments, communities, and individuals. Yet they are an extremely important part of the African health problem. They affect the entire food chain, including production, storage, transportation, and processing. Efforts to improve food safety should not be limited to agriculture or any other single element of the food system. Food-borne diseases are caused by biological disease agents and chemical and physical contaminants. Contamination by aflatoxin and other mycotoxins are a serious health problem for which known solutions exist. Regulatory mechanisms are needed to avoid misuse of agricultural chemicals that lead to health risks in application and food residues. This point is also stressed by Nelson (chapter 6). Nonetheless, weaknesses in the African food control system, poor infrastructure, lack of public and private resources, and improper food handling make food safety improvements difficult.

As in the case of zoonotic diseases discussed by Torrey in chapter 4, there is an urgent and important need for a surveillance system that collects, analyzes, and shares epidemiological data to guide action to improve food safety. Furthermore, public awareness of basic hygiene and food safety measures and risks must be strengthened among farmers, consumers, processors, and street food vendors. More research is needed to prevent the formation of mycotoxins by fungi and to reduce the need for chemical pesticides through host-plant resistance and integrated pest and crop management, a point also raised by Nelson in chapter 6.

Improved food safety may increase the cost of food to the consumer, leading to a conflict between food security (expressed as access to enough food) and food safety (expressed in terms of relative risk) (Caswell and Bach 2007). If poor households without sufficient resources to acquire enough food to meet their calorie and nutrient needs are confronted with an increase in the price of food brought about by activities to lower the risk of illness, they may experience more hunger and nutrient deficiencies. Although such a trade-off between access to enough food and a lower risk of illness is unethical, it is nevertheless not uncommon and should be considered by governments as they introduce food safety regulations. What is an acceptable risk level, and what would it take to achieve it while still moving toward a situation in which all Africans have access to enough food to meet their energy and nutrient requirements?

Demographic Changes, Future Food Demand, and Health Implications

Africa is likely to experience a large increase in the demand for food owing to population growth, income increases, urbanization, and related changes in consumer tastes and preferences. As shown by Torrey (chapter 9), Sub-Saharan Africa has experienced high population growth rates, and, although the rates are falling, the decrease in growth rates is slow. The population of Sub-Saharan Africa is likely to at least double between 2000 and 2050. Torrey observes that the big question is what will happen to fertility rates. Will the demographic transition in the region be slower or faster than that seen outside of Africa? Torrey expresses concern that in many African countries fertility rates are falling only slowly, if at all. Although surveys show that young African women generally want fewer children than their parents' generation, intrahousehold power structures and lack of access to reproductive health care, contraception, and family planning make such a desire difficult to achieve.

Population growth, together with changes in the age structure and the diet transition resulting from urbanization and income increases, will place strong pressures on the African food system. Torrey estimates that the region produces enough food to meet the biological needs of its population if available food is distributed according to need—which, of course, it is not. She further estimates that, adjusting for changes in calorie requirements due to changes in the age structure and urbanization, dietary energy requirements for the population of the region will double between 2000 and 2030. Assuming that the distribution of food access does not change, this estimate implies that even if the region can double the availability of food over the 30-year period (of which 10 have already passed), the proportion of the population that suffers from dietary energy deficiencies will stay at current rates. In addition, the region is facing widespread micronutrient deficiencies (see Watson and Pinstrup-Andersen, chapter 2, and Herforth, chapter 7) and a nutrition transition that is causing increasing overweight, obesity, and chronic diseases, particularly in urban areas. If food security goals are to be achieved, the need for urgent action to turn the food system toward the achievement of health goals is obvious.

Poverty, malnutrition, and poor health contribute to low productivity and are themselves outcomes of such low productivity, making increased food production difficult. Infectious and parasitic diseases are widespread and, together with malnutrition, cause more than half the deaths in the region. They also cause low productivity within and outside the food system (see also Sahn, chapter 11). Although poverty and unequal income distribution play a key role in the degree to which individuals and households have access to food, poor infrastructure and poorly functioning markets hamper the physical distribution of food from food-surplus to food-deficit areas. These factors, as well as lack of access to appropriate knowledge, technology, inputs, and credit, also keep food production at low levels. Policy interventions should address these areas of concern if future African food demands are to be met.

Complementary Action for Short-Term Solutions

Poverty-reducing policies promote agricultural productivity, improve rural infrastructure, and strengthen domestic markets and are needed to create sustainable health and nutrition improvements, but their impact takes time. In the short term, complementary programs and policies, such as income and transfer programs and primary health care, are needed. Alderman (chapter 10) presents a menu of such programs and their pros and cons for use in Africa. A large share of the Africans who, as mentioned in chapters 2 and 3, suffer from chronic hunger, malnutrition, and health problems are defenseless against income shocks caused by production, market, or employment losses, including droughts and pest attacks (as discussed by Nelson in chapter 6).

Without safety nets or some other insurance mechanism, income shocks can result in severe suffering, further nutrition and health deterioration, and death. The choice of program and targeting mechanism must be context specific and take into account existing knowledge about household behavior and gender-specific intrahousehold decision-making processes. Conditional transfers that provide food or cash on the condition that recipient households meet certain requirements, such as taking their children to the health clinic periodically, have proven successful in several middle-income developing countries with reasonable health infrastructure. Low-income developing countries, including many in Sub-Saharan Africa, would have to make investments in rural health care facilities for households to meet such health care conditions.

Large Economic Returns from an Integrated Approach

Programs and policies of the kind discussed by Alderman may be expensive and require institutions and infrastructure not currently available in some countries. It is important, however, to view such programs not as unproductive handouts, but as investments in human resources and future economic growth and stability. The returns to such investments can be high (Sahn, chapter 11). Recognizing that health and nutrition are intrinsically important measures of well-being, Sahn concludes that "by raising the productivity of the workforce, good health will help transform the African food system into a modern sector that contributes to economic growth and poverty alleviation." As several chapter authors argue, human health is an important outcome of economic growth. In chapter 11, Sahn shows that economic growth is influenced by the quality of human resources, which, in turn, are strongly influenced by health status. Thus, health improvements can break the vicious circle or downward spiral of poverty, malnutrition, and poor health across generations and help avoid the poverty traps discussed by Barrett in chapter 12.

The economic and productivity implications of poor health and health shocks are particularly pronounced in rural areas of Africa, where the food system is the main source of income and employment. The productivity consequences are likely to be most severe for farmers and others who undertake hard physical work. Furthermore, the nutrition effects of health shocks will be direct and severe among semi-subsistence farmers, who may not be able to provide the labor needed to bring the crop to harvest. Sahn suggests that the link between health and productivity is particularly important for women partly because of the role women play in food production, food preparation, and child care and partly because of their special vulnerabilities related to reproductive health (see chapter 13).

A review of several estimates of the economic impact of changes in health status from methodological, analytical, and empirical perspectives leads Sahn to recommend targeted policies and interventions to improve health and nutrition. The design and implementation of such interventions "inevitably focuses attention on the complexities of the constraints that jointly hold back the poor from being swept up into the virtuous circle of improved health and poverty reduction" instead of ending up in a poverty and ill-health trap of the kind discussed by Barrett in chapter 12.

The Poverty/Hunger/Ill-Health Trap

Barrett reports that the ultra-poor, those who make less than half-a-dollar a day, are likely to also be malnourished and in poor health. In fact, ultra-poverty, poor health, hunger, and malnutrition are mutually reinforcing conditions that push people into a poverty trap, defined as a "self-reinforcing mechanism that causes poverty to persist" (Azariadis and Stachurski 2007, 33; cited by Barrett in chapter 12). Referring to recent research, Barrett suggests that major health shocks may be the leading cause of collapse into long-term poverty. Widespread hunger and malnutrition (chapter 2) combines with prevalent infectious diseases (chapter 3) to cause poor health and ultra-poverty, with severe negative effects on human well-being, cognitive development, and individual and national incomes (chapter 11).

As discussed by Herforth in chapter 7 and emphasized in chapter 12, the well-being of the rural poor depends heavily on the natural environment. Adverse weather patterns and the degradation of natural resources may cause severe economic and health hardships. Health and environmental shocks may initiate a downward spiral leading to poverty/ill-health traps from which it may be very difficult to escape. This risk points to the importance of strategies that integrate health, food, nutrition, and environment, according to several chapter authors. Barrett suggests that "food systems are the natural locus for such strategies" and that "all past cases of rapid, widespread progress out of poverty have been causally associated with the transformation of food systems." Increased crop yields have been particularly important in reducing poverty in countries outside Africa. In Africa, however, both crop yields and poverty rates have stagnated. Barrett finds it "difficult to envision... substantial progress in freeing Sub-Saharan Africa from its apparent ultra-poverty/hunger/ill-health trap without significant advances in the continent's food system."

Effective action to unlock the poverty/hunger/ill-health trap will be country- and context-specific. Barrett suggests four broad principles to guide the design and implementation of such action: (1) build and protect household-level productive assets; (2) improve the productivity of poor people's assets; (3) improve risk management options for the ultra-poor; and (4) facilitate favorable transitions out of agriculture.

The Need for Gender Specificity

The concept of poverty traps and the need for more related research appear to be much on the minds of Cramer and Wandira (chapter 13) when they argue that "understanding the factors that keep women from escaping poverty can help elucidate the reasons why past interventions have not been successful." Women are key players in the African food system, accounting for 70 percent of farm labor and performing 80 percent of food processing. The large increases in food supplies called for by Torrey in chapter 9 will have to be met primarily by women farmers. But, as emphasized by Cramer and Wandira, women must be given the power to do so. They will require access to land rights, water use rights, credit, extension services, and well-functioning markets for inputs and outputs. In many areas smallholder farmers, most of whom are women, are attempting to raise their incomes through better access to output markets, and supermarkets are offering new market opportunities. But these opportunities also present smallholders with new competitive conditions, requirements for improved food safety (chapter 8), and demands for consistency in quantity and quality—requirements they may have difficulties meeting. Although diversity in farming systems, called for by Herforth in chapter 7, may result in more diverse diets and consequently better nutrition, complex farming systems may make it harder for farmers to increase their marketable surplus and earn higher incomes.

Agricultural projects and policies must take context-specific gender norms and women's time demands and constraints into account. Both women and men should be involved in developing priorities and implementation strategies for projects and research for the food system. The time demands on poor women in rural Africa, many of whom are malnourished and in poor health, are heavy. These demands include time for farming, child care, care for sick household members and orphans, and fetching of water and firewood. Cramer and Wandira conclude, "Improving the health of women in Sub-Saharan Africa is a key component in boosting productivity in the agricultural sector and in general."

Cramer and Wandira identify the very limited communication between agricultural and health research as an obstacle to women's ability to meet nutrition and health goals. They suggest that agricultural and health development professionals collaborate in future research and implementation to help achieve the Millennium Development Goals related to health and nutrition. They point to several topics on which research is needed, including intrahousehold relations, positive deviants, women's health and agricultural production, and gender-specific poverty traps. They also call for more work to better understand why existing knowledge is not resulting in desired action.

Capturing Synergies to Achieve the Millennium Development Goals

In chapter 14, von Braun, Ruel, and Gillespie make a strong case for strengthening the linkages between agriculture and health to achieve reductions in poverty, malnutrition, and poor health. The chapter brings together much of the substance from previous chapters with a focus on the research and policy interventions needed to accelerate progress toward achieving the Millennium Development

Goals (MDGs). The authors claim that the MDGs provide an opportunity to effectively link agriculture and health but that the framework for doing so is missing. The MDGs fail to provide "the set of instruments to effectively exploit the synergies between agriculture and health and to achieve joint policy formulation." Both agriculture and health are important for most of the MDGs, and close collaboration between the two sectors may capture important synergies.

The Hunger Task Force, one of 12 task forces established to guide government policy aimed at achieving the MDGs, discusses the importance of linking health and agriculture; "a discussion of how to implement these integrated policy approaches, however, is lacking" (von Braun, Ruel, and Gillespie, chapter 14). The MDGs were perceived as the policy targets within countries' poverty reduction strategy papers (PRSPs), which could but in most cases failed to design and implement multisectoral action. Unfortunately, the failure of the health and agricultural sectors to work together is typical and not limited to the MDGs. Although the World Health Organization (WHO) and the United Nations Children's Fund (UNICEF) have suggested comprehensive health strategies, attempts to design and implement them have met strong resistance from within both sectors. The authors conclude that the existence of disincentives to collaboration between the health and food sectors means that "agriculture and health policies and programs tend to remain locked in sectoral silos" (von Braun, Ruel, and Gillespie, chapter 14). Chapter 14 lists the challenges that would have to be confronted to break down the silos, along with success factors and suggestions on how to orient national policy frameworks to promote synergies between the two sectors.

The Bottom Line

An integrated, multidisciplinary, systems approach to research and development in human health and the food system, with due consideration to natural environment issues, offers great advantages over single-sector approaches, irrespective of whether the goal is improved health, improved nutrition, improved food systems, or sustainable management of the natural environment. In fact, the achievement of all four goals can be pursued in a systems approach. Any trade-offs among them can be explicitly identified and assessed, and double, triple, and quadruple wins are possible. Given the strong interactive relationships that exist among health, the food system, and the natural environment, existing firewalls between them should be broken down. Nowhere is that more obvious than in efforts to achieve the Millennium Developments Goals for Africa.

CHAPTER 2

∿∿∿∿∿

The Nutrition Situation in Sub-Saharan Africa

Derrill D. Watson II and Per Pinstrup-Andersen

Abstract

Hunger and malnutrition are widespread in Sub-Saharan Africa. The region as a whole is not on track to achieve either the World Food Summit goal (halve the number of people suffering from hunger by 2015) or Millennium Development Goal 1 (halve the proportion of people suffering from hunger by 2015). Life expectancy is low while fertility, child mortality, and population growth rates are high. The prevalence of hunger has increased dramatically in the Democratic Republic of Congo (DRC), where about 43 million, or about three-fourths of the population, now suffer from hunger or food insecurity. Tanzania has also experienced a significant increase in the number of hungry people. Great progress has been made in Ethiopia, Ghana, and Nigeria, but the rest of the countries in the region have seen little change in the number of people suffering from hunger or food insecurity. These facts point to two conclusions: first, the World Food Summit (WFS) goal and Millennium Development Goal 1 (MDG 1) can be achieved in Africa only by turning the DRC around; and second, the remainder of Sub-Saharan Africa could accomplish MDG 1 (only one country in the region is on target to achieve the WFS goal and 12 are on track to achieve MDG 1). Recent increases in the economic growth rates of several countries in the region offer hope for improvements in human well-being, including reduced poverty, better nutrition, and less hunger, although the 2009 world economic recession makes progress more difficult. Thus, although the region as a whole is not on track to achieve the MDGs, a renewed emphasis on hunger alleviation could accomplish MDG 1 for most of the countries of Sub-Saharan Africa.

Introduction

Globally, hunger and malnutrition affect the lives of more than 1 billion men, women, and children. As the Food and Agriculture Organization of the United Nations (FAO) compellingly states, hunger "saps strength and dulls intelligence. It destroys innocent lives, especially children. And by weakening a nation's workforce, hunger cripples a nation's growth" (FAO 2007c). In few areas is the need to overcome hunger and malnutrition more urgent than in Sub-Saharan Africa.

Malnutrition may take several forms: hunger, hidden hunger, and obesity. In this chapter, "hunger" refers primarily to energy and protein deficiencies. Yet even when people consume sufficient calories, they may suffer from deficiencies of important micronutrients, such as iron or vitamin A, which can cause lifelong health problems and retard human development. These deficiencies are commonly referred to as "hidden hunger." Finally, when people's net energy intake is excessive, they can experience obesity and the chronic diseases that go with it. These three types of malnutrition are increasingly found side by side in developing countries around the world, highlighting the need for new thinking on how to improve total health and well-being in a variety of contexts. Although the primary focus of this chapter is hunger, it refers to hunger and malnutrition where appropriate to include micronutrient deficiencies, overweight, and obesity problems.

Hunger and malnutrition are twin killers responsible for or closely associated with more than half of the documented deaths of children under age five in the developing world (Figure 2.1). Curable diseases like diarrhea become fatal without proper nutrition, and conversely, the survival rates of many diseases improve dramatically when their victims have adequate nutrition. Life expectancy at birth is lower in Sub-Saharan Africa than in any other region of the world—a mere 50 years compared with an average of 67 in all developing countries (Table 2.1). This low life expectancy stems in large part from the region's child mortality rate, also the highest in the world. Approximately 145 of every 1,000 children die before the age of five in Africa, twice as many as in other developing countries and 20 times the rate in industrialized countries.

The next section breaks down the distribution of hungry people across regions, focusing particularly on hunger in Africa using several different measures of hunger and malnutrition. The remaining sections analyze recent trends to show what the results will be in 2015 if these trends continue unchanged. Most of the negative hunger trends observed in Sub-Saharan Africa are caused by the collapse of the Democratic Republic of the Congo (DRC). If the DRC is removed from the data set, there is hope that Sub-Saharan Africa could accomplish the first Millennium Development Goal (MDG 1) by 2015 with reasonable additional effort.

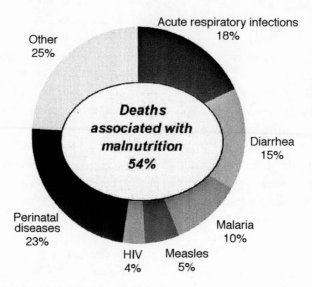

Figure 2.1   Deaths associated with malnutrition, 2002
SOURCE: Blössner and de Onis 2005; WHO 2004.

Table 2.1 Life expectancy and under-five mortality rate by region, 2000–07

Region	Under-five mortality rate	Life expectancy
West and Central Africa	169	50
East and Southern Africa	123	50
South Asia	78	64
Developing-country average	74	67
Middle East and North Africa	46	69
East Asia and Pacific	27	72
Latin America and Caribbean	26	73
Central and Eastern Europe and Commonwealth of Independent States	25	68
Industrialized countries	6	79

SOURCE: UNICEF 2009b.

Measuring Hunger and Malnutrition

There are several measures of the incidence of hunger and malnutrition, including FAO data on adult undernourishment, World Health Organization (WHO) data on the prevalence of underweight children under five, and data from the United Nations Children's Fund (UNICEF) on the incidence of low-birth-weight children. The first two of these measures are combined with the under-five mortality rate to form the Global Hunger Index.

The FAO estimates the number and percentage of people who have inadequate caloric intake on the basis of total food consumption and distribution in each country. This measure is the broadest one available on population-level nutrition statistics, providing yearly estimates in each country using minimal data requirements. The FAO data are usually three-year averages around the date cited to smooth year-to-year fluctuations.

The chief disadvantages of this data set are the number of assumptions made to create the estimates, the uncertainty of the national data on the consumption and distribution of available food, and the failure to consider hidden hunger or obesity. Furthermore, although it is widely recognized that people's caloric needs differ according to activity, height, age, weight, basal metabolic rate, climate, and other factors, it would be infeasible to measure each individual's caloric needs. Smith, Alderman, and Aduayom (2006) estimate hunger in Sub-Saharan Africa based on household expenditure surveys (HESs), concluding that the HES measures of hunger are more closely correlated with other MDGs and so are likely to be more accurate. The primary difference between the FAO data and the HESs lies in assumptions about household food availability rather than in methodology. Because FAO estimates are available for more countries and more years, the FAO data on hunger prevalence are the broadest available for measuring hunger.

The most recent available FAO (2009b) data use a three-year average over the period from 2004 to 2006. FAO estimates that in 2005 some 873 million people suffered from hunger around the world (Figure 2.2). One-fourth of the people suffering from hunger lived in Sub-Saharan Africa (212.3 million), with another fourth in India (251.5 million), 127.4 million in China, and 178.7 million in the rest of Asia. Within Sub-Saharan Africa, 40.5 percent of the hungry people (86.5 million) were found in East Africa. A further 54.3 million were found in Central Africa, with 36.7 million in Southern Africa, and 34.7 million in West Africa (Figure 2.3). Rapidly increasing food prices during 2007–08 are likely to have increased the number of people suffering from hunger and malnutrition. FAO (2009b) estimates that during this period over 120 million additional people joined the undernourished, 20 million of whom are in Sub-Saharan Africa.

Although more hungry people live in Asia than in Sub-Saharan Africa, the prevalence of hunger in Sub-Saharan Africa as a whole is a staggering 30 percent, with only 21 percent of South Asia's population suffering from hunger and a mere 9.5 percent in East Asia and the Pacific (Figure 2.4). Reducing hunger and malnutrition in Africa is key to improving health, life spans, and child welfare.

Within Sub-Saharan Africa, the highest prevalence of hunger is in Central Africa, where more than half of the population (57 percent) is in need (Figure 2.5). That number is rising rapidly. East and Southern Africa fare rather better,

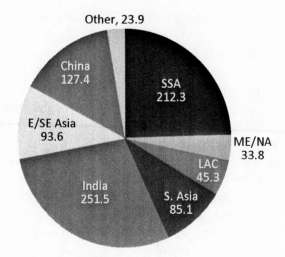

Figure 2.2 Millions of people suffering from hunger globally, 2005
SOURCE: Based on data from FAO 2009b.
NOTE: SSA = Sub-Saharan Africa; ME/NA = Middle East and North Africa; LAC = Latin America and the Caribbean; S. Asia = South Asia; E/SE Asia = East and Southeast Asia.

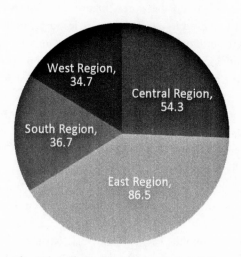

Figure 2.3 Millions of people suffering from hunger in Sub-Saharan Africa, 2005
SOURCE: Based on data from FAO 2009b.

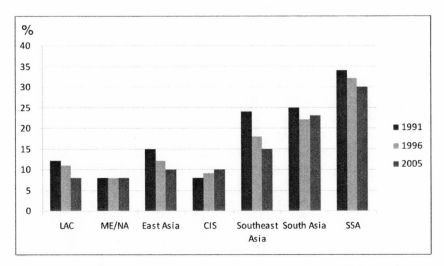

Figure 2.4 Percentage of population suffering from hunger globally by developing-country region, 1991, 1996, and 2005
SOURCE: Based on data from FAO 2009b.
NOTE: LAC = Latin America and the Caribbean; ME/NA = Middle East and North Africa;
E. Asia = East Asia; CIS = Commonwealth of Independent States; SSA = Sub-Saharan Africa.

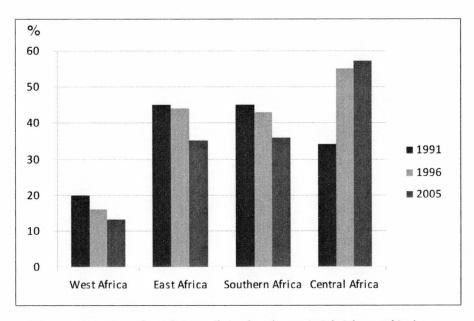

Figure 2.5 Percentage of population suffering from hunger in Sub-Saharan Africa by region, 1991, 1996, and 2005
SOURCE: Based on data from FAO 2009b.

and the situation is improving, although 35 percent and 37 percent still suffer from hunger respectively. West Africa is the one bright spot, where only 13 percent of the population is deemed to have insufficient energy intake.

Another measure of the scope of hunger is found by considering the number of children between zero and five years old who are significantly underweight for their age, as measured by WHO and UNICEF. Their data consider children to be significantly underweight if their weight-for-age is more than two standard deviations below the median. These estimates have the advantage of focusing on one of the most vulnerable groups in society and account to a certain extent for food allocation within households.

WHO (2009e) estimates that 112 million children are significantly underweight while UNICEF (2009b) places that number at 148 million. It is not clear why there is such a large difference between the two estimates, but the error margin in estimates of this nature is likely to be large. Well over two-thirds of the world's underweight children live in Asia, with more than one-third of them found in India alone (Figure 2.6; UNICEF 2009b). Ethiopia and Nigeria account for 10 million hungry children—roughly 7–9 percent of the total. The rest of Sub-Saharan Africa accounts for approximately 22–29 percent of the world's underweight children (UNICEF 2009b; WHO 2009e). More than one in four children in Sub-Saharan Africa (27–28 percent) are underweight, compared with almost one in two in South Asia and one in six in East Asia (Figure 2.7).[1]

A third measure of hunger—the number of children born with significantly low birth weight—focuses on the welfare of pregnant women and their infants

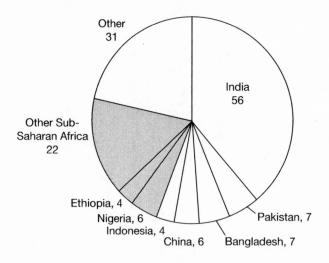

Figure 2.6   Millions of underweight children, 2000–07
SOURCE: Based on data from WHO 2009e.

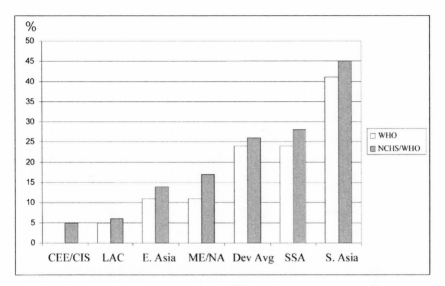

Figure 2.7   Prevalence of underweight children by region, 2007
SOURCE: Based on data from UNICEF 2009b.
NOTE: NCHS = National Center for Health Statistics; CEE/CIS = Central and Eastern Europe/
Commonwealth of Independent States; E. Asia = East Asia; Dev Avg = developing-country average;
S. Asia = South Asia.

(Figure 2.8). Of the three measures covered, this one is perhaps least susceptible
to measurement error, the vagaries of cross-country comparisons, and confounding individual variation. It is, however, confounded by how women are treated in
a society or community. Lower birth weight may reflect a lack of care given to
pregnant women. Low birth weight has also been on the rise in developed countries because improvements in medical technology and techniques have saved the
lives of many preterm children who would not have survived birth before. This
measure also fails to account for women who have not been pregnant and men.

As Figure 2.8 shows, half of the world's 20.6 million low-birth-weight children
are in South Asia, with 20 percent in Africa and 10 percent in East Asia. Low-
birth-weight children are also significantly more prevalent in South Asia than
elsewhere, with 29 percent of children being born underweight, compared with
15 percent for West and Central Africa and 13 percent for East and Southern Africa
(Figure 2.9).

Each of these measures highlights that Asia, and particularly India, has the
largest number of hunger victims. Child welfare is also lowest in South Asia, as
both newborns and children under age five are most likely to be underweight in
South Asia. After South Asia, however, the children in Sub-Saharan Africa are
in greatest need. Furthermore, the prevalence of hunger in South Asia has been
decreasing over the past 20 years, whereas it has increased in Sub-Saharan Africa.

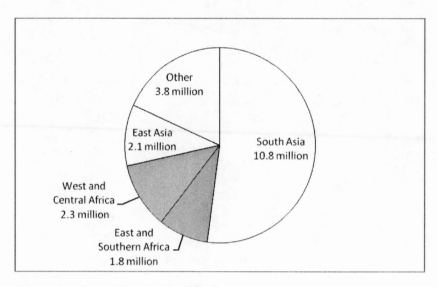

Figure 2.8 Millions of low-birth-weight children, 2000–07
SOURCE: Based on data from UNICEF 2009b.

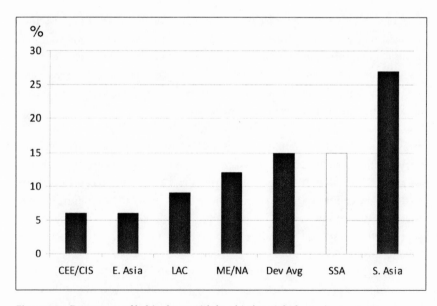

Figure 2.9 Percentage of babies born with low birth weight by region, 2000–07
SOURCE: Based on data from UNICEF 2009b.

If these trends continue, Sub-Saharan Africa will account for an increasing share of the world's hungry and malnourished. It is imperative to take action now to reverse the rising tide of hunger in Sub-Saharan Africa (see Figure 2.11 later in this chapter).

Hidden Hunger

Even if people consume enough calories to meet their daily energy requirements, they may not consume sufficient quantities of key micronutrients. Moreover, without vitamin supplementation, it is unlikely that anyone who does not consume enough calories will consume sufficient micronutrients. Table 2.2 shows the estimated prevalence of certain micronutrient deficiencies by country in Sub-Saharan Africa. Iron deficiency is the most prevalent micronutrient deficiency in the region, ranging from 37 percent of preschool-age children to 86 percent, followed by vitamin A, affecting 17–70 percent of preschool children, and zinc, with 9–61 percent of adults at risk. Goiter, or iodine deficiency, is least prevalent, with rates ranging from less than 5 percent to 42 percent. Deficiencies of different micronutrients are not necessarily correlated with each other. Some countries (like Angola and the Democratic Republic of the Congo) are highly susceptible to all micronutrient deficiencies for which data have been collected, whereas others are at high risk of one (like Eritrea and Ethiopia) or more.

Micronutrient deficiencies can result in a number of illnesses and conditions. Iron-deficiency anemia can cause permanent damage to children, harming learning ability, stunting growth, and altering bodily chemical balances. Vitamin A deficiency can lead to blindness and death and is particularly prevalent in Sub-Saharan Africa and Southeast Asia (WHO 2009e). Lack of vitamin A increases the risk of child death from diarrhea and measles. Iodine, which can be readily added to salt and is found in seafood, helps prevent goiter and mental retardation. Zinc is important for bone growth, metabolism, and mental and emotional growth and stability. It also reduces the risk and impact of diarrhea, stunting, wasting, and pneumonia and lowers the risk of miscarriage (Hotz and Brown 2004).

Possible solutions to micronutrient deficiencies include vitamin supplementation and enrichment or fortification of foods. Breast milk is a significant, natural, cheap, readily available source of vitamin A for children. Salt can be iodized at a cost of pennies per ton. Supplementation is no substitute for proper diagnosis, however. Calis et al. (2008) studied 381 Malawian preschool children with severe anemia and found that iron deficiency was not a significant cause of anemia, but vitamin A deficiency and numerous diseases (such as malaria, HIV, and hookworm) were.

Table 2.2 Micronutrient deficiencies in Sub-Saharan Africa, by country, 1998–2004

Country	Iron (preschool) children affected, %)	Vitamin A (preschool children affected, %)	Iodine (total goiter rate, %)	Zinc (adult population at risk, %)	Economic impact (% of GDP lost)
Angola	72	55	33	46.0	2.1
Benin	82	70	<5	16.5	1.1
Botswana	37	30	17	17.1	0.6
Burkina Faso	83	46	29	13.3	2.0
Burundi			42	46.5	2.5
Cameroon	58	36	12	27.7	0.8
Cape Verde				16.6	
Central African Rep.	74	68	11	22.7	
Chad	76	45	24	21.1	1.2
Comoros				49.9	
Congo, Dem. Rep.	58	58		57.5	0.8
Congo, Rep.			36	42.9	1.9
Côte d'Ivoire				20.8	
Djibouti				37.3	
Eritrea	75	30	10	32.4	1.1
Ethiopia	85	30	23	21.7	1.7
Gabon	43	41	27	18.6	1.1
Gambia	75	64	20	36.1	1.3
Ghana	65	60	18	21.0	1.1
Guinea	73	40	23	33.9	1.4
Guinea-Bissau	83	31	17	29.0	1.5
Kenya	60	70	10	32.9	0.8
Lesotho	51	54	19	31.2	0.8
Liberia	69	38	18	59.2	1.2
Madagascar	73	42	6	32.9	0.8
Malawi	80	59	22	34.2	1.4
Mali	77	47	42	11.1	2.7
Mauritania	74	17	21	14.0	1.3
Mauritius				29.5	
Mozambique	80	26	17	60.5	1.2
Namibia	42	59	18	14.2	0.8
Niger	57	41	20	9.4	1.7
Nigeria	69	25	8	12.8	0.7
Rwanda	69	39	13	39.8	1.1
Sao Tome and Principe				36.7	
Senegal	71	61	23	25.3	1.3
Seychelles				18.8	
Sierra Leone	86	47	16	56.5	1.4
Somalia				17.1	
South Africa			16	19.7	0.4
Swaziland	47	38	12	20.5	0.6
Tanzania	65	37	16	37.5	
Togo	72	35	14	22.9	1.0
Uganda	64	66	9	23.8	1.0
Zambia	63	66	25	38.0	1.3
Zimbabwe	53	28	9	43.4	0.7

SOURCES: UNICEF 2004, based on existing surveys; for zinc, Hotz and Brown 2004.
NOTE: GDP = gross domestic product.

Obesity

The third form of malnutrition, obesity, generally results from excessive caloric intake relative to the body's metabolic needs and a person's activity level. It may also be a symptom of other health problems, including thyroid problems and genetic predisposition. A body mass index (BMI) of more than 25 indicates overweight, and a BMI of more than 30 signals obesity.[2] Overweight and obesity are primarily of concern because of their links with chronic diseases, such as Type 2 diabetes and heart problems.

As urbanization increases the proportion of adults engaged in sedentary work, caloric needs decrease. As globalization spreads the marketing influence of highly processed, high-calorie, low-nutrient foods worldwide and they penetrate into more and more areas, calorie consumption increases. The combination of these factors and others has contributed to what the WHO calls a global obesity epidemic. Yet as people change consumption patterns from high-nutrient, low-calorie foods to low-nutrient, high-calorie "junk" foods, obesity may mask hidden hunger.

It has long been assumed that obesity and overweight are largely problems of developed countries, where nearly half of the population is overweight. OECD (2009) shows that the United States has the highest percentage of obese adults, at 34 percent—representing a 12 percent increase since 2000 and a 100 percent increase since 1978. Even though South Korea has the lowest incidence of obesity, at 3 percent, this rate represents a 50 percent increase over only 10 years. Furthermore, 30 percent of the South Korean population is overweight.

During the past 20 years obesity has become an increasing problem across the developing world as well. WHO data show that in 8 of 45 Sub-Saharan African countries, more than 10 percent of children are overweight or obese, and in 20 more countries children have a 5–10 percent chance of being overweight or obese. In Comoros, more than one-fifth of the children are overweight or obese. Roberts (2004) reports that South Africa's prevalence of adult obesity is comparable to that of the United States and that 40 percent of Moroccans are overweight.

The increasing prevalence of obesity makes solving hunger much more difficult, particularly since obesity and hunger may be present within the same family in low-income areas (de Menezes Toledo Florêncio et al. 2001). Cultural attitudes and the AIDS virus make the situation more difficult as well. Arne Astrup, then-president-elect of the International Association for the Study of Obesity, noted that AIDS often leads to weight loss, creating a cultural bias against losing weight lest one be identified as HIV-positive (Roberts 2004). Thus fighting malnutrition does not simply involve increasing calorie consumption. To reduce hunger and obesity, a holistic health perspective should be taken that focuses on nutrition, education, lifestyle patterns, household decision-making dynamics, culture, sanitation, and water purity.

The World Food Summit and Millennium Development Goals

To encourage countries to take needed actions to combat hunger, the FAO convened the World Food Summit (WFS) in 1996. The summit's objective was to renew the political commitment to reducing hunger and malnutrition and engender greater public awareness of the seriousness of the associated problems. Close to 10,000 participants gathered in Rome with leaders and representatives of 185 governments. In signing the Rome Declaration and the associated seven-point Plan of Action, they pledged their support for the ongoing quest to eradicate hunger from the world, with an immediate view to decreasing the number of people suffering from hunger to half of its 1990 level by no later than 2015. The goals of the WFS and its 2002 follow-up, the World Food Summit Five Years Later, were reaffirmed in the final report of the 2009 Madrid High-Level Meeting on Food Security for All.

Despite the increased attention these summits directed to the problems of hunger and malnutrition, progress to date has been spotty at best. For the world as a whole, the number of hungry people fell slightly before the 1996 summit but increased again before the follow-up summit five years later. Overall, the number of hungry people declined by only 22 million between 1990 and 2001. After the follow-up summit, the level of hunger surpassed its 1991 level by 2005 (873 million). With the increase in food prices since then, FAO (2009b) estimates that the number of hungry people has increased by more than 120 million to surpass 1 billion in 2009.

A straight-line extrapolation of 1990–2005 data, representing business as usual, would bring the number of hungry people to about 860 million by 2015. Including rough estimates for 2007 and 2009, which do not come from country-by-country data, would raise the number of hungry people in 2015 to 990 million, an increase

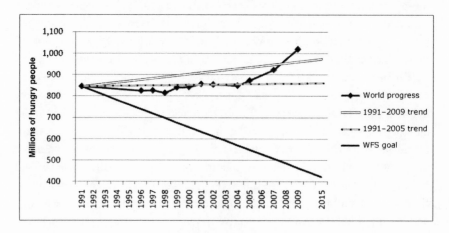

Figure 2.10   Progress toward meeting the WFS goal globally, 1991–2015
SOURCE: Observations from FAO 2009b; extrapolations by authors.

of 150 million from the 1990 level (Figure 2.10). It is important to remember that extrapolations are not predictions, but merely outcomes that are reasonable to expect under business as usual. Should the world's governments decide to place a priority on reducing the prevalence of hunger, the numbers could be very different.

Although the number of people suffering from hunger and malnutrition increased at the global level, it decreased rapidly in China. In fact, most of the progress on the world scale has been made by China, which reduced the number of hungry people by 50 million between 1991 and 2005. If China is not included, the global increase in the number of hungry people between 1990 and 2005 is much sharper. Two other countries that have seen changes almost as large are India (with 40 million more hungry people) and the Democratic Republic of the Congo (32 million more).

This bleak picture is worst in Sub-Saharan Africa, where the number of hungry people increased from 174 million in 1991 to 212 million by 2005 and may have risen to 265 million by 2009 (Figure 2.11). At present trends there will be between 250 and 270 million hungry people by 2015 in Sub-Saharan Africa instead of the targeted 87 million, an increase of 40–60 percent. As shown in Figure 2.12, much of this increase has occurred in Central Africa, where the incidence of hunger doubled during the 1990s. In the other three subregions of Africa, the incidence of hunger was largely unchanged until the food crisis, with a slight decrease in West Africa and slight increases in Southern and East Africa. The chapter will consider the importance of Central Africa again shortly.

In 2000, the MDGs reinforced the work of the World Food Summit by calling for halving the share of the population suffering from hunger between 1990 and 2015. The actual document signed by the governments of the world did not contain specific numeric targets, only a declaration that they would work to decrease hunger and malnutrition and improve other important targets. The targets were added after the fact and were designed to be in line with earlier declarations. For most countries, meeting the MDG for hunger will be easier than meeting the World Food Summit goal because population growth naturally reduces the share of people suffering from hunger even if the number of hungry people remains constant. For the countries of Sub-Saharan Africa, with their high rates of population growth, the MDG is a much easier hurdle.

In fact, before the food crisis, the world experienced a real decline in the proportion of people suffering from hunger—from 16 percent in 1991 to 13 percent in 2005. This decline led to an expectation of a rate of 10.9 percent by 2015, which is at least close to the goal of 9.5 percent. The food crisis brought the share of people suffering from hunger back up to 15 percent in 2009, implying that little to no progress will be made by 2015.

Progress has been somewhat slower in Sub-Saharan Africa than elsewhere. The share of the population suffering from hunger fell from 34 percent in 1991 to

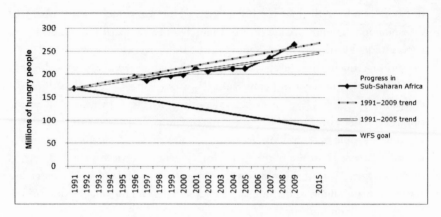

Figure 2.11   Progress toward the World Food Summit goal in Sub-Saharan Africa,
1991–2015
SOURCE: Observations from FAO 2009b; extrapolations by authors.

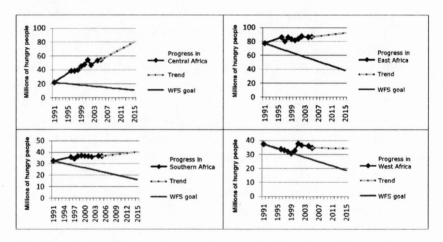

Figure 2.12   Progress toward meeting the WFS goal in Sub-Saharan Africa, by region
SOURCE: Observations from FAO 2009b; extrapolations by authors.

30 percent in 2007, rising slightly to 31.6 percent in 2009. This pattern suggests that the prevalence of hunger will be at least 10 percentage points higher than promised by 2015. Breaking this figure down by subregion is again instructive. West Africa appeared to be on track to meet the MDG, thanks largely to progress in Ghana, until 2004. Similarly, East and Southern Africa show significant progress, reducing hunger from 44 to 35 percent and from 45 to 37 percent, respectively. In Central Africa, however, the percentage of people suffering from hunger has increased dramatically from 36 percent to 58 percent. Current trends indicate that the share of the population suffering from hunger in that region will have more than doubled by 2015.

Contribution of the Democratic Republic of the Congo

The doubling of the incidence of hunger in Central Africa, whether measured by the number of people or the percentage of the population, represents the primary change in Africa. What has caused this dramatic increase in hunger? Considering the changes by country (Figure 2.13), it is readily apparent that nearly all the change has come from the Democratic Republic of the Congo[3] (DRC), known as Zaire until 1997. In 1991, the DRC had the third-largest number of hungry people in Africa, and by 1997 there were more hungry people there than in any other African country. Since 1991, the DRC has seen a larger increase in the number of hungry people (32.5 million) than any other country in the world. No other African country has experienced such a large change in the number of hungry people during this time period, and only China and India—with more than 20 times the population—have seen a larger change.

The DRC is remarkable for a number of reasons. It has the fifth-lowest gross domestic product (GDP) per capita in Sub-Saharan Africa and the lowest gross national income per capita. The annual growth rate of GDP is lower in the DRC than anywhere else in Sub-Saharan Africa (-6.3 percent). Its official economy is the most dependent on agriculture, with 59 percent of GDP coming from agriculture. The government spends less on health per person than any other country in the world. Since 1990 the official development assistance (ODA) going to the DRC has increased 10-fold. It receives twice the ODA of any other African country

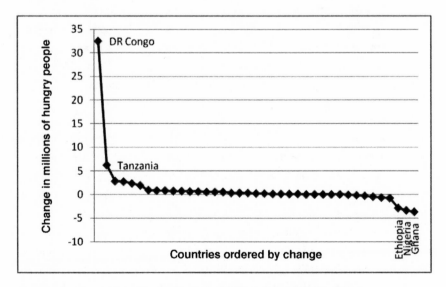

Figure 2.13   Change in millions of hungry people in Sub-Saharan Africa, by country, 1991–2005
SOURCE: Based on data from FAO 2009b.

and has the highest ODA per capita. The Freedom House measure of good governance shows that, although the DRC does not have the worst governance in Africa, its score has averaged 6 out of 7 throughout the past decade, worse than the average score of 4.

Geography has played an important role in the DRC. Although it is not technically landlocked, only a narrow corridor links the bulk of the country in the center of Africa to the Atlantic seashore, making trade with the outside world difficult. On the other hand, the DRC has been blessed with more rain each year than any other country in Africa and with mineral wealth. Unfortunately, as shown by Ross (1999), Bannon and Collier (2003), Englebert and Ron (2004), Mehlum, Moene, and Torvik (2006), and a host of others, great mineral wealth can be a mixed blessing, leading to armed conflict and economic stagnation rather than continual development, particularly where governance is already weak.

War has been particularly devastating in the DRC, and it is certain that progress will remain elusive until the conflict can be brought to an end. Yet the First Congolese War did not begin until 1996, by which point the incidence of hunger had already more than doubled. To what extent the increase in hunger led to the first war is an open question that has not yet been adequately researched. It appears, however, that any explanation of why Sub-Saharan Africa is not on target to accomplish the WFS goal and the MDG must focus on the DRC.

Considering the progress of Sub-Saharan Africa without the DRC, the situation looks very different. Half of the difference between the expected incidence of hunger in 2015 and the WFS goal is caused by the DRC. Without the DRC, the number of hungry people in Sub-Saharan Africa was largely unchanged from 1991 to 2005, and the percentage of the population suffering from hunger decreased dramatically because of rapid population growth. In fact, the remainder of Sub-Saharan Africa was within 2 percentage points of being on target to accomplish the MDG before the food price swings of 2007–08.

This situation suggests two things. The first, already mentioned, is that for Sub-Saharan Africa to succeed, it is essential that the DRC get turned around. The second is that with only a little more effort and support, including the correction of any negative effects of the recent food and economic crises, the remainder of Sub-Saharan Africa could accomplish the MDG for hunger. This is one of the best pieces of news to emerge for the MDGs.

Figure 2.13 depicts the change in the number of hungry people in each country, ordered from largest increase to largest decrease. The vast majority of countries saw relatively little change in the number of hungry people. Only nine countries saw a change of more than 1 million people (Ghana, Nigeria, and Ethiopia with large decreases and the DRC, Tanzania, Kenya, Madagascar, Burundi, and Zambia with large increases).

The fact that the changes have been small in number does not mean that they have not been important. Many countries in Africa had few hungry people to begin with, so a small change in the number of hungry people is large relative to the previous level. Eleven countries have seen more than a 50 percent increase in the number of people suffering from hunger already, the exact reverse of the WFS goal, and six more are on target to reach that same point by 2015. Nonetheless, population has risen much faster than the number of hungry people, implying that most countries in Sub-Saharan Africa are experiencing progress toward the MDG.

In addition to considering the change in the number or percentage suffering from hunger, IFPRI has developed a Global Hunger Index (GHI) to provide a more inclusive measure of hunger (von Grebmer et al. 2009). It is determined by aggregating the three variables: the percentage of the population suffering from hunger, the percentage of children under the age of five who are underweight, and the under-five mortality rate expressed as a percentage. Each year's GHI is based on data from a span of years; the 1990 GHI is based on data from 1988–92, and the 2009 GHI is based on data from 2002–07 (von Grebmer et al. 2009). Table 2.3 summarizes Sub-Saharan African countries' progress in reducing hunger as reflected in three different measures—the number of people suffering from hunger (WFS goal), the percentage of people suffering from hunger (MDG 1), and the GHI.

Population growth in Sub-Saharan Africa is high enough to put any country with a decreasing number of hungry people on track to accomplish the MDG by 2015. Even some countries where the number of hungry people is slowly increasing are on track. That is why a number of countries are likely to achieve the MDG whereas few countries are on track to achieve the WFS goal. The GHI provides a balance between these two measures: most countries are making some progress according to the GHI, but few are on target to decrease hunger by half by 2015. There is broad agreement between the MDG and GHI on which countries are making progress. This fact should be no surprise since one-third of the GHI comes from the data used for the MDG. It is comforting, though, that child mortality and underweight prevalence appear to move similarly with hunger in the broader economy.

Table 2.3 Progress in Sub-Saharan Africa by goal (number of countries)

Progress	WFS 1991–2005	MDG 1991–2005	GHI 1990–2004
On target to halve hunger by 2015	1	12	4
Some progress	8	15	24
No progress/slow worsening	13	5	9
Serious worsening	17	7	1

SOURCES: FAO 2009b; von Grebmer et al. 2009.

Conclusions

Combating hunger and malnutrition is one of the greatest challenges the world faces today. The right to food was enshrined in the Universal Declaration of Human Rights by the United Nations in 1948. This right was reaffirmed by numerous speakers, including Secretary-General Ban Ki-Moon and Pope Benedict XVI, at the 2007 World Food Day. On that occasion the secretary-general declared, "The world has the resources, the knowledge, and the tools to make the right to food a reality for all" (UN 2007). This chapter has shown, however, that the right to food is not a reality for hundreds of millions of people, and with business as usual, that vision will not be fulfilled as promised in the World Food Summit goal and the Millennium Development Goals.

The number of hungry people in Sub-Saharan Africa has doubled since 1970, increasing by 100 million even while the number of hungry people in the rest of the world has decreased by 200 million. Over time, the problem of hunger is being concentrated in the countries of Sub-Saharan Africa. In 1991, roughly 20 percent of the people suffering from hunger lived in Sub-Saharan Africa. By 2002, halfway between when the MDG and WFS goals were set and when they were due to be met, 24 percent of the people suffering from hunger lived in Sub-Saharan Africa. If current trends continue, nearly 30 percent of the world's hungry people will live in Sub-Saharan Africa by 2015. The increasing marginalization of Africa will be an impediment to future development efforts unless prompt action is taken now at every level.

There is good news too, however. Though the number of hungry people in Africa has been increasing, the rate of increase has slowed since 1970. Furthermore, some countries are making significant progress in reducing the share of the population suffering from hunger. The subregion of West Africa is on target to achieve the MDG by 2015.

One of the striking conclusions of the analysis in this chapter has been the dominant role of relatively few countries in determining regional and subregional trends. Just as China alone has reduced hunger by more than the total world change, nearly all of the increase in the number of hungry people in Africa during the 1990s can be attributed to the increasing incidence of hunger in the DRC, where three times as many people—more than 70 percent of the population—suffered from hunger in 2005 as did in 1991. Similarly, West Africa is on track to accomplish the MDG largely because Ghana had already done so by 2002. Most countries in Sub-Saharan Africa saw only small changes in the number of hungry people.

To understand global and regional trends, researchers must examine the individual countries causing the greatest shifts and study the shifting patterns of hunger reduction within those countries. The more specifically and precisely these changes in hunger can be measured, the easier it will be to determine the underlying causes of hunger and the binding constraints preventing its reduction. This understanding will give policy makers and other concerned groups the tools they need to combat hunger in their specific regions.

The hunger trends in Sub-Saharan Africa are dominated by the changes in the DRC. It will be impossible to achieve the regional MDG for hunger without turning the situation there around. Yet the rest of Africa has a much brighter prospect because most countries have experienced little change in the number of people suffering hunger. Thus renewed efforts could still achieve the MDG for hunger in the rest of Sub-Saharan Africa (that is, excluding the DRC) by 2015.

As these efforts unfold, it is important to pay attention not only to the goal deadline of 2015, but also to the long-term ability of households and families to feed themselves. If, as seems likely unless current trends change, the WFS goal and MDGs are not met by 2015, the world will have to press on and continue fighting against hunger, poverty, and malnutrition. As Johannes Rau, former president of Germany, declared:

> The fight against hunger calls for patience, endurance, great commitment and persuasiveness. We need patience and endurance because the fight against hunger is long and hard. We should not allow ourselves to become disheartened if progress is sometimes less than we had hoped, or if we suffer set-backs in some areas, and must keep our eyes firmly fixed on our goal: a world without hunger (Rau n.d., 1–2).

There is hope. Progress is being made in many areas. These goals are attainable, but more must be done in order to make them a reality. That which we can do, we must.

Notes

1. Before 2006, nutritional status was determined using only children from the United States as a reference population. These data came from the National Center for Health Statistics/WHO. WHO has now moved to a new reference population including children from Brazil, Ghana, India, Norway, Oman, and the United States. The 2009 *State of the World's Children* is the first to use the new reference population, so both sample populations are reported for comparability with earlier results.

2. BMI is calculated by dividing a person's weight in kilograms by the height in meters squared. It is less accurate for elderly people, tall people, and people with large amounts of lean-muscle mass.

3. Also known as Congo-Kinshasa.

CHAPTER 3

Disease Burdens of Sub-Saharan Africa and
Their Interactions with Malnutrition

Onesmo K. ole-MoiYoi

Abstract

To control disease, integrated solutions are needed that incorporate strategies with synergistic components, enabling partner organizations to work together to achieve the goal of reducing the burden of disease and malnutrition. Synergistic components must include

- recognition of country and regional priorities for socioeconomic development;
- commitment and support by Sub-Saharan African governments;
- holistic approaches to disease control that recognize the interplay between disease and malnutrition;
- community involvement in policy formulation, project planning, implementation, and evaluation;
- application of innovative and appropriate technologies;
- development of capacity in Sub-Saharan Africa for all aspects of disease control; and
- donor agency coordination.

According to the *World Development Report* (World Bank 2008), the overarching global challenges of the 21st century, including ending hunger and poverty, sustaining the environment, providing security, and managing global health, will be difficult to achieve without significant improvements in agricultural productivity. Both agricultural productivity and animal and human health will be adversely affected if insufficient attention is paid to holistic strategies to mitigate malnutrition and the spread of infectious diseases.

Background

Most countries in Sub-Saharan Africa are mired in a profound poverty problem and are not on track to achieve most of the Millennium Development Goals (MDGs). Civil strife and poor governance are major contributors to this lack of progress, and extreme poverty raises the likelihood of not only violent conflict and the collapse of states into lawlessness, but also falling health indicators.

The Africa of the 21st century is faced with a heavy burden of disease, combined with ill-equipped medical systems and underdeveloped technological capacity. In addition, the perceived risk of infections and other health problems discourage foreign investment and trade, thus further exacerbating marginalization and poverty. A major challenge for the governments of Sub-Saharan Africa and the international development community is thus to bring scientific and technological advances in the biological sciences to bear on the health priorities of poorer countries.

Five of the MDGs focus on health-related challenges where progress has been slow: (1) eradicate extreme poverty and hunger; (2) reduce infant mortality; (3) improve maternal health; (4) combat HIV/AIDS, malaria, tuberculosis, and other diseases with access to essential medicines; and (5) reduce the proportion of people without access to safe water and improved sanitation. These challenges are intensified by problems of gender inequity, lack of basic infrastructure, environmental degradation, and climate change, all of which have direct and indirect detrimental effects on health and agricultural productivity.

Recent advances in biomedical research, particularly in genomics and bioinformatics, increase the probability of developing both new and improved childhood vaccines. These advances have already led to the development of additional multivalent vaccines and regimens that show great promise against conventional viruses and bacterial infections.

Some of the pathogenic agents causing the diseases under consideration here, such as intestinal worms, are entirely controllable with better access to affordable drugs, enhanced community education programs, and mobilization and delivery of public health services. Others—namely HIV, the tubercle bacillus, the malaria parasites, and the agents causing African trypanosomiases—are not conventional. Each of these diseases has confounding biological phenomena characteristic of the host-agent interface that complicate the development of therapies against it.

Disease and Malnutrition

The burdens of disease and malnutrition, each reinforcing the other, continually conspire to weaken African populations and are at the core of Sub-Saharan

Africa's perennial dilemma of a vicious circle of poverty and underdevelopment. Undernourishment is considered the major cause of Sub-Saharan Africa's high prevalence of acquired immunodeficiency syndrome (AIDS), which predisposes people to a multitude of infections caused by viruses, bacteria, protozoa, and intestinal worms. Infection stimulates specific and nonspecific host defense mechanisms. The capacity to mount these molecular and cellular self-defense pathways is directly influenced by the host's macro- and micronutrient status. Observations in populations, even those with adequate caloric intake, have shown that micronutrient malnutrition is associated with alterations in tissue integrity at the portals of entry of infectious agents such as reduction or lack of mucous secretions that trap and remove foreign agents, loss of ciliated respiratory tract epithelium, alterations in normal intestinal flora, and a diminution in the capacity for phagocytosis of invading organisms (Grimble 1994).

The synergism between infection and malnutrition is especially clear in areas of poor basic sanitation where bacterial infections and worm infestations are common causes of diarrhea, which is often associated with blood loss and malabsorption of nutrients. Poverty and lack of education also have a deleterious influence on eating habits (Grimble 1994). Generalized infection with fever causes hypercatabolism, which is often aggravated by anorexia, with a resultant loss and ultimately depletion of body nutrient reserves (Filteau and Tomkins 1994).

The combination of disease and malnutrition is responsible for Sub-Saharan Africa's high mortality rates for infants (9.5 percent) and children under age five (16 percent). Although these rates are gradually decreasing, they are still far above those of the rest of the world, including South Asia (UNICEF 2008a). The two-way links between disease and poverty in the adult population, which are such a prominent feature of HIV/AIDS and agricultural productivity, are discussed in chapter 5.

Malaria and intestinal helminthic infestations often coexist and are major contributors to caloric and micronutrient malnutrition. The most vulnerable populations are pregnant women, infants, and children, who are often already malnourished. On the one hand, anemic pregnant women with malaria and intestinal infestations are at a high risk of giving premature birth and of bearing infants with low birth weight (LBW), while on the other hand, premature and LBW infants are at a higher risk of early childhood mortality and impaired growth as well as impaired cognitive development (Stephenson, Latham, and Ottesen 2000; Steketee 2003). Because of preexisting conditions prior to pregnancy, some of these adverse consequences may pass from generation to generation.

To break this vicious circle of malnutrition, infection, and immunological decompensation, disease control measures need to be instituted alongside appropriate nutritional interventions. Therapeutic efforts based on food enrichment, such as adding vitamins to staple foods, have had appreciable success. A more recent approach is the biofortification of major staples eaten by populations in the developing world. This novel strategy employs recent advances in the biological sciences to speed up the selection and propagation of crops with desirable traits, such as enrichment in major micronutrients for which deficiencies are common. This is further discussed in chapter 14.

Control of Infectious Tropical Diseases

As previously stated, many diseases and malnutrition are mutually reinforcing. This chapter will consider vector-borne diseases, helminthic infestations, and animal protozoan diseases that have profound effects on the nutritional status of populations in Sub-Saharan Africa.

Malaria

Within the Task Force on MDG 6 is the Working Group on Malaria, which has sought to develop a framework for relieving the burden of malaria, a disease that infects 300–500 million people annually worldwide. Although malaria is endemic in Asia, Southeast Asia, and Central and South America, the highest prevalence and severest morbidity and mortality from this protozoan parasitic infection occur in Sub-Saharan Africa. Malaria causes more than 1–2 million deaths (WHO 2000) of mostly children. It has been estimated to cause economic losses totaling US$12 billion a year and to retard Sub-Saharan Africa's economic growth by 1.3 percent annually. For people living in highly endemic areas, this loss translates into the spending of up to 25 percent of the family's income on combating malaria.

Mosquito malaria vectors breed astonishingly well in many human-made environments in rural, urban, and periurban areas, including in discarded plastics that are an eyesore across Sub-Saharan Africa and the rest of the developing world, cans, abandoned pools, and old tires. In urban and periurban areas, mosquitoes have adapted amazingly well to breeding sites that are often highly polluted with elevated levels of heavy metals and other toxins. With efforts to increase agricultural productivity, examples of mosquito breeding sites also include rice paddies and maize fields. In the latter, maize pollen has been identified as an excellent nutrient for mosquito larvae so that it is used in ex *vivo* propagation of malaria. Malaria parasites have also adapted remarkably well to survival in mammalian hosts, having evolved means to transit through the circulatory system, which is a most hostile environment. These protozoa have also evolved precise mechanisms of entry and survival in liver cells and erythrocytes, within which they multiply. Malarial parasites, perhaps more than any other disease-causing agent, have influenced human evolution with a selection pressure that has given rise to sickle cell hemoglobin (HbSS) and various other erythrocytic disorders.

These erythrocytic traits, which are associated with milder forms of malaria and thus better survival, include HbC, HbE, HbF, α and β thalassemias, and glucose-6-phosphate dehydrogenase deficiency (Nagel 2004).

The sickle cell trait (HbAS) in the heterozygous state confers protection against the development of life-threatening parasitemia, perhaps because the variant HbAS is more difficult to digest by the parasite, which relies on hemoglobin as a source of amino acids. HbAS also predisposes red blood cells to mechanical deformation and thus premature removal from the circulation. The incidence of cerebral malaria in children with the sickle cell trait is reported to be at the level of 90 percent relative to normal controls (Hill et al. 1992).

Tolerance to malaria or premunition has also been described. These patients are parasitemic but have no disease symptoms. Such a potential polymorphism has been identified in human chromosome 5, which might confer resistance to malaria in disease carrier populations in East Africa (Hernandez-Valladares et al. 2004). Identification of such asymptomatic individuals, who provide a significant pool for mosquito infection, and their treatment is essential if the disease is to be effectively controlled.

The most common and virulent malarial infections are caused by *Plasmodium falciparum*. The full genome of a clone of *P. falciparum* has been sequenced (Gardner et al. 2002). The genome, which has 23 chromosomes, is 23 megabytes (Mb) in size and encodes about 5,300 genes, 60 percent of which have little or no predicted sequence similarity to proteins from other organisms. Surprisingly, only 14 percent of the predicted proteome sequences are enzymes. For this reason many important features of the *P. falciparum* metabolism that would be useful as targets in the search for more specific chemotherapeutic agents remain unclear. The complete absence of biosynthetic pathways for amino acids and the homologues of their transporters perhaps serve to emphasize the parasitic life-style of this obligate, intracellular pathogen. Relative to other eukaryotes whose genomes have been sequenced, the *P. falciparum* genome has a large number of genes that encode proteins that mediate immune evasion. Among these is the *var* family that has 59 genes, which encode erythrocyte membrane protein 1 (PfEMP1), a highly polymorphic group of molecules expressed on the red blood cell surface membrane, fully exposed to detection by the mammalian immune system (Baruch et al. 1995; Su et al. 1995; Horrocks et al. 2004). It has been postulated that the high rate of switching of the expression of *var* genes provides a high degree of antigenic variation and evasion of mammalian host immune destruction. Other gene families that appear in clusters in the genome of *P. falciparum* exhibit high sequence heterogeneity, which may also contribute to parasite genomic diversity. The availability of the genome sequence is facilitating a better understanding of *P. falciparum* parasite biology, including a better definition of loci for important phenotypes such as drug resistance and perhaps virulence.

Among the significant metabolic alterations seen in patients with malaria living in a disease-endemic area in Brazil is a decrease in transport proteins such as albumin and transferrin as well lower levels of cholesterol and total lipids, which may be secondary effects of fever and gluconeogenesis (Pereira et al. 1995). As a disease, malaria exacerbates anemia in populations that are already ravaged by iron and folate deficiencies.

MALARIA IN PREGNANCY

It has been documented that *P. falciparum* malaria is more common in pregnant than in nonpregnant women (Steketee et al. 2001). The effects of low-pressure blood flow in the placental venous bed combine with those of parasitized erythrocyte adherence to endothelial cells, which causes clogging of the blood vessels, to lower the oxygen available for the fetus. Unlike other human parasites, malaria has clear and substantial adverse effects on pregnancy, nutrition during pregnancy, and pregnancy outcomes (van den Broek 2001; Brabin 1991; McGregor, Wilson, and Billewicz 1983).

In general, cytoadherence, which disrupts microvasculature blood flow, causes low oxygenation to vital organs with resultant dysfunction and is thus central to the pathophysiology of malaria. Cytoadherence may thus be among the major factors favoring parasite sequestration and replication, especially in pregnancy. Evidence suggests that the main mediators of cytoadherence are the *P. falciparum* erythrocyte membrane proteins1 (PfEMP1). In pregnancy, this phenomenon may occur under circumstances where it is difficult to document the presence of malaria parasites in the maternal circulation. A combination of low capacity for oxygen transport due to the malaria-induced anemia and nutrient deprivation, as well as host immune responses, contributes to intrauterine growth retardation (IUGR) and premature birth (Ismail et al. 2000; Menendez et al. 2000; Garner and Brabin 1994). Even with minor or moderate bleeding during delivery, the anemia of pregnancy predisposes the mother to hypotension, shock, and death.

CONTROL MEASURES FOR MALARIA

It has been shown that preemptive treatment of pregnant women in prenatal clinics for malaria in Sub-Saharan Africa helps improve pregnancy outcomes. To avoid the adverse consequences of disease, Roll Back Malaria and other initiatives have advocated this approach, as well as the addition of micronutrients to diets for pregnant women (Nahlen 2000).

In spite of several declarations in the past 20 years, including the World Health Organization's Roll Back Malaria (RBM) initiative and the Abuja Declaration and Plan of Action on Roll Back Malaria, the disease continues to be a major threat in much of Sub-Saharan Africa. The Abuja Declaration, which was an affirmation of the RBM initiative, was impressive in its representation and commitment to setting up the Plan of Action for the control of malaria (Roll Back Malaria/World Health Organization 2003). Of the 50 countries in Sub-Saharan Africa in which malaria is endemic, 80 percent were signatories to the declaration. Nineteen heads of state attended the summit, and the rest were represented by vice presidents, prime ministers, and ministers of health. Four of the founding agencies were international and included the World Bank, the World Health Organization (WHO), the Food and Agriculture Organization of the United Nations (FAO), and the United Nations Children's Fund (UNICEF). All the major global developments agencies were also prominently represented. The Abuja Declaration advocated a holistic strategy including the use of insecticide-impregnated bed nets, the availability of affordable antimalarials, and the control of mosquito larvae. The latter had been and continues to be largely ignored in many malaria control programs.

It has been difficult to implement proposed RBM interventions, however, partly because of inadequate funding and logistics. Recently the Global Fund to Fight AIDS, Tuberculosis, and Malaria, which is the world's largest funder of malaria control programs, has been advocating for higher levels of funding and has proposed the establishment of country-led initiatives with clearer objectives, targets, and follow-up assessment of impact.[1]

Lessons learned from a multitude of well-meaning but random and uncoordinated interventions carried out over the past 50 years reveal that no single solution is likely to succeed in the control of malaria. Long-term, holistic, and sustainable solutions are needed.

WHO'S ERADICATION CAMPAIGN AGAINST MALARIA

WHO's post–World War II Global Malaria Eradication Campaign eliminated malaria from vast areas of Southern Europe, the United States, and, to a lesser extent, parts of Latin America, where the disease had been endemic (Najera 2001). The tools used in this highly successful eradication campaign included extensive aerial spraying, albeit using DDT, and environmental management. In Sub-Saharan Africa, the eradication campaign was abandoned in 1969 because it was considered logistically, socially, and politically impractical, given the then-emerging picture of the adverse effects of DDT on the environment. The fact that effective and affordable drugs were also available at that time gave credence to the rationale for abandoning the eradication campaign in Sub-Saharan Africa.

After the eradication campaign was abandoned in Sub-Saharan Africa, the gradual emergence of global drug resistance in *P. falciparum* led to the advocacy for a new strategy, which was based on developing new drugs for treating malaria rather than continuing with any measure of disease prevention.

PARASITE GENETIC VARIABILITY AND DRUG RESISTANCE

Plasmodium falciparum uses genetic variability not only to evade recognition and destruction by the mammalian immune surveillance mechanisms, but also to develop resistance to anti-malarials. WHO's Malaria Eradication Campaign was abandoned in Sub-Saharan Africa in 1969 not only because of the ill-advised use of DDT, but also for logistical reasons. Disease control was further frustrated by the appearance of drug-resistant parasites. Over the years, global resistance to first-line drugs has continued to develop. As a result, chloroquine and sulfadoxine/pyrimethanine are not recommended for use across Sub-Saharan Africa, and resistance to amodiaquine is increasingly being reported in East Africa. Unlike South America, where resistance to mefloquine appears to be widespread, this is not yet the case in Sub-Saharan Africa.

The recent advances in genomics have allowed the identification of several *P. falciparum* genes associated with drug resistance, which include dihydrofolate reductase (*pfdhfr*), dihydropteroate synthase (*pfdhps*), chloroquine resistance transporter gene (*pfcrt*), multidrug resistance gene (*pfmdr1*), and Ca^{2+}ATPase gene (*pf*ATPase). The drug resistance phenotype is often associated with amplification or mutations in such genes.

Because monotherapy is likely to lead to resistance, WHO's recommended combination therapy, with derivatives of artemisinin, such as artemether/lumefantrin (AL - Coartem®), artesunate/mefloquine (AS-MR), artesunate/amodiaquine (AS-AQ), and artesunate/sulphadoxine (AL-SP), is being widely implemented (Nosten and White 2007).

MONITORING FOR THE EMERGENCE OF DRUG RESISTANCE

Monitoring for the appearance of drug resistance in epidemiological surveys has been especially challenging. Drug resistance to anti-malarials is sometimes conferred by mutations involving single-nucleotide polymorphisms (SNPs) in the drug resistance loci. PCR-based amplification of the drug resistance–associated genes allows for monitoring the appearance of SNPs associated with parasite resistance to anti-malarials that can be performed on an epidemiological scale (Crameri et al. 2007). For example, in a recent study in Thailand that analyzed SNPs of genes that confer drug resistance to mefloquine in *P. falciparum,* it was established that amplification of *pfmdr1* was the most important determinant of resistance to this particular drug as well as to reduced sensitivity to artesunate treatment. These SNP-based studies hold promise for improving the efficiency and accuracy of epidemiological surveys for drug resistance and for predicting treatment failures at the level of the individual patient.

Genomics can thus be used to develop more efficient methods of monitoring the emergence of drug resistance in infectious agents as well as other diseases. Additionally, studies focusing on analyses of genome-wide diversity among *P. falciparum* isolates from diverse geographical regions revealed a strong positional correlation with gene function. Using groups of drug-resistant isolates, genomic regions showing lower diversity were sought in comparative studies with drug sensitive parasites. Large regions of low diversity (selective sweeps) among chloroquine-resistant (CQ®) parasites were found on chromosome 5, 7, and 11 and those of pyrimethamine resistance (PYR®) on chromosomes 13 and 14. The low-diversity regions on chromosomes 7 and 13 contained the loci for the well-known sweeps for *pfcrt* and *pfdhfr*, respectively (Volkman et al. 2007). These studies illustrate the power of genome-wide population genetic analyses in the identification of selective sweeps bearing loci for important phenotypes, such as drug resistance.

With the availability of the genome sequence for *P. falciparum*, there is renewed interest in the development of new drugs against malaria. Some of these efforts involve novel multinational platforms of public-private partnerships such as the Medicines for Malaria Venture (http://www.mmv.org). Perhaps these public-private initiatives will make innovative contributions in overcoming what will continue to be one of the major obstacles for the control of malaria—namely, the cost and the length of time it takes for any promising compounds to reach licensure.

VACCINES FOR MALARIA

It was hoped that with the advent of molecular biology and the cloning of the genes encoding the circumsporozoite (*Pf*CSP) surface protein of the human-infective stages of *P. falciparum*, the sporozoites would provide candidate antigens with which vaccines would be easily developed. For more than 25 years, a good deal of effort has been directed at developing anti-malarial vaccines using recombinant DNA technologies. There have been many false starts, but, according to WHO, more than 70 vaccine candidates were at different levels of development in 2004 (http://www.who.int/vaccines/aboutus.shtml). So far, the only vaccine candidates that have conferred any degree of protection have been those based on *Pf*CSP. Such a vaccine has been tested in one- to four-year-old children in Mozambique and reduces new *Falciparum* infection by about 10 percent and the incidence of severe disease by 58 percent (Alonso et al. 2004). Clearly there is a need to develop better vaccines, and investigations are focused on developing attenuated, sporozoites-based vaccines (Luke and Hoffman 2003).

The assumption that vaccines based on the surface proteins of *P. falciparum* sporozoites would be efficacious was based on the relative ease with which anti-viral and anti-bacterial vaccines had been developed. Malaria parasites are multihost, intracellular protozoa that have much larger genomes and have evolved very sophisticated and complex ways of survival. The emerging picture on the immunity to malaria is that its basis is both antibody- and cell-mediated. Scientists' understanding of the molecular and cellular aspects of immunity to malaria is improving, but the use of available information for vaccine development is still rudimentary.

The available evidence already suggests that not one, but perhaps several vaccines will be needed for the control of malaria. The vaccines may cover the three categories: antisporozoite (pre-erythrocytic), asexual (erythrocytic) stage vaccines, and transmission-blocking. Unfortunately, during the past 25 years of work on vaccine development, millions have continued to die of malaria—mostly children in Sub-Saharan Africa and Southeast Asia.

LESSON FROM THE WHO MALARIA ERADICATION CAMPAIGN

In the current pursuit of new drugs and the development of recombinant vaccines for malaria, the lesson that has been forgotten from the WHO campaign is that mosquito control and environmental management were the basis for successful malaria eradication more than 50 years ago. None of these elements feature prominently in current control programs in Sub-Saharan Africa. Although DDT was a major component of the WHO campaign, it is no longer the best option for many reasons, including the availability of biopesticides, such as native *Bacillus thuringiensis* israeliensis (*Bti*) and *Bacillus sphericus* (*Bs*) toxins that have considerably fewer adverse effects on the environment.

THE NEED FOR A HOLISTIC STRATEGY FOR CONTROLLING MALARIA

In spite of many claims, silver-bullet strategies for controlling malaria, including treating the infection in patients or using bed nets or insecticide-treated nets, have not succeeded in reducing disease incidence. In a general way, affordability and drug resistance pose a challenge for the former approach, and insecticide resistance among mosquitoes owing to natural selection (mosquitoes learning to bite before bedtime) for the latter.

One of the most strongly advocated interventions for the control of malaria in Sub-Saharan Africa is the use of bed nets, especially insecticide-treated nets (ITNs). Although the use of protective netting should correlate with a decrease in the incidence of malaria, the use of such protection is low in countries that are most affected by the disease. The Sub-Saharan African country with the highest percentage of bed-net use in under-fives is Congo Brazzaville at 68 percent, but in that country only 6 percent of bed nets are treated with insecticides. Ethiopia has one of the lowest rates of use, at 2 percent, and although all are ITNs, the low rate of use suggests a serious problem with effectiveness in relation to the relative intensity of disease transmission and sustainability of the program. The data available for East African countries reveal the following ratios of conventional bed net/insecticide-treated bed net coverage in under-fives, respectively: Tanzania, 31 percent/16 percent; Uganda, 22 percent/10 percent; and Kenya, 15 percent/5 percent. Central and West African countries together average 16 percent/7 percent, and the average for the whole continent is 15 percent/8 percent (UNICEF 2008a, Health Table 3).

It is becoming increasingly obvious that a holistic strategy for the control of malaria is required. Such an integrated campaign against malaria would include not only the availability of affordable, artemisinin-base combination therapy and the distribution of insecticide-treated bed nets, but also the control of mosquitoes at larval stages, the identification and treatment of the malaria carrier population that has a polymorphism for malaria resistance, and closely working with communities in the disease endemic areas. The latter is critical if a sense of ownership of disease control programs is to develop and interventions are to be sustainable. With coordination and monitoring, these interventions can significantly reduce sickness and death from malaria in Africa, even before any new drugs or vaccines are available.

APPLICATION OF A HOLISTIC STRATEGY FOR THE CONTROL OF MALARIA: PRELIMINARY EVIDENCE

There is evidence that such a holistic strategy is effective for the control of malaria in several ecoregional zones, including periurban areas, highland areas, and irrigated rice-growing areas in Kenya. The latter are new, but the cultivation of rice is rapidly spreading into many areas of Sub-Saharan Africa (Jacob et al. 2007).

In the highlands of Kenya, more than 85 percent of mosquito breeding sites are human-made, consisting of pits made by brick layers, pools from abandoned fishery projects, as well as unexpected sites such as holes in tree trunks. Epidemiological studies in urban, coastal Kenya similarly reveal that breeding sites for mosquitoes are standing water, discarded plastics, cans, ,and old tires. Environmental degradation is thus a major contributor to the spread of malaria. The availability of this information on mosquito breeding sites is essential in setting up effective control programs (Mwangangi et al. 2006; Githeko et al. 2006).

Environmental management and larval control are crucial and will require concerted efforts targeted at minimizing human–mosquito contact (insecticide-treated nets and biological repellents) and treatment of the disease using affordable drugs such as artemisinin-based combinations. A participatory approach that actively involves the affected communities is fundamental to sustainable mosquito and disease control.

Parasitic Infections

Hookworms, roundworms, whipworms, flukes, and protozoa infect millions of people in the developing world and are major contributors to malnutrition, causing considerable morbidity and mortality in areas where poor hygiene and poor water supplies are common. Anemia, poor appetite with weight loss, and intestinal discomfort are the commonest presenting signs in intestinal helminthic infections (Dreyfuss et al. 2000).

The roundworm (*Ascaris lumbricoides*) is one of the most prevalent intestinal parasites, infecting more than 1.5 billion people or about 25 percent of the world population. Roundworms can be up to 12 inches long and exert enormous nutritional and metabolic demands on their mammalian hosts. In high densities, they also cause intestinal obstruction requiring emergency surgery.

The hookworms (*Ancylostoma duodenale and Necator americanus*) are most prevalent in Sub-Saharan Africa, Southeast Asia, and China, with the latter having an estimated 200 million infected people. Like roundworms, the global hookworm burden is estimated at more than 1 billion (Crompton 1999, 2000). The hookworm causes intestinal blood loss as well as iron deficiency. Hookworms are one of the major parasites, infesting up to 30 percent of pregnant women in certain parts of the developing world (WHO 1994; Taylor and Parker 1987).

The whipworm (*Trichiuris trichiura*) infects more than 600 million people worldwide, causing diarrhea and abdominal pain and other symptoms. Schistosome infections (*S. hematobium* and *S. mansoni*), amebiasis, and giardiasis are also common causes of diarrhea associated with poor appetite and retarded growth (Stephenson 1987). Although filariasis is endemic in more than 80 countries, infecting more than 120 million people in India and Sub-Saharan Africa, there is little evidence to suggest that it contributes to adverse nutritional outcomes.

FLUID AND ELECTROLYTE MALNUTRITION

Diarrhea causes losses of water and electrolytes with resultant fluid and electrolyte malnutrition (FEM). Intestinal worm infestations contribute to iron, nutrient, and micronutrient losses, either directly or by induction of anorexia and malabsorption. Diarrheal diseases caused by rotavirus or bacteria, such as shigellosis and salmonellosis, are associated with malabsorption of amino acids, sugars, and lipids as well as losses of zinc, iron, and vitamin A (Glass 2006). Vitamin A deficiency worsens lesions in the digestive tract, exacerbating malabsorption.

CONTROL OF HELMINTHIC INFECTIONS

Unlike the therapy of many other tropical diseases, highly effective, relatively inexpensive, and safe broad-spectrum anthelmintics, such as albendazole and mebendazole, are available. It has been recommended that routine mass deworming should be introduced where parasitic infections are prevalent and where protein-energy malnutrition (PEM) and anemia are prevalent in humans. The WHO has recommended five anthelminthic drugs for use in controlling intestinal nematodes. These drugs include albendazole, levamisole, mebendazole, pyrental, and praziquantel, which can be used to improve the health, developmental, and nutritional status of girls and women. After the first trimester of pregnancy, pregnant and lactating women can ingest single oral doses of these drugs (WHO 1996, 1998, 1999).

Similarly, routine efforts to treat children with schistosomiasis using metrifonate or praziquantel seem highly desirable, both to rid children of potential serious pathology and to improve their nutritional status. More attention needs to be given to population-based chemotherapy for these infections, along with intensification of public health and other measures to reduce their transmission, including improved sanitation and water supplies. Although the logistics may prove challenging and vary from one region of the world to another, such efforts would improve the health and nutritional status of millions of the world's children (MacLeod 1988).

Infection-associated Metabolic Alterations

In some cases, infection-induced metabolic alterations are defensive responses by the host attempting to cope with the infecting agents. In other cases, they are driven by parasite factors, and in still others, the reactions are appropriate, but sometimes excessive. These changes may influence protein, carbohydrate, and lipid metabolism and thus the host's nutritional status. The most prominent of these metabolic changes is perhaps the synthesis of molecules that mediate innate host defenses such as acute phase reactants and cytokines. These inflammatory responses are primarily mediated by tumor necrosis factor (TNFα), interleukin 1 (IL-1), and IL-6. A secondary response occurs with the action of catecholamines, cortisol, and glucagon. TNFα induces higher energy consumption and increases protein and lipid metabolism. TNFα is also an inducer of anorexia and weight loss with the inhibition of lipoprotein lipase production and depletion of fat reserves (Starnes et al. 1988).

In full-blown gluconeogenesis, the amino acids are deaminated and become a source of glucose. Such a state induces the release of pro-inflammatory cytokines, namely IL-1, IL-6 and TNFα. These cytokines induce the synthesis of acute phase reactants including complement factors, C-reactive protein, α1-acid glycoprotein, α1-antitrypsin, α1-antichymotrypsin, ceruloplasmin, haptoglobin, fibrinogen, α2 macroglobulin, and serum amyloid (Fleck 1989). The diversion of available amino acids for synthesis of acute phase reactants occurs to the detriment of maintaining optimal levels of housekeeping proteins such as albumin, hemoglobin, immunoglobulin, and transferrin (Kosek, Black, and Keusch 2006).

Malaria, although to a lesser extent than bacterial endotoxin, induces the release of cytokines including TNFα (which plays a critical role), IL-1, and interferon gamma (IFNγ). In turn these cytokines induce the release of additional pro-inflammatory cytokines such as IL-8, IL-12, and IL-18. A compensatory mechanism balances these reactions with the release of anti-inflammatory cytokines including IL-6 and IL-10 (Hoffman, Campbell, and White 2006). In malaria, cytokines are responsible for fever, malaise, and other signs of disease. It has been established that TNFα (cachectin) causes cachexia directly or indirectly through activation of IL-1.

It is noteworthy that altered levels and activities of TNFα and other cytokines occur in many infections, including amebiasis, leishmaniasis, trichuriasis, and tuberculosis. In these diseases the balances between cytokine, chemokine, and stimulatory molecules determine the type of immune response mounted by T cells, which can differentiate along a Th1 or Th2 pathway. Th1 cells produce IFNγ and IL-2 and enhance macrophage defense, resulting in parasite killing and delayed-type hypersensitivity reactions. Th2 responses release deactivating cytokines (IL-4, IL-5, IL-6, and IL-10), which favor B cell activation and antibody production (Hoffman, Campbell, and White 2006).

Protein-Energy Malnutrition

The effects of severe protein-energy malnutrition (PEM), *kwashiorkor,* are well known and include chronic diarrhea, compromised mucosal immunity, and dysfunction of both the classical and alternate complement pathways, thus predisposing the host to Gram negative and other infections (Fresno, Kopf, and Rivas 1997).

Deficiencies of micronutrients, including iron, zinc, selenium, copper, other minerals, and vitamin A play roles in PEM, and these roles are being better defined. Iron and zinc are required as co-factors in metalloenzymes involved in macrophage phagocytic functions. The zinc and iron deficiencies seen in PEM also contribute to a decrease in T-cell responses and diminution in IL-2, NF_KB, and IFNγ production, with resultant dysfunction of cell-mediated immune responses. Malnourished hosts with PEM are thus predisposed to developing infections caused by bacteria, intracellular parasites, viruses, and pathologic protozoa. Although the ever-present hazard of combined infections and malnutrition threatens the health of all those living in poverty, the most vulnerable groups are pregnant women, infants, and children. The synergism between malnutrition and infection and their adverse effects on immunological functions has recently been reviewed (Scrimshaw and Sangiovanni 1997; Beisel 1996).

Although children under the age of five years would appear to be at especially high risk, there are few controlled interventional studies, which are difficult to carry out, demonstrating the effects of improved diets on the frequency and severity of infections, especially in childhood. One study in the Punjab confirms what has been known in the developed world—that combining infectious disease control and provision of adequate nutritional supplements is the best strategy for promoting good health (Taylor and Parker 1987).

Many of the children who live beyond the age of five years in the developing world are those who have been exposed to both malnutrition and disease and survived. These children are seldom left without some form of permanent sequelae. Given the difficulties inherent in setting up comparative studies, assessing the long-term impact of PEM is a challenge. The consequences of micronutrient mal-nutrition and PEM may include physical, psychological, and cognitive deficits that may not allow affected children to achieve their optimal potential in adult life. Stunted growth, behavioral alterations, and learning disabilities may all have lifelong effects. For instance, chronic iron-deficiency anemia and iodine deficiency may cause mental retardation and poor psychomotor development, even if some of the underlying causes are corrected (Scrimshaw and Sangiovanni 1997). There is thus abundant evidence in support of coordinated programs that use a holistic approach aimed at controlling infectious diseases and improving nutritional sta-tus in a timely manner, while at the same time making family-planning services widely available.

Investing in animal productivity is the most obvious way to control PEM. Al-though reducing animal production risks requires developing broadly applicable technologies to meet many challenges, the main challenge is to protect animals against endemic and epidemic diseases. The others are to identify and conserve animal genotypes that remain productive under biotic and abiotic stresses and that are most suited for the diverse ecosystems in Sub-Saharan Africa and to develop nutrient-rich feeds that are also suited to varied local environments.

Among the most important diseases that constrain livestock productivity in Sub-Saharan Africa are trypanosomiasis, tick-borne diseases (including theileri-osis, or East Coast fever [*Theileria parva*]), tropical theileriosis (*Theileria annulata*), bovine tuberculosis, contagious bovine pleuropneumonia, and African swine fever. Among these diseases, the most widespread and challenging malady is African trypanosomiasis, which affects human beings, livestock, and wildlife in the com-munities that are most vulnerable.

African Trypanosomiasis

African trypanosomes, hemoflagellate protozoan parasites that cause sleeping sickness in human beings and *nagana* in livestock, are transmitted by tsetse flies, disease vectors belonging to the genus *Glossina*. These flies infest 10 million square kilometers of Sub-Saharan Africa. It is estimated that more than 60 mil-lion people in 37 countries and a much larger number of livestock, including cat-tle, pigs, and camels, are at risk for trypanosomiasis (Pepin and Donelson 2006). Trypanosomiasis is thus a major public health burden and an impediment to live-stock production in much of Sub-Saharan Africa.

HUMAN AND ANIMAL TRYPANOSOMIASIS

Recent epidemics of human trypanosomiasis have occurred in areas of civil unrest such as the Democratic Republic of the Congo, Angola, southern Sudan,

Mozambique, and Uganda. In many countries in Central and West Africa, the disease continues to be endemic. It is estimated that these countries have more than 300,000 patients with sleeping sickness, with 40,000 new cases each year. In livestock, the disease remains widespread, with an estimated cost to African agriculture of US$4.5 billion (FAO 2003b).

The pathogen *Trypanosoma brucei* consists of three subspecies, two of which infect human beings. *Trypanosoma brucei rhodesiense* is found in East and southern Africa, *T. brucei gambiense* in West and Central Africa, and both species occur in Uganda. In West Africa, human African trypanosomiasis (HAT) presents as a chronic disease that might last for several years with minimal debilitation of the infected individual. Because infected individuals may travel during the course of infection, however, the chronic nature of the disease facilitates transmission of the parasite to wider areas, which has important epidemiological implications. In East Africa *T. b. rhodesiense* HAT is an acute disease that lasts weeks or months with severe disability, causing the patient to remain at home (Molyneux and Ashford 1983). This pattern has serious economic implications for affected families and communities. Large epidemics remain a constant threat as well. The most dramatic of such epidemics occurred during the 1890s, when 67 percent of the population around the Great Lakes in East Africa was infected (Boothroyd 1985). Lesser epidemics have occurred throughout the 20th century, particularly during times of civil strife. In the 1960s HAT was no longer considered a major public health problem, but it returned to alarming levels in the 1990s (Smith, Pepin, and Stich 1998).

T. brucei brucei is not infectious to human beings because it is lysed by apolipoprotein L-1, which occurs in the high-density lipoprotein (HDL) fraction of human serum (Vanhamme et al. 2003). In livestock and wildlife in Sub-Saharan Africa, however, it causes an animal African trypanosomiasis (AAT), a wasting disease called *nagana*. AAT in livestock and wildlife is also caused by other pathogenic parasites, including T. *congolense* and *T. vivax,* both of which are also transmitted by the tsetse fly. *Trypanosoma evansi* and *T. suis* are the main pathogens of trypanosomiasis in camels and pigs, respectively.

INFECTION IN THE TSETSE VECTOR

During the trypanosome life cycle, the parasites shuttle between mammals and several species of blood-sucking tsetse flies belonging to the genus *Glossina*. In the tsetse fly, the parasites go through several developmental stages for adaptation to the vector's digestive and salivary internal milieu; the trypanosomes change from anaerobic to aerobic metabolism, which is accompanied by alteration of their carbon source from glucose to proline. The latter is the main energy source for the tsetse fly during flight (Vickerman 1985; van Weelden et al. 2003). Tsetse flies infest Sub-Saharan Africa over a belt that stretches from south of the Sahara to north of the Kalahari, between 15° north and 15° south, respectively.

DISEASE PATHOPHYSIOLOGY

The mammalian-infective stages of the different species of trypanosomes, the metacyclics, are transmitted into the skin in the saliva of the tsetse vector during feeding. The metacyclics, each of which is completely covered by a coat consisting of about 10 million copies of a single glycoprotein known as the variable surface glycoprotein (VSG), proliferate at the site of a bite, transforming into blood-stream forms and then spread through the lymphatics into the bloodstream.

In mammals, bloodstream trypanosomes—each of which, like the predecessor metacyclics, expresses only one predominant VSG—multiply rapidly and appear in sequential waves of parasitemia. HAT infection with *T. b. rhodesiense* is an acute, severe, febrile illness with severe malaise, which progresses rapidly to meningo-encephalitis. Deterioration into a stuporous state with malnutrition, cachexia, and coma occur within months. In contrast, *T. b. gambiense* causes a chronic infection where waves of parasitemia also occur, but the disease is insidious (Molyneux and Ashford 1983). As trypanosomiasis progresses, the general clinical presentation includes excessive body wasting, intermittent fever, increasing severity of headache, malaise, lymphadenopathy, cardiac complications, and central nervous system disease with daytime sleepiness, nocturnal insomnia, and behavioral disorders. With continued damage to the central nervous system, stupor and coma appear. In West African trypanosomiasis, the central nervous system symptoms may take months or years to become severe. Unless treated, HAT and AAT are fatal.

In livestock, recurrent waves of parasitemia are also a characteristic feature of the disease. Mature cattle exhibit severe weight loss, whereas younger cattle show decreased growth rates. In females, the reproductive system is often severely affected, causing infertility or spontaneous abortions. This outcome imposes a heavy economic burden on the affected countries, where animal productivity may drop by as much as 85 percent of its optimal potential (Kooy 1991). If the infection is left untreated, the infected animal eventually succumbs to anemia, heart failure, or opportunistic bacterial infections, which take advantage of the compromised immune system (Molyneux and Ashford 1983).

THE VARIABLE SURFACE GLYCOPROTEIN (VSG)

The mammalian bloodstream has active and latent elements of the immune system and is thus a hostile environment to any invading microorganisms. Because trypanosomes are completely exposed to the mammalian blood stream and tissues, these parasites have evolved sophisticated mechanisms to evade destruction by the immune system. The parasite generally expresses only one VSG at a given time in a population.

With every wave of trypanosome parasitemia that has organisms bearing a particular VSG, the immune system mounts an antibody-mediated response that eliminates the parasites bearing that particular surface coat. With the elimination of a population of trypanosomes with the dominant VSG, the number of parasites in the blood decreases. During infection, however, a small number of trypanosomes undergo antigenic variation by switching to the expression of a new VSG, unrecognized by the population of antibodies directed against the previously dominant VSG. Trypanosomes with the new VSG appear and multiply rapidly, the levels increase again, giving rise to the new wave of parasitemia. Thus, the infected animal must mount a new immune response. The waves of parasitemia that are characteristic of trypanosomiasis in mammals are thus due to sequential switches in the VSG displayed by the parasite (Molyneux and Ashford 1983; Kooy 1991). Antigenic variation occurs at a rate of 1×10^{-2} to 1×10^{-6} per parasite per doubling time (Turner 1997).

In the trypanosome genome, a single gene encodes each VSG, and generally only one gene is expressed at a given time (Pays et al. 1983). The VSG genes are all part of a large family comprising more than 1,000 different genes, each encoding a different VSG protein (Borst 1986). Throughout its mammalian infection, the parasite can switch between the different genes in what appears to be an almost stochastic manner. With sequential waves of parasitemia, immunological exhaustion ensues, leading to an immunodeficiency syndrome. Much like AIDS, the phenomenon of antigenic variation renders victims of trypanosomiasis defenseless. Hence in both HAT and AAT, opportunistic bacterial, viral, protozoan, and other infections associated with progressive fever, headaches, lethargy, and body wasting are usually the cause of death.

NUTRITIONAL DEFICIENCIES IN TRYPANOSOMIASIS

In trypanosomiasis caloric, macro-, and micronutrient malnutrition occur. Trypanosomes are present in large numbers in the circulation during infection, and nutritional deficiencies occur partly because of the heavy parasite load and the ensuing competition for nutrients. The deficiencies are exacerbated by the presence of anorexia, diarrhea, and the fever-induced high metabolic rate. Another major contributor to nutritional deficiencies is the wasteful diversion of amino acids, sugars, lipids, and the host's protein synthetic machinery to make large amounts of IgM and IgG antibodies to fight against each new variant of the parasite's VSG with each recurrent wave of parasitemia.

Several host factors play pivotal roles in the pathophysiology and nutritional deficits in trypanosome infections. Prominent among these is cachectin/TNFα, which, as already indicated, is a potent, multifunctional, polypeptide cytokine that was independently isolated from trypanosome infections and then subsequently shown to have complete sequence identity to TNFα. As suggested by the name, cachectin/TNFα has been shown to induce cachexia. Cachectin/TNFα, which is produced by macrophages, induces the release of fat from storage depots and reduces the concentration of enzymes needed to synthesize and store fat. Persistent production of cachectin/TNFα occurs in trypanosomiasis, chronic infection, and malignancy, giving rise to a syndrome of anemia, anorexia, and weight loss (Tracey and Cerami 1990). Massive weight loss is thus a common feature of trypanosomiasis, with death occurring in untreated hosts from immunological exhaustion and resultant intercurrent infections. The control of AAT would thus greatly contribute to improved livestock productivity and alleviation of PEM.

CONTROL MEASURES FOR TRYPANOSOMIASIS

The control of HAT and AAT can be effected by three approaches: (1) drug treatment of infections directed against the various species and subspecies of parasites causing trypanosomiasis; (2) development of vaccines against the metacyclic or bloodstream forms of the trypanosomes; and (3) control of the tsetse fly vectors, in order to reduce new infections in human beings and animals from tsetse fly bites. The three potential interventions have been suboptimal: drugs are costly, toxic, and often not available; vaccines have not been developed nor are they likely to be; and control of the vector faces logistical challenges.

The control of animal trypanosomiasis would drastically improve the productivity of livestock and open up a substantial part of the 10 million square kilometers of tsetse-infested areas in Sub-Saharan Africa to agriculture.

CHEMOTHERAPY FOR TRYPANOSOMIASIS

Different kinds of drugs are needed to treat the different forms and stages of human and animal trypanosomiases. There is great hope that survival from trypanosomiasis will improve as a result of agreements between the pharmaceutical industry and the World Health Organization to donate, so far, three of the five effective drugs for the treatment of sleeping sickness: eflornithine, melarsoprol, and pentamidine. Pentamidine is used to treat the initial phase of T. b. gambiense HAT infections, whereas melarsoprol and eflornithine are recommended for the second phase and the advanced central nervous system phase of T. b. gambiense, respectively. Treating the initial phase of HAT T. rhodesiense infection requires suramin, the free availability of which is still under discussion. The drug of choice for treating animal trypanosomiasis is suramin, which is costly and not readily available to those who mostly need it—namely, nomadic communities. In addition to the challenges of availability and affordability of these agents, drug resistance is widespread (Pepin et al. 1994).

VACCINE DEVELOPMENT

Beyond the difficulties encountered with the availability and efficacy of drugs for trypanosomiasis, the likelihood of developing a conventional vaccine against trypanosomes is slim, given the splendor displayed by these protozoa in the practice of antigenic variation, a phenomenon that has evolved to circumvent mammalian immune assault. The VSG completely covers the surface of metacyclic and bloodstream trypanosomes and shields any of the invariant antigens from exposure to the mammalian immune system. That recombination of trypanosomes also occurs in tsetse fly vectors (Tait 1980), thus widening the repertoire of genes encoding the surface coat in these parasites and rendering the prospects of developing such a VSG-based vaccine hopeless (Pepin and Donelson 2006).

STRATEGIES FOR TSETSE VECTOR CONTROL

Because of the obstacles to developing a conventional vaccine against trypanosomes, the widespread resistance to the drugs in the market, and the uncertainty about the sustainable availability of the drugs, the control of the tsetse vectors must be a central component of an integrated, long-term strategy for vector and disease management for both HAT and AAT. Tsetse flies can be manipulated applying knowledge of their behavior. The integrated pest management options include determining how tsetse flies find mammalian hosts. Field investigations have revealed that tsetse flies use both olfactory and visual cues to locate hosts. Tsetse flies are thus attracted by certain colors and odors and repulsed by others. Different-colored traps, predominantly black and blue, were found to attract tsetse flies. This finding is the basis for essentially all trap technologies used by organizations involved in controlling the species of tsetse flies that transmit AAT. Similar studies also revealed that tsetse flies are attracted to fresh buffalo urine. A program has been set up to encourage farmers to trap tsetse using appropriately designed traps along with fermented cow urine, which works as well as fresh buffalo urine. Although trapping can dramatically reduce the number of vectors of the livestock disease by more than 99 percent, bringing these technologies into full operation in communities in tsetse-infested areas has presented some difficulties. Problems include the short color-steadfastness of the clothing material, theft of the cloth, and dismantling of traps by baboons.

Studies on tsetse bloodmeals revealed that tsetse flies do not feed on certain animals, such as the waterbuck. Component volatiles, originally isolated and characterized from the waterbuck, have now been produced. Farmers use the waterbuck repellent in livestock collars designed to hold a dispenser. This method of controlling tsetse is especially convenient for nomadic communities (Gikonyo et al. 2003).

The need for continuing to improve these artificial baits, which will allow a dramatic reduction of tsetse populations at affordable cost, is underscored by their lack of adverse effects on the environment.

NEW APPROACHES TO TRYPANOSOMIASIS CONTROL

Developing more effective control of human and animal trypanosomiasis will require an integrated approach with research in several areas, including discovery of new drugs, improvement of tsetse control, development of better and cheaper diagnostic reagents, and the identification of the basis of natural trypanotolerance of indigenous African breeds for use as a basis for breeding. Studies on drug discovery should identify more effective and less toxic compounds to treat acute and chronic HAT and AAT infections. This effort will be greatly aided by the "Tritryp" Project that led to the completion of sequencing of three parasite genomes, namely, *Trypanosoma brucei gambiense, T. cruzi* and *Leishmania major* (El-Sayed et al. 2005).[2] Such genomic information will help scientists identify unique pathways for the design of more specific and less toxic chemotherapeutic agents against trypanosomes. One stumbling block in this effort is that the pharmaceutical industry lacks financial incentives to develop new drugs against trypanosomes and other orphan diseases. The creation of public-private partnerships, such as the partnership for Drugs for Neglected Diseases Initiative, is a promising strategy that addresses the gaps in the drug development process, which has prevented promising new drugs for neglected diseases from reaching clinical trials.

TSETSE FLY VECTOR GENOMICS

Current vector control methods are based on trapping that exploits visual and odorant attractants and repellents of the tsetse flies. The sterile insect technique (SIT) has been found effective in reducing tsetse populations in one contained situation—the island of Zanzibar. Efforts are being made to expand the use of SIT into mainland Africa, but SIT is fraught with a multiplicity of problems. Among these are the large numbers of irradiated, therefore sick, male tsetse flies required to compete effectively with normal males, the solitary nature of tsetse flies, the large number of species that transmit trypanosomiases of both livestock and humans, and the difficulties of rearing some of these species in the laboratory to produce the large numbers required for SIT.

Findings from future genomic studies on the vector have the potential to significantly improve upon existing vector control strategies. For example, knowledge of the genes encoding the fly receptors for attractants and repellents would vastly improve trapping efficiency and enhance the repellent-bearing collars that are currently in use. Additionally, the genes encoding mediators of host–parasite interactions are vital for the development of genetically engineered lines that are unable to transmit trypanosomes, which can be immediately used in the ongoing SIT release programs. This application of refractory strains in SIT would reduce the cost of the projects and would also increase the efficacy of their application in HAT-endemic areas (Aksoy et al. 2005).[3]

Recent studies have identified and cloned genes that may mediate vector competence in tsetse. One of these encodes a *Glossina* proteolytic lectin that mediates the differentiation of bloodstream-form trypanosomes into procyclic or midgut forms, while the other is a trypanolysin that causes rapid lysis of bloodstream-form trypanosomes, and its expression seems to be highest in species that are more refractory to trypanosome infections (Amin et al. 2006). Interestingly, the expression of both of these genes is induced by a blood meal. For GM *Glossina* or any GMO vector to be effective in decreasing disease transmission, such a vector has to genetically stable to compete effectively with its wild type counterpart.

Climate Variability and Disease Risk

Climate change may have profound and far-reaching influences on all biological and physical life-support systems, including human survival. It will thus have an impact on environmental, plant, animal, and human health, with attendant influences on disease trends and agricultural productivity. Other confounding factors include changing human rural and urban settlement patterns, population growth, travel, trade, migration, erratic disease control, and the emergence of pesticide and drug resistance by vectors and agents of disease, respectively.

Continued epidemiological surveys of vector-borne diseases are needed to determine the consequences of climate change on the spread of these diseases into new areas bordering disease-endemic regions. For instance, available evidence suggests that the biological activity and geographical distribution of malarial parasites and their vectors are sensitive to climate factors, especially temperature and precipitation. The risk of malaria epidemics increases five-fold in the Indian subcontinent with the appearance of the El Niño–Southern Oscillation phenomenon (Martens et al. 1995).

Similar observations have been made for the incidence of malaria and yellow fever in East Africa (Githeko et al. 2006). Changes in precipitation will also influence the distribution of other vectors and the incidence of disease. The vectors include those for trypanosomiasis, schistosomiasis, onchocerciasis, filariasis, and tick-borne diseases, as well as diarrheal diseases of viral and bacterial origin.

Biofortification of Staple Crops: A Potential Solution

A biofortification program, HarvestPlus (H⁺CP), has been developed by a consortium of institutions—the Consultative Group for International Agricultural Research (CGIAR) and its partners (HarvestPlus 2009). HarvestPlus addresses the important problem of micronutrient malnutrition, which is the cause of widespread morbidity and significant mortality predominantly affecting children and pregnant women in the developing world. At times, it occurs in areas where caloric intake is adequate. The micronutrients selected are vitamin A, iron, and zinc. The mandate of H⁺CP is to develop means of correcting micronutrient deficiencies in low-income countries employing, predominantly, selective breeding for the biofortification of staple crops.

These micronutrient deficiencies have serious but preventable consequences for health. Vitamin A deficiency is the leading cause of visual impairment and blindness in children in the developing world. Although the details are not fully understood, the inability to modulate gene expression in vitamin A deficiency, especially in mucosal tissues and other portals of entry of many infectious agents, may underlie the predilection to diseases caused by bacteria and viruses that are agents for common childhood illnesses. These diseases are the main causes of death for a significant number of such children living in high-risk areas.

Iron-deficiency anemia is also widespread and is a leading cause of poor growth and development. With iron deficiency, decreased cellular and humoral responses, impaired cytokine function, and poor oxygen carrying capacity all predispose to infection (Nussenblatt and Semba 2002). It is not surprising that a deficiency of zinc, which is such an important cofactor and modulator of the functions of many enzymes including metalloenzymes and DNA and RNA polymerases, would result in growth retardation and varying degrees of mental decompensation. That significant reduction in childhood illnesses can be achieved with zinc supplementation additionally derives from the role of zinc in the mediation of phagocytic, cytokine, and T- and B-lymphocyte functions in host defense (Scrimshaw and Sangiovanni 1997). Zinc is also a cofactor in systems that thwart the effects of membrane-destabilizing toxins secreted by infectious agents causing diarrheal, skin, and lung diseases.

The H⁺CP micronutrient initiative had been preceded by a project that was supported by WHO and UNICEF and carried out between 1995 and 2002 by the CGIAR. H⁺CP works with a large number of stakeholders, including universities from developed and developing countries, as well as national agricultural research systems. The strategy employed in H⁺CP includes activities in germplasm screening, genotype and environmental interactions, functional gene discovery, breeding, and identification of elite clones employing both classical and genomic-based approaches such as marker-assisted selection and intussusception.

After Phase I of H⁺CP, several micronutrient-fortified staples are already developed. These staples include high-iron rice for Asia, high-iron maize and beans, and high beta-carotene sweet potatoes for Africa. Community-based efficacy trials designed to examine whether vitamin A and iron status of high-risk populations can be improved by consumption of micronutrient-enriched staples are promising.

The availability of these varieties is likely to have a positive and immediate impact on the health of vulnerable populations. Innovative research will continue to be needed to find appropriate metabolic pathways to enhance fortification and better ways of overcoming the challenge of bioavailability of micronutrients in fortified staples. Such is the case for the bioavailability of iron in high-phytate diets. The bioavailability of a nutrient requires the presence of not only of an appropriate synthetic pathway, but also proper processing of the micronutrient, transport and storage in suitable organelles, postharvest stability, and mobilization for uptake during digestion.

Although the availability of genome data for many of the staple crops being fortified will facilitate gene discovery, detailed functional genomics will continue to be required in monitoring the stability of the genotypes and their expression of micronutrients in various environments and seasons, a phenomenon that has been referred to as "the triple helix" (genetics × environment).

Successful implementation of any solution coming out of research to problems facing farmers will, in each case, require a concerted effort involving research organizations, policy makers, national institutions, and the farmers themselves. For those solutions to become sustainable and contribute to poverty reduction, farmers will need to develop and nourish a sense of ownership of such science-based interventions. The acceptability of some biofortified staples may present such a challenge.

The H$^+$CP is indeed an interdisciplinary and global alliance of research and implementing organizations that are addressing the problem of micronutrient deficiency, which is considered by all stakeholders to be a great priority that has not been met. Applying cutting-edge science to the production of sufficient and safe food for the alleviation of poverty and the attainment of MDGs is a unique contribution that the CGIAR and its partners can continue to make.

Notes

The author would like to thank Dr. Mushtaq Ahmed, associate dean for medical education, Aga Khan University East Africa, and his associates for helpful discussions on the subject of this chapter and Linda B. ole-MoiYoi for comprehensive editing.

1. For an update on Roll Back Malaria, see http://www.rollbackmalaria.org/. globalad vocacy/pr2008-01-25.html. Information on the Global Fund can be found at http://www .theglobalfund.org/en/.

2. See also http://www.sciencemag.org/cgi/content/abstract/309/5733/404, http://www .tigr.org/new/press_release_07-14-05.shtml, and http://www.wellcome.ac.uk/doc_WTX02 6056.html.

3. See also http://www.vectorbase.org/Sections/Other/addtl_org_includes/glossina_ge nome_project.pdf.

CHAPTER 4

~~~~~~~~

Animals as a Source of Human Diseases: Historical Perspective
and Future Health Risks for the African Population

E. Fuller Torrey

Abstract

Animals and humans are intimately connected by diseases. Many of the earliest diseases affecting humans, such as hepatitis and malaria, are thought to have been passed down as humans evolved in Africa from primate ancestors. Other diseases, such as anthrax and brucellosis, spread from animals to *Archaic Homo sapiens* when these hominids began to systematically hunt the animals. The greatest number of human diseases, including measles and tuberculosis, originally came from animals domesticated by *Homo sapiens*. The transmission of diseases from animals to humans continues to occur, as AIDS tragically illustrates.

Africa has the world's largest number of mammalian species and thus the greatest potential reservoir of new microbes to infect humans. It also has a large number of disease-transmitting arthropods, contaminated water supplies, and a major problem with malnutrition, all of which favor disease transmission. Minimizing such transmission will require attention to four factors: (1) changes in the relationship between animals and humans, such as the greater intimacy that comes when animals and humans share living space; (2) changes in modes of travel, such as paved roads and new airports, which facilitate the rapid transmission of infectious diseases; (3) changes in food production and processing, such as the change from the slaughter of individual animals to the simultaneous slaughter of hundreds; and (4) changes in ecology and environment, such as urbanization, deforestation, and global warming, all of which may increase disease transmission.

The largest impediment to controlling the transmission of animal diseases, both in Africa and elsewhere, is the lack of coordination between national and international agencies that have responsibility for animal health and those that have responsibility for human health. By coordinating such agencies, African nations could provide a model for the rest of the world.

Introduction

Africa is a continent of firsts. Five million years ago, it gave birth to the first hominids, some of whom carried diseases they had inherited from their primate ancestors. Approximately 1.5 million years ago, Africa was the site of what may whimsically be regarded as the first experiment in nutrition—the cooking of meat using fire. And approximately 75,000 years ago, Africa was the site of the evolution of the first humans, *Homo sapiens,* armed with the ability to think about themselves, understand others, think about the past and the future, and write chapters for books about nutrition and disease. This was the modern human.

This chapter will discuss the relationship between animals and human disease. It will first discuss heirloom infections and then infections transmitted from animals when hominids began hunting them. Next, it will discuss the domestication of animals and the profound change domestication wrought in animal-human relationships. It will then address the transmission of infectious agents from animals to humans and cite examples of human diseases acquired from animals: measles, tuberculosis, AIDS, and other diseases. In considering the future, the chapter will then survey opportunities for the transmission of additional infectious agents from animals to humans, a process that creates new human diseases. Finally, the chapter will conclude by assessing what can be done to minimize the creation of new human disease, thus promoting better health for Africans and people everywhere.

Before beginning, it is useful to acquire some perspective on the place of humans in the microbial world. Humans are merely one of 4,500 species of mammals, encompassing everything from aardvarks to zebras. All mammalian species together constitute less than one-tenth of 1 percent of the estimated 30 million living animal species (Margulis and Schwartz 2001, 208), including between 300,000 and 1 million different species of bacteria and approximately 5,000 species of viruses. Thus, from the point of view of a microbe looking for an animal to parasitize, humans are at best an incidental hors d'oeuvre at the banquet table of life.

From the human point of view, however, it is a different story. When researchers at the University of Edinburgh compiled a list of 1,415 microbes known to cause diseases in humans, they reported that 868, or 61 percent, of the microbes are known to be currently transmitted from animals to humans (Taylor, Latham, and Woolhouse 2001). This list did not include microbes that were transmitted from animals to humans in the past and then underwent mutation, such as the measles virus. If all microbes causing human disease that came from animals either past or present were included, the list would include at least three-quarters of all human infections. Thus, from a microbe's point of view, the relationship between animals and humans is of little importance, but from the human point of view, it is exceedingly important.

Heirloom Infections

Heirloom infections in humans are caused by microbes that were passed from our primate ancestors to early hominids and then from hominids to modern humans as they evolved. Since bacteria have existed for 3.5 billion years and viruses and protozoa for perhaps 2 billion years or more, it is not surprising that every form of life that has evolved has been infected with these microbes.

Most heirloom infections are harmless, living unobtrusively on our skin or in our intestines for our entire lives. Many of these microbes perform useful functions—intestinal bacteria, for example, aid with food digestion. Humans share many of these heirloom microbes with other primates and other animal species. For example, a study of 12 protozoa found in human intestines reported that 11 of them are also found in the intestines of monkeys (Cockburn 1977).

Although the vast majority of infections humans have inherited from their primate ancestors are harmless, some may cause disease. Most herpesviruses are thought to be heirloom infections, including herpes simplex 1 and 2, which cause chronic infections of the mouth and genitalia; varicella-zoster virus, which causes chickenpox; and Epstein-Barr virus, which causes mononucleosis and some forms of cancer. Similarly, the two viruses that cause most cases of hepatitis and some liver cancers are thought to be heirloom infections. Most serious, the protozoa that cause malaria are thought to have been passed along from primates to humans in the course of evolution. Malaria is one of mankind's oldest and deadliest diseases and continues to devastate Africa, where it is the third leading cause of death, behind only HIV/AIDS and pneumonia and other respiratory infections (Medilinks 2008).

Thus it should be clear that *Homo sapiens* was never free from infectious diseases. If the Garden of Eden existed, Adam may have had herpes cold sores, Eve may have had hepatitis, the mosquitoes circling around them may have been carrying the malaria parasite, and the snake was almost certainly carrying salmonella bacteria.

Infections of Hunters

Approximately 1.5 million years ago, a remarkable event occurred. Some *Homo erectus* in Africa were sitting around a fire, which they had only recently learned to control, and one of them accidentally dropped a gazelle leg he had been eating into the fire. By the time he retrieved it, the meat had become partially cooked, and *Homo erectus* noted that the meat tasted better. What he did not know was that the cooking also made the meat easier to digest and more nutritious. In one experiment, mice raised on cooked meat gained 29 percent more weight than mice raised on uncooked meat (Gibbons 2007). The cooking of meat was probably one reason the brain capacity of *Homo erectus* increased in size by approximately 50 percent over the brain of its predecessor, *Homo habilis*.

From that time onward, hominids increasingly became hunters. By the time *Homo erectus* evolved into multiple species of *Archaic Homo sapiens* approximately 400,000 years ago, the hunting of animals had become very important. One species of *Archaic Homo sapiens*, Neanderthal man, who lived between 230,000 and 30,000 years ago, regularly killed horses and other big mammals. According to one account, "they were so good at hunting that their diet consisted almost entirely of meat" (Zimmer 2001, 301).

Hunting brought hominids into a closer relationship with animals than they had previously had. For about 4 million years in Africa, hominids and animals had lived relatively separate lives. When hunting became common, however, hominids became physically proximate to animals in the process of skinning, butchering, and ultimately eating them. The animals, of course, carried their own set of microbes, some of which hominids had not previously been exposed to. Hominids hunted the animals, and the animals' microbes hunted the hominids.

One example of an infection acquired by hominids through hunting during the Paleolithic period was the *Taenia* tapeworm. The infection was acquired by eating undercooked meat from wild cattle (aurochs) or wild boars (Hoberg et al. 2001). In most individuals, tapeworms cause no clinical symptoms, but in some they may cause abdominal pain, weight loss, or, if they go to the brain, seizures. Another macroparasite acquired by hominids at this time was the roundworm *Trichinella spiralis*, which may infect an individual's heart muscle or brain; it may originally have been transmitted through the eating of undercooked meat from wild horses, boars, or bears.

Other diseases transmitted from animals to hominids during this period include anthrax, brucellosis, Q fever, tularemia, and glanders. The first three are thought to have been transmitted to humans from wild ancestors of cattle, sheep, and goats. The ancestors of cattle are thought to have been indigenous to Africa, so the earliest infections probably occurred there. The ancestors of sheep and goats were probably not indigenous to Africa, so the earliest infections would have taken place when *Homo erectus* migrated to the Middle East. Anthrax is a bacterial disease that begins as skin ulcers in humans; if untreated, approximately one-quarter of people with anthrax die. Brucellosis in humans is characterized by a relapsing fever and muscle and joint pain. Q fever in humans produces a fever, and in some cases pneumonia or hepatitis. Brucellosis and Q fever may also occasionally be fatal. Tularemia is a bacterial infection spread from rabbits or squirrels, and glanders is a bacterial infection acquired by humans from infected horses and mules. Both diseases produce skin ulcers in humans, and occasionally pneumonia, and may be fatal.

All five of these diseases continue to occasionally be transmitted from animals to humans, as they have been for hundreds of thousands of years. The microbes causing all of these diseases had presumably been carried by the animals for thousands, or even millions, of years and only began to threaten hominids when the relationship between animals and hominids changed, as when hominids began hunting animals. This theme—that diseases are associated with changing relationships between animals and humans—will be a recurring one in this chapter.

The Domestication of Animals

A profound change in the relationship between humans and animals occurred approximately 11,000 years ago, when humans began domesticating animals. The change brought not only many advantages to humans, but also many diseases, which were transmitted from animals to humans. The domestication of animals occurred concurrently with the domestication of plants. The sequence of these two events has been debated, but they probably occurred simultaneously and influenced each other. For example, using an animal to pull a plow significantly increases the area that can be cultivated. Similarly, the parts of domestic crops that cannot be used by humans can be used as feed for domesticated goats, pigs, and cattle.

The first animals domesticated specifically for food were sheep and goats. The wild ancestors of both lived in the Zagros Mountains in what is now western Iraq. Domestication would not have been difficult, since both sheep and goats are herd animals and tend to follow a dominant leader; both are also relatively placid and breed easily in captivity. The value of sheep and goats for early humans should not be underestimated. For example,

> [t]he goat can provide both the primitive peasant farmer and the nomadic pastoralist with all his physical needs, clothing, meat, and milk as well as bone and sinew for artifacts, tallow for lighting, and dung for fuel and manure (Clutton-Brock 1981, 57–58).

In addition, goat's milk can be made into cheese, its wool can be used for clothing, and its skins can be used for both clothing and water containers. Goats can also be used to help clear land by eating shrubs and low-hanging tree branches. They are hardy and adaptable and thrive in a variety of climates, including semi-desert.

The next animals domesticated were pigs and cattle. In *A History of Domesticated Animals*, Frederick Zeuner claimed that, after dogs, "the domestication of cattle was the most important step ever taken by man in the direction of exploitation of the animal world" (Zeuner 1963, 240–241). Cattle can be used for meat, milk, butter, and cheese. Their hides can be used to make shoes, clothing, and shields for fighting. Their dung can be used as fertilizer, mixed with mud for building mud huts, or burned as fuel. Even their horns can be used as weapons. It is thus not surprising that many cultures have revered cattle.

Humans' domestication of cattle, however, is somewhat surprising. The original wild cattle, known as aurochs, were six feet tall and said to be "fierce, swift, and agile" (Perkins 1969, 178). Nonetheless, their domestication occurred in the Fertile Crescent in southwestern Asia, as well as, apparently independently, in Africa.

African domestication of cattle most likely occurred in the eastern Sahara region approximately 9,000 years ago. Until 6,000 years ago, this region was green and had regular rainfall (Kröpelin et al. 2008). Recent genetic studies suggest that this region's indigenous wild cattle, the humpless *Bos Taurus*, were domesticated early and spread across North Africa (Hanotte et al. 2002). At some later date another breed of cattle, the humped *Bos indices*, known as zebu cattle, was introduced into Africa through Egypt or the African east coast. The two types of cattle interbred, and today's African cattle have varying degrees of genes from each.

Evidence for the independent African domestication of sheep, goats, or pigs is lacking, and it is thought that they were introduced into Africa through Egypt approximately 6,000 years ago. Similarly, chickens are thought to have been initially domesticated in Southeast Asia and introduced to the east coast of Africa by traders. Dogs may have been independently domesticated in Africa as well as elsewhere in the world. Besides these species, Africa can claim to have independently domesticated only the guinea fowl (Diamond 1997, 389).

It should be emphasized that the domestication of animals profoundly changed the human-animal relationship. For millions of years, primates and their hominid descendants had lived on the same plains with, but separated from, other animals. Their major interactions occurred when one tried to make a meal of the other. That period was followed by a few thousand years when hominids systematically hunted some animals, skinning and butchering them to use as clothing and food.

The Transmission of Disease

The domestication of animals brought with it entirely new relationships. Wild animals that humans had previously gazed at from afar now stood domesticated in humans' backyards. In colder weather, humans and animals often shared a common living space, as indeed still occurs in many parts of the world. Because the domesticated animals represented a significant part of a family's wealth, humans cared for sick animals and sometimes assisted in the birth of animal offspring. In Papua New Guinea, for example, it is not uncommon for women to suckle piglets when a mother pig is unable to do so. In all cultures, children play with the baby offspring of domesticated animals, even kissing them.

The contact between humans and animals following domestication brought about a new relationship not previously seen in human history. Because each animal, including each human, carried its own set of microbes, the new relationship ensured that these microbes would be readily exchanged. Each time a cow coughed in a hut shared with humans, each time a child kissed a baby lamb, each time the feces of a goat or chicken inadvertently contaminated the family food supply, microbes that may have been entirely novel to humans were transmitted to them from the animals. Similarly, the microbes carried by humans were transmitted to the domesticated animals.

All microbes, like other organisms, undergo continuous evolution, a process that is inherent in life itself. One of the most common ways for microbes to evolve is by invading the tissues of other animals, including humans. From the point of view of a microbe, a human is merely a useful vessel in which to reproduce and evolve. If the human develops a disease because of that process, the disease is incidental to the microbe's reproduction and evolution. As Jared Diamond observed, "Diseases represent evolution in progress, and microbes adapt by natural selection to new hosts and vectors" (Diamond 1997, 209).

Microbes are remarkably resourceful in finding ways to move from animals to humans. One way is to be passed along as part of the evolutionary chain, as illustrated by the heirloom infections. A more common mode of transmission is direct, which occurs, for example, when the bite of a dog transmits rabies or when humans acquire anthrax, tularemia, or other diseases by skinning and butchering infected animals. Another common mode of transmission is through the contamination of food or water by, for example, the feces of an infected animal. In Africa, however, the most common way microbes move from animals to humans is by being carried by arthropod vectors. The protozoan that causes malaria, carried from animals to humans by mosquitoes, is the most important example of this process. Mosquitoes also carry many viruses from animals to humans in Africa, causing widespread diseases, such as yellow fever, West Nile virus disease, and Rift Valley fever, and more localized diseases, such as o'nyong nyong disease, chikungunya, Bwamba fever, Bunyamwera fever, Sindbis fever, and Semiliki Forest fever. Ticks are also important arthropod vectors, carrying the rickettsiae that cause the African spotted fevers and the virus causing sandfly fever. Flies carry diseases from animals to humans as well; the most important example is the tsetse fly, which carries the protozoan that causes African sleeping sickness, a disease of great historical importance in many parts of Africa.

Once a microbe has successfully moved from an animal to a human, in the vast majority of cases, nothing happens. Humans have complex immune defenses, including lymphocytes, antibodies, and cytokines, that neutralize or kill almost all invading microbes. The immune system is under the control of a large number of genes; some humans are therefore more susceptible to infections with some microbes than others because of differences in their genes. When the polio virus or tuberculosis bacteria infect a human, for example, the likelihood that the microbe will actually cause disease is largely determined by the person's particular configuration of genes, called genetic susceptibility.

Two other factors figure prominently in the outcome of the disease. One is the state of the person's immune system. If the immune system is suppressed, as in individuals with AIDS or individuals being immunosuppressed for the treatment of cancer, the microbe is more likely to cause infection. This factor is especially pertinent to Africa, where many individuals already have impaired immune systems because of malnutrition and malaria; the additional effects of HIV in suppressing the immune system make individuals much more susceptible to other infectious diseases, including, most prominently, tuberculosis. The other determining factor is the relative strength of the microbe. Many microbes have different strains, with some strains being much more powerful than others. Such differences are commonly seen, for example, in epidemics of influenza, in which some strains of the virus cause mild disease whereas others, such as that which caused the 1918–1919 pandemic, are often lethal.

Once a microbe has been successfully transmitted from an animal to a human and has set up an active infection, the microbe may or may not undergo mutations and change. Sometimes, it changes just a little, as in the case of the influenza virus. In other cases, it changes so much that its origin can be ascertained only by genetic analysis. An example of this drastic change is the human measles virus, which many believe to have been originally transmitted to humans from cattle as the rinderpest virus. In some cases, the human microbe has undergone so much mutation it is difficult to ascertain its origin.

Examples of Diseases Transmitted from Animals to Humans in Africa

Among the many diseases that have been transmitted from animals to humans, this chapter will focus on three, all of which are among the leading causes of deaths in Africa—measles, tuberculosis, and AIDS.

Measles

The virus that causes measles is widely believed to have evolved from the rinderpest virus, which causes disease in cattle. As already noted, the humpless taurus cattle were apparently domesticated from an indigenous species in the eastern Sahara about 9,000 years ago. Later, the humped zebu cattle were introduced from Asia and bred with the taurus cattle. Rock art in the Sahara region dated to 7,000 years ago depicts the herding of humpless cattle as well as sheep (Gifford-Gonzalez 2000). The use of cattle in Africa spread rapidly on an east-west axis in the Saharan region, but it spread southward very slowly. The reason, according to anthropologist Diane Gifford-Gonzalez, is that a series of diseases spread from wild animals to the cattle, killing many of them. The most severe of these diseases included malignant catarrhal fever, carried by young wildebeests; Rift Valley fever, carried by rodents and ungulates; East Coast fever, carried by African buffalo; foot-and-mouth disease, also carried by buffalo; and trypanosomiasis (sleeping sickness), caused by a protozoan parasite carried from cattle to cattle by the tsetse fly.

The rinderpest virus was dramatically introduced into Africa in 1889. The Italian army invaded what is now Ethiopia and Somalia and imported cattle from India to feed its troops. These cattle were infected with rinderpest, which then quickly infected the African domestic cattle. Rinderpest swept across Africa over a seven-year period, virtually wiping out the cattle in many areas. It also spread to other wild animals and caused widespread mortality among buffalo, wildebeests, giraffes, bushpigs, eland, and kudu. Since many African tribes, such as the Masai, were highly dependent on cattle for survival, the rinderpest epidemic also caused widespread famine. One Masai man described the corpses of cattle and humans as being "so many and so close together that the vultures had forgotten how to fly" (Plowright 1982, 16).

The human measles virus, a direct offspring of the rinderpest virus, is apparently an adaptation of the rinderpest virus to humans. Studies of the molecular structure of the two viruses show that they differ very little.

Whether measles existed in Africa before the 1889 rinderpest epidemic is uncertain. Although some evidence suggests that measles may have existed in ancient times, tracing the history of measles anywhere in the world is problematic because until recently it was confused with smallpox, chickenpox, rubella (German measles), and other diseases characterized by a rash. In addition, measles, like rinderpest, is a herd disease, and a community must be 250,000 persons or greater to maintain the infection. Until urbanization in recent years, most African communities were not this large. Thus, it seems likely that measles had been introduced by traders plying the African coasts in earlier centuries, but because of the dispersed population, it died out.

Although measles is now mistakenly regarded in Western countries as a relatively benign illness, it is in fact a serious disease that can have major, even fatal, consequences. It attacks the victim's immune system and may go to the brain. It is most severe in individuals who are malnourished or infected with other diseases such as tuberculosis and AIDS. Until recent years, measles in Africa was said to contribute to 10 percent of all childhood deaths, or about 5 percent of all African deaths (Cliff, Haggett, and Smallman-Raynor 1993, 194), making it the seventh leading cause of death on the continent. Since 2000, however, a massive campaign to vaccinate African children against measles has become one of the most successful public health campaigns ever undertaken. Between 2000 and 2005, it was estimated that deaths from measles in Africa decreased from 396,000 per year to 36,000 per year (UN News Centre 2007).

Tuberculosis

Tuberculosis is the eighth leading cause of death in Africa. The bacterium that causes the human form of the disease, *Mycobacterium tuberculosis*, is closely related to the bacterium that causes the bovine form of the disease, and for many years it was believed that tuberculosis had spread to humans from cattle. More recent genetic analysis has suggested that human *Mycobacterium tuberculosis* is more closely related to the form of bacterium carried by goats and that they, rather than cattle, were the source of the human disease (Espinosa de la Monteros et al. 1998). Still other researchers have suggested that the human form of tuberculosis was an heirloom infection that hominids acquired from their primate ancestors and that humans passed it to cattle rather than cattle to humans (Gibbons 2008).

Two aspects of tuberculosis are especially noteworthy. First, it is a disease of crowding, both among animals and among humans. Among cattle, for example, "it is a universal experience that the incidence of bovine tuberculosis increases in proportion to the density of the cattle population, i.e., to the size of the herds and the space allotted to the cattle when they are kept indoors" (van der Hoeden 1964, 15). Similarly, monkeys that live in the wild are free of tuberculosis, whereas "the monkey in captivity is the most susceptible of all animals to tuberculosis" (Steele and Ranney 1958, 910). This transmission is often caused by spread of the disease from humans to captive primates.

Thus, it is easy to imagine that the bacteria causing tuberculosis had existed for millions of years among wild goats with no apparent disease but that once goats were domesticated and herded 10,000 years ago, the disease became manifest and was transmitted to the humans who had domesticated the goats. This is a theme that will recur throughout this chapter: changes in the relationship between animals and humans often lead to changes in disease.

Second, for tuberculosis, as for most infectious agents, genetic susceptibility to becoming infected is important. It was long known that many people became infected with the bacterium that causes tuberculosis, yet only a few developed the disease. It is now known that carrying certain genes predisposes a person to developing clinical tuberculosis once he or she becomes infected with the bacteria (Bellamy et al. 1998); presumably, carrying certain other genes confers resistance.

These genetic differences explain why only some people develop clinical disease although many others may be subclinically infected.

Tuberculosis has been a devastating killer, especially since urban crowding began in the Western world in the 17th century. In 1680, John Bunyan called it "the captain of all these men of death" (Dubos and Dubos 1952, 8). According to one estimate, tuberculosis has "probably killed 100 million people over the past 100 years" (Frieden et al. 2003, 887). Tuberculosis has been especially deadly in Africa, which has only 11 percent of the world's population but accounts for 34 percent of the world's deaths from tuberculosis (Chaisson and Martinson 2008). Moreover, the situation has grown worse in recent years with the rise of AIDS. In individuals with AIDS, whose immune systems are suppressed, tuberculosis spreads rapidly and accounts for up to 40 percent of deaths in AIDS patients (Chaisson and Martinson 2008). The situation has become so dire that in 2005 the ministers of health for Sub-Saharan African nations held a special conference in Abuja, Nigeria, and declared a tuberculosis emergency (Makombe 2005).

AIDS

According to the World Health Organization, AIDS is the leading cause of death in Africa, accounting for approximately 20 percent of all deaths. It is caused by a human modification of a retrovirus that has probably existed in primates for millions of years, causing little or no illness in them. The human immunodeficiency virus-1 (HIV-1), which causes the most severe form of AIDS, is a combination of viral strains carried by two species of monkeys in central Africa (Bailes et al. 2003). The two monkey strains infected chimpanzees, producing a new strain of simian immunodeficiency virus that was then transmitted to humans who were probably butchering chimpanzees for use as "bushmeat." HIV-2, which causes a less severe form of AIDS, is a human modification of a retrovirus carried by a species of monkey in West Africa.

Primates have probably carried simian retroviruses for millions of years, and humans have probably been hunting primates for bushmeat for thousands of years. Simian retroviruses have likely been transmitted to humans many times during past centuries, through a bite by a live monkey, for example, or a cut on the hand of a human who was skinning an infected primate. These individual humans may have become infected and perhaps even died, but nobody knew because the disease was not transmitted to others and thus no epidemic occurred. Isolated human deaths from unknown diseases do not come to public attention in most parts of the world. Why then did the AIDS epidemic begin when it did? Probably because something changed.

The epidemic of human AIDS began in Africa because of social change. To spread from one human to another, HIV-1 and HIV-2 require close personal contact—usually an exchange of body fluids such as occurs during sexual intercourse or the sharing of a common needle for intravenous injections or drug abuse. In the 1960s colonial rule was ending in Africa and civil wars broke out. Urbanization increased, followed by social breakdown and widespread prostitution. Developed countries were experiencing a sexual revolution in general, and a gay revolution in particular, as well as increased intravenous drug use and the sharing of needles. Indeed, if one set out to create the most favorable social circumstances for spreading a sexually transmitted microbe from Africa to the rest of the world, the circumstances of the late 20th century would provide a perfect model.

One technological advance in particular is thought to have played a role in the dissemination of AIDS—the introduction of plastic disposable syringes after World War II. Previously, syringes for injections had been made of glass, were relatively expensive, and had to be sterilized before being reused. The introduction of inexpensive plastic syringes, designed to be discarded after a single use, made them much more widely available in developing countries. The World Health Organization has estimated that approximately 12 billion plastic syringes are sold each year, sufficient for two injections per year for every man, woman, and child on the planet if the syringes are discarded after use (Hutin, Hauri, and Armstrong 2003).

Unfortunately, many of the plastic syringes are reused, often with no attempt at sterilization between uses. Studies have shown that in many countries at least 50 percent of injections are given with reused, unsterile plastic syringes; in some countries the figure has been reported to be as high as 90 percent of injections (Simonsen et al. 1999). Laypeople commonly believe that injections are more efficacious than medicine given by mouth; giving injections is therefore big business, and in developing countries they are frequently given by untrained "injection doctors," "needlemen," and a variety of traditional healers (van der Geest 1982). Thus, the introduction and wide dissemination of plastic syringes provided ideal circumstances for the spread of infectious agents that are primarily transmitted by the spread of bodily fluids. In Africa, the use of unsterile syringes is thought to have played a major role in the spread of the viruses causing AIDS as well as those causing hepatitis B and C.

AIDS has had a devastating effect on health in Africa, causing 2 million deaths there each year. In Botswana, one of the hardest-hit countries, 39 percent of the adults are thought to be infected with HIV, and in some Sub-Saharan countries, 15 percent or more of children have been orphaned by AIDS (Lamptey et al. 2002).

Other Diseases

Measles, tuberculosis, and AIDS are three important African diseases that were originally transmitted from animals to humans, but there are many others.

Pertussis (whooping cough), the 15th leading cause of death in Africa, is caused by a bacterium, *Bordetella pertussi*, that is closely related to bacteria carried by pigs, sheep, dogs, cats, rats, horses, rabbits, and some primates. Current thinking is that the pertussis form of the bacteria probably spread to humans from pigs. Smallpox is another disease that has devastated Africa and much of the world. Its origins have been long debated, since closely related viruses affect monkeys, rodents, cows, cats, and water buffalo. Many suspect that water buffalo were the original source of smallpox, since the buffalo were initially domesticated in Southeast Asia, where human smallpox was first recorded (Hare 1967). Diarrheal diseases are the fourth leading cause of death in Africa. One common cause is bacterial members of the *Escherichia coli* family, which are responsible for many outbreaks of diarrhea caused by contaminated food and water. *Escherichia coli* are widely distributed among cattle, most of whom are asymptomatic carriers; the bacteria may spread to humans through the consumption of undercooked beef or unpasteurized milk.

The most common causes of diarrheal diseases are bacteria in the salmonella family. *Salmonella typhi*, which causes typhoid fever, is the best known, but approximately 2,500 other salmonella serotypes are known. Salmonella bacteria are carried by many species of reptiles and birds, and these species are thought to have been their origin. Because chickens are widely kept in many parts of Africa, they are the principle immediate source of salmonella infections. The bacteria can spread to humans through direct handling of infected chickens or the eating of undercooked meat or eggs. Experiments have shown that the salmonella bacteria remain viable in eggs cooked "sunny-side up" or "over easy" as well as in boiled or fried eggs in which the yolk remains liquid (Hedberg et al. 1993). Thus, any food to which eggs have been added is a potential source of salmonella poisoning. The bacteria can also infect other foods. For example, the largest salmonella outbreak in the United States occurred in Illinois and Wisconsin in 1984 and sickened an estimated 200,000 people; the source was milk contaminated with salmonella bacteria (Miller, Hohmann, and Pegues 1995).

Acute respiratory diseases, especially pneumonia, are the second leading cause of death in Africa, surpassed only by AIDS. Among the causes of acute respiratory diseases, influenza is potentially the most lethal. The virus that causes influenza is carried by ducks and other water birds, including herons, gulls, and terns. These birds have probably carried influenza viruses for millions of years, and it was only when ducks became domesticated, probably originally in Southeast Asia, that influenza became a major problem. Like virtually all peoples of the world, Africans have been widely infected during influenza pandemics, such as the one in 1918–19.

Another epidemic disease that has periodically spread to Africa is bubonic plague. It is caused by the bacterium *Yersina pestis*, which evolved from a similar bacterium widely distributed among rats and other rodents in Southwest Asia. Human plague was first recorded when rats joined the caravans of traders going back and forth between the Middle East and China; such caravans passed directly through the area where the rats were indigenous. This initial epidemic, called the plague of Justinian, occurred in the 6th century CE.

Since that time, bubonic plague has surfaced periodically around the world, especially in port cities where infected rats arrive on trading ships. The deadliest epidemic was the Black Death of the 14th century, which is estimated to have killed as much as one-third of Europe's population. The most recent epidemic began in Hong Kong in 1894 and slowly spread around the world: "In 1900 it struck Africa, Australia, New Zealand, London, Cardiff, Astrakhan in Russia and, finally, the west coast of the United States" (Marriott 2002, 123).

The aforementioned examples have focused on human diseases spread from animals that have been or still are major sources of mortality in Africa, but many other diseases that spread from animals to humans rarely cause death. One example consists of rhinoviruses, which cause many types of the common cold. For many years it was thought that rhinoviruses originally spread to humans from horses, but scientists now believe that the viruses originated in cattle and were then modified after spreading to humans.

Another such example is the bacterium that causes human stomach ulcers, *Helicobacter pylori*. Dogs, cats, horses, cows, pigs, sheep, and some primates carry this bacterium, but sheep have emerged as the most likely source of its spread to humans. The evidence to support this conclusion comes from rural Sardinia, where sheep are widespread. It has been reported that 98 percent of shepherds are infected with *Helicobacter pylori*, a rate more than twice as high as Sardinians who are not shepherds (Dore et al. 1999). The bacterium may be transmitted in the sheep's milk, which shepherds sometimes drink raw.

Looking to the Future: The Importance of Changes

Understanding past transmissions of infectious agents is important for limiting the spread of existing disease and affecting the emergence of new human diseases in the future. What lessons can be learned from the past, and how can these lessons be used to affect Africa's future?

Changes in the Relationship between Animals and Humans

As the previous discussion has shown, any change in the relationship between animals and humans may change the transmission of infectious agents between them. This fact is especially pertinent in Africa, which has more wild mammalian species than any other area on earth. As such, Africa is a reservoir for more unknown infectious agents, which are carried by these animals and which, as the relationship between animals and humans changes, could be transmitted to humans for the first time. Thus, in doomsday scenarios in which an Ebola-like infectious agent kills many people, Africa is the most likely origin of such agents.

Changes in the relationship between animals and humans can have many causes. In the southern Sudan, for example, an increase in cattle raiding has led families to keep their cattle much closer to home—even in their living quarters— where they can be watched. As the African middle class increases in size, they are likely to increasingly adopt Western modes of pet keeping. In North America and Western Europe, it is now common for dogs and cats to live intimately with their owners, even sleeping with them and eating food from their plates. This kind of intimacy is also likely to increase in Africa. Another change in relationship is occurring as Africans, faced with poverty and malnutrition, increasingly hunt, skin, and eat various wild animals as bushmeat.

Changes in Modes of Travel

As modes of travel have changed in the past, humans have been increasingly exposed to infectious agents that had been previously geographically isolated. This phenomenon was strikingly illustrated by the bacteria causing bubonic plague, which was carried by rats and their fleas along caravan routes and then by ships around the world.

A recent illustration of this principle was the spread of the virus causing severe acute respiratory syndrome (SARS) from southern China in 2003. The virus spread to humans from palm civets and other animals for sale in open-air markets for use as bushmeat. Before widespread air travel, such outbreaks were confined to the immediate area. Carried by international air passengers, however, the SARS epidemic spread to 30 countries on five continents within a few weeks.

On February 21, 2003, for example, a man with SARS stayed overnight at a hotel in Hong Kong and infected at least 17 other guests. Some of these guests then flew to Hanoi, Singapore, and Toronto, spreading SARS to individuals in these cities. In Toronto, 24 people died from SARS, and the city was virtually shut down. Another man, after visiting his sick brother in a hospital, boarded a flight for Beijing and infected 22 other passengers on the flight, 5 of whom died (Olsen et al. 2003). Retrospective analysis of the passenger seating list on the flight revealed that passengers who had sat immediately in front of, or to the side of, the infected man were the most likely to have become infected.

Air travel has thus made all areas of the world susceptible to infections by microbes, including those carried by animals. An epidemic may begin on one side of the world and within hours be carried to the other side of the world. In Africa, therefore, a SARS-like virus can suddenly arrive at, or an Ebola-like virus can be rapidly carried away from, an airport in Addis Ababa, Bamako, Capetown, or Yaoundé. And as roads are improved in the more remote areas of the continent, infectious agents will go to or from the airport to these areas even more rapidly.

Changes in Food-Production and -Processing Methods

Since animals are a major source of protein in human diets, changes in the methods of animal food production and processing can produce important changes in human exposure to disease. Until recently, animal food production in Africa consisted of the slaughter of a single chicken, duck, sheep, goat, or cow in the family yard, often to celebrate a holiday or a special event such as a marriage. In recent years, however, many urban areas in Africa have witnessed the introduction of mass slaughterhouses and mechanized food production, often accompanied by insufficient safeguards and inspection programs. When a single diseased animal is consumed by an extended family and neighbors, the illness is restricted to that small group. When diseased animals are included in mass food production, however, the resulting illness may affect many more people.

Another example is mad cow disease. Bovine spongiform encephalopathy (BSE), also known as mad cow disease, is caused by a prion, a strange and poorly understood microbe that affects the brains of cows. When humans become infected, they develop memory loss, seizures, involuntary movements, and dementia, and these symptoms usually progress to death. With the rise of giant agribusinesses, cattle are now slaughtered in mechanized factories where attempts are made to use every possible part of the carcass. One procedure involves the recovery of animal fat and protein to make products that are used as pet foods. In the 1980s in Britain, a change was made in this recovery process that made it more likely that brain tissue, and thus prions, would be included. Prions then got into the British beef supply, resulting in an epidemic of BSE with more than 150 deaths.

A cautionary example of how even minor changes in food production may produce profound changes in the distribution of diseases are the changes in fish farming that occurred in southern China. Fish there are farmed in ponds and then sold as food. When it was discovered that fish grew bigger when the pond was fertilized by animal feces, it became common practice to hang cages of pigs, chickens, and ducks directly over the pond so that their feces would drop in the water. The animals drank water from the pond, and wild ducks swam in it.

The influenza virus, which is carried by ducks, is known to mutate when it passes through pigs. Such mutations produce new strains of the virus, some of which can be lethal for humans. The modification of fish farming in southern China in recent decades has produced optimal conditions for the influenza virus to pass from ducks to pigs and back to ducks again, producing new strains of the virus. It is thought that this process is increasing the number of strains of influenza available to spread worldwide, including the strain known as the "bird flu" presently spreading in the world with a high human mortality rate. The lesson to be learned is that any change in the method of food production that alters the relationship among animals may have unforeseeable and unintended consequences for human health.

Problems in food processing also exist in many parts of Africa. The lack of clean water for cleaning foods, cooking, and drinking is widespread. Food intended for human consumption is also regularly contaminated by flies and other insects that may be carrying infectious agents. This problem is especially severe in African family compounds where domestic animals and humans live together; in such situations, a fly may have to travel only a few feet to carry an infectious agent from animal feces in the yard to food on the table.

Changes in Ecology and Environment

Many African countries are undergoing profound ecological and environmental changes, including urbanization, deforestation, and global warming. Most cities in Africa have at least doubled in population in recent decades, and some have tripled or more. The existence of megacities with populations of 10 million or more is relatively new. New York, in 1950, was the first such city, but by 2015 the world is expected to have 21 megacities, including Lagos and Cairo (Zwingle 2002).

Large cities promote the dissemination of diseases in many ways. Some infectious agents, such as the measles virus, require a concentrated population of 250,000 or more in order to survive. As the population of Africa become increasingly urbanized, it is likely that other infectious agents will exploit such concentrations of individuals. Urbanization also promotes the spread of microbes through the contamination of urban water supplies, poor sewage systems, trash heaps that support rodents, and crowded living conditions. As one expert noted in 1998, "The mega cities of the tropics, with their lack of sanitary systems, serve as incubators for emerging zoonoses—they represent the most difficult zoonotic diseases risks of the next century" (Murphy 1998, 434).

Deforestation is another ecological change that may produce alterations in human diseases. In many African countries, deforestation is taking place as simpler forms of agriculture are being replaced by the large-scale growing of cash crops. Another cause of deforestation is the need for firewood and charcoal for cooking; the rising price of cooking oils makes the cutting down of trees increasingly attractive to those living in poverty.

The possible effects of deforestation on disease transmission can be illustrated by Argentine hemorrhagic fever. This South American virus, carried by rodents, increased sharply among humans following the conversion of grasslands to maize cultivation, a change that favored an increase in the rodent population (Morse 1995). In North America, deforestation followed by reforestation has resulted in a rapid rise in the deer population. The deer carry ticks that in turn carry Lyme disease, and since the 1990s, there has been an epidemic of human Lyme disease in the northeastern United States (Steere 2001).

Global warming is another environmental change that will almost certainly increase the distribution of some infectious diseases in Africa, as elsewhere. As temperatures rise, disease vectors such as mosquitoes will be found in increasingly broad areas. For example, Addis Ababa, Ethiopia, is situated at an altitude of 7,000 feet and has previously been relatively free from malaria; with global warming, this will no longer be the case. Global warming is likely to also exacerbate the cycles of drought that have traditionally plagued many parts of Africa. This change will, in turn, decrease food production and increase malnutrition and susceptibility to disease.

What Can Be Done?

What can be done to minimize the transmission of infectious agents from animals to humans and thus the development of diseases? It is important to minimize future dangers. A 2003 report from the U.S. Institute of Medicine was sobering, claiming that "none of its members are sanguine about what the future may hold with regard to microbial threats to health. . . . Today's outlook with regard to microbial threats is bleak on a number of fronts. . . . Microbial threats present us with new surprises every year" (Smolinski, Hamburg, and Lederberg 2003, 245). The recent emergence of human epidemics of animal-borne infectious agents should be a wake-up call: AIDS, SARS, West Nile virus, bird flu, and in Africa, probably Lassa fever, Marburg hemorrhagic fever, and Ebola hemorrhagic fever. As the director of the U.S. Centers for Disease Control and Prevention noted in 2004, "11 of the last 12 emerging infectious diseases that we're aware of in the world, that have had human health consequences, have probably arisen from animal sources" (International Society for Infectious Diseases 2004).

The single most important step to take is to develop an extensive surveillance system to detect new and recurrent infectious disease outbreaks as early as possible. Currently, the most effective such system is the Program for Monitoring Emerging Diseases, or ProMED, an Internet reporting system administered by the International Society for Infectious Diseases, using foundation funding. This useful warning system is constrained in Africa by incomplete disease surveillance in many countries. In 2000, the World Health Organization (WHO) launched the Global Outbreak Alert and Response Network, but like many WHO endeavors, it has been slow to reach its potential because of the politics of that organization.

A fundamental problem at both the international and national level is a lack of coordination between agencies that have responsibility for animal health and agencies that have responsibility for human health. Influenza, for example, is a disease of great importance for both poultry and humans. Internationally, the World Organization for Animal Health (Office International des Epizooties, OIE), based in Paris, has responsibility for animal diseases, whereas the World Health Organization, based in Geneva, has responsibility for human diseases. Coordination between these two agencies has traditionally been poor. This lack of coordination at the international level is mirrored by a lack of coordination at national levels, both in Africa and elsewhere.

A basic cause of this lack of coordination of disease information is a gulf that has long existed between veterinarians, the specialists in animal diseases, and infectious disease physicians, the specialists in human diseases. The two groups have been trained in different schools and have worked in different professional worlds for more than a century. The relative lack of veterinarians in African countries exacerbates the problem further. Although it has become increasingly clear that most emerging human infectious diseases originate in animals, little effort has been made to close this gulf. The lack of coordination between animal- and human-disease specialists was highlighted again during the recent bird flu epidemic.

One model for such coordination is Denmark, which has developed "a zoonosis center as an element of its national public health institution . . . uniting veterinary and human health professionals" (Smolinski, Hamburg, and Lederberg 2003, 170).

Another way to minimize the threat of animal-carried infectious agents is to educate the public. Studies in the United States have shown that most people are unaware of the transmission of infectious agents from animals to humans. Beginning in childhood, people need to be taught not only to enjoy animals, but also to respect them as possible sources of disease. It is useful for people to know that Donald Duck is the source of the virus causing influenza, Mickey Mouse may be carrying the hantavirus, Bambi spreads Lyme disease, Big Bird carries the West Nile virus, and even Barney, beloved of small children, is quite likely to be carrying salmonella bacteria, as all reptiles do (Torrey and Yolken 2005).

CHAPTER 5

How AIDS Epidemics Interact with African Food Systems
and How to Improve the Response

Stuart Gillespie

Abstract

Recognition of the complex, long-wave aspects of the AIDS crisis has been slow to dawn. Sub-Saharan Africa, particularly southern Africa, continues to be the epicenter of the crisis. There are many key interactions between rural livelihoods, HIV transmission and AIDS impacts. Food insecurity and AIDS not only coexist in many regions of Africa, but also interact in potentially vicious circles. Against this backdrop, implementation of HIV-responsive approaches to ensuring food and nutrition security—at a scale that matches the epidemic—remains limited. This chapter briefly reviews what is known about how HIV interacts with food systems in Africa and the remaining knowledge gaps that must be addressed. Some of these gaps relate to understanding of the interactions, but many are operational, relating to what can be done to respond more effectively.

Introduction

Among the multiple causes and consequences of AIDS epidemics, the vicious circle between AIDS and food insecurity is a growing concern, particularly in Sub-Saharan Africa, where HIV is hyperendemic in several countries. The coexistence of and interactions between AIDS and hunger are further accentuated at present by the ongoing food crisis.

It is useful to start by examining the evolution of the AIDS epidemic in Africa, using data from UNAIDS, released in July 2008 (UNAIDS 2008). At that time, globally, more than 25 million people had died since the first case was reported in 1981, from a total estimate of 65 million infected. The epidemic appears to have stabilized, albeit at exceptionally high levels of new HIV infections and AIDS deaths. An estimated 33 million people were living with HIV in 2007. The annual number of new HIV infections has declined from 3.0 million in 2001 to 2.7 million in 2007. Overall, 2.0 million people died from AIDS in 2007, compared with an estimated 1.7 million in 2001. Although the percentage of people living with HIV has stabilized since 2000, the overall number of people living with HIV has steadily increased as new infections occur each year and HIV treatments extend life. New infections still outnumber AIDS deaths.

The AIDS epidemic in Sub-Saharan Africa continues to be a major regional development crisis with impacts that will be felt for decades to come. The region accounted for 67 percent of all people living with HIV and for 75 percent of AIDS deaths in 2007. An estimated 1.9 million people were newly infected with HIV in Sub-Saharan Africa in 2007, bringing to 22 million the number of people living with HIV. In addition, Sub-Saharan Africa has more than 12 million orphans (UNAIDS 2008).

Sub-Saharan Africa's epidemics vary significantly from country to country in both scale and scope. Adult national HIV prevalence is less than 2 percent in several countries of West and Central Africa, as well as in the Horn of Africa, but in 2007 it exceeded 15 percent in seven southern African countries (Botswana, Lesotho, Namibia, South Africa, Swaziland, Zambia, and Zimbabwe) and was greater than 5 percent in seven other countries, mostly in Central and East Africa (Cameroon, the Central African Republic, Gabon, Malawi, Mozambique, Tanzania, and Uganda). Southern Africa continues to bear a disproportionate share of the global burden of HIV, with 35 percent of all HIV infections and 38 percent of AIDS deaths in 2007 having occurred in that subregion.

In sum, epidemics in southern Africa are fully fledged, generalized epidemics affecting the overall population (sometimes referred to as hyper-epidemics). In East Africa, epidemics are more concentrated in specific population subgroups or geographic areas. West Africa, in general, has lower prevalences than in East Africa, and AIDS is not a significant problem in North Africa.

It is not entirely clear why AIDS has hit southern Africa so hard—socioeconomic variables, cultural factors, and sexual behavior all play a role. Poverty, income inequality, gender inequity, high mobility, multiple concurrent partnerships, the lack of male circumcision, and the prevalence of co-infections are factors that have been identified and need further examination (Gillespie, Kadiyala, and Greener 2007).

AIDS epidemics are multidimensional, long-wave phenomena. A wave of HIV infection is followed by increased incidence of opportunistic infections and, several years later, by the AIDS death wave (the latter now being attenuated to some extent by the rollout of antiretroviral drugs, as discussed later). Beyond these effects, depending on a host of variables, there lies a stream of economic and social impacts at household, community, and national levels. Several countries (including

Kenya, Lesotho, Malawi, Namibia, Rwanda, Swaziland, the United Republic of Tanzania, and Zimbabwe) have recently brought down infection rates, although it is not clear how they achieved this decline—whether by proactive prevention strategies, AIDS deaths, the epidemic's reaching its natural peak, or all of these.

The massive push for universal access to treatment, care, and support led to access to antiretrovirals (ARVs) for 3 million people by the end of 2007. Focusing only on the most-affected countries of Sub-Saharan Africa, however, reveals a mixed picture. Of the hyperendemic countries, all (except Botswana) fall within the range of 20–40 percent ARV coverage for advanced HIV. About two-thirds of Africans living with HIV who qualify for therapy are thus still not receiving drugs. AIDS is a long-wave threat, and the fact that the disease disproportionately strikes the most productive members of society sets it apart from other health shocks. Owing to the vast numbers of people currently infected with the virus, and the continuing need for ARV therapy (as HIV incidence remains high), the effects of AIDS will last for many, many years to come.

What Are the Links between AIDS, Agriculture, and Food and Nutrition Security?

Food and nutrition interact with HIV in several ways at different levels. One interaction, between malnutrition and disease, gets straight to work in the human body directly after an individual has become infected with HIV. The importance of nutrition for immune function was understood 40 years ago when the term NAIDS ("Nutritionally Acquired Immune Deficiency Syndrome") was first used (Scrimshaw, Taylor, and Gordon 1968).

Another vicious circle, schematized in Figure 5.1, revolves around a household's degree of access to the food it needs. On the upstream side of viral transmission, food insecurity may put poor people at greater risk of being exposed to HIV—for example, through forced migration to find work or through poverty-fueled adoption of transactional sex as a "survival" strategy. And on the downstream side, the various impacts of chronic illness and premature mortality on household assets and resources are well documented. Throughout, it is the poor, and especially poor women, who are most vulnerable to the HIV-hunger nexus because they are least able to reduce their exposure to the virus, to gain access to and sustain treatment, and to mitigate the impacts of the disease.

Globally, the primary livelihood base of most people infected or affected by AIDS is agriculture. In East and southern Africa, AIDS epidemics are already having serious consequences for agriculture by affecting adults at the height of their productive years, making it difficult for poor people—especially poor women—to provide food for their families.

But it is important to guard against simplistic assumptions. The critical constraint, for example, may not be labor power—it may be a lack of cash due to the

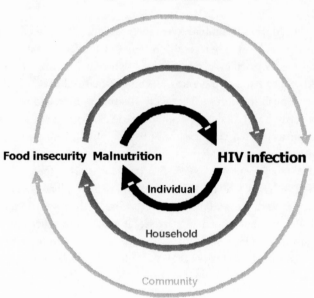

Figure 5.1   Spirals within spirals: Interactions between food insecurity, malnutrition, and HIV infection
SOURCE: Friis, Gillespie, and Filteau 2008.

new financial demands brought by the illness. Some studies show a limited current aggregate impact on agriculture, but aggregated data (presented as means or averages) may mask differences in impacts within communities. This apparent limited impact may change when young adults, who are disproportionately at risk from HIV, are expected to become household heads. Nothing is static in this epidemic. Moreover, unknowns still exist—for example, the long-term impacts that AIDS imposes by fracturing the intergenerational transfer of knowledge and skills from farmers to their children.

Important interactions exist between hunger (Millennium Development Goal 1) and most of the other Millennium Development Goals (MDGs). Likewise, the AIDS epidemic—especially in southern Africa—will influence the ability of several countries to reach most of the goals (beyond MDG 6, which explicitly focuses on AIDS, malaria, and tuberculosis). There is evidence that AIDS affects food production, income generation, and nutrition (MDG 1), reduces school attendance (MDG 2), disproportionately affects girls and women (MDG 3), increases child mortality (MDG 4), adversely affects maternal health (MDG 5), interacts significantly with malaria and TB (MDG 6), and reduces time allocated to ensuring a safe and sanitary environment and protecting farmland from degradation (MDG 7). Finally, the focus on "an active global partnership for development" in MDG 8 represents one important means of addressing a complex, multisectoral issue such as the HIV-hunger nexus.

Concepts

In this section, several conceptual tools are provided to help navigate the universe of causes and consequences of HIV and AIDS, highlighting interactions with food and nutrition insecurity at several levels. This discussion starts with the virus and how it infects the human body, interacting with an individual's nutritional status.

Nutrition and immunity in HIV-positive individuals can interact in two ways (Figure 5.2). First, HIV-induced immune impairment and heightened subsequent risk of opportunistic infection can worsen nutritional status. HIV infection often leads to nutritional deficiencies through decreased food intake, malabsorption, and increased utilization and excretion of nutrients, which in turn can hasten death (Semba and Tang 1999). Second, nutritional status modulates the immunological response to HIV infection, affecting the overall clinical outcome. Immune suppression caused by malnutrition is similar in many ways to the effects of HIV infection (Beisel 1996).

Turning from the individual to the level of households and communities, interactions can be conceptualized using an adaptation of the sustainable livelihoods framework (Gillespie 2006). Figure 5.3 portrays the dynamics of household and community interactions with HIV and AIDS as an iterative cycle.

HIV and AIDS both affect, and are affected by, people's livelihoods. The macro context, conditions, and trends will to some extent determine the vulnerability of different livelihood systems to upstream HIV exposure and to the downstream impacts of AIDS. After HIV has entered a household or community, the type and severity of its impacts on assets—mediated by institutional structures, processes, and programs—will determine the type of strategies that the household adopts.

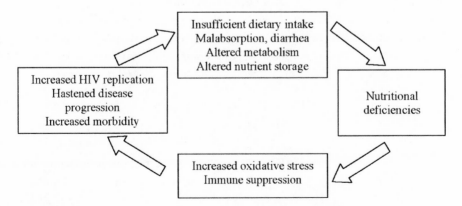

Figure 5.2   The vicious circle of malnutrition and HIV
SOURCE: Semba and Tang 1999.

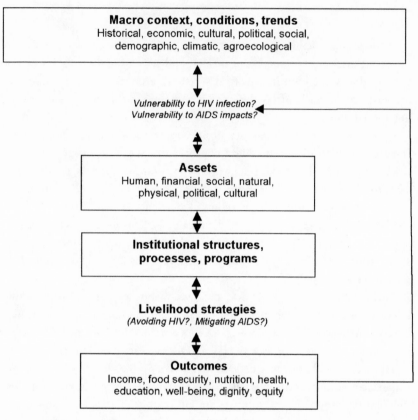

Figure 5.3   Adapting the livelihoods framework to HIV and AIDS
SOURCE: Author.

These strategies will differ, among other ways, in terms of their ability to (1) reduce people's exposure to HIV and (2) increase their resilience to AIDS impacts. Such strategies and responses in turn lead to various outcomes, including food and nutrition security. Finally, the diagram shows how these outcomes are also inputs— for better or worse—into future vulnerability or resilience. And so the cycle turns.

Structure of the Chapter

This chapter continues by reviewing the key evidence concerning the upstream links between food insecurity and HIV—that is whether, and through what pathways, situations of food insecurity put people at greater risk of being exposed to and infected by the virus. This discussion is followed by an examination of what is known about the downstream (or post-infection) side—how AIDS-related disease and premature mortality exacerbate or precipitate food insecurity or malnutrition.

The discussion tracks the path of the virus. On the upstream side, it starts by examining the role of macro-level conditions and the differences between countries before zooming in on communities, households, and ultimately individuals to try to understand what factors and processes confer greater risk and vulnerability to HIV infection. Following HIV infection in an individual, this discussion then tracks the effects of the virus as they extend from the individual, identifying key pathways and types of impact at different levels, from individual to household and community and finally to national and regional levels.

From this basic understanding of the key interactions, the chapter goes on to discuss options for responding to them, highlighting key agricultural and other food and nutrition-related interventions, interspersed with boxed operational research challenges.[1]

Do Poverty and Food Insecurity Increase Exposure to HIV?

The International Picture

At the country level there is a weak positive relationship between national wealth and HIV prevalence across countries in Sub-Saharan Africa, where higher prevalence is seen in the wealthier countries of Southern Africa (Gillespie, Kadiyala, and Greener 2007). Strong urban–rural economic linkages, good transport links, and high professional mobility may translate into both higher incomes and higher HIV incidence. National poverty rates, on the other hand, do not show a strong association with HIV prevalence (Figure 5.4). But there is a clear and significant pattern of association between income inequality and HIV prevalence across African countries—countries with greater inequality have higher HIV prevalence (Figure 5.5); the relationship is less pronounced in Asia and Latin America.

These results are simply bivariate associations using national cross-sectional household survey data, so they do raise the potential for simultaneous causality. That is, it is not clear which comes first—income inequality or HIV infection. They do point, however, to the need to dig deeper into the issue of inequality between people, as is done in the next section.

Household- and Community-Level Vulnerability to HIV Exposure

Evidence of the association between HIV transmission and household socioeconomic status is mixed (Wojciki 2005; Nyindo 2005; Buvé et al. 2001; Gillespie, Kadiyala, and Greener 2007). Whereas early studies tended to find positive correlations between economic resources, education, and HIV infection (such as Ainsworth and Semali 1998), as the epidemic has progressed, it has increasingly been assumed that this relationship is changing. But evidence of the degree, type,

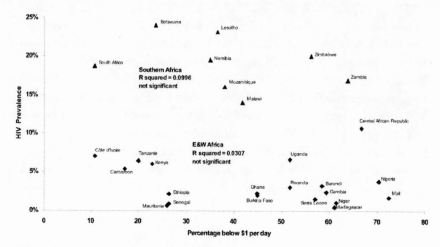

Figure 5.4   HIV and poverty in Africa
SOURCES: Economic data from UNDP 2006; HIV prevalence data from UNAIDS/WHO 2006.
This graph from Gillespie, Kadiyala, and Greener 2007 was charted by Robert Greener (UNAIDS).

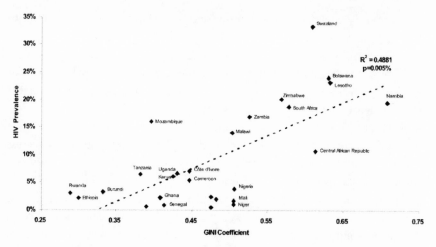

Figure 5.5   HIV and income inequality in Africa
SOURCES: Economic data from UNDP 2006; HIV prevalence data from UNAIDS/WHO 2006.
This graph from Gillespie, Kadiyala, and Greener 2007 was charted by Robert Greener (UNAIDS).
NOTE: The Gini coefficient is a measure of income inequality ranging between 0 and 1, where
0 corresponds to perfect income equality and 1 corresponds to perfect income inequality.

and dynamics of the influence of socioeconomic factors on rates of HIV transmission in different settings and at various stages of the AIDS epidemic is still
rudimentary.

In most countries, relatively rich and better-educated men and women have
higher rates of partner change because they have greater personal autonomy and

spatial mobility (Gregson et al. 2006; Hargreaves and Glynn 2002). Although the richer and better educated are likely to have better access to reproductive health care, condom use is generally low in Africa and other parts of the developing world. Preexisting sexual behavior patterns (from pre-HIV times) therefore make the richer more vulnerable to HIV infection, especially in the early stages of the epidemic, when information about the virus and how to protect oneself is usually low (Anderson et al. 1991). At a later stage, however, it has been argued that individuals with higher socioeconomic and educational status tend to adopt safer sexual practices once the effects of AIDS-related morbidity and mortality become more apparent, adding greater credibility to HIV prevention messages (De Walque et al. 2005). A recent review of the association between education and HIV risk bears out this finding (Hargreaves et al. 2008)

Another currently postulated dynamic is that poverty (possibly itself fueled by AIDS) is increasingly placing individuals from poor households at greater risk of exposure to HIV through the economically driven adoption of risky behaviors. Poverty and food insecurity are thought to increase sexual risk taking, particularly among women who may engage in transactional sex to procure food for themselves and their children. Women's economic dependence on their partners may also make it difficult for them to insist on safer sex (for example, condom use), as discussed later. In addition, poor people are more likely to be food insecure and malnourished, which in turn may lead to a weakening of the immune system and increased HIV risk.

Several studies adopting ethnographic methodologies do suggest that material poverty increases the risks of contracting HIV mainly through the adoption of high-risk behaviors. The respondents to an ethnographic study in the Southern Province of Zambia (Byron, Gillespie, and Hamazakaza 2006) identified frequent droughts and limited wage labor opportunities, following the closure of companies in the wake of economic liberalization, as the "push" factors behind women's increasing resort to transactional sex.

In another qualitative study in Malawi, certain social groups were found to continue to engage in high-risk behaviors, despite knowing the risks. The backdrop was the ongoing collapse of the peasant household's coherence as a unit of production as livelihood portfolios veered (1) from self-sufficient unpaid labor performed within the household (especially by women and children) toward cash-earning piecemeal work (or *ganyu*); (2) from agriculture toward non-agriculture with income-earning turning increasingly to trade and services, including sexual services; and (3) from household toward individualized work, whereby every able-bodied person works, including women and youth, to earn cash to cover their subsistence needs. Women and girls are now undertaking *ganyu* labor beyond the confines of the village, with poor women at particular risk as transactional sex is increasingly incorporated into *ganyu* contracts (Bryceson and Fonseca 2006).

Examining nationally representative data, using DHS data from eight countries, Mishra et al. (2007), however, find a positive association between an asset-based wealth index and HIV status. This relationship was stronger for women, and it was clear that HIV prevalence was generally lower among the poorest individuals in these countries. This result is partly accounted for by an association of wealth with other underlying factors. Wealthier[2] individuals tend to live in urban areas where HIV is more prevalent and to be more mobile; they are more likely to have multiple partners, to engage in sex with nonregular partners, and to live longer—all factors that may present greater lifetime HIV risks. On the other hand, they tend to be better educated, with better knowledge of HIV prevention methods, and are more likely to use condoms—factors that reduce their risk relative to poorer individuals. Controlling for these associations, however, does not reverse the conclusion—there is no apparent association between low wealth status and HIV.

Such cross-sectional studies are, however, unable to distinguish between the effect of economic status on HIV infection and the effect of HIV infection on economic status, and they are unable to control for the fact that individuals from richer households may survive longer with HIV, and thus are more likely to be present in the population to be tested, thereby increasing HIV prevalence rates. Such limitations can be overcome by using prospective cohorts to track HIV incidence. Three recent studies shed some light here—one from Zimbabwe suggests incidence peaks in poorer groups (Lopman et al. 2007), one in KwaZulu Natal, South Africa, suggests it peaks in the middle asset-wealth class (Bärnighausen et al. 2007), and one in Limpopo Province, South Africa, finds no relation between HIV incidence and wealth (Hargreaves et al. 2007).

A few other longitudinal studies shed light on socioeconomic differentials in HIV transmission. A nationally representative rural panel data survey (2001–04) in Zambia sought to determine the ex ante socioeconomic characteristics of prime-age adults who died (Chapoto and Jayne 2006). When ranked by asset levels, wealthier men were 43 percent more likely to die of disease-related causes than men in poor households, with no clear association among women. Digging deeper, they find that within the group of relatively poor women, those having some form of formal or informal business income are 15 percent less likely to die of disease-related causes than those without any such income—suggesting that efforts to provide greater income-earning opportunities for poor women may make at least a modest contribution to reducing female prime-age mortality.

Individuals: Who Is at Risk?

HIV infection rates in young women are usually the highest of any subgroup in the most-affected countries (UNAIDS 2008). A recent nationally representative study in Zambia, for example, found more than 60 percent of the prime-age deaths between 2001 and 2004 were women (Chapoto and Jayne 2006). The marginal probability of dying from disease and AIDS-related causes rises steeply from age 15, peaking between ages 30 and 34 for females, and between 50 and 54 for males. Young, single women were at most risk.

Another major source of individual risk—and one that sets HIV apart from most other diseases—is the prior death of at least one adult in the same household. In Zambia, this risk was found to be the single most important factor influencing the probability that a prime-aged individual would die from illness and AIDS (Chapoto and Jayne 2006). Irrespective of gender and income status, individuals experiencing a prior death in their household are six to seven times more likely to die of disease-related causes than individuals in households with no prime-age deaths in the past eight years.

Poverty, Food Insecurity, and HIV: Pathways and Interactions

Links between socioeconomic conditions and HIV risk and vulnerability are complex. A major analytical challenge is to define the causal pathways operating from distal socioeconomic factors to proximal individual behaviors and ultimately physiological factors. Different socioeconomic factors may affect health at different times in the life course, operating at different levels (for example, individual, household, and neighborhood) and through different causal pathways (Gillespie, Kadiyala, and Greener 2007).

GENDER AND ECONOMIC ASYMMETRIES

The issue of gender is front and center to any discussion of HIV and poverty. Gender inequity shapes power relations, sexual relations, and thus risk. Women are at greater risk of HIV infection than men for many reasons. Biologically, a greater area of tissue is exposed to the virus during intercourse, and women are more likely to have other sexually transmitted diseases (STDs) and less likely to seek treatment. If untreated, STDs may quadruple the risk of HIV transmission (Galvin and Cohen 2004). Socioculturally, women's relative powerlessness also increases risk. Women are less likely to negotiate condom use, inside or outside of marriage. Some men coerce adolescent girls into sex in the mistaken belief they can rid themselves of the virus. Other practices are highly risky for women, including genital mutilation and dry sex. The male partner is often considerably older than the female, further unbalancing the power differential, and the norms of virginity and silence restrict adolescent girls' access to information about sex and increase their risk of experiencing sexual coercion.

Women's socioeconomic dependence on men and their unequal access to resources, opportunities, and assets, including land, often place them at high risk. Economic asymmetries within a couple are reinforced by various contextual factors, such as family and peer pressures, social and economic institutions, and pervasive and deeply entrenched gender-based inequalities. In a study of four communities in the Southern Province of Zambia, respondents blamed women. Women were perceived to move around and "give love for money"—women who some believe could otherwise work hard and did not need to have sex for money. The fact that men, often much older than girls or women, pay for sex was rarely mentioned as a cause of the problem (Byron, Gillespie, and Hamazakaza 2006).

Using a combination of data sources on HIV status at the individual level and poverty and inequality measures at the community level, a study in Kenya found—conditional on a set of individual and community characteristics—gender inequality between young women and adult men to be significantly correlated with an individual's HIV positive status (Beegle and Ozler 2007). This effect is stronger for young females, especially in western Kenya, where HIV prevalence is highest, and is robust to various definitions of economic inequality between young women and older men. Other evidence points to significant positive associations between larger age differences between partners, value of economic transactions, and unsafe sexual behaviors (Luke 2005; Hallman 2004).

In Botswana and Swaziland, a groundbreaking study found that food-insecure women were 70 percent more likely to have unprotected transactional sex than food-secure women, with the same pattern repeated for a host of other variables reflecting power and control over sexual relations. For men, food insufficiency was associated with only a 14 percent increase in the odds of reporting unprotected sex and was not associated with other risky sexual behaviors (Weiser et al. 2007). Although food insufficiency is certainly influenced by income, it is a distinct entity with different causes and consequences—there are many steps between an aggregated household income variable and the ability of an individual woman to obtain, control, and use income to buy food. A specific focus on protecting and promoting access to food may thus decrease exposure to HIV, especially among women.

MOBILITY

The link between mobility and the spread of HIV is determined by the structure of the migration process, the conditions under which it occurs, including poverty, exploitation, separation from families and partners, and separation from the sociocultural norms that guide behaviors within communities (Crush, Frayne, and Grant 2006). Mobility can increase vulnerability to high-risk sexual behavior as migrants' multilocal social networks create opportunities for sexual networking. Mobility also makes people more difficult to reach for preventive, care, or treatment services (Zuma et al. 2003; Boerma et al. 2003; Bärnighausen et al. 2007).

In East and Southern Africa, plantations and related agricultural industries (typically producing tea, coffee, tobacco, sugarcane, and rice) are often associated with situations of significant risk. Risks may be enhanced by regularized single-sex migration; high and seasonal demands for agricultural labor on estates; the fact that workers move on their own, sometimes from considerable distances, and are lodged in single-sex dormitories; long and often irregular pay intervals; and a dependent population of occasional or commercial sex workers from nearby villages or further afield (Ngwira, Bota, and Loevinsohn 2001; Byron, Gillespie, and Hamazakaza 2006). Ownership structures, the national policy environment, and the economics of the industries are all important drivers of HIV transmission risk.

MALNUTRITION AND ILL HEALTH

Nutrition is the pivotal interface between food security and health security. An individual's susceptibility to any disease depends on the strength of the immune system, which among other factors is affected by nutrition, stress, and the presence of other infections and parasites. The risk of infection with HIV is heightened by high prevalences of such cofactor conditions, which decrease immune response in HIV-negative persons and increase viral load in HIV-infected persons (Stillwaggon 2006). Worms cause malnutrition through malabsorption and intestinal bleeding, and they weaken the immune response by forcing its chronic reaction to the non-self invaders. Infectious and parasitic diseases and malnutrition thus create an environment of enhanced risk.

Malnutrition, particularly involving vitamin A deficiency, is also associated with an increased risk of sexually transmitted diseases (STDs), including genital ulcers and cervical HSV (herpes simplex virus) shedding (Semba et al. 1998; Mostad et al. 2000), which in turn has been found to increase the risk of HIV transmission (Auvert et al. 2001; Galvin and Cohen 2004).

In sum, when examining the interplay between poverty, food insecurity, and HIV transmission, while it is true that poor and food-insecure individuals and households are likely to be hit harder by the downstream impacts of AIDS, their chances of being exposed to HIV in the first place are not necessarily greater than wealthier individuals or households. Approaches to HIV prevention need to cut across all socioeconomic strata of society, and they need to be tailored to the specific drivers of transmission within different groups—with particular attention to the vulnerabilities faced by youth and women and to the dynamic and contextual nature of the relationship between socioeconomic status and HIV.

How Does AIDS Affect Food and Nutrition Security?

This section, like the previous one, tracks the path of the virus—this time starting with the individual who has become infected with HIV, moving out to the household and the community to examine evidence for the impacts of HIV-related morbidity and mortality on food and nutrition security, and then extending upward and outward to consider what is known about broader macroeconomic effects.

Individual Impacts

In addition to greater vulnerability and risks of becoming exposed and infected with HIV (as already described), women have greater vulnerability to the downstream effects of HIV and AIDS than men (Gillespie and Kadiyala 2005a). The extra burden of care brought on by AIDS is falling on the shoulders of millions of women, with implications for their health, nutritional well-being, psychosocial status, and those of their dependent children.

Of the many types of individual impact, the violation of women's rights to property is one of the most serious. A recently widowed woman may be expected to leave her husband's village after his death, and she may lose control over land and other assets they may have been jointly using as a family. In a Zambian study, one to three years following the death of their husbands, widow-headed households, on average, had control of 35 percent less land than what they had before their husband's death (Chapoto, Jayne, and Mason 2007). In some cultures "widow inheritance"—where a woman is expected to marry the brother of the deceased—is the only way a widow can retain rights to her husband's land. Widows may be left destitute, more susceptible to HIV, and more vulnerable to further consequences of AIDS.

Household and Community Impacts

The threat that HIV and AIDS pose for food security was first recognized in the late 1980s (Gillespie 1989). Many studies in Sub-Saharan Africa have since shown that subsistence farmers are vulnerable to the impacts of AIDS because the disease reduces the resources that households can devote to agriculture. Labor loss occurs not only as a result of sickness and premature adult death, but also as a result of the reallocation of labor to nurse the ill, while working capital and income are siphoned off to pay mounting medical bills. The specific levels and types of vulnerability depend on the characteristics of families, livelihoods, and farming systems.

AIDS has also significantly affected commercial agriculture, and there is increasing evidence that companies shift the costs it entails (replacement worker costs, paid sick leave, lost wages, and productivity losses) to employees in a variety of ways (Rosen and Simon 2003). Agricultural extension is being hit hard too by the sickness and death of extension agents, who are at particular risk because of their mobility. Other occupational groups are hit hard as well—for example, fishing communities (Box 1).

At more aggregate levels, as rural communities with high HIV prevalence face increased labor shortages, widespread reductions in household incomes and increased cash constraints may also depress demand for labor and nontradables. There is some evidence from Malawi that reductions in labor demand may lead to wage declines, posing serious problems even for poor households not directly affected by AIDS (Dorward and Mwale 2006).

In one of the few studies to quantitatively examine the community-level impacts of AIDS-related prime-age adult mortality, Jayne, Chapoto, et al. (2006) in Zambia analyzed nationally representative longitudinal survey data collected on a panel of 5,420 households from 393 rural standard enumeration areas (or villages) in 2001 and 2004. Village fixed-effects models on differenced outcomes were estimated to measure the relationship between adult mortality rates and area of land under cultivation, crop output, and per capita income at the community level, controlling for time-invariant unobservable characteristics and initial community conditions. The impact, at this time and place, was found to be modest—a rise in community-level adult mortality rates from 0 to 24 percent was associated with a 6 percent decline in land area cultivated at the community level.

Using anthropological and ethnographic methods, Drinkwater, McEwan, and Samuels (2006) examined two communities, one periurban and one rural, in two studies 12 years apart in Zambia's Copperbelt and Central Provinces. They used the concept of "cluster" as the unit of analysis. The objective was to understand how individuals, households, and production networks adapted or disintegrated over time as a result of AIDS-related ill health and death. The position of the person who is chronically ill or has died was found to be a key determinant of the resilience of the socioeconomic unit. For example, the death of a primary producer[3] was likely to negatively affect the surviving household or cluster members' welfare. One interesting finding was that prime-age mortality tended to be more concentrated among "secondary producers"—that is, younger adults who would in future be expected to become primary producers. This finding suggests the full impact of AIDS on agriculture should be viewed over a relatively long—even intergenerational—period of time.

In Rwanda, Donovan and Bailey (2005) found that death-affected households showed few significant differences in crop production compared with matched nonaffected households without a death or illness. But relatively small "death effects" may be a reflection that pre-death measurements occurred during the illness period, when the household was already adjusting to AIDS. The measured "death effect" in such cases would thus underestimate the extent to which the household was initially affected and had to change.

The importance of protracted HIV-related illness (not just death) is borne out by a study of tea estate workers in Kenya, which was one of the first to rigorously quantify the impact of HIV and AIDS on individual labor productivity during disease progression (Fox et al. 2004). A retrospective cohort design was employed to study the productivity and attendance of tea estate workers who died or were medically retired because of AIDS-related causes between 1997 and 2002 in western Kenya. After adjusting for age and environmental factors, HIV-positive individuals plucked between four and eight kilograms a day less in the last 18 months before termination. They used significantly more leave days and more days doing less strenuous tasks in the two years before termination than did comparison pluckers. Tea pluckers who stopped working because of AIDS-related causes earned 16 percent less in their second year before termination and 18 percent less in the year before termination. These results may be underestimates given that workers often bring unrecorded "helpers," but they do show a significant drop-off that starts years before the employee must terminate work.

The impacts of AIDS on agriculture (and indeed other sources of livelihood) are not one-time events. They are processes, often hidden and slow-burning but potentially very destructive. AIDS can exert its effects over a relatively long period of time while rendering other stresses and shocks both more likely and more severe in their effects. Following a shock to household income, households in Malawi affected by AIDS were found to take up to 18 months to stabilize, with a new equilibium income that was about half the pre-shock income levels (Masanjala 2006). Similar findings had been reported earlier in Kenya (Yamano and Jayne 2004). Such limited resilience is likely to increase vulnerability to other shocks.

Impacts are also context specific, differing by community and by household in type and degree, and they depend on a range of demographic, economic, and sociocultural factors and processes. They also depend of course on sustained access to effective antiretroviral therapy. Vulnerability to AIDS impacts may be viewed as a function of the type and degree of socioeconomic change in relation to the ability to respond to such change. Where there is flexibility and a diversity of possible responses, households may be more resilient. Where response options are limited, households are more vulnerable—responses taken under duress may be costly and unsustainable.

Box 1: AIDS, Food Security, and Fishing

Fishing is a major source of livelihood in Africa, especially in the Lake Victoria basin, where it employs around 500,000 people. Fishing communities are at particularly high risk of HIV exposure. A recent comparative study of fisherfolk and other high-risk groups in selected countries (Kissling et al. 2005) showed prevalence rates among fisherfolk of 24 percent in Uganda and 31 percent in Kenya—four to six times higher than rates in the general population and about twice as high as rates among truck drivers, who are conventionally considered a high-risk group. Prevalence rates among the many women working in fishing communities is not known but is likely to be even higher owing to the subordinate economic and social position they occupy.

Several risk factors have been implicated, including a demographic structure with high rates of single men in sexually active age groups; high rates of mobility and migration; easy availability of cash income on a regular basis, without tangible investment or savings opportunities; poverty and gender inequality that marginalize women in commercial transactions, making them vulnerable to sexually exploitative relations (including "fish for sex"); poor health service infrastructure and condom availability; generally poor health and hygiene status in fishing camps; a subculture of risk taking, hypermasculinity, and perception of low social status among many fishermen; widespread alcohol consumption; and finally, limited options for livelihood diversification (Allison and Seeley 2004; Seeley and Allison 2005; Tanzarn 2006).

In terms of impacts, HIV and AIDS can seriously affect the livelihoods of fishing communities as well as the viability of the entire fishery sector. Families lose income, assets, and the capacity to invest in their future. Communities experience declining living standards, reduced economic options, and the progressive erosion of social cohesion and caring capacity. In addition, long-term stewardship of fisheries resources becomes undermined as fishing communities lose important knowledge and management skills. Recent research has also suggested that fisherfolk will be among those untouched by planned initiatives to increase access to antiretrovirals in coming years (Seeley and Allison 2005).

These risks and impacts emanate beyond the fisheries sector through mobile and part-time fishing populations and the high volume of daily interactions through trade and markets. The multiplier effects of the loss of productive labor and declining productivity may affect rural incomes more broadly. Nutrition vulnerability—not only of the fishing community itself, but also of other communities that depend on fish and fish products—is likely to increase. Fish is one of the main (or only) affordable sources of animal protein and micronutrients of poor households in this region. Young children in particular may be severely affected, given the significant risk of cognitive impairment associated with micronutrient deficiency.

In this context, the notion of "coping" has become a clichéd, catch-all term for such responses. "Coping" is, more often than not, an externally applied value judgment that may not correspond to what is actually happening in the present—and almost always neglects the likely future consequences. Many responses are those of distressed households without much conscious strategy—"struggling not coping," as Rugalema (2000) pointed out. Responses may have a veneer of coping, but the costs may need to be paid further down the line (as occurs, for example, when a child is denied schooling).

Given that many impacts are revealed in actual responses that households and communities make in the face of AIDS, these responses should be examined for their effectiveness and sustainability. Where households are not subject to additional stresses such as drought, and when viewed over a relatively short reference period (for example, a couple of years), there are some indications from the literature that traditional responses can mitigate the worst effects of AIDS. Complex factors, however, determine the success of these strategies. These factors include the sex, age, and position in the household of the ill or deceased person, the household's socioeconomic status, the type and degree of labor demand in the production system, the availability of labor support to affected households, other livelihood opportunities, available natural resources, the availability of formal and informal sources of support, including credit and interhousehold transfers, the length of time that the epidemic has been affecting the rural economy, and the existence of concurrent shocks such as drought or commodity price collapses (Gillespie and Kadiyala 2005a).

Impacts on the Agricultural Sector

Using demographic projections and household survey evidence, Jayne, Villarreal, et al. (2006) consider the likely consequences of the AIDS pandemic for the agricultural sector of the hardest-hit countries of East and Southern Africa. They suggest that although AIDS is projected to erode population growth to roughly zero in the seven hardest-hit countries, the net result is a roughly stable number of prime-age adults over time. AIDS-related agricultural labor shortages are likely to induce labor migration out of the urban informal sector into agriculture. For poorer smallholder households, they suggest that land will remain a primary constraint on income growth. AIDS-induced decapitalization of highly afflicted rural communities—meaning a loss of savings, cattle, draft equipment, and other assets—may come to pose the greatest limits on rural productivity and livelihoods for these communities.

Using data from Malawi, Dorward and Mwale (2006) highlight the challenges in determining the nature and magnitude of broader impacts of HIV and AIDS on labor markets and wages. Although affected households may face increased labor shortages, widespread reductions in household incomes and increased cash constraints will also depress labor and nontradable demand in rural communities with high HIV incidence. Reductions in family labor may also lead to a shift out of more labor-demanding cash crops. Depressed labor demand could cause wages to fall, posing serious problems even for poor households not directly affected by HIV and AIDS. They find some evidence for such a shift, driven primarily by reductions in labor hiring by better-off households with HIV-induced cash constraints. The introduction of labor-saving technologies in such a context could be damaging—cash transfers may be more appropriate. The effect of cash constraints is highlighted in Box 2 in the context of the huge 2008 food price hikes.

Moreover, where AIDS does depress unskilled wages, this effect is likely to increase inequality within rural communities and impose further pressures on poor people and their livelihoods—perhaps also increasing their risk of HIV exposure. Jayne, Villarreal, et al. (2006) also point to the inequality-driving aspect of capital asset loss. Unlike the loss of labor and knowledge, which represent a loss to entire communities, capital assets lost by afflicted households are generally redistributed within the rural economy rather than lost entirely.

Macroeconomic Impacts, Poverty, and Inequality

At a macro-level, the impacts of HIV and AIDS are not clear—at least not yet or not using current models. Most estimates in high-prevalence countries indicate a reduction of about 0.5–1.5 percent in growth of gross domestic product (GDP) over a 10- to 20-year period (Piot, Greener, and Russell 2007), which is significant but not catastrophic. Many important aspects of development are econometrically invisible, however, such as women's work, the loss of information in social systems including intergenerational knowledge fracture, the loss of social capital as networks and information channels erode, relational goods, and the effects on millions of children as they see their parents weaken and die.

Box 2: Food Price Crisis and the AIDS Response

The food price crisis—superimposed as it is on a broader and deeper livelihoods crisis in Southern and East Africa—strengthens the multipronged rationale for linking food and nutrition security with AIDS programming. It also makes it much harder to achieve and sustain such integration.

How Could Higher Food Prices Affect HIV Prevention?

- Acute food insecurity has been associated with unprotected transactional sex among poor women.
- Sudden increases in food insecurity often lead to distress migration as people search for work and food, which may enhance risk of HIV exposure, both for the person moving and for other adults who may remain at home.
- Household food insecurity may translate into increased adult malnutrition with possible detrimental effects for immune status. Maternal undernutrition is associated with low birth weight among infants, who will be at higher risk of vertical (mother-to-child) HIV transmission.

How Could Higher Food Prices Affect Care and Treatment?

- Individuals who are malnourished at the onset of therapy have much lower survival rates.
- Adults living with HIV require 10–30 percent more energy than before they were infected, and children may need up to 100 percent more. The rising cost of food may seriously constrain the ability to ensure an adequate nutritional intake, leading to more frequent and severe opportunistic infections and a more rapid progression to AIDS.
- For people being treated for HIV, nutrition is important for the following reasons: (1) good nutrition reduces side effects and thus improves treatment adherence; (2) some drugs are more effective when accompanied by good nutrition; (3) HIV increases an individual's calorie requirements and appetite; and (4) access to good nutrition is needed to prevent the dilemma of choosing between purchase of food or medicine (as purchasing power declines). There is some evidence that urban-dwelling patients interrupt treatment when they return to rural areas because they can no longer afford to live in the city. Any significant dropoff in adherence induced by such effects could have serious implications for the development of viral resistance to first-line drugs. There is also evidence of food assistance being cut back (for example, from 12 to 9 months in the The AIDS Support Organization program in Uganda) as a result of food price hikes.

How Could Higher Food Prices Affect Mitigation of AIDS Impacts?

- Food-insecure households suffer more severe and enduring livelihood impacts from concurrent health and economic shocks, which undermine resilience and foreclose options to adapt to any stress.
- Children may be taken out of school to work for cash or food. Besides being denied an education (including on HIV prevention), they may be at greater risk of being exposed to HIV out of school.
- The increase in the costs of supporting an orphan may result in a decline in fostering of orphaned children and possibly a reduction in the quantity and quality of essential care and support programs for orphans and vulnerable children.
- The struggle to work to raise income to buy food affects intrahousehold time allocations. Care for the youngest children (feeding, health care, and psycho-social stimulation) is often compromised.

Given that the concern here is primarily with deprivation, manifested by food insecurity and malnutrition, it is important not to be overly focused on aggregates or means that effectively mask subnational differentials. As already shown, strong evidence indicates that inequalities (socioeconomic, gender) drive the spread of HIV infection and that AIDS itself increases these inequalities—a potentially vicious circle that is not captured by income means.

Two drivers of inequality have been discussed—declining unskilled wage rates and decapitalization of affected households. Land acquisition by better-off households is likely to increase as widows and orphans fail to keep access or ownership rights to land after the death of the husband or father. The fear of such a loss may also prevent AIDS-affected households from renting out land as a response— another example of the intertwining of vulnerabilities and inequities (in this case, relating to gender and HIV). The AIDS epidemic is thus intertwined with the way in which power, authority, value, and opportunity are distributed within societies. Such land acquisition trends could lead to aggregate production increases at the community level while simultaneously increasing inequality, poverty, malnutrition, and HIV incidence.

The majority of impact studies offer cross-sectional household-level "case-control" snapshots. Besides suffering from an inability to track the dynamics of interactions over time, such studies do not related household-level effects to more aggregated sector-level or national-level impacts. Nor do they shine a clear light on what is happening within households, such as intrahousehold division of labor, caregiving, and other resources—and especially impacts on women and children. Yet another problem with the notion of "household coping" is its implication that all members of a household are affected equally. One participant at the IFPRI 2005 conference in Durban pointed out that the "extended family" in most cases meant "extended women."

How to Improve the Response to the HIV-Hunger Nexus

At the outset, it is worth reiterating the rationale for responding to the documented interactions between HIV, AIDS, food security, and nutrition. It is a *dual* rationale—first, to raise the likelihood that food and nutrition security policies and programs can achieve their original objectives in the context of a severe AIDS epidemic, and second, to contribute meaningfully to a broad-based multisectoral response to HIV and AIDS. These are the two primary mutually reinforcing objectives for any intervention. In terms of the Millennium Development Goals, goals 1 (hunger) and 6 (HIV) need to be addressed in an integrated fashion in Southern Africa, and progress toward them will probably follow similar tracks.

This chapter began by highlighting the long-wave nature of AIDS epidemics and the different waves relating to the causes and consequences of HIV and AIDS. Attempts to attenuate these waves are conventionally grounded in the three core pillars of AIDS policy: prevention, care and treatment, and mitigation. An HIV timeline, as in Figure 5.6, illustrates the entry points for the three strategies.

It is important to understand the main role of food and nutrition research, policy, and programming in terms of the dual objectives listed and in terms of these core strategies. The strategies themselves can overlap and reinforce each other. Care, treatment, and mitigation can be preventive. Programs aimed at improving the well-being of people infected or affected by HIV and AIDS may reduce transmission risk. Where social protection schemes protect orphans or other vulnerable children, they may be less likely to engage in risky sexual practices than if they were left to fend for themselves. The community as a whole gains a preventive advantage since prevalence is contained and so are the wider risks of exposure. At the community level, there may be positive-sum solutions linking mitigation and prevention. For example, women who are widowed by AIDS may be left with landholdings that they can no longer cultivate and livestock that they can no longer manage. At the same time, there may be young adults in the community who have no land or livestock of their own; with poor livelihood prospects they may be at heightened risk of HIV infection. Social innovations that secure the widows' entitlements, allowing them to exchange a fair share of the production for the young adults' labor would be of benefit to both.

In the face of the challenges posed by the HIV–hunger nexus, there is no convenient magic bullet for intervention and no blueprint. Truly multisectoral involvement is required. This approach is fundamentally different from simply adding more (usually vertical) HIV activities onto sectoral plans. Mainstreaming starts when decisionmakers internalize AIDS as a development issue and engage in a critical review of existing policies and programs through the lens of their growing knowledge of AIDS interactions. It is a process involving continual reflection and the progressive application of principles and processes for responding rather than pulling predesigned interventions off the shelf.

Yet despite the growing understanding of the interactions between HIV and food security, and the increasing lip service paid to them, actual multisectoral

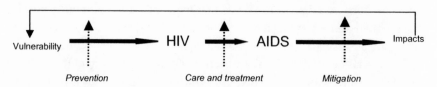

Figure 5.6   The HIV timeline showing core strategies
SOURCE: Author.

responses remain thin on the ground. Responses that match the size of the problem are overwhelmingly health oriented, single-sector, and usually vertical in
design and delivery, with a few scatterings of mostly small-scale innovation. Rhet-
oric abounds, but most development organizations remain locked in comforta-
ble systems and timelines that simply do not align with the long-wave dynamics
of AIDS.

Against the backdrop of the epidemic, it has become easy to succumb to a
convenient state of denial or a creeping sense of professional paralysis. Recently,
the concept of "normalization" has been used to refer to the ways in which people
"adjust . . . reality to take account of the miseries of AIDS" (De Waal 2006). A
recent study by the Regional Network on AIDS, Livelihoods, and Food Security
(RENEWAL) in Zomba, Malawi (Peters, Kambewa, and Walker 2007) documents
how villagers are similarly striving for normality. Rather than ignoring or denying
the abnormal circumstances of the rising toll of HIV-related illness and death,
they try to control these circumstances, making huge efforts to channel them into
the normal and normative ways of their society. A similar process of normalization occurs at the level of development policy in Africa.

In April 2005, the International Food Policy Research Institute (IFPRI) convened the International Conference on HIV/AIDS, Food, and Nutrition Security
in Durban, South Africa. The conference concluded with an emphasis on a twin-
track strategy aimed at strengthening household and community resistance to
HIV and resilience to AIDS through (1) preserving and augmenting livelihood
opportunities (including agriculture) for affected communities, and (2) ensuring
appropriate social protection systems (including food and nutritional assistance)
for those who need them. In short, this twin-track approach (1) secures livelihoods, and (2) protects vulnerable groups.

Policy needs to draw upon what is working already in communities where
proactive responses are underway. This approach is quite distinct from any
notion of leaving it to the communities to "cope." Rather, it involves maximizing
learning from community innovations about what works, where, and why. Where
households and communities' capacity to respond effectively has been exceeded,
a broad-based social protection system offering minimal benefits or specifically
targeted support programs will be important for mitigation in the short and
medium term. These two strategies should be pursued simultaneously in a con-
tiguum approach, based on the different comparative advantages of all stakeholders from households to national governments and international agencies.

Securing Livelihoods

Discussing livelihood security and AIDS in Africa means discussing agriculture.
Because agriculture is the fundamental livelihood base of most people affected by

HIV and AIDS and because food security is an increasing concern to them as impact waves hit, the agriculture sector must take a proactive stance in the face of the epidemic. Stakeholders (from farmers to policymakers) need to progressively re-view agricultural situations through an HIV lens in order to respond more effectively (Loevinsohn and Gillespie 2003).

To the agriculture professional who asks, "Why should I bother about AIDS?" the answer is simple. If the agricultural sector in Africa fails to proactively take HIV and AIDS into account, it will not be able to achieve its primary objective of improving food production and access. Similarly, international agricultural organizations supporting African agriculture need to mainstream AIDS to remain relevant, or the first Millennium Development Goal—eradicating extreme poverty and hunger—will remain a hopeless dream. First and foremost in this context, the rationale for bothering about AIDS is one of professional self-interest.

Another reason for the agricultural professional to be engaged is that developments important to the professional—and to Africa's poor and hungry—*are* in fact happening in many places in Africa. Communities are responding, community-based, nongovernmental organizations (NGOs) are actively innovating, and governments are beginning to go beyond declarations on paper to put in place AIDS-responsive programs. A major conference organized by IFPRI in Durban in 2005, the 2006 Africa Forum organized by Project Concern International in Lusaka, along with several sessions at both the 2006 and 2008 International AIDS Conferences in Toronto and Mexico City, respectively, not only demonstrated the huge demand for knowledge, but also several interesting intervention options and grassroots innovations aimed at tackling the interactions between hyperendemic AIDS and hunger.

Conventional wisdom prioritizes technologies and crops that save labor in the context of AIDS. Although such technologies may be appropriate for certain types of households and regions, this recommendation has been overgeneralized (Jayne, Villarreal, et al. 2006; Dorward and Mwale 2006). Labor-saving technologies may even be harmful if they further drive down wage rates that are already falling owing to HIV-induced cash-constraints on ability to hire. Emphasis may need to be placed on other ways of assisting these households, such as cash transfers to help them hire labor (see Adato and Bassett 2008 for a state-of-the-art review).

Donovan and Bailey (2005) found that Rwandan households, facing high population density and very small average agricultural holdings, appear to use labor replacement strategies rather than labor-saving technologies to deal with labor shortages. They found a disturbing trend of households' shifting away from crops that provide erosion control, thus endangering future soil fertility. Because affected households ex post tend to be in the lower income groups, agricultural policy that can generate rural income growth from diverse sources will assist these and other poor households.

What does an HIV-responsive agricultural policy or program look like? Table 5.1 shows how re-viewing agriculture through an HIV lens results in adjustments and initiatives within the rubric of policy, programs, and research. The lens is bifocal, reflecting both the upstream prevention of HIV infection and the downstream mitigation of AIDS impacts.

Just as mitigation can be preventive, so some modifications to agricultural practice can both prevent HIV exposure and mitigate AIDS impacts, such as protecting women's property rights and providing options for youth to engage in farming through, for example, the JFFLSs.

Though few have been evaluated and most are small scale, an increasing number of HIV-responsive agricultural interventions are now being implemented. Examples include conservation farming, tractor hire services, postharvest and processing technologies in the Bondo and Busia districts of Kenya (Bishop-Sambrook 2003), agricultural support and training, vocational training and provision of credit and loan schemes in Lesotho, Tanzania, Uganda, and Zimbabwe (White 2002), pit farming in Zambia, and community grain banks in Malawi (Connolly 2003). Others have focused on promoting agrobiodiversity and indigenous knowledge (Du Guerny 2004; Gari and Villarreal 2002).

There is thus significant scope for agricultural policy to become more HIV-responsive, both to further AIDS-related objectives and to help achieve agricultural objectives. Land–labor ratios and the relative degree of substitutability between household resources, among other factors, will determine the possible responses to HIV and AIDS. If policy becomes more HIV-responsive, it will stay relevant and effective. By mainstreaming HIV/AIDS into the policy process and carefully monitoring results, policymakers will help build up evidence of what works in different contexts, enhance learning, and ultimately leave people better equipped to address the multiple threats of the epidemic.

Protecting Vulnerable Groups

This section differentiates interventions aimed at providing food and nutritional assistance to vulnerable groups from broader social protection interventions, although the latter will not be considered in detail here.

FOOD AND NUTRITIONAL ASSISTANCE

According to the World Health Organization, individuals living with HIV (PLHIV) who are asymptomatic need to increase their energy intake by 10 percent, and symptomatic individuals should increase their intake by 20–30 percent (WHO 2003b). People on antiretroviral (ARV) treatment in resource-poor settings may lack access to sufficient quantity and quality of food to complement their treatment, offset side effects, and encourage adherence. Current research shows that

Table 5.1 Re-viewing agriculture through an HIV lens

Policy	Programming	Research
Adopting agricultural commercialization policies that take account of the extra risks posed by evening markets and the need for people to travel far to sell their produce.	Integrating information about HIV into agricultural extension programs.	What are the implications of such changes for inequality within rural communities, and for risk of individuals being exposed to the virus through the adoption of risky livelihoods or behaviors?
	Fostering convergence of social and health services with agricultural support to ensure food, health, and care preconditions for nutrition security as well as access to preventive health technologies and information, including treatment of STDs and availability of condoms.	
Reducing the need and desire to migrate by incentivizing adoption of local livelihood strategies in and around the community; extending the growing season with small-scale irrigation; diversifying products; agroprocessing; strengthening existing, and creating new, market linkages; and developing the farm input supply chain.	Establishing vocational training for youth, including orphans, such as Junior Farmer Field and Life Schools (JFFLSs), as pioneered in Cambodia and adapted in Kenya and Mozambique.	To what extent, and under what conditions, does AIDS erode agricultural assets (land, labor, capital, and knowledge) or investment incentives?
	Using cooperatives and farmer organizations as entry points for mitigation, care, and support activities in communities such as by developing income-generating activities, savings mechanisms, health insurance, or a social fund to provide care for orphans.	How important are these effects relative to other health and nonhealth factors (such as malaria, tuberculosis, drought, price variability, and poor infrastructure) in influencing agricultural decision making at the household level (about such things as land use, crop choice, input use, and output marketing)?
Using appropriate policy reform to overcome barriers to participating in agricultural production and marketing by affected households, such as their depleted resource base, their need to be close to home to tend to the sick, loss of key skills; and their inability to take on risk.	Preserving agricultural knowledge through the HIV-aware and gender-proactive agricultural extension capacity; JFFLSs can bridge gaps in intergenerational knowledge transfer.	How do these impacts play out over time?
	Bypassing capacity constraints through better communications, such as rural radio.	
	Reducing women's domestic work burden, such as by using labor-economizing methods of food preparation, water supply, and fuel supplies.	How do they influence overall agricultural sector performance and the ability of the agricultural sector to serve as an engine of pro-poor economic growth?
Generating community-level incentives for interhousehold labor exchange.	Introducing poultry and small stock to improve diets.	
	Smoothing peaks and avoiding bottlenecks in labor demand.	
Pursuing land tenure arrangements to protect the occupancy and inheritance rights of widows and orphaned children.	Where labor is constrained, reducing labor intensity of systems of cropping (including improved seed varieties, zero or minimum tillage, intercropping), soil conservation (using soil-holding grasses, not labor-intensive ridging), animal husbandry (rearing smaller stock such as poultry), pest control (using trap crops to attract pests away from crops), and postharvest storage.	

SOURCE: Author.

good nutrition is as important to the efficacy of medical interventions as it is to peoples' ability to resist and mitigate infection. Castleman, Seumo-Fosso, and Cogill (2004) highlight the importance of maintaining adequate food consumption and nutrition levels for all PLHIV, regardless of whether they are taking ARV treatment. Research has also shown that independent of ARV treatment, weight loss remains a predictor of mortality in HIV-infected individuals (Tang et al. 2002; Mangili et al. 2006). Clear evidence now shows that malnourished individuals starting ARV therapy are far more likely to die (by an estimated six times) in a given period than well-nourished individuals (Paton et al. 2006).

With regard to ARVs, given the improbability that large numbers of people can meet and sustain drug adherence thresholds of greater than 95 percent, there is a significant likelihood that viral resistance will develop and spread, undermining the efficacy of existing drug regimes. A whole new and very expensive second-line drug regime may soon be required to respond to such resistance. Side effects are one reason for such poor adherence, and there is evidence that malnutrition makes such side effects worse. This situation further strengthens the case for improving understanding of how to mainstream nutritional support into HIV responses. Nutritional support of asymptomatic HIV-positive individuals may delay the need for ARVs, though more research is needed here.

A recent study was undertaken in Kenya to highlight key constraints, opportunities, and challenges relating to interventions aimed at strengthening the nutrition security of people living with HIV on antiretroviral treatment. Through collaboration between the Academic Model for the Prevention and Treatment of HIV/AIDS (AMPATH) and RENEWAL in western Kenya, qualitative research was undertaken on a short-term nutrition intervention linked to the provision of free antiretroviral treatment for people living with HIV in late 2005 and early 2006. Patients enrolled in the food program while on treatment regimens self-reported greater adherence to their medication, fewer side effects, and a greater ability to satisfy increased appetites. Most clients reported weight gain, recovery of physical strength, and the resumption of labor activities while enrolled in dual programs. Such improvements catalyzed increased support for HIV-positive individuals from family and community (Byron, Gillespie, and Nangami 2008).

Most nutrition-relevant research in the context of AIDS is clinical research that relates primarily to interactions within the individual body and their implications for health policy. A strong focus on *clinical* nutrition and HIV currently exists in the context of issues such as infant feeding, mother-to-child transmission, and the safety and efficacy of ARV therapy among malnourished populations (WHO 2005c). There have been few corresponding attempts to link nutritionists with agricultural economists or program managers to investigate the broader issue of household and community-level nutrition security, policy, and programming in the context of AIDS. Work is needed to clarify ways of bridging the gap between short-term nutritional support to individuals and longer-term livelihood security programming for communities affected by AIDS. Such interdisciplinary research will need to be matched by intersectoral action on the part of the agriculture and health sectors in such environments. A focus on nutrition security—through ensuring the food, health, and care preconditions for long-term nutritional well-being—can help reveal opportunities for effectively linking health services with agriculture, food, and nutrition policy in the context of HIV and AIDS.

Most nutrition-relevant responses to date have revolved around delivery of food aid. Food assistance remains a widely employed safety net in the context of HIV and AIDS, despite a paucity of evaluations of impact on HIV-related target groups (Egge and Strasser 2006). Key areas of expected impact include increases in daily food consumption by all household members, in money available for other needs, and in household food security. These key effects should in turn generate a cascade of secondary effects measurable by indicators such as anthropometrics, treatment adherence, school attendance, productivity, and the degree of reliance on risky response strategies and on caregivers. Food aid, however, tends to be targeted to certain types of people rather than according to the determinants of vulnerability, and this approach may lead to significant inefficiencies. Not all female-headed households, for example, are vulnerable, nor are all orphan-fostering households. Drimie and Mullins (2006) discuss ways in which a livelihoods approach can guide analysis to a better understanding of who is actually at risk or vulnerable, why, and how to improve their resilience.

Box 3: Nutrition Research Challenges

What long-term options exist for ensuring and sustaining nutrition security within affected households and communities? What does nutrition "through an HIV lens" look like, and what are the operational implications of rethinking nutrition from this perspective? Does nutrition offer an entry point for forging better links between public health and agricultural responses to AIDS—thus improving both food and health security? How should the need for short-term nutritional support be balanced with long-term strategies to ensure nutritional security in affected households? How should linkages between food assistance and livelihood activities and strategies for income security be developed and promoted to ensure sustainable food security for HIV-infected individuals and their households? How can improvements in nutrition security achieved through short-term interventions be sustained over time without eroding acquired benefits? What is the cost-effectiveness of nutrition interventions for PLHIV and their households, and what are the implications for scaling up such interventions? What role does nutrition play in new approaches to social protection in the context of AIDS?

Where food assistance is required, there is an emerging consensus on the need for multiple criteria to target beneficiaries. Useful criteria include the presence of a chronically ill adult and high dependency ratios (including the number of orphans). Analyzing community health surveillance data, Egge and Strasser (2006) suggest that targeting efficiency could be improved by first differentiating households according to wealth category (using, for example, assets as a proxy) and then applying other criteria such as chronic illness. Some key research challenges regarding integrated HIV and nutrition responses are highlighted in Box 3.

SOCIAL PROTECTION

"Social protection" means different things to different people. Definitions in common currency are mainly differentiated by the degree to which the envisioned protection extends to enhancing livelihoods, includes social insurance as well as assistance, and is advocated as a right rather than a reactive form of relief (Adato, Ahmed, and Lund 2004). Increasingly recognized as an essential part of social policy, social protection systems have been used to enable individuals, families, and communities to reduce risk, mitigate the impacts of stresses and shocks to their livelihoods, or both. They may also be used to support people who suffer from chronic incapacities to even secure livelihoods, including people living with HIV. Interventions may include conditional and unconditional cash transfers, direct distribution of food or nutritional supplements, school-based food programs, price subsidies, agricultural inputs, public works programs, social health insurance, asset insurance, life insurance, and microfinance. In the context of AIDS, there is still little experience to build on, though there are signs that this lack of experience is now changing.

The scope of this rapidly growing field of enquiry and experimentation goes well beyond the focus of this chapter—it thus aims simply to highlight some of the pertinent concerns and research challenges (see Box 4 for the latter). The reader is referred to a recent comprehensive review by Adato and Bassett (2008). In Zambia in 2007, an evaluation by the United Nations Children's Fund (UNICEF) found that in poor, AIDS-affected households that received community-based cash transfers, food consumption had increased, despite a recent drought, and the incidence of illness had declined in both children and adults.

Box 4: Research Challenges in Social Protection

Key research questions include: What types of community change, innovation, and adaptation (resilience) are underway? Are community-driven approaches an untapped resource for addressing the AIDS–food insecurity nexus? How does social capital contribute to resilience and response? What is needed to strengthen, sustain, or rebuild social capital in the face of losses of the individuals whose links and contributions are part of the community's "stock" of social capital? What determines an effective community response ("community AIDS competence"), and what lessons can be learned and applied to scaling up effective responses? How can community collective action be maximized to fill labor and other resource gaps opened up by AIDS? How can incentives and opportunities for communities be created to protect the entitlements of affected households, enabling them to exchange on fair terms what they have (such as land they can no longer cultivate) for what they need (such as food)? What are the limits of community-driven responses to AIDS? What is an appropriate balance between government-led social protection policies and schemes and community-led responses? How can national policy and programming learn from, and scale up, local responses while staying responsive to local conditions and not undermining local agency? How community-government partnerships be facilitated to this end?

As mentioned, women and children are likely to be particularly vulnerable to HIV and AIDS. Gender inequity can be addressed through gender-transformative interventions—interventions that not only recognize and address gender differences, but also go a step further by creating the conditions whereby women and men can examine the damaging aspects of gender norms and experiment with new behaviors to create more equitable roles and relationships. Guaranteeing women's property and inheritance rights will be particularly important (Piot, Greener, and Russell 2007; Weiser et al. 2007; Global Coalition of Women and AIDS 2007). Steps need to be taken to document women's land tenure security in areas of high HIV prevalence, raise public awareness, and reform legislation where necessary, including customary law and practice. Strategic litigation opportunities may be sought and legal precedents progressively established through test cases, while ensuring women's access to legal structures and processes. The issue of women's land tenure security is one of direct concern both to agriculture and to social development.

Conclusions

Poverty, food insecurity, malnutrition, and hunger have been around a lot longer than the human immunodeficiency virus. AIDS is one of many sources of vulnerability and stress, exposing the fragility of people's livelihoods, especially in Southern Africa. The fact that HIV and AIDS interact wth food insecurity and malnutrition necessitates a more integrated analysis of food systems and the dynamics of food and nutrition insecurity.

Gains have been made in this field in recent years. At a political level, there is the 2006 UN Political Declaration on HIV/AIDS, which recognized the need "to integrate food and nutritional support, with the goal that all people at all times will have access to sufficient, safe, and nutritious food to meet their dietary needs and food preferences for an active and healthy life, as part of a comprehensive response to HIV/AIDS" (UN 2006a, 4). UNAIDS recently published a policy brief outlining key approaches to responding to interactions between HIV and food insecurity (UNAIDS, WFP, and WHO 2008). The agency also now recommends that governments set aside a percentage of their antiretroviral treatment budget for nutritional interventions.

But new challenges are emerging. The dramatic recent rise in food prices is putting extra strain on households and communities struggling with food insecurity, HIV, and other livelihood shocks and stresses. The food price crisis simultaneously accentuates the negative interactions between food, nutrition, HIV, and AIDS, while also making it harder to effectively address them by ensuring the food security of vulnerable households. In this context, a strengthened focus is needed on (1) assessing, monitoring, and tracking vulnerability, food insecurity, and the interactions between HIV and hunger; (2) linking sustained food and nutritional assistance with treatment programs in areas of chronic food insecurity; (3) building bridges between the agriculture and health sectors to ensure longer-term support to livelihoods where HIV and hunger coexist; and (4) strengthening the resilience of vulnerable households by enhancing local capacity and providing options and incentives for safe livelihood strategies. Such measures need to be complemented by effective state-led systems of social protection, including transfers of food, cash, or vouchers.

A locally adaptable "HIV lens" can be applied to programs related to agriculture—the engine of rural growth in Africa—to reveal simple modifications that can improve such programs' impacts on both hunger and AIDS. Vicious circles can be reversed. Improving rural livelihoods and agricultural production can help reduce both the spread of HIV and the impacts of AIDS. Programs that reduce the need for poor people to migrate to look for work (by restoring degraded land, for example) can reduce their risk of being exposed to the virus.

On the flip side, applying a "food and nutrition lens" to the core AIDS program strategies of prevention, care, and treatment can likewise reveal potential synergies. Individuals who are malnourished when they start antiretroviral therapy are far more likely to die in a given period than well-nourished new patients. Good nutrition also improves the efficacy of the drugs, reduces their side effects, and improves adherence to treatment regimens. Such effects will generate both short-term benefits to the patient and major long-term benefits as better adherence slows the development of drug-resistant strains. Linking nutrition with treatment will also reduce poverty. Several organizations, including the U.S. Presidential Emergency Program for AIDS Relief (PEPFAR), are beginning to address these implications, but responses need to be far more integrated and systematic, not just add-ons. They must be founded on an active link between agriculture and health programming, with nutrition security as the pivotal interface.

Synergies between research, capacity, and communications, if exploited, may ultimately enhance and sustain impact. Ownership, local relevance, and policy impact are strongly associated. Locally prioritized research is more attuned to the national and regional setting, and the findings are thus more actionable. The reverse link is stronger too: implementation can generate policy-relevant operational research priorities. Outreach, as such, becomes easier when research is embedded in local systems—in a sense, the process of "reaching out" has already been done before the study findings are known, by anchoring the research priorities in the local context. This reality does not negate the importance of generating international public goods. Several key research issues may not be high priorities for any single country but may be of major importance for the region as a whole—examples are the environmental impacts of AIDS and interactions with another long-wave process, climate change. A balance is needed. Networks like RENEWAL (www.ifpri.org/renewal) have sprung up in recent years to find this balance and to catalyze and scale up scientific and operational learning in real time.

Looking ahead, there is a growing need for operational research and better evaluations of programmatic attempts to deal with the HIV-hunger nexus. The demonstrated diversity of impacts requires a diversity of researchers, working collaboratively across disciplines. Bridges need to be built between social scientists, epidemiologists, public health specialists, nutritionists, and agricultural economists. Above all, the scale of effective responses must be increased to maximize impact. Large-scale epidemics need large-scale responses, but these responses need to be tailored to the particular drivers and impacts in different locations for different vulnerable groups.

Notes

1. This chapter builds upon earlier work in which this author has recently been involved, including Gillespie and Kadiyala (2005a), Gillespie (2006), Gillespie, Kadiyala, and Greener (2007), and Gillespie (2008), updating the scientific and operational evidence bases with the findings of recent studies. The following section draws considerably on a recent review by Gillespie, Kadiyala, and Greener (2007).

2. It is important to note that most studies focus on *relative* poverty and *relative* wealth in the context of generalized chronic poverty. In most cases, it is only the highest one or two quintiles (or possibly three in middle-income Southern African countries) that can be thought of as representing the nonpoor, using the standard poverty line definitions or the $1- or $2-a-day measures adopted for the purpose of global comparison. Comparisons are thus between wealth*ier* and poor*er* groups.

3. Note that the primary producer is not necessarily the head of the household or cluster. Rather, the role refers to the principal producer in the household or cluster who owns key assets, is able to organize labor, and is ultimately responsible for food.

CHAPTER 6

Pest Management, Farmer Incomes, and Health Risks in Sub-Saharan
Africa: Pesticides, Host Plant Resistance, and Other Measures

Rebecca Nelson

Abstract

In the African context, crop pests affect human health through multiple pathways. "Pests" include the diverse mammals, birds, insects, weeds, mollusks, and microbes that compete with humans for use of agricultural products. Available crop loss estimates are impressive (and dubious), suggesting that biotic stresses significantly reduce food security for African smallholders. Reduced food supplies contribute to malnutrition, and reduced incomes lead to inadequate access to purchased food and medical care. In addition to reducing crop yields and value, pests can reduce food quality and safety. The use of pesticides has direct health implications as well. Pest complexes and related health challenges vary among production systems. Traditional cropping systems are oriented to the production of diverse crops without favoring massive pest outbreaks. Increasing population pressure can lead to system degradation, input-intensive production, agroecological intensification, or all of these. On degraded soils, the parasitic weed *Striga* is a severe problem. Stressed systems also favor the accumulation of mycotoxins such as aflatoxin, which are a huge health burden in Africa. Intensification can lead to pest outbreaks as well, provoking the heavy use of pesticides. Heavy pesticide use can lead to the loss of natural biological control mechanisms, causing further losses as well as toxicity to humans. Agroecological intensification implies increasing and diversifying crop production through methods that improve soil and crop health. Improving farmers' access to well-adapted, pest-resistant crop varieties and facilitating their agroecological intensification will have positive effects on human as well as ecosystem health.

Introduction

The majority of Africans are smallholder farmers who depend on rainfed agriculture for their livelihoods. Sixty-four percent of the population of Sub-Saharan Africa is rural, and 60 percent of the economically active population derives its livelihood from agriculture (FAO 2006b). Most farms are a hectare or less in size. For smallholder farmers, family food security may be affected by any of a wide array of biotic or abiotic stresses that reduce the quantity or quality of their crop yields. Biotic threats to crop productivity include chronic or periodic predation by insect or mammalian pests; infection by viruses, fungi, bacteria, or nematodes; and competition or parasitism by weeds. For purposes of this chapter, the diverse taxa that harm crops will be collectively referred to as "pests."

Agricultural pests have both obvious and non-obvious implications for crop yields and quality, and they also interact with human health in both straightforward and insidious ways. The mechanisms by which pests and pest management affect human health include indirect effects resulting from lost production and direct effects resulting from pesticide exposure and effects on food safety. For smallholders who depend substantially on consuming the food they produce, crop losses due to biotic (and abiotic) stresses reduce food availability and can therefore compromise nutrition. Crop losses also imply lost income, which lowers the family's ability to purchase food and health care. Although pesticide use is lower in Africa than in many other regions, exposure is uncontrolled in high-value crops and cropping systems. Mycotoxins produced by molds attacking maize, groundnut, and many other crops are likely to be a major public health burden in Africa.

African cropping systems are diverse, and the pests and pest complexes associated with them are diverse as well. Pest complexes can be characterized by crop, agroecosystem, or both (see, for example, Pingali 2001). Because the purpose of this chapter is to reflect on the conceptual and policy issues concerning pest-related effects on farmer incomes and health risks in Sub-Saharan Africa, a simplified framework will be used. At the risk of oversimplifying a panorama that is famously diverse and complex, this chapter does not attempt to characterize the diversity of African production systems and their associated pest complexes, but rather presents the following four syndromes as potentially useful caricatures: the traditional scenario; the degraded scenario; the input-intensive scenario; and the agroecologically intensive scenario. For each, examples of pest scenarios and their health implications are given.

The first scenario is the "traditional" one. Most African agriculture is still practiced in traditional, labor-intensive systems with minimal inputs. Practices such as intercropping and fallowing tend to maintain pest populations at tolerable levels as a result of the complexity inherent in the systems. Pest management in such systems is thus not an explicit, distinct activity, but rather an outcome of the diversified production system. Traditional production systems are coming under increasing pressure from rising populations, changing climate, labor migration, and other factors. These pressures lead to changes that affect the natural resource base and the pest complexes with which farmers must contend.

How production systems evolve depends substantially on the context. How people respond to the pressures upon them varies with such factors as the inherent productivity of the system and the extent of market integration. Farmers producing crops on relatively favorable lands and who have access to markets for their produce have incentives and opportunities to use inputs that are inaccessible to farmers in more remote and unfavorable conditions.

The second scenario, then, is the "favorable" one, which entails input-intensive production. Ironically, favorable conditions may lead to agroecological disasters. Many pest syndromes are the direct result of intensification (Thomas and Waage 1996). Indiscriminate intensification leads to monocultures based on a narrow genetic base of crop varieties. Insecticides are among the inputs applied, but this convenient control measure has a tendency to backfire when pesticides kill the pests' natural enemies and pests develop resistance to the chemicals applied. Natural areas around crops are lost, eliminating the natural habitats of the insects that prey on pests, reducing these predators' ability to withstand pesticide pressures. These conditions favor the buildup of pest populations, which can undermine the profitability of the system. Overexposure to pesticides by farm workers erodes health, and pesticide residues may affect consumers and imperil markets.

The third scenario is the "unfavorable" one. Under unfavorable conditions, the natural resource base is often fragile and farmers lack economic resources to invest in explicit pest-control measures like pesticides. Resource degradation typically involves reduction in biological diversity, depletion of soil fertility, and reduced availability of water. The decline in ecosystem health leads to poor plant health, making crops more vulnerable to pest problems. Certain pests, such as parasitic weeds of the *Striga* and *Alectra* genera, are characteristic of degraded production systems or plants under stress (Gacheru and Rao 2001; Oswald and Ransom 2001). The low productivity of such systems reduces the food and income that can be derived from them, leading to malnutrition and human ill health.

The forth scenario is the "sustainable" one. Given appropriate opportunities, outreach, and incentives, there is the possibility of sustainable intensification based on traditional or agroecological principles. Sustainable intensification involves cover crops, leguminous constituents, or both. Although legumes can improve soil fertility, livelihoods, and nutrition, the susceptibility of many legume species to pests and diseases can be an obstacle to increased integration of legume species in cropping systems.

Crop Losses Attributed to Pests

Accurate data on crop losses are difficult to obtain in general, and this is particularly true in poor countries with weak agricultural research and extension systems. Thus, it is not surprising that data on losses due to pests in Africa are of limited quality and quantity. Abate, van Huis, and Ampofo (2000) state that there is no adequate information on the economic significance of pests under farmers' conditions, and doubtless the same applies to the state of knowledge concerning the nutritional significance of pest losses. Available sources of data on pest-induced yield losses include estimates by Oerke and colleagues (Oerke et al. 1994; Oerke 2006), the CABI Crop Protection database (CABI 2004), statistics from the Food and Agriculture Organization of the United Nations (FAO), the national studies sponsored by the Rockefeller Foundation for some countries, and published surveys and experimental research studies. The HarvestChoice project, recently initiated with the support of the Bill and Melinda Gates Foundation, has undertaken to improve the quality and utility of pest-related information (Wood 2008; http://www.harvestchoice.org/). This information will allow better allocation of resources and improved focus for policy analysis and formation. Nonetheless, for the present no credible source of accurate information is available on the pest-induced crop losses associated with the four scenarios mentioned.

Available data, though scant and dubious, suggest that pests cause significant losses overall. Maize, groundnuts, and beans are important crops in East Africa; losses on these crops give a general sense of the pest burden. Based on the 2005 estimates available through FAOSTAT, maize is grown on 9.8 million hectares in the region, with an average yield of less than 1.5 metric tons per hectare. Beans are grown on 3.7 million hectares, with an average yield of about 690 kilograms per hectare. The groundnut figures are similar to those of beans, with 3 million hectares of production and yields of 620 kilograms per hectare. Oerke and Dehne (2004) estimate that 55 and 60 percent of the maize and groundnut crops in East Africa are lost to pests, respectively. Grisley (1997) interviewed farmers to obtain their estimates for losses in beans and maize. Farmers in Kenya's Murang'a district estimated that they lost 47 percent of their maize to three insects and two pests and another 10 percent to two diseases. Farmers in this area estimated that they lost 34 percent of their beans to six insect pests, and another 11 percent to three diseases. The farmers' estimates are reasonably similar to estimates made by researchers based on formal experiments. The farmers interviewed by Grisley (1997) estimated that they lost 11 percent of their maize yield to stemborers. De Groote et al. (2001) compared sprayed and unsprayed fields, sampling 194 fields over three seasons, drawing on five ecosystems. They concluded that 13.5 percent of maize yields were lost to stemborers, with losses higher in dry areas (21 percent). These estimates do not take full account of postharvest losses, which can be considerable.

These estimated averages may give some idea about how pest losses affect productivity, but more information is needed to understand how these losses affect food supplies at the national and household levels. Major pest outbreaks are relatively rare but devastating and require national or international preparation, monitoring, and response. Chronic or patchy losses are less likely to drive effective responses, but it is important to understand the objective and perceived risks they present, as well as the emotional and practical responses they elicit. When losses are chronic and relatively stable or predictable, people will adjust to the expected yield and make the management decisions they feel they can afford. For the bean pest complex, for example, farmers expect heavy losses at certain times of year and time their bean crops to avoid those months.

Examples of major pest outbreaks include cassava mealybug and mosaic disease (CMD). The CMD epidemic that started in the late 1980s caused losses estimated at US$1.2–2.3 billion. In some areas people virtually abandoned their basic staple; at the height of the epidemic, the equivalent of 60,000 hectares of cassava production was lost in Uganda alone (Thresh and Cooter 2005). For these catastrophic events, key management decisions cannot be made at the farm level, but require intervention at the national or international levels. There is an obvious need for public investment in monitoring the threats of such outbreaks and ensuring readiness through preemptive breeding and the development of biological control strategies. The most successful case of a massive biological control campaign, against the cassava mealybug (Herren and Neuenschwander 1991), showed an overwhelmingly favorable cost-benefit ratio (Zeddies et al. 2000). This example and others provide inspiration and hope for the success of classical biological control, for instance in the cases of the diamondback moth in horticultural systems in Eastern and Southern Africa and of the millet head miner in West Africa (McKnight Foundation CCRP 2009).

Such coordinated efforts are rarely taken for the pest complexes that affect most cropping systems; individual farmers must contend with their pest challenges as best they can. There are 24 arthropod pests that cause economically significant losses across the continent and many more that are of local importance (Abate, van Huis, and Ampofo 2000). For the majority of African farmers, who grow their crops largely for home consumption under marginal economic circumstances, chemical pest control options are not physically or economically accessible. Among the inputs they might apply, fertilizer would be a higher priority than pesticides. The threat of drought reduces incentives to apply any type of input.

If losses are patchy, it is even harder for farmers to take cost-effective action. For high-value crops, farmers who are able to purchase pesticides may apply economically unjustified quantities as an "insurance policy." That is, given a level of risk perceived as unknown and a large financial stake in avoiding pest losses, farmers may spray their crops as a safety measure (Rossing, Daamen, and Hendrix 1994). Because of a poor understanding of damage-pest relationships, farmers may overreact to minor pest damage that would have no economic implication. For farmers cultivating under marginal conditions, the threat of crop loss may reduce the incentive to apply fertilizer or otherwise invest in productivity. Whereas some pest effects are overestimated, the damaging effects of others are invisible or non-obvious, such that they are poorly understood and ineffectively managed. Farmers are generally better at managing more visible phenomena but can be ineffectual when it comes to diseases (Bentley and Thiele 1999; Isubikalu et al. 1999). Mycotoxins represent an extreme case of invisible damage. This topic will be further addressed later in this chapter.

The Pesticide Picture

Just as information on crop losses in Africa is far from satisfactory, data on pesticide use in Africa are scant (Abate, van Huis, and Ampofo 2000). Available information, such as it is, largely pertains to expenditures on pesticides in given countries or regions. These data show that Africa has the lowest rates of pesticide consumption of all world regions. A hectare of land cultivated in Africa receives pesticide treatment costing an average of US$3.04, whereas the European counterpart hectare receives pesticides worth US$37.86 (Abate, van Huis, and Ampofo 2000, based on FAO sources). Farmers engage in relatively little use of pesticides on most food crops. Exceptions include pest-vulnerable legumes such as cowpea (Isubikalu et al. 2000), as well as vegetables grown for food and cash (discussed later). The relatively low use of pesticides in much of African agriculture is both good and bad—good in that pesticide use imposes health and environmental costs (Pimentel et al. 1991; Pimentel et al. 1992; Pimentel and Greiner 1997) and bad in that this condition reflects the general lack of market integration of much of the African farming population.

Although the intensive pesticide use that characterized Asia in the wake of the Green Revolution is not seen in Africa overall, pesticide use is on the rise and is intensive in certain types of production systems. For example, the East African smallholder farmer sector has moved substantially to a cash crop economy, particularly for production of horticultural crops. Government policies encourage the use of pesticides (Abate, van Huis, and Ampofo 2000). This shift is worrisome; pesticides are an unhealthy solution to pest problems, particularly under tropical conditions (Stubbs, Harris, and Spear 1984; Pingali, Marquez, and Palis 1994; Antle, Cole, and Crissman 1998), and they are often ineffective owing to pest resurgences.

Most pesticides used are applied on commercial crops such as cotton, vegetables, coffee, and cocoa, as well as being used to control outbreaks of locusts

(Matthews, Wiles, and Baleguel 2003). Production of cash crops can be pesticide-intensive, and workers are generally not protected from exposure to pesticides (Gomes, Lloyd, and Revitt 1999; London et al. 2002; Williamson, Bal, and Pretty 2008). Because of a lack of protective clothing and proper training, occupational exposure levels are high and are presumably associated with negative health impacts (Williamson, Bal, and Pretty 2008). Water and food are contaminated through the reuse of empty pesticide containers (Ondieki 1996).

Other breaches of "safe use" include the employment of children in pesticide application. Cocoa production, like that of many other tropical plantation crops, has a long history of dependency on intensive pesticide use. In West Africa, pesticides are often applied by children. A study conducted by the International Institute for Tropical Agriculture estimated that more than 150,000 children were employed in applying pesticides on cocoa plantations in three countries in West Africa, most of them in Côte d'Ivoire (IITA 2002).

Five percent of the pesticides used in Africa are applied in campaigns aimed at migratory pests such as locusts and armyworms (Ondieki 1996). For example, an estimated US$100 million was spent on pesticides for locust control in Africa from 1985 to 1989 (Brader 1989, as quoted by Ondieki 1996), and 3.3 million hectares were treated with pesticides in Algeria, Libya, Mauritania, Morocco, and Tunisia to control a locust outbreak between late 2003 and mid-2004 (USAID 2004). This large-scale spraying has unintended negative consequences for other pests, including the elimination of natural biological controls for other pests, such as millet head miners (Baoua 2007), as well as causing problems such as crop phytotoxicity, and bird mortality (Ondieki 1996). In addition, this strategy involves international donations of large quantities of pesticides, sometimes outdated or banned in their country of origin (Ondieki 1996), not all of which are used in the spray campaigns. This practice has led to the buildup of stocks of unused pesticides, which are stored in unsafe ways. The FAO (1999) has estimated that 20,000 tons of toxic pesticide waste is stored under tenuous conditions in Africa, posing threats to human and environmental health.

The IPM Picture

With the advent of the agricultural chemical industry in the wake of World War II, the concept of pest control took shape around the idea of eliminating individual pests as constraints to crop production. The downsides of reliance on chemical control soon became evident. Pesticides had toxic effects on nontarget organisms, and pest populations tended to explode when their natural enemies were killed and the pests developed resistance to the pesticides (Devine and Furlong 2007; Pimentel et al. 1992). The problems associated with the pest control mentality led to the idea of integrated pest management (IPM), which initially involved using a combination of methods to maintain individual pest populations at acceptable levels. IPM has evolved considerably since the term came into use in the 1960s. The emergence of systems thinking led eventually to the idea of integrated crop management, recognizing that the interrelated components of an agroecosystem need to be considered together. In addition to providing productivity, the system should be designed to optimize costs and benefits related to efficiency, health, and environment, as well as to consider cultural values, equity, and other social criteria.

In Asia, the Green Revolution led to an initial overuse of pesticides in rice production. This overuse, in turn, resulted in outbreaks of pests such as the brown planthopper, with concomitant morbidity and mortality to the humans who handled the pesticides (Loevinsohn and Rola 1998). The IPM concept was widely implemented, largely through the FAO's Intercountry IPM Program (Kenmore 1991). This program worked with farmer field schools (FFSs) to reduce pesticide use and bring a more agroecologically oriented approach to rice production. To the limited extent that the Green Revolution has arrived in Africa, this approach to IPM is appropriate. That is, when cropping systems are sufficiently intensified to make it economically feasible for farmers to focus explicitly on pests, the concomitant problem or risk of pesticide abuse needs to be addressed, as in the case of the intensive horticultural systems mentioned later in this chapter. To the extent that neither the benefits nor the hazards of input intensification have been felt, an explicit focus on IPM and pesticide reduction may have limited relevance (Orr 2003; Orr and Ritchie 2004). A more holistic approach, integrating crop, soil, and pest management as well as issues related to market integration, is critical in view of the constraints and resource limitations that farmers face (Abate, van Huis, and Ampofo 2000; Snapp and Minja 2003). Working with FFSs in East Africa, Okoth, Khisa, and Thomas (2002, 18) observed that "the mono-crop (rice), mono-focus (pest management) of the FFS, as practiced originally in Southeast Asia, would not work in East Africa." This trend in FFSs toward integrated crop management and beyond is not limited to Africa; as IPM implementation through FFSs has evolved in many parts of the world, it has broadened to subsume more and more aspects of agroecologically based productivity, leading to an approach that can better be described as "integrated crop management," or ICM (see, for example, van de Fliert and Braun 1999).

That said, it is still worthwhile to reflect briefly on the elements of IPM that may be of relevance to African farmers in the context of an ICM approach. These interrelated elements would include the use of diversity for risk and pest management, the use of pest-resistant crop germplasm (noting potential for conflict or harmony with the use of diversity), the use of introduced biological control agents and biopesticides, and habitat management to increase the effectiveness of natural enemies of crop pests. The use of biological diversity and biological control are mentioned in the cases described later in this chapter. Natural enemies and parasidoids may keep pest populations in check if pesticides are not overused. For example, habitat management has been shown to be effective for cereal stem and cob borers (Borgemeister et al. 2005). A negative correlation was seen between abundance of nearby grasses and borer incidence. Wild hosts are reportedly highly attractive to ovipositing female moths, though the wild grasses do not allow high rates of larval survival. A short fallow with a legume or cover crop reduced losses by 5- to 11-fold compared with continuous maize cultivation. Intercropping was also effective in reducing infestation and losses.

Not all pests have plentiful natural enemies, perhaps in part because many staples are non-indigenous (maize, cassava, and sweetpotato are all relatively recent arrivals on the continent). Introduced biological control agents may be necessary to manage some pests. In addition, biological pesticides may be useful as a substitute for purchased inputs, as well as potentially less toxic (although biological pesticides are not necessarily innocuous). *Tephrosia vogelii*, a shrub that grows wild in various parts of Southern Africa, is also used as a "living fence" and as a fallow crop to enhance soil fertility. Infusions of the fresh leaves can be used as a biopesticide spray for horticultural or other crops (Kuntashula et al. 2006). Its leaves, when crushed and powdered, can be used to protect stored grain from insect damage (Koona and Dorn 2005).

Although there are many reasons to advocate for agroecological methods, the overall dominance of the "pesticide paradigm" in places where farmers can afford and gain access to agricultural inputs speaks to the challenge of implementing nonchemical control strategies. The use of diversity and biological control are not necessarily simple or straightforward to implement. For example, although diversity generally reduces pest and disease pressure, in some cases increased host diversity increases pest or disease problems (Thurston 1992). In addition, labor is limited in most households, many potentially useful practices entail high labor input, and opportunity costs may ultimately prevent their implementation. The successful design and implementation of integrated pest or crop management requires an understanding of farmers' priorities, perceptions, beliefs, and constraints (time and other resources). Participatory approaches enhance the likelihood that this understanding will inform the technology development and implementation process (see, for example, Snapp and Minja 2003).

Agroecosystem Trajectories and Their Associated Pest Scenarios in Africa

In nondegraded traditional systems (the first scenario described earlier), inherent pest pressures are often kept at tolerable levels as a consequence of the suites of cultural practices such as intercropping, rotation, low host density, and burning. Crop diversity is often a feature of such systems. More than 100 different plant species have been documented in the home gardens of the Chagga of Tanzania, for example, including more than 40 different types of bananas (Thurston 1992 and references therein). Diverse traditional systems enhance natural enemy levels and tend to keep pest levels low (Abate, van Huis, and Ampofo 2000). In addition, crop diversity buffers the farmer against a range of climate and pest risks; if one crop or variety suffers from a drought or pest, perhaps another will produce enough to support the family. One of the main types of traditional systems practiced in Africa and elsewhere in the humid tropics is slash-and-burn agriculture, also known as swidden agriculture or shifting cultivation. Under low population pressures, this system can provide an effective way to handle pests and loss of soil fertility, the two biggest problems of tropical agriculture.

Farmers complement these indirect pest management tactics with active tactics. Hoeing to remove weeds is the most commonly practiced of the explicit pest management activities, a response to the strong and obvious effect of weeds on crop yields (for example, according to Oerke and Dehne [2004], 17 percent of the maize crop is lost to weeds in Central Africa). Other cultural practices carried out to reduce pest losses include careful timing of planting and harvest; use of clean planting material (for example, obtaining planting material for cassava from high-altitude locations where virus pressure is low); mechanical control (for example, picking egg masses or conspicuous insects and digging trenches to trap locusts or armyworms); and use of plants or plant extracts with antipest qualities to protect crops in the field and in storage (Abate, van Huis, and Ampofo 2000).

Although a thorough analysis of traditional African pest management strategies is beyond the scope of this chapter, this fascinating subject is of relevance in the design of agroecologically sound approaches to agricultural intensification in Africa. Thurston (1992) details plant disease–related strategies in his book *Sustainable Practices for Plant Disease Management in Traditional Farming Systems,* and Abate, van Huis, and Ampofo (2000) review insect pest management strategies in traditional African agriculture. For the purposes of this chapter, the question is, what is the relevance of traditional practices to the pest management challenges of contemporary African farmers? It is likely that diversified and agroecologically managed agricultural systems could have a plethora of positive health implications for agroecosystems and their human constituents. Assuming that much can be gained by combining indigenous knowledge with agroecological theory and experimentation, how can this promise be realized in the context of the continent's diverse social, cultural, and economic contexts?

Traditional systems are being eroded as population pressure increases, the natural resource base is depleted, market forces affect cropping patterns, and climate patterns change. Strategies that were viable under low human densities or subsistence economies give way to new scenarios. For example, when population densities permit 15–30 hectares to be managed extensively to feed each person, the slash-and-burn system can be regarded as sustainable (Thurston 1992). As population pressure increases, however, slash-and-burn approaches become destructive. Slash-and-burn with shortened fallows is one of the many pathways that lead to degraded agroecosystems characterized by declining soil fertility and reduced biodiversity (the unfavorable, degraded scenario described earlier). Such outcomes are typical where market access is relatively poor and conditions are relatively unfavorable. Where market access is relatively good and conditions are relatively favorable, a distinct pathway typically leads to input-intensive systems (the favorable, input-intensified scenario described earlier). A third way, leading to agroecologically intensified systems characterized by the integration of legumes and the practice of integrated crop management, should be made more practically and economically viable through favorable policies, research and development (R&D), and other incentives. Some of the pest issues associated with the favorable and unfavorable scenarios, and agroecological approaches to their management, are considered here.

Cases

Favorable Systems with Market Access: Diamondback Moth in the Production of Vegetables in East Africa

Under favorable conditions with good market access, intensive horticultural systems are profitable for smallholders and provide vegetables to enhance the nutrition of both producer households and their urban customers. Brassica crops, such as cabbage (*Brassica oleracea* var. *capitata*), collard (*Brassica oleracea* var. *acephala*), and rape (the Ethiopian mustard *Brassica carinata*), are important vegetable crops in East and Southern Africa, contributing to both livelihoods and nutrition in a maize-based diet (see, for example, Said and Itulya 2003). These crops are grown for home consumption and also for local markets. In Kenya, for example, annual average cabbage production exceeds 256,000 tons (Macharia, Löhr, and De Groote 2005). Unfortunately, intensive horticulture in the tropics is notorious for the high use of pesticides.

The management of diamondback moth illustrates some of the problems and solutions that can be implemented. Pests are the principal constraint to *Brassica* production, with the diamondback moth (*Plutella xylostella*) the most important. Diamondback moths are more and more damaging, often causing complete loss of the crop (Kibata 1996; Ayaıew 2006). Farmers mainly control diamondback moth through pesticide application, but chemical control is increasingly difficult and even uneconomical. As also observed in Asia, diamondback moths rapidly acquire resistance to the pesticides applied (Mwaniki et al. 1998; Ayalew and Ogol 2006). Farmers are driven to apply cocktails of pesticides at increasing frequency (Löhr 2001 and references therein). In some cases, the pesticides have become so ineffective that "some trials in farmers' fields in Kenya have shown significantly and consistently higher DBM [diamondback moth] populations in the λ-cyhalothrin treatments than in untreated plots (Macharia, personal communication)" (Ayalew 2006, 919). This counterproductive effect is attributed to insecticide resistance in the pest, coinciding with pesticide susceptibility in the predators and parasitoids that normally reduce pest populations.

Ayalew and Ogol (2006) characterized the occurrence of diamondback moths and its parasitoids in Ethiopia. Surveying 194 brassica fields in 13 areas of the country, they identified eight primary hymenopterous parasitoid species from five families. Parasitism rates ranged from 4 to 80 percent, and rates of parasitism showed a strong negative correlation with diamondback moth populations. Overall, higher diamondback moth density was associated with high rates of pesticide use and low rates of parasitism. In some areas where pesticides were sprayed weekly or even more frequently, pest levels were among the highest. Areas without a history of pesticide use showed fields with the highest rates of parasitism and lowest rates of pest occurrence. As seen for management of the brown planthopper in Southeast Asian ricefields, pesticides are often not only a poor solution to the problem, but in fact major contributors to the problem.

In Southeast Asian rice fields, natural biological control is generally effective if varieties with some degree of resistance are grown without pesticide use, because of the effectiveness of natural biological control (Huan et al. 2005; Schoenly et al. 1996; Way and Heong 1994). Such natural biological control may be less effective in Africa, where many important crops have been introduced and thus have not co-evolved with natural enemies of the crop pests (Abate, van Huis, and Ampofo 2000). Introduced biological control agents can be effective when indigenous ones are inadequate, as illustrated by the brilliant success of the biological control campaign that solved the outbreak of cassava mealybug (Herren and Neuenschwander 1991). Thinking along these lines, Macharia, Löhr, and De Groote (2005) assessed the potential impact of biological control of the diamondback moth in Kenyan cabbage production. In their survey of 68 cabbage producers in six districts, they found that 16 percent of production costs went to pesticides. All of these farmers relied on pesticides for diamondback moth control, most spraying on a calendar-driven basis. They were increasing their applications because of increasing pest pressure, anticipating a 98 percent yield loss if they did not control the pest. This finding reflects farmers' sense of total dependency on pesticides, even though the chemicals are declining in their efficacy and cost-effectiveness. Based on many years of research, Macharia, Löhr, and De Groote (2005) estimated that 30 percent of current losses could be abated through the use of biological control. Combined with a 50 percent decrease in the needed pesticide application, the authors estimated that more than US$28 million in economic surplus would be gained by the use of biological control. This result includes the cost of the research and extension work, while considering the benefits only to cabbage producers in Kenya. Because the benefits would also likely apply to producers of other vegetables (such as kale, cauliflower, and broccoli) and producers in other countries in the region, this total appears to be a very conservative estimate of benefit. The investment–benefit ratios depend on the assumptions made but provide a compelling case for investment even under the worst-case scenario.

The whitefly problem in horticultural systems in East Africa is another illustration of the problems associated with the "pesticide treadmill" and its downsides. For diamondback moths, whiteflies, and a range of other pest challenges, intensive but agroecologically sound approaches to managing the cropping system are needed so that pests are kept at acceptable levels. In addition to biological control, components of an ecological integrated pest management (IPM) system might include the use of pest-resistant varieties, intercropping, rotations, and botanical (for example, neem-based products) and biological pesticides (*Bacillus thuringiensis*). For whiteflies that vector the cassava mosaic virus, Fondong, Thresh, and Zok (2002) found that intercropping reduced whitefly populations and disease incidence, perhaps slowing the spread of the disease to adjacent areas; this reduction did not, however, affect disease severity within the primary fields analyzed. Semaganda et al. (2003) noted that intercropping enhanced the activity of the whitefly's natural enemies. In their survey of factors related to the diamondback moth in Ethiopia, Ayalew and Ogol (2006) found that intercropping showed a negative correlation with diamondback moth intensity. Said and Itulya (2003) conducted experiments on the effects of intercropping on diamondback moths and found that intercropping suppressed diamondback moth populations and increased food production per unit of land.

Unfavorable Systems I: Mycotoxins

Mycotoxins are naturally occuring toxic and carcinogenic substances that are produced by certain molds (fungi of the genera *Aspergillus, Fusarium,* and *Penicillium*) that grow on many foodstuffs both before and after harvest. Mycotoxins that pose human health risks include aflatoxins, deoxynivalenol (DON, also known as vomitoxin), fumonisins, ochratoxins, and ergot alkaloids. Among the most potent and notorious of these is aflatoxin, which is produced by the fungus *Aspergillus flavus*. Maize (corn) and groundnut (peanut) are among the most vulnerable crops to aflatoxin contamination. These two crops are the foundations of the diet of millions of Africans, especially in the eastern and southern regions of the continent. Fungal infection and aflatoxin accumulation is highest when crops are subjected to water stress and insect damage in the field and to suboptimal storage conditions (Herrman 2002). Because these conditions often prevail, African populations are at risk for ingesting large quantities of aflatoxin (Sibanda, Marovatsanga, and Pestka 1997).

Effects of aflatoxin exposure include stunting, liver cancer, and even death. A strong association has been reported between high aflatoxin levels in women and low birth weight of their offspring (DeVries, Maxwell, and Hendrickse 1990). Hendrickse (1997) notes the widespread aflatoxin contamination of human breast-milk in tropical Africa (more than 30 percent of samples from Ghana, Kenya, Nigeria and Sudan). A study in West Africa found a link between aflatoxin levels in children's blood and stunting (Gong et al. 2002). Among the 480 children in Benin and Togo analyzed in a cross-sectional study, 99 percent had been exposed to aflatoxin, and higher levels were associated with reduced growth. Maize was the main source of contamination for this group (Egal et al. 2005). Hendrickse (1997) makes the case that kwashiorkor can be attributed to aflatoxicosis. Liver cancer is the fifth most frequent cancer worldwide. Incidence of liver cancer is 2–10 times higher in developing countries than in developed countries (Henry et al. 1999). The two key risk factors for liver cancer are hepatitis and aflatoxin, and there is a strong interaction between the two: the risk of liver cancer from aflatoxin consumption is 30 times greater in individuals who have been exposed to hepatitis (Henry et al. 1998, as cited in Henry et al. 1999). Azziz-Baumgartner et al. (2005) suggest that the high incidence of liver cancer found in eastern Kenya is attributable to chronic aflatoxin exposure. Sporadic outbreaks of aflatoxin in drier parts of Kenya have been reported (Onsongo 2004). In 2004, 125 deaths attributed to acute aflatoxin poisoning were reported in eastern and central provinces (Lewis et al. 2005; Azziz-Baumgartner et al. 2005). Williams et al. (2004) hypothesize that aflatoxicosis may be one of the most important and least-recognized health problems in the developing world, since existing evidence suggests that aflatoxicosis may compound health problems such as malaria and HIV/AIDS.

In Europe and the United States, aflatoxin levels in human and animal food are tightly regulated because of its carcinogenic, immunosuppressive, growth-retarding, and toxic effects (Robens and Cardwell 2003). This regulation entails losses to producers in the United States; for example, maize from three southern U.S. states valued at US\$85–100 million was destroyed because of excessive aflatoxin in 1998 (Betran, Isakeit, and Odvody 2002). Aflatoxin regulation can be used as a nontariff trade barrier to the detriment of African producers. The tension between protection of producers and consumers is problematic in the African context; stringent international standards, such as those of many European countries, make it difficult for developing countries to market their goods internationally, but a lack of monitoring and regulation puts consumers at risk. Codex Alimentarius, an international body tasked with facilitating world trade and protecting international public health, has taken on board the concerns for fair trade and for health by adopting moderately stringent limits for aflatoxin (Henry et al. 1999).

International regulators apparently feel powerless to reduce aflatoxin contamination and instead have promoted vaccination against hepatitis (Henry et al. 1999). This approach may reduce liver cancer risk, but it may not protect populations from the immunosuppressive and other toxic effects of aflatoxins. A more comprehensive approach to reducing aflatoxin risk is necessary to improve the overall health of African populations at risk for high levels of aflatoxin consumption. Such an approach would involve risk assessment in relation to weather; participatory farmer training on reducing aflatoxin in crops before harvest, in processed and stored crops, and in diets; and crop breeding to reduce vulnerability to fungal infection and aflatoxin accumulation. To reduce the genetic susceptibility of crop varieties to *A. flavus* and other mycotoxigenic fungi, African breeding programs need to establish the capacity to test for the relevant fungi and the mycotoxins. Establishing this capacity is now a high priority for the Kenyan maize-breeding program (Gethi 2009). Similarly, capacity to test for aflatoxin can empower farmer organizations to identify sources of contamination and to develop ways of avoiding them. The farmer union National Smallholder Farmers' Association of Malawi (NASFAM) in Malawi, for example, has implemented an aflatoxin-monitoring and -tracing system to facilitate groundnut commercialization. Highly contaminated samples were traced to households that shelled their groundnuts with the aid of water to soften the shells. This diagnosis led to the demand for better access to small machines to reduce the drudgery and pain involved in manual shelling of groundnuts (Chinyamunyamu 2007).[1]

Unfavorable systems II: Parasitic weeds. The parasitic weeds *Striga* and *Alectra* are huge constraints to African cereal and legume production under poor soil fertility and moisture conditions. Sauerborn (1991) contends that *Striga* is the single most important biotic constraint to food production in Africa. These flowering plants attach to the roots of their host plants and debilitate them by sucking away nutrients and water, as well as through toxic effects. Among the many *Striga* species in Africa, three are agriculturally important: *Striga gesnerioides* attacks cowpea, *S. asiatica* infests cereal crops in Southern Africa, and *S. hermonthica* is predominant in cereals in East and West Africa. In West Africa, approximately 40 million hectares of cereal-based systems are severely infested by *Striga*, and almost 70 million hectares are moderately infested (Lagoke, Parkinson, and Agunbiade 1991). *Alectra vogelii* is another parasitic weed that attacks cowpea. Each parasitic weed plant produces a phenomenal number of tiny seeds (60,000 per plant), each of which can remain viable in the soil for decades, awaiting the chemical signal characteristic of its host root (reviewed by Berner, Kling, and Singh 1995). In traditional rotations with long fallows, intercropped species, tolerant traditional varieties, and healthy soils, *Striga* is not a major threat to crop production. As those traditional practices give way to simplified and shortened cropping systems, the problem becomes acute or even devastating.

In Malawi, for instance, the traditional millet- and sorghum-based system of precolonial times has been converted into a maize-based system. Malawi is among the poorest countries in Africa. Soil fertility is low, and as populations rise, farming is being practiced on more marginal lands. Farmers, isolated from markets, use little fertilizer and almost no pesticide. Farmers thus simultaneously confront reduced soil fertility and lower and more unpredictable rainfall patterns. While difficult for farmers, these conditions favor *Striga*. In southern and central Malawi, about two-thirds of fields with depleted soils are infested with *Striga* (Snapp and Minja 2003). Levels of infestation vary and are patchy even within fields. Once a field becomes severely infested, it becomes extremely difficult to eliminate because of the "seed bank," and farmers are forced to abandon their fields.

The Malawi Government Guide to Agricultural Practice (1995, as cited by Snapp and Minja 2003) recommends that *Striga* and other parasitic weeds be managed by hand pulling and burning. This practice may eventually reduce the seed bank, but scientists and farmers know that it may not greatly benefit the existing crop, because much of the pest's damage is done before the weed emerges and becomes vulnerable to hand-weeding (Riches et al. 1993). A number of other solutions to the *Striga* problem are promising but likely out of the reach of Malawian smallholders with extreme resource constraints. Genetic studies have suggested the potential for resistance breeding against *Striga* (see, for example, Gethi and Smith 2004; Berner, Kling, and Singh 1995), but no varieties currently available to Malawian farmers have significant resistance (Kabambe and Mloza-Banda 2000, as cited in Snapp and Minja 2003). A new *Striga* management technology has recently been released in Kenya, involving a maize hybrid that is able to withstand the systemic herbicide imazapyr. Seeds of the resistant maize are coated with the herbicide, which then protects the germinating plant from attack by the parasitic weed (Kanampiu et al. 2003). Given the variable accessibility of hybrid seed to Malawian farmers (Smale and Phiri 1998) and their lack of pesticide use, it is not apparent that this technology will be widely used in Malawi. It may be more readily accessible to farmers in Kenya, who are generally more integrated into markets. This contrast is suggested by the responses of Kenyan and Malawian farmers to a recent pest outbreak in pigeonpea; 30 percent of Kenyan farmers applied pesticides to control the pest outbreak, whereas virtually none of the Malawian farmers did so (Minja et al. 1999).

Various integrated approaches to *Striga* management have been suggested, based on overlapping sets of principles. The approach presented by Berner, Kling, and Singh (1995) focuses on the use of crop rotation with selected "trap crops" (nonhost cultivars that are efficient in causing *Striga* seed to germinate without allowing the pest to complete its life cycle). In this approach, crop rotation is complemented with the use of *Striga*-free planting material, as well as biological control, host resistance, and host seed treatments. Snapp and Minja (2003) note that the management of soil fertility can virtually eliminate the negative impact of *Striga* and suggest an integrated crop management strategy focused on the simultaneous improvement of soil and plant health. A particularly effective trap crop is the legume *Tephrosia vogelii*, a leguminous plant native to Malawi that is widely used as a green manure and biopesticide. Intercropping maize with *Tephrosia* increases maize yields through enhanced soil fertility and probably through a direct negative effect on *Striga* (Snapp and Minja 2003). Intercropping with the legume *Desmodium* also has a dramatic suppressive effect on *Striga* (Khan et al. 2002), as well as repelling stemborer and providing fodder for livestock.

So What to Do? Implications for Policy

Pests have a substantial influence on productivity and food safety in Sub-Saharan Africa and thus on human livelihoods and health. The approaches needed to address pest-related problems depend on the contexts in question. The different scenarios outlined here suggest different policy implications that would promote alternative pathways toward agroecologically sustainable intensification. For high-value cropping systems in which pesticide use is high and hazardous (the favorable, input-intensive scenario), it is necessary to ensure that people handling pesticides are aware of the health risks and how to minimize them. It is worthwhile to seek alternative ways of reducing pest damage while minimizing pesticide use; in high-value systems where pests are limiting, such alternatives may be cost-effective and welcomed as such. In cropping systems where profitability is inherently low (the unfavorable, degraded scenario), farmers' options are severely limited by their resource constraints. In these systems, it is critical to seek integrated solutions that address farmers' priorities and acknowledge their limitations. Farmers may be more motivated to reduce risk and to optimize their returns to small investments of cash or labor than to maximize yield (Rohrbach and Snapp 1997, as cited in Snapp and Minja 2003). For the most resource-limited farmers, addressing overall risk and returns is likely to be more effective than a narrow focus on one or more pests. Successfully addressing the constraints of smallholders, in general, requires working closely with them throughout the process of priority setting, system design, technology development, and implementation.

For both the input-intensified and the degraded-constrained contexts, the goal is to move from unsustainable practices to a more ecologically sound system that protects and enhances the health of the people, soil, and ecosystem more broadly (the fourth scenario). An integrated analysis of agroecosystem and human health, which considers the diversity of crops and diets as well as resiliency versus shocks and stresses (Peden 1998), is likely to provide a stronger basis for motivating and informing positive change than the analysis of single aspects of the system. To move in the direction of better agroecological pest management, increased investment in research and development is needed in a number of areas. For both high-value and subsistence-oriented agriculture, the use of agroecological principles, together with a participatory experimental approach, is the necessary basis for designing production systems that are sustainable and robust with respect to biotic and abiotic stresses. Traditional production systems are a rich source of inspiration for agroecologically sound management practices. An important component of integrated crop management would be the use of crop varieties, multilines, or populations that are resistant or tolerant to key pests. For many crops of cultural and nutritional importance in Africa, limited effort has been made to breed for pest resistance and tolerance in locally adapted germplasm. For example, many legume crops hold great potential for increasing soil health, incomes, and nutrition, but their contributions are constrained by their extreme vulnerability to pests. Substantial natural variation for resistance exists in the germplasm of many crops and can be used through conventional, marker-assisted, and participatory breeding. The potential role for genetic engineering in improving resistance to pests in the African context is an open question (Gressel et al. 2004). Transgenic technologies are available for viruses and insects and could be valuable for protection of crops that lack adequate levels of native resistance. For sweetpotato, for instance, weevil problems have defied attempts at breeding and integrated management, and breeders see use of the *Bacillus thuringiensis* (Bt) toxin gene as a potential solution to a hitherto intractable problem (Mwanga 2007). Although millions of hectares of Bt maize are grown in many countries, it is not clear if and when Bt sweetpotato will be deployed. This issue is as much a policy one as a technical one. Interestingly, opposition comes largely from factions in the United States and Western Europe, where pesticide use levels are much higher than in Africa (Oerke and Dehne 2004).

Scientists are trained to look at specific components of specific problems. Although this approach is a natural consequence of disciplinary structure of the research establishment, it is not necessarily an effective way of addressing major problems. An integrated approach may be needed, for example, to reduce the aflatoxin problem. As with many other problems, even the basic outlines of the problem are currently ill defined. To rationally and effectively drive policy, more data are needed to assess the body load and health effects of aflatoxin exposure in Africa. To allow meaningful sampling and the design of effective interventions, observed levels of toxin should be related to expected levels based on environmental conditions and management practices. In maize, plant stress is an important predisposing factor for toxin accumulation, so a key step will be a coordinated effort to enhance access to well-adapted, drought-tolerant varieties. Breeding programs must also build in resistance to insect damage, fungal attack, and toxin accumulation, along with the other traits that farmers and consumers need. An understanding of the underlying inheritance of these traits is needed for efficient trait improvement. Bringing all this together requires investment and dedication. But a scientific achievement like the production of a superior crop genotype is often just the starting point for successful pest management. To improve farmers' capacity to manage pests, to enhance their livelihoods, and to reduce their health risks, farmers need access to knowledge and technology, as well as the capacity and incentives to use them with confidence. Understanding and investing in the many dimensions of a systems approach will bring closer the ideal of an agroecologically sound African agriculture (Lewis et al. 1997).

Notes

1. Further information on aflatoxin management is available at the website for the International Crops Research Institute for the Semi-Arid Tropics (ICRISAT; http://www .icrisat.org/aflatoxin/).

CHAPTER 7

～～～～

Nutrition and the Environment:
Fundamental to Food Security in Africa

Anna Herforth

Abstract

Nutrition, food production, and the environment are inextricably linked. The way people obtain food affects the environment and the ecosystem services it provides, which in turn affect food security and human nutrition. As detailed in chapter 2, food insecurity in Sub-Saharan Africa is widespread and persistent, and malnutrition, land degradation, water issues, soil nutrient loss, and eroding crop genetic diversity threaten present and future livelihoods. Food security, which calls for foods to meet dietary needs and food preferences for a healthy and active life, necessarily implies consistent access to a diverse diet. Furthermore, food security rests on continued provision of ecosystem services. Considering these nutritional and environmental underpinnings, genuine food security cannot be achieved in Africa through growth in cereal production and incomes alone, but also requires agricultural crop diversity. Policies are needed to encourage a food system that will result in dietary diversity for all segments of society while maintaining ecosystem services, using indicators of food security more closely tied to nutrition and the environment. Emerging challenges, including rising rates of obesity, HIV/AIDS, climate change, and food price volatility, and case studies of existing policies in Sub-Saharan Africa strengthen the case for agricultural diversification and the use of updated indicators to achieve food security.

Framework: The Relationship between Nutrition and the Environment

The environment is the foundation for food security and nutrition. Ecosystem services are the basis for food production and the caloric and nutrient yields necessary for human nutrition. Adequate nutrition is necessary for humans' ability to work and to seek food. How people seek and produce food, from crop choices to agricultural use of fossil fuels and water, affects the environment, which in turn affects nutrition by dictating which crops can be grown where and when and what they will yield (Figure 7.1).

Components of "the environment" include biodiversity, soil, water, climate, and ecosystems, all of which provide ecosystem services. Table 7.1 shows examples of how each affects food security and human nutrition and is affected by food-seeking behavior.

Food security, which requires foods to provide adequate nutrition, depends on ecosystem services rendered by each environmental component. Ecosystem services are "the various ways that organisms, and the sum total of their interactions with each other and with the environments in which they live, function to keep all life on this planet, including human life, alive" (Chivian and Bernstein 2008, xi). The Millennium Ecosystem Assessment (2005a) delineates four types of ecosystem services: (1) supporting services, such as nutrient cycling and soil formation; (2) provisioning services, such as food, fresh water, wood, and fuel; (3) regulating services, such as water purification and climate and disease regulation; and (4) cultural services, providing opportunities for aesthetic, recreational, and spiritual needs. The services ecosystems provide make food production possible. Soil and water are the building blocks of food, with essential support from microbes and animals. Food security dwindles without healthy soil, adequate water, and an ecosystem that supports microbes, natural soil fertilizers and aerators, insect pollinators, and pest controllers.[1]

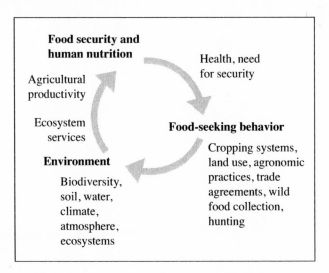

Figure 7.1   The environment, food security, and food-seeking behavior
SOURCE: Author.

Table 7.1 Components of the environment, how they affect human nutrition, and how they are affected by human food-seeking behavior

Component	How it affects nutrition	How it is affected by food-seeking behavior
Biodiversity		
• Wild biodiversity	• Affects the diversity of foods and medicines available for human consumption	• Competition for space between wilderness and farming affects ecosystems, habitats, and number of species

• Agrobiodiversity
  –crop species and varieties
  –noncultigens
  –insects
  –microbes
	• Affects yields
	• Affects use and development of varieties that are particularly high yielding, nutrient-rich, or adapted to specific environments
		• Cultivation or gathering based on desired characteristics affects genetic diversity in crops and wild species
		• Cropping systems, trade agreements, marketing and transportation, and cultural and consumer preferences affect number of species and varieties grown
		• Agronomic practices affect insect diversity, including pollinators, pests, and predators

Soil		
• Nutrient content • Structure • Biodiversity (microbes, microfauna)	• Affects yields • Affects nutrient content of crops	• Species grown, continuous cultivation, and other agronomic practices (tilling, mulching, fertilizing, etc.) affect fertility (nutrient content and structure) and soil biodiversity
Water		
• Irrigation water • Drinking water	• Affects yields • Affects cleanliness and safety of food and drink • Affects exposure to waterborne and insect vector-transmitted disease	• Water resource management affects water quantity and quality • Agrochemicals and soil erosion affect water quality • Irrigation can increase yields but overirrigation can cause salinization • Conservation practices and choice of drought-resistant varieties can conserve water

Climate	
• Temperatures	• Fuel use in food production and transportation releases greenhouse gases
◦ Affects yields	• Livestock activities produce 1/5 of all greenhouse gases (Steinfeld et al. 2006)
• Weather and storms	• Land use changes for crop production affect carbon sink; alley cropping and forest regeneration increase it
◦ Affects what crops can be grown where and when	• Soil erosion, conservation tillage, and other cropping practices affect soil carbon sink
◦ Affects wild food availability	
◦ Affects exposure to infectious disease (such as malaria)	
Ecosystems	
• Capacity to provide foods	• Land use changes affect ecosystem size; rainforest destruction and desertification are largely irreversible changes
◦ Affects land fertility	• Food system–resultant climate change endangers certain ecosystems
◦ Affects wild food availability (such as ocean fish, Brazil nuts)	

SOURCE: Author.

Background: Food Insecurity, Malnutrition, and Agriculture in Sub-Saharan Africa

The linkages between agriculture, the environment, and nutrition and food security are especially direct in Sub-Saharan Africa, where more than two-thirds of the population depends on agriculture for their livelihood (World Bank 2007b; Dixon, Gulliver, and Gibbon 2001). The vast majority of these are smallholder farmers, who are typically net buyers of food, relying on their agricultural production for income as well as for directly consumed food. For the urban poor, too, the kinds of foods available and accessible determine food security. Therefore agricultural solutions will be of utmost importance for increasing food security in Sub-Saharan Africa.

Food Insecurity Is a Problem

According to the United Nations, "Food security exists when all people, at all times, have physical and economic access to sufficient, safe, and nutritious food to meet their dietary needs and food preferences for a healthy and active life" (FAO 1996b). No indicator is consistently used across Sub-Saharan Africa to measure the prevalence of food security according to that (or any) definition, but approximations show that food insecurity is widespread. The Food and Agriculture Organization of the United Nations (FAO) estimates that one-third of people in Sub-Saharan Africa are food insecure or "undernourished," based on an indicator of caloric availability (FAO 2008b).[2] Others have estimated significantly higher levels of food insecurity in Sub-Saharan Africa using household expenditure surveys (Smith, Alderman, and Aduayom 2006). Poverty is closely related to food insecurity, and more than 46 percent of the population in Sub-Saharan Africa lives on less than $1 per day (UN 2005); the rate is higher in rural areas than in urban (World Bank 2007b). With business as usual, the proportion of food-insecure people in Sub-Saharan Africa will stay constant at one-third of the population, and the number of food insecure will rise to 265 million by 2015 (Pinstrup-Andersen and Herforth 2008).

Malnutrition Disables Productive Lives

Poverty and food insecurity manifest themselves as malnutrition, and in a vicious circle, malnutrition causes poverty through loss of productive capacity. The number of malnourished children in Sub-Saharan Africa has increased over the past decade; the percentages of stunted and underweight children have stayed constant at about 35 percent and 24 percent, respectively, since 1995 (SCN 2004). These high rates of child malnutrition contribute greatly to making mortality rates for infants and children under five years of age in Sub-Saharan Africa the highest in the world (UNICEF 2007). Malnutrition accounts for 35–56 percent of all child deaths, mostly because malnourished children are much more likely to die from disease than well-nourished children (Pelletier et al. 1995; Black et al. 2008).

More common than death from malnutrition is disability: malnutrition limits work productivity (see chapter 11). In Sub-Saharan Africa, this means reduced agricultural productivity, which compounds the problem of food insecurity. Malnutrition in childhood reduces learning potential, as well as adult work capacity, earning capacity, and productivity (Martorell 1995; Haas et al. 1995; Victora et al. 2008). Both protein-energy malnutrition and micronutrient malnutrition (often called "hidden hunger") contribute to lost productivity. Deficiencies in iodine and iron in infancy and young childhood result in irreversibly impaired mental development. Even mild iodine deficiency reduces IQ by 10–15 points, limiting productive capacity (Maberly et al. 1994); 43 percent of the African population is iodine deficient (SCN 2004). Iron-deficiency anemia not only impairs mental development and physical growth in children (Lozoff 2007; Shafir et al. 2008), who consequently have a lower potential for productivity in adulthood, but also reduces work capacity in adults (Haas and Brownlie 2001). National rates of iron-deficiency anemia among children under age five in Sub-Saharan African countries range from a low of 47 percent to a high of 86 percent (MI et al. 2004). Vitamin A deficiency causes reduced immune function and blindness; 32 percent of children under five in Sub-Saharan Africa are vitamin A deficient (SCN 2004).

Macro- and micronutrient malnutrition also worsens the progression of HIV/AIDS (see chapter 5). This interaction is important to consider in Sub-Saharan Africa, where about 5 percent of adults live with the disease; in some countries, rates are much higher (UNAIDS 2008). Those with HIV/AIDS die faster if they are generally malnourished (Fawzi 2003) or micronutrient malnourished (Baum and Shor-Posner 1998; Semba and Tang 1999). Better nutrition is needed to support immune function, and HIV/AIDS increases energy requirements (WHO 2003b). Also, given that antiretroviral treatments often must be taken on a full stomach, limited food compromises treatment for the disease.

Because of its high toll on human health, resources, and well-being, malnutrition reduces national and regional economic growth substantially. In most countries in Sub-Saharan Africa, malnutrition reduces gross domestic product (GDP) by 1–2 percent (MI et al. 2004). Losses come from reduced physical and mental capacity, as well as reduced school attendance and increased health care costs (World Bank 2006). Further losses result from the growing double burden of malnutrition—including overweight and related diseases—which is rising even in some rural areas of Sub-Saharan Africa (WHO/FAO 2003; Mendez, Monteiro, and Popkin 2005), where noncommunicable diseases carry high rates of disabling complications (Beran and Yudkin 2006, Unwin et al. 2001). Malnutrition also reduces agricultural productivity, especially when compounded with disease (Haddad and Bouis 1991; Edgerton et al. 1979; see also Sahn, chapter 11, in this volume).

Weakened Ecosystem Services Underlie Food Insecurity

Low per capita agricultural productivity is a persistent challenge to livelihoods in Sub-Saharan Africa. Yields and yield advances are significantly lower for Sub-Saharan Africa than for other regions of the world (World Bank 2009). Population in the region is growing at a rate of 2.2 percent per year (UNFPA 2009), whereas agricultural productivity has risen at a rate of only 1.3 percent per year since 1980 (Coelli and Rao 2005). Although average yields are still rising, there is wide variation between fields, with the poorest farmers often seeing the least improvement, if not declines. This situation is related to governments' perennially low investment in agriculture, but the weakening of ecosystem services also plays an important role.

Given the inheritance system in much of Africa whereby family land is divided among sons, a larger population means that each successive generation has less land to till on average. There has been a rapid decrease in mean farm size; for example, from 1960 to 2000, average landholdings in Kenya and Ethiopia shrank 50 percent (Jayne et al. 2003). Average landholdings in other Sub-Saharan African countries declined 25–45 percent in the same time period (Figure 7.2). The increased pressure on land has changed farming practices, often resulting in lower productivity. Farmers are more likely to continuously crop their land for decades

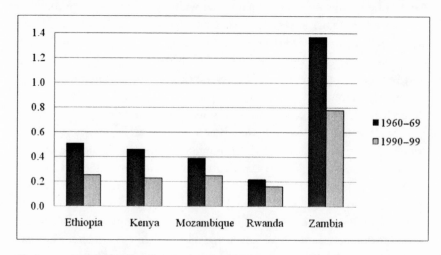

Figure 7.2   Average landholding size in selected African countries, 1960–69 and 1990–99
SOURCE: Data from Jayne et al. 2003.

(Liu et al. 2007), unable to let it lie fallow because of the ever-pressing need for food and income. Low crop diversity worsens the situation because continued dependence on one or two crops mines the same nutrients from the soil year after year. The process can be very rapid: a research group in Kenya found that both soil nitrogen and soil organic carbon declined 37–73 percent in the first four years of cultivation (Solomon et al. 2007).

Nutrient mining in Sub-Saharan Africa, exacerbated by continuous cropping and low diversity, causes declines in crop productivity (Sanchez 2002). Experimental data from the highlands of Kenya (Ngoze et al. 2008) illustrate yield declines in relation to number of years of continuous cropping: there, soils lost more than half of their productivity after 35 years of continuous cultivation. When asked why they would need to take action to improve productivity, farmers in a similar situation in Zambia commonly responded, "The soils are tired" (Gladwin et al. 2002, 125). Furthermore, soil nutrients are important not only for yields, but also for the mineral content of foods. The occurrence of zinc, iodine, and selenium deficiencies in humans is geographically correlated with respective soil deficiencies (Graham et al. 2007; Hartikainen 2005).

Soil erosion contributes to productivity losses through loss of nutrients as well as the physical base for cultivation. Severe dry and rainy seasons in much of Africa make bare, exposed soil extremely vulnerable to wind and water erosion. Although the exact estimates are debatable, erosion may be reducing productivity across Sub-Saharan Africa by 0.5 percent a year (Lal 1995).

The result is that steady soil depletion, shown as yearly negative nutrient balances, is occurring in all African countries except Libya, Mauritius, and Reunion (Figure 7.3; Henao and Baanante 2001). African soils are ancient and weathered to begin with; erosion, increasingly intensive cultivation, and practices such as low use of fertilizer and few organic amendments degrade them further. The rate of nutrient loss in Sub-Saharan Africa is five times higher than the average rate of replacement by fertilizers (World Bank 2007b). Valuing nutrients at the price of fertilizer, nutrient depletion is estimated to cost 7 percent of agricultural GDP in the region (Drechsel, Kunze, and Penning de Vries 2001).

Soil lost from fields often ends up as siltation in watersheds, reducing water quality (Scherr and Yadav 1996), which is particularly problematic for Sub-Saharan Africa, where lack of adequate water is a major constraint to yields as well as human health. Most farms there rely on rainfall, with only 4 percent of agricultural land irrigated (Gruhn, Goletti, and Yudelman 2000). Although low water use limits annual yield potential, expansion of irrigation may be limited since the available water supply for many parts of Sub-Saharan Africa is projected to decrease by up to 10 percent by the end of the century because of climate change (de Wit and Stankiewicz 2006). Moreover, irrigation must be taken up with care, because overirrigation can cause waterlogging and salinization, reducing arable

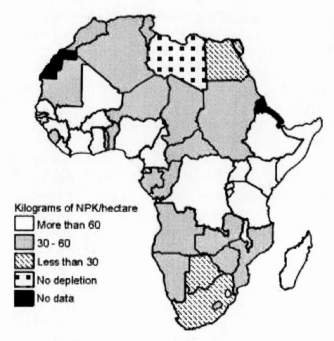

Figure 7.3   Average annual nutrient depletion in Africa, 1993–95
NOTE: NPK = nitrogen, phosphorus, and potassium.
SOURCE: Henao and Baanante 2001, Figure 1.

land. It is extremely difficult to restore saline soils. Salinity affects nearly 3 percent of arable land in Africa as a whole and much more in certain regions, such as in Kenya, where nearly 15 percent of arable land is saline (UNEP 2007; Mashali et al. 2005).

Changing food preferences in Africa, especially in urban areas, are also implicated in water and land scarcity. The demand for animal source foods is increasing more rapidly than the demand for grain in Africa (FAO 2006a)—a situation that will greatly increase water requirements. Beef production, for example, requires 15–35 times more water than wheat or sorghum cultivation (Clay 2004). In addition, increased livestock grazing is likely to result in further land degradation. Most of the human-induced soil degradation in Africa has resulted from overgrazing (Pinstrup-Andersen and Pandya-Lorch 1994).

In all, 5 to 10 million hectares are lost annually to severe degradation, including desertification, with the result that 1.4–2.8 percent of total cropland, pasture, and forest may be lost between 2000 and 2020 (Scherr and Yadav 2001). In Sub-Saharan Africa, it is estimated that 60 million people will be forced to migrate from desertified areas by 2020 (UNCCD 2004). This migration would increase pressure on arable land and cities, further straining the ecosystem services that

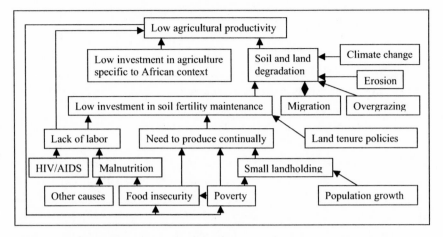

Figure 7.4   A causal map of low agricultural productivity in Sub-Saharan Africa

are the foundation for food security. See Figure 7.4 for a visual representation summarizing the causes of low agricultural productivity in Sub-Saharan Africa.

Environmental degradation is associated with food insecurity and malnutrition. In West Africa, child under-five mortality is highest in areas of high soil degradation (UNEP/GRID-Arendal 1998). Ecosystem type is associated with infant mortality rate: drylands, which provide the most limited ecosystem services in terms of soil fertility and water availability, have the highest rates of infant mortality (Millennium Ecosystem Assessment 2005a). Maps of rainfall and poverty in Kenya reveal that those living in the driest areas tend to have higher poverty rates and poorer-quality housing than those in areas that receive more rainfall (WRI et al. 2007); accepting poorer-quality housing rather than less food when resources are limited is a typical coping strategy. Another study in central Kenya corroborates these trends: farms with "low" and "medium" soil natural resources were found to yield roughly half the farm income of farms with "high" soil natural resources (Shepherd and Soule 1998). Although these relationships lack a clear causal direction or pathway, even where poverty and food insecurity push people to live on poor-quality land, lack of ecosystem services is likely to exacerbate their vulnerability.

Nutrition and the Environment: Components of Food Security

Solutions to food insecurity clearly need to take into account the malnutrition situation and its environmental underpinnings in Sub-Saharan Africa. Nutritious diets and environmental sustainability are often thought of as separate goals apart from food security, but they are undeniably a part of food security itself.

Many definitions of food security have been used, reflecting the evolution of the term and varying concepts of what it means (Pinstrup-Andersen and Herforth 2008; Pelletier, Olson, and Frongillo 2006; Maxwell and Frankenberger 1992). The United Nations definition is used here because it is the most widely used internationally and the one to which 182 countries agreed at the 1996 World Food Summit.

Nutritious Diets Are Inherent in Food Security

The UN food security definition makes clear that access to a nutritious diet is inherent in food security: "Food security exists when all people, at all times, have physical and economic access to sufficient, safe, and nutritious food to meet their dietary needs and food preferences for a healthy and active life" (FAO 1996b). Nutritional quality, as well as caloric adequacy, is essential; sufficient calories without the needed balance of macro- and micronutrients would make a "healthy and active life" impossible.

The definition is also unambiguous that nutritional needs should be met by *food*; consuming an all-maize or all-rice diet and staving off micronutrient deficiencies with vitamin supplements does not constitute food security. Rather, continuous access to a diverse diet is the defining characteristic of food security.

The inclusion of food preferences in the definition of food security is also important. People must be able to obtain foods that do not violate personal ethics, religious norms, or cultural traditions—a set of conditions generalized as "food preferences." Indigenous and traditional crops and foods, which are often important culturally, nutritionally, and ecologically, seldom receive attention in agricultural development projects, which tend to focus on the same common commodity crops around the world.

Ecosystem Services Are Necessary for Food Security

The 1996 World Food Summit consensus also emphasized the importance of environmental integrity and sustainable development in achieving food security. Out of seven commitments that 182 heads of state and government representatives made at the summit, two deal with sustainable agriculture. One states:

> We will pursue participatory and sustainable food, agriculture, fisheries, forestry and rural development policies and practices . . . which are essential to adequate and reliable food supplies at the household, national, regional and global levels, and combat pests, drought and desertification, considering the multifunctional character of agriculture (FAO 1996b).

The World Food Summit Plan of Action then details the steps needed to implement this goal (FAO 1996b). The leaders who signed the Declaration on World

Food Security thus affirmed that ecosystem services are directly related to food security and health, beyond theoretical considerations or far-off effects on future generations. Although the terms "environment" and "sustainability" were not included in the wording of the food security definition itself, the World Food Summit Declaration and Plan of Action clearly recognize the fundamental importance of ecosystem services to food security.

The Framing of Food Security: Mere Caloric Adequacy

Despite the multifaceted definition of food security, too often "food security" is used synonymously with "caloric adequacy"—a misconception strengthened by the fact that the only measurement of food security used around the world continues to be national-level per capita calorie availability (FAO 2003a).[3] That measure was developed when protein-energy malnutrition was the main identified nutrition problem, just as the Green Revolution was providing a solution (Pinstrup-Andersen and Herforth 2008). Considering that the UN food security definition now clearly includes the need for access to a diverse diet that meets food preferences, as well as the directive to produce food sustainably, it is striking that the global measurement of food security has not moved beyond the concept of caloric adequacy.

Measuring food security in terms of per capita calorie availability frames the food security problem as inadequate calories and steers development thinking toward a solution that involves increasing calories, while neglecting other facets of meeting nutritional needs. This approach to the problem has pushed research and policy agendas heavily toward staple crops; the vast majority of agricultural research focuses on starches at the centers of the Consultative Group on International Agricultural Research (CGIAR) and national agricultural research centers. Discourse about food security routinely implies increased production or provision of staples, sometimes including oil and pulses in addition to grains. This narrow focus on calories results in an incomplete solution to the problem of food insecurity, bypassing solutions that might better increase access to a diverse diet.

In addition to overlooking the need for dietary diversity, the current measurement of food security as per capita calorie availability fails to generate political priority for environmental sustainability of food production. It sets a paradigm of planting starch crops that generate the maximum food calories per unit of land, although cultivating a diversity of crops has greater possibilities for protecting ecosystem services. Moreover, the calculus of available food made by the FAO counts only well-known commodities, leaving out traditional crops and wild foods entirely. If traditional and wild foods are not recognized as contributing to food security at local levels, there is little political incentive to protect wild areas or agroforestry systems to ensure food security. Plans for achieving food security typically do not consider ecosystem services, such as direct food provisioning through wild foods, or supporting services of pollinators.

Reframing the Food Security Agenda: Nutrition and the Environment as Fundamental

Ending food insecurity, associated with poverty, malnutrition, and poor agricultural productivity, requires a reorientation of thinking about the foundation of food security. Past agricultural projects have not reduced overall food insecurity in Sub-Saharan Africa for many reasons, including many that fall outside the realm of agriculture, such as wars, governance problems, and natural disasters. But part of the reason that food security has not improved—and in fact has worsened in recent decades—is that too many agricultural policies and programs function within a conventional paradigm of staple and export crops, as if the identity of crop grown matters little as long as it provides calories or can be sold. This paradigm is based on a faulty understanding of food security as merely adequate calorie availability, an underestimation of the barriers to gaining access to diverse diets, and a lack of connection of production systems to ecosystems.

For household nutrition, local and regional availability of diverse diets, and maintenance of ecosystem services, it matters not only how much is grown, but also what is grown and how. Policies and programs aimed at reducing food insecurity in Sub-Saharan Africa need to treat nutrition and the environment as fundamental to food security—not just as ideals, but as practical drivers toward the goals of improved productivity, livelihoods, and food security toward which every nation strives.

The Case for Agricultural Diversity for Food Security: A Means to Improving Nutrition and the Environment

The Nutrition Side: Agricultural Diversity Is Needed for Access to Diverse Diets

The poor are often unable to afford and obtain a sufficiently varied diet to meet their nutritional, particularly micronutrient, needs. In Sub-Saharan Africa, 69 percent of calories come from cereals, roots, and tubers (FAO 2000). A diet so high in starches is an impediment to meeting nutritional needs. Interventions to address nutrition often involve micronutrient supplementation, fortification, and more recently biofortification. These solutions are important and likely to lead to rapid reductions in malnutrition-related mortality. They do not, however, address the basic and fundamental problem of inadequate access to a varied diet.

As discussed, dietary diversity is crucial for genuine food security, which encompasses nutritional quality and food preferences. Because of its empirical association with caloric and nutrient adequacy and, in turn, positive child growth and nutritional status (Ruel 2003), dietary diversity has itself been proposed as a measure of household food security (Hoddinott and Yohannes 2002; FAO 2007b). Dietary diversity is generally quite low in Sub-Saharan Africa. In a study using household-level data from 12 countries in Sub-Saharan Africa, 8–63 percent of households were found to consume diets low in diversity—that is, they consumed fewer than four out of seven food groups[4] (Smith, Alderman, and Aduayom 2006).

Dietary diversity usually increases with income; the ability to purchase food also helps avert seasonal variation in food availability on farms (Torlesse, Kiess, and Bloem 2003). Accordingly, the straightforward policy solution to food insecurity would be to improve incomes through some combination of national economic growth, targeted income generation for the poor, and possibly reduced prices for essential goods, including staple grains. Many staple and export crop–oriented agricultural programs aim to increase farmers' household income under the assumption that the household could then more easily purchase foods to make up a diverse diet. Income growth is important but not sufficient, however, to rid Sub-Saharan Africa of food insecurity.

Most immediately, income increases will not achieve food security for Africa because in many parts of Africa, the components of a diverse diet are simply not available. Figure 7.5 shows that per capita availability[5] of nonstarch commodities is too low to meet human needs. Pulses are the protein source (complementary with grains) most accessible to the majority of poor households in Sub-Saharan Africa. Only 26 grams of pulses are available per capita per day, however, providing only about 10–15 percent of the daily adult protein requirement.[6] Slightly more than 200 grams of fruits and vegetables are available, about half the World Health Organization minimum requirement of 400 grams (WHO/FAO 2003). Inadequate supply pushes up the prices of these dietary components and contributes to continued food insecurity. Although it appears that there are enough starchy roots and cereals per capita,[7] unequal distribution means that adequate amounts are often inaccessible to the poor. With current per capita availability of other dietary components dramatically *below* human needs, there is little hope that the poorest can get access to sufficient quantities of nonstaples. It has been observed before that insufficient local food availability limits household purchases of food (Pinstrup-Andersen 1985).

Figure 7.6 shows the quantities of fruits, vegetables, pulses, cereals, and starchy roots available as food in Sub-Saharan Africa from 1987 to 2003 (FAO 2009a). Although quantities of cereals and starchy roots have increased over the years,

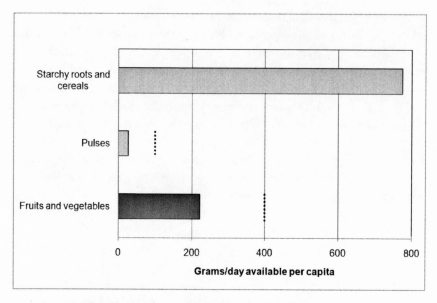

Figure 7.5   Per capita food availability in Sub-Saharan Africa, 2003
NOTE: Dotted lines represent approximate quantities that would fulfill dietary needs for pulses and fruits and vegetables under a scenario of perfect distribution. These quantities are based on WHO/FAO guidelines for fruits and vegetables and on the adult protein requirement for pulses (accounting for protein intake from cereals and assuming low intake of animal-source foods).
SOURCE: Author, based on data from FAO 2009a.

quantities of fruits and vegetables have risen at a more modest rate, and quantities of pulses have remained very low. Increases in starches have been important, but there has been relatively little policy attention to increasing the availability of other dietary components. This oversight has limited opportunities to reduce prices of nonstaples, which would make them more accessible to the poor.

Compounding the insufficient availability of nonstaples is lack of access to markets. Sub-Saharan Africa has the highest proportion of people with poor access to markets in the world. Only 20 percent of the rural population is able to reach a viable market in less than two hours, and nearly 35 percent must travel five hours or more (World Bank 2007b). Inadequate and poorly maintained roads and cold chains make it difficult to transport food, particularly perishable food, from areas of higher to lower availability. This lack of infrastructure, the inadequate availability of markets, and the time and cost involved in reaching them together create a barrier to obtaining diverse diets, with the result that home production or wild collection may be among the few ways to get consistent access to a diverse diet.

Another dimension of lack of access to food involves how income is used within a household. Assumptions about perfect intrahousehold allocation of resources that achieves maximum food security for all household members generally do

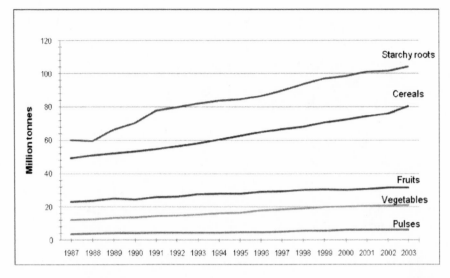

Figure 7.6   Food quantities in Sub-Saharan Africa, 1987–2003
SOURCE: Author, based on data from FAO 2009a.

not bear out. Several factors affect how income is spent, including the form of the income, whether it comes regularly or in sporadic large payments, and who controls it (Pinstrup-Andersen 2006). Women's control of income in particular tends to have a more positive effect on household and child nutrition than men's control of the same income (Smith et al. 2003; Nyariki, Wiggins, and Imungi 2004). Often, the crops controlled by women are horticultural.

Improved national and household income needs to be combined with crop diversification in Sub-Saharan Africa to ensure food security. There is strong evidence that households with home gardens consume more fruits and vegetables than those without home gardens (Bushamuka et al. 2005; Chakravarty 2000; Faber, Smuts, and Benade 1999; Faber et al. 2001; HKI 2003; Maxwell, Levin, and Csete 1998; Talukder et al. 2000). Of course, these households continue to consume staple crops as well, so it is likely that the added produce increases their dietary diversity. In Kenya and Tanzania, a longitudinal study of smallholder, semi-subsistence farmers found that the number of crops cultivated was strongly associated with dietary diversity (Herforth 2010).

This is not to say that smallholder production should be subsistence oriented. On the contrary, nonstaple crops offer significant opportunities for value addition, and farmers may be most likely to diversify production if they can market their produce for good returns. Crop diversification can affect dietary diversity by increasing income security (reducing farmers' risk in depending on only one or a few key crops) and by increasing harvests of minor crops, which women typically

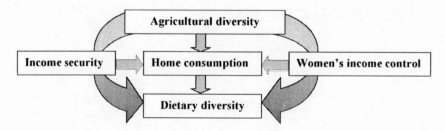

Figure 7.7   Pathways from agricultural diversity to dietary diversity
SOURCE: Author.

sell (Figure 7.7). These nonstaple crops are often most suitable for value addition, such as bundling, drying, and specialized marketing.

The Environmental Side:
Maintenance of Ecosystem Services Depends on Diversity

Crop diversity is also key to maintaining and restoring ecosystem services for food production. An increase in fertilizer use is sometimes suggested as the best solution to declining crop productivity, because it would increase yields and reduce land degradation and deforestation. Although increased fertilizer use would indeed be helpful, as in the case of supplementation for improved human nutrition, it cannot completely replace the need for diversity, for several reasons.

First, the poor in Africa often cannot easily get access to fertilizers because of poverty combined with the high expense of fertilizer in Sub-Saharan Africa (Sanchez 2002), and remoteness from markets. As a result, fertilizer use in Africa is low. Fertilizer subsidies and government programs can solve this problem to some degree, but they require good infrastructure to transport the fertilizer, as well as farmer trust. Manure can also be purchased, but the price for manure, as for chemical fertilizer, is prohibitive for many.[8]

Realistically, rehabilitating soils in Sub-Saharan Africa may depend on crop diversification and agronomic practices made possible by diversification, such as crop rotation and alley cropping. Legumes are often more easily accessible than fertilizers in rural Sub-Saharan Africa, and their production improves soil nitrogen, generally the most limiting nutrient in the region (Mafongaya et al. 2006; Sanchez 2002). In Malawi, farmers unable to afford fertilizers or wary of government promises were more willing to plant legumes to increase soil fertility (and household food security) than to depend on temporary government fertilizer subsidies (Bezner Kerr et al. 2007; Msachi, Dakishoni and Bezner Kerr 2009).

Second, intercropping can simultaneously reduce costs and increase productivity, which could reduce poverty and the desperation that drives natural resource degradation. Grain crops intercropped with beans often yield better than cereals alone: gains in cereal yields as high as 50–250 percent have been reported from intercropping with legumes in Malawi (Mafongaya et al. 2006). An average of 60 percent gains in maize yields, plus additional cowpea yield, were shown in a three-year maize-cowpea intercropping trial in Zimbabwe (Lough et al., as reported in Graham et al. 2007). Case studies elsewhere demonstrated that rice-legume crop rotation reduced inorganic fertilizer use by 30 percent (Pingali and Rosegrant 1994), and using legumes as green manure saved farmers 22 percent on production costs, in addition to increasing yields almost threefold (Altieri, Rosset, and Thrupp 2001). Legumes can also significantly increase vegetable yield (Mafonyaga et al. 2006), possibly through their effects on soil fertility or other effects of diversity such as soil biota or pest biocontrol. In a review of 286 interventions in 57 countries using a set of resource-conserving agricultural practices including multicropping, the overwhelming majority showed increased yield, while also adding to ecosystem services through water use efficiency and carbon sequestration (Pretty et al. 2006).

Third, there is evidence that fertilizers alone cannot completely maintain soil quality even if regularly applied. A study in Kenya found that despite complete inorganic fertilization,[9] productivity in soils that had been continuously cultivated for 35 years or more was only one third that of newly converted soils and could be restored only with the addition of soil organic matter (Kimetu et al. 2008).[10] Restoring soil organic carbon specifically, which cannot come from fertilizer alone but involves agronomic practices, has been found to be necessary to improve yields (Lal 2007). Swift et al. (1994) present strong evidence that applying mixtures of organic and inorganic fertilizers often results in higher productivity than either alone. Yet in another study, yield was shown to decline over time with continuous cropping of rice, even given adequate application of both soil organic matter and fertilizer, because of subtle changes in soil chemistry that prevented plants from using nutrients efficiently (Cassman 1999). Despite management of soils with fertilizers and other soil amendments, multicropping or fallow periods may be necessary to maintain productivity of soils.

Fourth, unlike use of fertilizers, agricultural diversification may encourage soil biodiversity. Crop species diversity is associated with greater soil diversity, including microbes and fauna (Brussaard, de Ruiter, and Brown 2007). Some evidence indicates that greater soil biodiversity may increase resistance against plant diseases and other stresses. In conditions of limited water and nutrient availability, soil biodiversity is associated with more efficient water and nutrient use and greater crop productivity (Brussaard, de Ruiter, and Brown 2007).

Finally, agricultural diversity, like dietary diversity, is likely to provide "insurance" against imbalances that lead to problems. In a paper reviewing the ecosystem functions of a variety of organisms in agricultural landscapes, Swift et al. (2004,

126–27) conclude, "The simplest rule for managing landscapes is . . . to say that if the vegetation is diverse then the associated diversity and functions will be taken care of." The complexity of the relationships between environment and productivity—like those between diet and health—means that diversity may provide the greatest resilience and security for yields, with the fewest unintended consequences.

Worth noting is that although legumes stand out for increasing soil fertility and yields when they are used in crop rotations, in intercropping, or as soil amendments, legumes cannot be the only path to diversification. Gains from legumes are not automatic and require a base amount of soil fertility (phosphorus in particular) to effectively fix nitrogen. In addition, legumes are often susceptible to disease, which in part reflects the scant attention they have received in agricultural research and development over recent decades.

Beside legumes, mixed livestock-cropping systems foster nutrient cycling and productivity, as crop residues feed livestock and livestock wastes improve soil quality. Adding livestock to smallholder farms can have positive impacts on dietary diversity and nutrition as well.

Planting nonleguminous herbs can also increase productivity, either through soil fertility or pest resistance, the effects of which are often difficult to distinguish in field settings (Box 7.1). Farmers in Uganda observed that soil fertility and nematode resistance increased when they planted amaranth in their tomato fields (Hart 2005). Marigolds, onion, and garlic can function as pest deterrents when planted around vegetable fields. Because pests can remain dormant in the soil through low seasons, seasonal crop rotation is sometimes the only way to control pests.[11] Furthermore, diverse plant species provide habitat to many insect species, increasing the potential for biocontrol of pests and creating safe havens for pollinators. Chapter 6 in this volume provides more in-depth information on inter- and intra-species diversity and pest control.

Within-Crop Diversity Furthers Food Security

Within-crop diversity (many varieties of the same crop) is arguably as important to food security as between-crop diversity, because it allows a species to survive in varied environments, owing to the ecosystem service of genetic diversity. Low genetic diversity in farmers' fields presents the risk of catastrophic crop loss; it also lessens the chance of future productivity if crop varieties cannot be found to overcome pests or other stresses wrought by climate change. Following the example of Nikolai Vavilov, who in the first part of the 20th century traveled the world collecting seeds and documenting crop diversity to quell famine,[12] plant-breeding authorities continue to recognize that "plant genetic resources represent both the basis for agricultural development and a reservoir of genetic adaptability that acts as a buffer against environmental change. The erosion of these resources threatens world food security" (Esquinas-Alcazar 1993, 33). The effect of past and present genetic erosion on agriculture's ability to weather unpredictable climate change in the future remains uncertain.

Box 7.1—Case study: A soil-restoring plant with multiple functions

Tithonia diversifolia (a member of the Asteraceae/sunflower family) is a multifunctional plant that improves health and ecosystem services in unexpected ways. Experimental results from Kenya show that supplementing soil with *Tithonia*[13] increased phosphorus uptake and improved yields of maize (Ikerra, Semu, and Mrema 2006; Kimetu et al. 2008). In that experiment, *Tithonia* was used as a green manure to amend soils at different stages of continuous cultivation. *Tithonia* had its greatest effect on land that that had been converted to agriculture 80–100 years earlier, returning yields to levels seen in newly converted land. *Tithonia*, but not other treatments (manure, sawdust, biochar), also significantly increased the calcium, potassium, and magnesium content of maize grains (Kimetu et al. 2008).

Tithonia diversifolia is also used traditionally against parasites and diarrhea in Congo and Rwanda and has been shown to have antimalarial properties (Elufioye and Agbedahunsi 2004; Tona et al. 1998; Cos et al. 2002). Farmers who cultivate the plant around their fields thus may use it as medicine as well as a soil amendment for increased food security. This example shows how conserving biodiversity often aligns with agricultural gains as well as indigenous knowledge and health systems, which can be vital, especially in places where modern health services are not readily accessible.

Research on the yield effect of variety mixtures is promising, indicating gains from within-crop diversity in the field. In a review of the effect of variety mixtures versus single-variety cultivation, Finckh et al. (2000, 813) conclude that "mixtures generally stabilize yields and yield losses due to disease; abiotic stresses are also better buffered than in pure stands." Another study showed that rice fields planted with a variety mixture yielded more than single-variety fields (Zhu et al. 2000). Farmers in the Central African highlands plant bean variety and species mixtures to tailor their crops to specific growing conditions (Trutmann, Voss, and Fairhead 1993). Sociocultural reasons may also result in continued cultivation of several varieties; the pattern of maize diversity in Mexico differs significantly between ethnic groups beyond what would be expected from varying agroecosystems (Brush and Perales 2007), indicating that varietal diversity plays a role in satisfying food preferences.

Environmental and genetic diversity also increase nutritional variation between crop varieties, providing a larger smorgasbord from which to meet dietary needs. Recent research has uncovered as much as 33-fold differences in micronutrients and known health-promoting phytochemicals between varieties of maize, wheat, onions, bananas and apples (Harjes et al. 2008; Adom, Sorrells, and Liu 2005; Yang et al. 2004; Englberger et al. 2003; Liu, Eberhardt, and Lee 2001). Rather than a cue to breed lines with the highest content of each known health-promoting compound, the evident diversity between varieties is a reason to grow and consume many different varieties, to ensure intakes of known and unknown health-promoting components. Science will surely identify additional benefits in years to come from as yet undiscovered phytonutrients. The only way to capture their benefits now is to rely on diversity.

Biodiversity and Ecosystems at Large Support Food Security

Beyond agriculture, environmental integrity also promotes food security by protecting wild foods and gathering places. The Millennium Ecosystem Assessment (2005a) highlights the role of the environment in providing cultural services for human well-being, including sense of place, spirituality, and cultural heritage. These cultural services certainly include food, which is central to cultural and often personal identity. The ability to find or produce culturally important foods is an integral dimension of food security, often related to dietary quality as well as food preferences. This characteristic holds for all societies but resonates most clearly in the case of indigenous peoples (Lambden, Receveur, and Kuhnlein 2007). The world is replete with stories of indigenous groups for whom environmental degradation, resulting in acculturation to mainstream culture and foods, results in food insecurity and poor health (Herforth 2009; Johns and Eyzaguirre 2006; Johns and Sthapit 2004). Johns and Sthapit (2004, 145) note that "changes in land use, including disturbance, deforestation, and appropriation of natural areas, diminish opportunities for gathering and hunting the essential wild components of many traditional food systems." Wild foods, and supporting the environment needed to obtain them, often make significant contributions to dietary quality (Roche et al. 2007; Kuhnlein and Receveur 2007; Ogle, Hung, and Tuyet 2001; Grivetti and Ogle 2000; Burlingame 2000). The Millennium Ecosystem Assessment (2005b, 31) quotes a respondent of the AmaXhosa people in South Africa, "I am entirely dependent on the environment. Everything that I need comes from this environment . . . our health depends entirely on these sites." If their environment were destroyed "it means that our culture is dead." Achieving food security for *all* people involves protecting the foodsheds of indigenous peoples.

Policy Options

Policies that achieve genuine food security will be based on the understanding that (1) by definition, food security includes nutritional quality and the support of ecosystem services, and (2) the potential for food security in Sub-Saharan Africa is limited without agricultural diversification and maintenance of biodiversity. Respectively, two important policy options include the use of indicators of food security that reflect not only per capita calorie availability, but also nutrition and the environment, and policies and programs to support agricultural diversity and biodiversity.

Indicators to Guide Appropriate Actions toward Food Security

According to the agreement signed at the World Food Summit in 1996, every government agrees in principle that nutrition and ecological sustainability are important to food security. Despite this agreement, progress toward food security in Sub-Saharan Africa has been slight, and malnutrition and environmental degradation have worsened.

Part of the problem may be that the right data for guiding appropriate actions for achieving food security are not collected. Instead, data on grain yields and per capita calorie availability guide policy decisions. If the global community is to take seriously the understanding that food security means access to foods for a healthy and active life, indicators of food insecurity must account for more than calories. Collecting information on the types of foods available and accessible, and the impact of producing and transporting them on ecosystem services, may guide food security policies in a different direction than at present. Such indicators are needed to hold governments accountable for their agreements on food security and sustainability.

AVAILABLE FOOD DIVERSITY PER CAPITA

For genuine food security, it is important to ensure—and thus to measure—available food diversity per capita. This indicator would reveal insufficient per capita availability of fruits, vegetables, and legumes (as shown in Figure 7.5) within the context of food security decision making. It could affect policies such as subsidies, trade agreements, and direct extension to farmers to help increase the supply of relatively unavailable dietary components. Combined with systematically collected productivity data for all functional classes of food crops, this indicator would also help to spur research and development to develop more disease-resistant, drought-resistant, productive varieties of fruits, vegetables, and legumes, and not just cereals. If successful, production of those foods would go up and prices down, making diverse diets more universally available and accessible.

ACCESSIBILITY OF DIVERSE DIETS

Accessibility of diverse diets is also an important indicator to add to routine monitoring of food security. Household surveys that measure dietary diversity or household consumption estimate the accessibility of diverse diets based on household behavior, but they are rarely done at a national level. Smith, Alderman, and Aduayom (2006) argue for estimating food security using household measures of both energy insufficiency and dietary diversity; others have developed a validated household dietary diversity score (Swindale and Bilinsky 2006). It is also important to be able to estimate accessibility of diverse diets without relying on household data, however, because interviewing households is too costly and time-consuming for continuous monitoring. Estimates could be made fairly easily using data that most ministries of agriculture already collect: local availability and price data for a variety of foods. By compiling such data into the main dietary components (starches, legumes, fruits, vegetables, animal-source foods), officials could regularly make a supply-side estimate of accessibility of diverse diets. This routine monitoring of accessibility of diverse diets could create policy incentives to increase production or consumption of relatively inaccessible food groups.

ECOSYSTEM SERVICE IMPACTS OF PRODUCTION SYSTEMS

Indicators of the impacts of production systems on ecosystem services would allow governments to prioritize, through incentives or other policy instruments, those systems that best maintain ecosystem services and to realize benefits to food security from doing so. Many of these indicators are not yet well developed enough to use for policy decisions, so research is needed to develop simple, reliable indicators for estimating production impact on ecosystem services.

"Crop per drop"—yield obtained per amount of water used—is one such indicator. Soil nutrient costs per hectare (in the absence of fertilization) is another useful ecological indicator that could guide crop choices by indicating soil productivity gains or losses from production of specific crops, individually and in combination. Food miles also has been suggested as an indicator of fossil-fuel use linked to climate change, although total fossil-fuel use in production, not just that linked to transportation, is a better indicator (Pretty et al. 2005; Singer and Mason 2006). These indicators would be useful for generating policies that factor in externalities to bring food production more in line with conservation of ecosystem services.

Beyond tracking the productivity of individual crops, it would be useful to understand their productivity when planted together, making more regular use of an indicator of combined yield per hectare or land equivalent ratios (LERs). Such an approach is important in Sub-Saharan Africa, where many smallholder farmers grow complex polycrops to reduce risk and maximize use of land, nutrients, and water (Graham et al. 2007). More research to understand the interactions between crops and their effects on productivity can help extension efforts in Africa promote the most practical, productive cropping practices. Research can also endorse the notion that polycropping and crop rotation are rational and forward-looking means of generating food security rather than undesirable coping strategies.

Policies to Support Agricultural Diversity

Small farmers with few resources cannot be held individually accountable for producing a greater diversity of foods when it is costly to do so; it is the responsibility of governments concerned with food insecurity to create policies that support agricultural diversity and eliminate policies that create barriers to it. The main priorities for such policies are described here.

POLICIES TO ENABLE DIVERSE PRODUCTION SYSTEMS

Governments, multilateral institutions, and nongovernmental organizations (NGOs) all have a role in generating food security projects that enable diverse production systems. Agricultural program priorities and extension staff at least should not actively discourage farmers from growing a variety of foods, nor in most cases should farmers be given advice and incentives to convert the majority of their cropland into single staple crops. Efforts to incorporate traditional crops and local varieties into standard agricultural and health extension training is one way to recognize and promote traditional systems important to food security, as is being done in Kenya (Box 7.2). More research is needed on the potential agronomic and nutritional gains from planting variety mixtures within the same crop, but given the available positive evidence, policies to make planting variety mixtures as easy as monocropping may be the step most needed now. Such policies could include legalizing the sale of mixed seed or funding breeding programs to maximize yield from variety mixtures (Finckh 2008).

Box 7.2—Agricultural policy and food security case studies

Rwanda
The Government of Rwanda supports five main crops: rice, maize, potatoes, soybeans, and beans, as well as tea and coffee for export. Government support promotes regionalized production of crops, with the result that individual farmers produce fewer crops in favor of the one that the government supports in their region. The government website states, "A limited set of crops has had to be identified, with support from research and extension, as a tool with which to design

public actions in support of the agricultural sector. The crops ear-marked are those actually, or potentially competitive, so that their production maximizes household incomes" (Government of Rwanda, Ministry of Agriculture and Animal Resources 2008).

This policy approach reflects a strategy to exploit agriculture as an engine of national economic growth, and to increase individual household income for farmers. Nutrition and the environment, however, though essential for food security, are not at the heart of this policy. A narrow focus on a few crops ignores evidence that increased national or household incomes do not automatically improve household food security; further, it has an inherent male bias since in Africa men usually control commodity crops for sale. Women control minor crops, which are directly important for household dietary diversity, and can earn income from them, which often translates into family well-being. If the policy increases available calories per capita, Rwanda may well succeed at reducing "food insecurity" as currently measured—but it is less certain that it will attain nutritious food to meet dietary needs and food preferences for all people.

Kenya

The National Museums of Kenya has worked with Bioversity International (a CGIAR agency) and local NGOs for the past several years to promote production and consumption of traditional African leafy vegetables (Irungu 2007). Since the onset of the colonial period, these vegetables, such as amaranth, nightshade, and *Cleome* sp., have been supplanted by less nutritious, more resource-intensive crops such as cabbage. These traditional vegetables are now seeing a resurgence, however, as agricultural training staff connect farmers to reliable seed sources and markets. Because the traditional vegetables are adapted specifically to the agro-ecosystem, farmers can grow them using fewer fertilizer, water, and pesticide inputs than they can growing staples and exotic cash crops. Some evidence even suggests that these vegetables enrich the soil, making successive crops more productive (Hart 2005). For consumers, these traditional vegetables are a way to connect with traditional food culture that has been undermined during recent East African history. Furthermore the nutritional content of the vegetables is a selling point among urban consumers increasingly at risk of overweight, heart disease, and diabetes. Traditional vegetables are also useful for households affected by HIV because of their relatively low labor requirements and high micronutrient content.

The Kenyan Ministry of Agriculture is now promoting traditional vegetables alongside the major commodities and cash crops that have been its historical focus. A new national food and nutrition policy, currently being reviewed, is slated to include extension agent training and recommendations specific to traditional leafy vegetables. The government is also considering adding an indicator of dietary diversity as a standard item in its national surveys (P. Maundu, pers. comm.). These policy changes take an updated view of food security and hold great promise for improved nutrition and environmental sustainability in Kenya.

CONSERVATION OF CROP VARIETAL DIVERSITY

Conserving genetic diversity within crops is essential to the goal of supporting agricultural diversity. Genebanks serve an essential function of ex situ crop variety preservation, so that varieties can be given out, regenerated, and used in breeding new varieties. In situ conservation is also important because it allows continuous adaptation of crops to new environmental surroundings. Conservation strategies agreed upon in the 2001 International Treaty on Plant Genetic Resources for Food and Agriculture[14] should be incorporated into overall food security policies.

RESEARCH TO IMPROVE PRODUCTIVITY OF
VEGETABLES, LEGUMES, AND FRUITS

As shown in Figure 7.6, the availability of fruits, vegetables, and legumes has barely changed from 20 years ago, while that of starches has increased. Increased investment in research and development of these so-called minor crops is one strategy to make them more competitive and easier to grow, so they are more attractive and rewarding for farmers. Improving farmers' access to seeds will also be important to encourage production of these crops.

BETTER INFRASTRUCTURE TO ENABLE PROFIT
FROM MORE PERISHABLE FOODS

Producing cereals can be a practical choice for farmers with limited market access because cereals can be stored for longer periods than fresh produce. In some cases, farmers may be reluctant to produce crops other than cereals because without access to markets, they would be unable to sell the excess perishable crops. One case in northwestern Bangladesh showed that farmers who had been producing rice as a monocrop because of the dependable prices began producing fruits and vegetables as soon as a new bridge was built that would ensure rapid transport of these foods to Dhaka (Mirle 2006). A persistent priority in improved food security is improving infrastructure and providing better access to markets.

RESEARCH AND PROGRAMS TO BETTER USE UNDERUTILIZED CROPS

One of the main reasons many well-adapted crop varieties and wild and traditional foods are underutilized in food security programs and undercounted in food security measurement is that they are not well understood. Mainstream culture tends to stigmatize traditional crops and wild foods, which are typically well adapted to local ecosystems. Cataloguing and research are needed to understand what food resources are available, their growth habits, and their nutritional value, which may be useful even for niche markets within mainstream culture (Frison et al. 2006; Johns and Maundu 2006). This work may help assuage the tendency to discard understudied traditional crops that could be important to food security for their nutritional value, environmentally sustainable production, and income-generating potential.

Emerging Challenges Strengthen the Case for Crop Diversification and Updated Measurement of Food Security

Exacerbating problems of poverty and malnutrition, major challenges to the food system in Africa loom: accelerating urbanization and dietary shifts, volatile fuel and food prices, unpredictable climate change, and HIV/AIDS. These changes underscore the need for a diversity of food produced locally and efficiently, with productivity measured in environmental and nutritional, as well as economic, terms.

Urbanization and the Nutrition Transition

In developing countries around the world, consumers are shifting from traditional diets to eating patterns high in refined starches, oils, and added sugars (Drewnowski and Popkin 1997; Pingali 2006). This shift has led to a "nutrition transition," marked by increases in overweight, obesity, and related chronic diseases such as diabetes and heart disease (Popkin 1999a). Although undernutrition remains the major problem, adult overweight exceeds underweight among urban women in nearly all Sub-Saharan African countries. In a few countries, the same is true for rural women (Mendez, Monteiro, and Popkin 2005). Among urban women in Sub-Saharan Africa, almost one-third are overweight or obese (Mendez, Monteiro, and Popkin 2005). Prevalence of obesity in children, though still only 5 percent on average, is rising sharply in Africa, more rapidly than anywhere else in the world (World Bank 2006; SCN 2004). Diabetes prevalence in Sub-Saharan Africa is expected to more than double between 2000 and 2025 (IDF 2006).

Urbanization is highly associated with the nutrition transition in developing countries (Popkin 1999b, 2001). Increased availability of cheap, fast foods, snacks, and beverages in cities in developing countries, in addition to lifestyle changes toward more sedentary work and less time preparing food, are likely to affect the shift toward overweight and nutrition-related chronic diseases. Africa currently has the highest urban growth rate in the world, at roughly 3.5 percent growth per year (UN 2006b, Table A.6). Urban populations in Africa are projected to double between 2000 and 2030, at which point more than half of the African population will live in cities (UNFP 2007).

Urbanization and the nutrition transition will have a large impact on the food market in Africa, and the rural sector must be able to respond to this growing market. Urban demand for food may help lift the rural poor out of poverty. Yet wise policy decisions about food production and availability must be made to prevent the public health problems of rapidly rising obesity and diabetes rates seen in other developing countries.[15] Food security strategies need to take into account a dietary future that is already practically here.

Subsidies and favorable trade policies toward cheap refined grain products, edible oils, and sugars may in the short run improve caloric sufficiency and the purchasing power of the population, but in the not-very-distant longer run will lead to a sick population. Diet patterns typical of the nutrition transition show that although overall dietary diversity tends to increase with increasing incomes, the quantities consumed of vegetables and vegetable proteins (mainly pulses) decrease and animal fat and protein consumption increases steeply (Drewnowski and Popkin 1997). Poor availability and accessibility of good-quality fresh fruits and vegetables, as illustrated in Figure 7.6, is a problem for people at risk of obesity as well as those affected by undernutrition. There are strong economic reasons for high-calorie and "empty-calorie" food choices where sugars, starches, and high-fat animal products are far cheaper sources of calories than fruits and vegetables (Drewnowski and Darmon 2005). Diversification of food production to include more vegetables, fruits, and legumes can help to avoid the situation now seen in countries that have experienced this nutrition transition, where obesity has become the major nutrition problem. Consumption of animal-source foods, too, requires balance for both nutritional and environmental reasons: animal-source foods are concentrated sources of micronutrients that are desirable in undernourished populations, and livestock can be a pathway out of poverty for poor farmers. At the same time, overconsumption of animal-source foods is a risk factor for obesity and chronic disease, and production of these foods often relies on environmentally destructive production systems (Pimentel and Pimentel 2003; Steinfeld et al. 2006).

Avoiding the consequences of a nutrition transition will require continuous monitoring of the availability and the accessibility of fruits, vegetables, and legumes in particular. This monitoring will involve more institutionalized use of per capita fruit and vegetable supply data, as well as price data for refined starches, sugars, and high-fat animal products. With this information, policy instruments (such as addition or removal of agricultural product-specific subsidies or altered trade agreements) could be employed to better connect agricultural production to public health.

An Energy Problem: Unpredictable Food and Fuel Prices

According to FAO, world food prices rose 37 percent in 2007 (FAO 2008b); they have since fallen back substantially (FAO 2009c). High prices can be a shock for consumers and farmers who are net buyers of food—the vast majority of farmers in Sub-Saharan Africa (Barrett 2008). The World Bank estimates that the food and fuel price spike increased the number of people in extreme poverty by up to 150 million worldwide (World Bank 2009).

While the number of people living in poverty may have receded with the subsequent drop in food prices, intermittent shocks to food security can result in irreversible nutritional setbacks, especially when they affect young children and pregnant women. The unpredictability of food prices, including the fuel needed to farm and transport food, is an argument for more diverse, locally grown production to provide diverse diets close at hand. Having a basic level of local self-sufficiency in food production, including all components of a diverse diet, reduces vulnerability to global price shocks by lowering dependence on purchased and transported food.

Biofuel production is related to food security. The way most biofuels are currently produced, however, seems to negatively affect both nutrition and the environment. Because of the land use changes associated with their production, there is good evidence that biofuels release more greenhouse gases than they save from reduced fossil-fuel combustion (Searchinger et al. 2008). Furthermore, biofuel production typically leaves no crop residue so that soil organic matter steadily decreases with years of production, contributing to soil degradation. Ethanol (mainly from maize and sugarcane) and biodiesel (mainly from oil palm, soybean, and rapeseed) production occupies productive cropland and causes deforestation without contributing to food production. Policies supporting ethanol production exacerbate high food prices (World Bank 2009) and, if adopted in Africa, would result in more land converted to fuel crop production, decreasing the amount of land in Africa used to grow food (Box 7.3.)

Box 7.3—Biofuels in Ethiopia

In 2008 Ethiopia suffered widespread food shortages and severe acute malnutrition, with 6 million children at risk (UNICEF 2008b) and 10 million people needing food assistance (BBC 2008). Earlier the same year, the government reallocated 24 million hectares of land to *Jatropha* production for biodiesel. While not responsible for the concurrent famine, the policy likely contributed to food shortages by diverting land and water from food crops that withered in the drought early in 2008. The Ministry of Mines and Energy, which developed the biodiesel policy, asserts that the land used for *Jatropha* is unproductive anyway. This ministry, however, has no mandate to protect public health, and there is at present no nutrition department in Ethiopia to resist a policy decision potentially perilous to food security and child survival. Lack of institutionalized nutrition capacity or consideration in the government, combined with centralized control over land, allows such questionable policies to move forward.

Trade remains important, but policy responses in an era of increasingly un-predictable food prices would be remiss if they did not also increase local food self-sufficiency, which involves producing a diversity of foods and avoiding land-intensive biofuel production that competes with food production.

The Unknown Path and Timing of Climate Change

Climate change will likely have a profound effect on food production. Increased temperatures and changing rainfall patterns may make crops more difficult to grow, through abiotic stresses (like drought and rising temperatures) and biotic ones (like new opportunities for pests). Potato farmers in the highlands of Peru, for example, are switching to different potato varieties as their traditional varieties become susceptible to fungal blights with the onset of milder weather (Silberner 2008). Interestingly, scientists predicted this result several years ago (Hijmans, Forbes, and Walker 2000). Climate change is predicted to cause a 3–7.5 percent reduction in cereal productivity in Sub-Saharan Africa in the next 75 years (von Braun 2007b), and 25–250 million Africans could suffer from climate change–induced water shortages (Cohen et al. 2008). Other estimates are even more dire, predicting a 25 percent fall in agricultural productivity in Sub-Saharan Africa within the next 25 years as a result of climate change (Cline 2007). Climate change also threatens indigenous people who are dependent upon wild plants, animals, and predictable seasons for survival.

It is difficult to predict what climate changes will happen where and when, but experts and sensitivity analyses seem to agree on one point: change is assured (IPCC 2001). Stocks of old varieties in gene banks will become increasingly im-portant, for their own sake and for breeding new varieties that will be produc-tive under new environmental circumstances. Genetic diversity in the field, in addition to the gene banks, will also be important for continued adaptation to environmental changes through natural and farmer selection. Because one pre-dicted change is longer droughts in many areas (Cohen et al. 2008), productivity indicators that take into account water use efficiency, such as "crop per drop," will become increasingly important. Livestock production also will have to be considered in terms of its high water requirements, low land use efficiency, and significant contributions to greenhouse gas emissions, which have implications for the food security of the most vulnerable populations worldwide.

The Impact of HIV/AIDS

The epicenter of the HIV/AIDS pandemic is in Africa, where 22 million people are infected (UNAIDS 2008). This high rate of infection presents further challenges to food security.

HIV-affected people are more likely to become malnourished, which in turn hastens disease progression, leading to earlier death (Fawzi 2003). Decreased appetite and food intake and poorer absorption of nutrients are typical of HIV-infected individuals (Fawzi 2003), who frequently suffer from micronutrient deficiencies. Meeting nutritional requirements is even more important in HIV-infected individuals because of reduced resiliency; additionally HIV-infected people require up to 10–30 percent more calories than non-infected persons (WHO 2003b). Not surprisingly, work productivity is reduced in HIV-affected populations (Fox et al. 2004), so that food production is decreased, off-farm wages are reduced, and demands on other non-infected family members are higher (Gillespie and Kadiyala 2005b). Furthermore, people living with HIV are less able to travel long distances (AIARD 2003) and thus less able to use markets. The death of a male head of household due to AIDS is associated with a 68 percent drop in household crop value, along with deteriorating diets (Yamano and Jayne 2004). The disease also has impacts on ecosystem services: HIV-affected people are less likely to take steps to maintain soil fertility because it takes extra energy to do so, and future benefits are discounted in the face of a terminal disease (FAO 1994).

For those with HIV/AIDS, adequate nutrition can mean the difference between taking life-saving medication or not, between succumbing to an infection or overcoming it. In short, nutrition more starkly becomes the difference between life and death. Yet with increased physical constraints on labor and market participation, adequate nutrition becomes more difficult to get. To be responsive, agriculture must become more productive with less labor, place a higher premium on home production of a diverse diet, and improve infrastructure to permit better access to markets. Appropriate metrics for measuring the dietary and nutritional impact of cropping systems (for example, the functional diversity of crops produced as well as labor per unit of food) become even more important in the context of HIV/AIDS.[16]

Conclusions

To eradicate food insecurity, nutrition and the environment must be given higher priority. Rather than being viewed as longer-range benefits that can be addressed after caloric adequacy is achieved, nutrition and the environment are themselves fundamental to true food security. The thinking about food security by the development community, programmers, analysts, and policymakers needs to shift from one focused solely on caloric adequacy to one genuinely concerned with the provision of a diverse diet through environmentally sustainable means. Agricultural diversification and increased use of related indicators of productivity are key to improved food security in Sub-Saharan Africa. Indicators such as available diversity per capita, accessibility of a diverse diet, and water use efficiency add new dimensions to productivity and food security metrics, permitting a more complete picture of food insecurity and what needs to be done to address it. Understanding the nutritional and environmental underpinnings of food security is becoming increasingly important in light of emerging challenges facing Sub-Saharan Africa, particularly urbanization, growing rates of obesity, climate change, and HIV/AIDS. Rather than only increasing cereal yields or national wealth, policies that succeed in reducing food insecurity will be those that focus simultaneously on nutrition and the environment.

Notes

I am grateful to Alice Pell for the many conversations we had during the development of this chapter, which shaped the outline and richly contributed to my thinking in preparing it. Thanks to Per Pinstrup-Andersen, Jim Levinson, Muriel Calo, Selena Ahmed, Gina Lebedeva, and anonymous reviewers for thoughtful comments on drafts.

1. For examples of ecosystem services related to food and income security, see Chivian and Bernstein (2008, particularly Chapter 3).

2. According to the FAO, "Undernourishment refers to the condition of people whose dietary energy consumption is continuously below a minimum dietary energy requirement for maintaining a healthy life and carrying out a light physical activity" (FAO 2009a).

3. The FAO measure of calorie availability adjusts for estimated inequality in access using an income distribution curve.

4. The seven food groups were (1) cereals, roots, and tubers; (2) pulses and legumes; (3) dairy products; (4) meats, fish and seafood, and eggs; (5) oils and fats; (6) fruits; and (7) vegetables.

5. Food quantities available for human consumption include production and imports minus exports, livestock feed, seed, additions to stocks, and losses (FAO 2009a).

6. The protein requirement for adults is 0.8 grams per kilogram body weight per day (IOM–FNB 2005). Cereals also contribute to protein intake (the amount varying by crop), forming a complete protein in combination with pulses. Accounting for per capita milk availability of 81 grams (FAO 2009a), also a major protein source for the poor, contributes

another 6 percent to the daily adult protein requirement. Per capita meat, egg, and fish consumption (54 grams per capita per day) would contribute another 14 percent toward protein needs if equally distributed, but consumption of these foods is highly skewed toward the wealthy.

7. The available quantity of starchy roots and cereals is enough to provide 1,500–1,800 kilocalories per person per day, or roughly 50–60 percent of average adult daily caloric needs (FAO 2004).

8. This information came from information gathered by the author from Kenyan farmers during fieldwork in Kenya in 2008.

9. NPK 120-100-100 kilograms per hectare.

10. The fertilizer was found to be ineffective because without the necessary soil structure and chemistry conferred by soil organic matter, the applied nutrients leached into the subsoil (Kimetu et al. 2008).

11. This information came from information gathered by the author from Kenyan farmers during fieldwork in Kenya in 2008.

12. See Vavilov and Dorofeev (1992) and Nabhan (2009).

13. Applied at the rate of 6 tons of carbon per hectare.

14. Agreed in 2001 by the Convention on Biological Diversity and FAO (http://www.cbd .int/agro/treaty.shtml).

15. In Egypt, for example, 71 percent of women are overweight or obese (SCN 2004); in Mexico, age-adjusted mortality rates from diabetes have increased by 60 percent since 1980 (Rivera, Barquera, et al. 2004).

16. Chapter 5 in this volume by Stuart Gillespie further details the interaction of HIV/AIDS and African food systems.

CHAPTER 8

Food Safety as a Bridge between the Food System and
Human Health in Sub-Saharan Africa

Dorothy Nakimbugwe and Kathryn J. Boor

Abstract

The safety and wholesomeness of foods within a food system are an important
reflection of the adequacy of the system for the population that depends on that
food supply. A high prevalence of unsafe foods is as undesirable as an inadequate
food supply, because both ultimately result in poor human nutrition and health.
Diseases transmitted through foods interact in a vicious circle with malnutrition,
each compounding the public health burden of the other. The predominant causes
of food-borne illnesses are biological disease agents (bacteria, viruses, fungi, and
gastrointestinal parasites), but chemical and physical contaminants are also a
concern. In Sub-Saharan Africa, food-borne illnesses frequently go unrecognized,
unreported, and uninvestigated because of limited access to medical facilities,
limited diagnostic facilities at the available medical establishments, lack of national
surveillance systems, and limited resources for investigation of food-borne illnesses in these countries. It is clear, however, that diarrhea continues to be a major
cause of morbidity and mortality among Sub-Saharan African children. One key
strategy for strengthening food safety systems and reducing food-borne illnesses
is to develop effective food-borne illness surveillance systems to collect, analyze,
and share epidemiological data. These data must then be used as a basis for setting
priorities on the most critical food-borne risks that need to be addressed in order
to realize the highest impact. Other critical needs include development of basic
infrastructure for hygiene, such as access to toilet and hand-washing facilities, as
well as delivery of potable water for food-related businesses and for domestic use.
Education and communication with consumers is a critical component of a well-
functioning food system. Food system developments must be appropriate and
sustainable for the local community, region, and country. Ultimately, because the

safety of foods in a given food system is a critical factor affecting public health, strategies that effectively reduce food-borne illnesses by enhancing the safety of local, national, and international food systems will yield tangible improvements in the global public health profile.

Introduction

Food systems, when operating optimally, should guarantee food security for the populations that depend on them—that is, individuals, families, communities, nations, and regions—by ensuring that even those who are most vulnerable have physical and economic access to sufficient, safe, and nutritious food to meet their dietary needs, at all times and from non-emergency sources (FAO 1996a). For the purposes of this chapter, a "food system" is defined as consisting of multiple subcomponents including food production systems, food-processing systems, food-marketing and distribution systems, and food control systems. Food control systems include food laws and regulations, food control management, food inspection services, and epidemiological and food-monitoring laboratory services. The goals of food control systems are to provide consumer protection and ensure that all foods are safe, wholesome, and fit for human consumption; conform to safety and quality requirements; and are honestly and accurately labeled as prescribed by law during production, handling, storage, processing, and distribution (FAO/WHO 2002, 2004a, b). Education and communication with the consumer is a critical, overarching subcomponent of a well-functioning food system (WHO 2008a).

The safety of foods within a food system provides important criteria for evaluating the adequacy of the system. A high prevalence of unsafe foods is as undesirable as an inadequate food supply, because both ultimately result in poor human nutrition and health. Establishing and maintaining food systems that ensure protection of consumers and that extend over the entire food chain is a responsibility that requires the cooperation of all stakeholders, including producers, processors, food service establishments, and food vendors as well as law enforcement officials and consumers. To ensure the safety of a food system, control measures must be integrated into every aspect of the system "from farm to fork." The safety of farmgate produce should, for instance, be ensured by applying the principles of good agricultural practices (GAPs) as a minimum standard during on-farm production operations. Similarly, good manufacturing practices (GMPs) should be applied, as a minimum, to ensure the safety of processed foods. Thereafter good handling practices (GHPs) should be implemented to ensure food safety during storage, distribution, marketing, retailing, preparation, and consumption. Adoption of additional preventive approaches by the private sector, such as application of food safety programs including Hazard Analysis and

Critical Control Points (HACCP), contribute to further improvements in food safety (FAO/WHO 2004b). To ensure that each segment of the food system understands its role in protecting the quality and safety of the food supply, implementation and enforcement of mandatory requirements should be preceded and supported by information, education, and communication that is appropriately targeted and delivered to each audience (WHO 2008a).

It is currently widely recognized within and outside Africa that comprehensive systems for protecting the safety of the food supply there are underdeveloped (FAO/WHO 2005a). A Regional Conference on Food Safety for Africa held in Harare, Zimbabwe, jointly convened by the Food and Agriculture Organization of the United Nations (FAO) and the World Health Organization (WHO), recommended a strategic plan for improving food safety consisting of nine points (FAO/WHO 2005a):

1. food safety policies and programs;
2. legislative and institutional advancements;
3. standards and regulations;
4. food inspection programs and techniques;
5. food analyses and food safety testing laboratories;
6. monitoring of food-borne diseases and the safety of foods on the market;
7. participation in Codex Alimentarius;
8. communication and stakeholder involvement (including industry officials and consumers); and
9. national, regional, and international cooperation.

Although the details associated with these nine points were developed during evaluation of food safety challenges specific to Africa, the points represent essential universal components of systems capable of reliably delivering foods that are safe for human consumption. Many of these points are interrelated: for example, to effectively safeguard a food supply, foods must be tested for compliance with standards, such as by using microbiological or compositional criteria (point 5), and then a regulatory agency with appropriate authority must enforce the standards (point 3). One feature of effective enforcement is removal of foods determined to be unsafe from the marketplace. In parallel, consumers must have adequate resources, including access to information, to make informed decisions to protect their own health.

The Food Safety Situation in Sub-Saharan African Countries

Numerous efforts have been directed toward improving food security and the general nutrition and health of populations worldwide, but silent killers—food- and waterborne diseases—continue to persist around the globe (Mead et al. 1999; Kosek, Bern, and Guerrant 2003; WHO 2008b). In addition to the typical, short-term symptoms (such as diarrhea, vomiting, and fever), food-borne illnesses can lead to long-term or chronic health complications, including neurological, gynecological, or immunological disorders, which may result in multiorgan failure and death (Mead et al. 1999; WHO 2008c). Food-borne diseases also interact in a vicious circle with malnutrition, each compounding the public health burden of the other. The predominant causes of food-borne illnesses are biological disease agents (bacteria, viruses, fungi, and gastrointestinal parasites), but chemical contaminants are also a concern (Mead et al. 1999; WHO 2008c). Although the burden of food-borne diseases on global populations cannot be known for certain, but only estimated, because of the lack of uniform public health surveillance systems around the world (Lopez et al. 2006; WHO 2008c), unsafe food is estimated to result in disease for at least one person in three each year (WHO 2009c).

Many food-borne illnesses in Sub-Saharan Africa go unrecognized, unreported, and uninvestigated because of limited access to medical facilities, limited diagnostic facilities at the available medical establishments, lack of national surveillance systems, and limited resources for investigation of food-borne illnesses in these countries (Lopez et al. 2006; WHO 2008c). It is clear, however, that diarrhea continues to be a major cause of morbidity and mortality among children in Sub-Saharan Africa (Kosek, Bern, and Guerrant 2003). Overall, the WHO estimates that in Africa, food- and waterborne illnesses result in about 700,000 deaths a year among all ages (WHO 2007c).

At least partly because of the absence of comprehensive disease surveillance and reporting systems in Sub-Saharan Africa, the predominant sources of information on disease outbreaks in the region are newspaper articles, networks such as Safe Food International (http://regionalnews.safefoodinternational.org/), and the WHO Regional Office for Africa (http://www.afro.who.int/). Although these sources suggest a high incidence of food-borne illnesses in Sub-Saharan Africa, the data are neither comprehensive nor fully quantitative. Notably, these sources report repeated outbreaks in certain countries that frequently affect large numbers of individuals. When contamination of food or water is clearly identified as the cause of an outbreak, it presents an opportunity to identify and understand factors that contributed to that outbreak and then develop and implement effective interventions to prevent future outbreaks.

Food-borne diseases have contributed to the slow development observed in Sub-Saharan African countries (WHO 2008c). The high burden of food-borne diseases and the related health consequences for African populations deter progress toward achieving the health-related Millennium Development Goals (MDGs), which were an outcome of the 2000 United Nations (UN) Millennium Summit.

The MDGs are eight goals with measurable targets and deadlines intended to improve the lives of the world's poorest people by 2015 (UN 2001). The MDGs and goals relevant to global food safety include the following: between 1990 and 2015, eradicate extreme poverty and hunger and halve the proportion of people who suffer from hunger (MDG1 and Target 3), and reduce child mortality, and specifically reduce by two-thirds the under-five mortality rate (MDG 4 and Target 1). According to the UN (2008), about one-quarter of all children in developing countries are underweight and at risk of having a future blighted by the long-term effects of undernourishment. For Sub-Saharan Africa, 32 percent of the population is identified as at risk for long-term negative health consequences from undernourishment. Between 1990 and 2006, this figure was reduced by only 4 percentage points. Indeed, while the *Millennium Development Goals Report* (UN 2008) states that progress has been made in a number of areas such as increased primary school enrollment, enhanced gender parity among primary school students, reduced deaths due to malaria, and increased representation of women in elected government positions, relatively little progress has been made in the MDGs that relate most directly to improving human health in Sub-Saharan Africa, such as reducing poverty and hunger, improving child and maternal health, and stopping and reversing the spread of infectious diseases. The following statistic illustrates the size of the task: in Africa alone an additional 404 million people will need to gain access to improved sanitation and 294 million additional people will require safe water in order to meet the MDG targets by 2015 (UNICEF 2009a).

Food Safety Challenges in Sub-Saharan African Countries: Risks and Opportunities

The frequent, repeated, severe, and widespread occurrence of food-borne illnesses in Sub-Saharan Africa is evidence that the current food safety systems fail in their capacity to protect consumers from food-borne risks (WHO 2007c, 2008c). A food safety risk is a known or potential adverse health effect that could result from human exposure to a hazard present in foods. Food-borne hazards can be biological, chemical, or physical (Mead et al. 1999). Food safety system failures can have many causes, but they certainly reflect the weak food control systems present in Sub-Saharan Africa and the inability of multiple segments of the food system to proactively control food safety hazards. Other contributing factors include the existence of fragmented legislation; multiple, and often uncertain, jurisdictions; and weaknesses in surveillance, monitoring, and enforcement (FAO/WHO 2002). The absence of resources, enforceable policies (or reliance on outdated ones), regulatory mechanisms, and coordinated efforts in addressing public challenges also contribute (WHO 2007c). Thus, despite stop-gap efforts by multiple government and nongovernmental organizations, weaknesses remain in African food control systems, with grave consequences for food safety and human health.

A key strategy for strengthening food safety systems and reducing food-borne illnesses is to conduct comprehensive risk analyses to enable authorities to identify and prioritize hazards that should be managed through targeted interventions, including through effective risk communications (FAO/WHO 2006). Risk assessment is a scientifically based process consisting of hazard identification, hazard characterization, exposure assessment, and risk characterization. An assessment typically contains both qualitative and quantitative information (FAO/WHO 2006). The absence of effective surveillance systems for generating reliable epidemiological data in Sub-Saharan Africa directly impedes the ability to conduct effective risk analyses, specifically assessments of risk. Consequently it is difficult to design and implement appropriate interventions, including effective legislation, appropriate food safety standards, and information, education, and communication campaigns (WHO 2008c). A quantitative understanding of the disease burden of a population and how that burden is distributed across different subpopulations (such as infants and women) are important pieces of information for defining strategies for improving population health. For policymakers, disease burden estimates provide a baseline by which to measure the health gains that could be achieved by targeted actions against specific risk factors. The measures also allow policymakers to prioritize actions and direct them to the population groups at highest risk. To work toward achieving these ends, in September 2006 the WHO Department of Food Safety and Zoonoses launched an initiative to estimate the global burden of food-borne diseases from all major causes (WHO 2005d, 2008c). Under this initiative, the Food-borne Disease Burden Epidemiology Reference Group (FERG) was established as an external advisory group for the WHO on global food-borne disease epidemiology. FERG has been given a five-year charge to provide global estimates of food-borne diseases; strengthen the capacity of countries to conduct their own food-borne illness burden studies; encourage countries to use burden of food-borne illness estimates for cost-effective analyses of intervention and control measures; and increase member states' awareness of and commitment to implementing food safety standards (WHO 2008c).

Development of capacity for food-borne surveillance systems represents an opportunity to improve food safety and human health in Sub-Saharan Africa. One example of an emerging surveillance system is the WHO-initiated Global Salm-Surv (GSS), a network of laboratories and individuals involved in surveillance, isolation, identification, and antimicrobial resistance testing of *Salmonella* and other food-borne pathogens such as *Campylobacter* (WHO 2009d). GSS, which recently changed its name to Global Food-borne Infections Network (GFN) to reflect its widened scope beyond surveillance of infections from *Salmonella* spp., was set up to strengthen and enhance the capacities of national and regional laboratories around the world. GFN promotes integrated, laboratory-based surveillance and outbreak detection and response and fosters collaboration and communication among microbiologists and epidemiologists in human health, veterinary, and food-related disciplines. GFN had 1,211 members from 158 countries in June 2009, including representatives from 39 African countries (WHO 2009b).

In addition to the emergence of laboratory networks such as GFN, appropriate tools for public health investigations in developing countries are also becoming available. For example, the WHO recently published *Foodborne Disease Outbreaks: Guidelines for Investigation and Control* (WHO 2008a). The guidelines are intended for use by public health practitioners, food and health inspectors, district and national medical officers, laboratory personnel, and others responsible for investigating and controlling food-borne disease outbreaks.

Food systems around the globe that are considered to provide safe food products have managed either to prevent the occurrence of food safety risks (in the forms of biological, chemical, and physical hazards) or to control the frequency, severity, and extent of these risks when they do occur. Some foods are more likely to transmit food-borne illnesses to humans than others. These risks may arise from several factors, including the environment in which the foods are grown; the methods by which they are harvested, transported, distributed, and prepared for consumption; the form in which the foods are consumed; the target group for which the foods are intended; and the perishability or shelf stability of the foods. Within food systems, the most vulnerable points for food safety risks also represent points of opportunity to manage and control the risks. The following discussion describes biological, chemical, and physical risks presently encountered in Sub-Saharan African food systems and opportunities for public health improvements.

Biological Risks and Associated Opportunities

Diseases due to biological agents are major causes of death, disability, and social and economic disruption for millions of people around the globe. An estimated 14–17 million people die each year from infectious diseases, with the majority of deaths occurring in developing countries (WHO 2009a). Food-borne diseases contribute significantly to the burden of diseases worldwide (WHO 2008c). They are defined as diseases, usually either infectious or toxic in nature, caused by agents that enter the body through the ingestion of food (Mead et al. 1999). Food-borne infectious diseases frequently cause diarrhea and are therefore also commonly referred to as diarrheal diseases. Although their global incidence is difficult to estimate, diarrheal diseases were reported to result in 1.8 million human deaths in 2005 alone, with the majority of deaths attributable to ingestion of contaminated food and drinking water (WHO 2007c). A wide range of biological risks exist in food systems because of the unwanted presence of living organisms, including micro- and macro-disease agents such as bacteria, fungi, viruses, and parasites. Food-borne illnesses can be categorized as bacterial if they are caused by bacterial infection or intoxication; viral if they are caused by viruses; parasitic if they are caused by parasites; and noninfectious if they are caused by metals or foods containing naturally occurring toxins such as some mushrooms (CDC 2004a). Worldwide, prevalent food-borne illnesses caused by microbiological agents include cholera, campylobacteriosis, *Escherichia coli* infections, salmonellosis, shigellosis, brucellosis, and hepatitis A (WHO 2007).

Many, but not all, bacterial food-borne illnesses can be treated effectively with appropriate administration of commercially available antibiotics. In addition to antibiotic therapy, when medical interventions are sought and secured, food-borne illnesses are generally treated with rehydration therapy and supportive care for the patient (CDC 2004a). Although many bacterial food-borne illnesses can be effectively treated and cured, greater reductions in public health burdens can be realized through implementation of cost-effective disease prevention strategies (Curtis, Cairncross, and Yonli 2000; Bowen et al. 2007).

The fact that food-borne illnesses (whether biological, chemical, or physical) are largely preventable presents considerable opportunities for improved human health in Sub-Saharan Africa. Because diarrheal pathogens are usually transmitted by a fecal-oral route, simple interventions to improve and support effective personal hygienic practices—for example, through sanitary handling and disposal of fecal material and hand washing—present proven strategies for reducing food-borne and other infectious illnesses that can be transmitted from handler-to-food and from person-to-person (Curtis, Cairncross, and Yonli 2000). To illustrate, a study by the U.S. Navy showed that implementation of a hand-washing program reduced outpatient visits for respiratory infections by 45 percent among young recruits in training (Ryan, Christian, and Wohlrabe 2001). A meta-analysis of results from multiple studies suggested that washing hands with soap could reduce the risk of diarrhea by more than 40 percent in both developed and developing countries (Curtis and Cairncross 2003). Given the morbidity and mortality associated with diarrheal diseases each year (Kosek, Bern, and Guerrant 2003; Scott et al. 2007), promotion and support of effective hand washing have the potential for a considerable positive impact on public health. In recognition of the importance of hand washing in protecting public health, the Global Public-Private Partnership for Handwashing with Soap initiated the first Global Handwashing Day on October 15, 2008 (Health in Your Hands 2009), highlighting the UN General Assembly's designation of 2008 as the International Year of Sanitation.

In addition to the microbial diseases described, parasitic infestation of foods and humans also contributes to the food-borne illness disease burden around the globe. More than half of the world's population is estimated to be infected with one or more species of intestinal worms (Hall et al. 2008). Hookworms and the nematodes *Ascaris lumbricoides* and *Trichuris trichiura* are the most common parasites and appear to have the greatest negative impact on child health worldwide (Hall et al. 2008). Human infestations with intestinal parasites are correlated with negative indicators of nutritional status, as well as with developmental (language, social, and gross and fine motor) disabilities (Oberhelman et al. 1998). Ineffective food inspection (especially of meat and fish), lack of access to and affordability of human and veterinary drugs, lack of or inadequate education and information, poor personal hygiene, and handling of foods by infected humans can all accelerate the spread of infestations, with severe consequences. The WHO and other global health agencies recommend antihelminthic (deworming) treatments for all high-risk groups as a means to reduce the burden of disease from these organisms (WHO 2004c, 2005a). Reinfection with helminths is a common occurrence, so long-term control requires regular deworming in parallel with preventive interventions designed to reduce transmission, including access to a safe water supply, control of fecal waste, and good personal hygiene (WHO 2004c). Deworming treatments for children may result in only modest, short-term improvements in growth and nutritional status (Taylor-Robinson, Jones, and Garner 2009) in the absence of extra nutritional support (such as provision of extra calories, protein, and micronutrients) to treat underlying nutritional deficits that either resulted from or were worsened by worm infections. Significant permanent reductions in parasite loads among humans and animals used for human food will require investments in comprehensive human and animal health care strategies and educational interventions targeted at breaking cycles of infection (WHO 2004c).

Chemical Risks and Associated Opportunities

Chemical contaminants in foods can originate from several sources, including misuse of agricultural chemicals, naturally occurring sources (like mycotoxins produced by molds), and contamination of food and water sources with chemical waste from human activities such as mining and industrial processing. Misuse of agricultural chemicals can have multiple negative effects, including the presence of chemical residues in foods. This outcome can occur when treatment doses are too high or when treatments are incorrectly applied, such as when application is timed too close to harvest or slaughter. Several risk factors have been associated with the entry of industrial, household, or agricultural chemical contaminants into the food system. These factors include a high prevalence of small-scale food processors with limited resources, knowledge, and skills who are also not well supervised; lack of or poor regulation of imported foods and food ingredients, which can lead to dumping of substandard products; the presence of chemical residues (pesticides, herbicides, veterinary drugs) in foods as a result of inappropriate use due to illiteracy; inappropriate storage of agricultural chemicals together with foods or live animals; inadequate resources to administer effective, complete therapeutic doses of medicine to sick animals; use of obsolete, inappropriate, and substandard food-processing and preparation equipment resulting in contamination of processed food with equipment material fragments; and use of novel ingredients that have not been adequately tested for human safety.

Chemical contamination of water sources and the environment can negatively affect food systems, with direct consequences for consumers. In 2006, for example, approximately 500 tons of petrochemical waste were intentionally illegally dumped in at least 15 sites, ultimately entering water supplies around the city of Abidjan, Côte d'Ivoire. Eight people who were exposed to the waste died, and nearly 90,000 others needed medical attention (Polgreen and Simons 2006). Events such as this one also disrupt livelihoods for those who depend on the water bodies for food. The fish and seafood were rendered unfit for export markets, but fisherfolk continued to sell the contaminated fish and seafood, despite knowing about the contamination event, in a desperate attempt to avoid losing their livelihoods. These sellers poisoned their customers, further expanding the negative consequences of this contamination event.

Reductions in the incidence of chemical contamination events of water and the environment in Sub-Saharan Africa will require investments in the infrastructure (including regulatory authority) necessary to support safe and cost-effective disposal of hazardous waste for the entire spectrum, ranging from major corporations to individual homeowners. Effective education and communication strategies will be needed to ensure that each segment of society understands both the risks associated with potential hazards and its role in protecting the quality and safety of the environment.

In addition to consumption of industrial, household, or agricultural chemical contaminants that may be present in foods through human actions or error, ingestion of toxic substances that may be present naturally in foods—such as mycotoxins, cyanogenic glycosides, and algal toxins—also can result in severe intoxication (Sanders 2003). Because mycotoxins, such as aflatoxin and ochratoxin A, can be found at measurable levels in grains, pulses, and nuts, and because these staple foods are widely grown, consumed, and traded in Sub-Saharan Africa, this discussion focuses on issues associated with consuming mycotoxins, with a specific emphasis on aflatoxin.

Mycotoxins are secondary metabolites of molds, including those that can grow on important food crops such as groundnuts, maize, and other oilseeds (Gourama and Bullerman 1995; Jiang et al. 2005). Grains and pulses, along with dried fruits and vegetables, ground and tree nuts, and dried spices are highly susceptible to growth of molds, particularly in the warm and humid conditions frequently encountered in Sub-Saharan Africa. Contamination of foods with molds usually starts in the field, where several factors including inadequate manual labor coupled with lack of mechanization lead to delayed harvesting, thus increasing exposure to molds. Other factors that appear to favor mold infestation include varietal susceptibility, water stress during crop growth, and infestation with in-field pests such as weevils. The risk of mold infestation and spread in foods also increases when relative humidity and temperature rise and when products are physically damaged (Williams et al. 2004).

The most notorious mycotoxins in human foods are aflatoxins, which are produced by *Aspergillus flavus* and *A. parasiticus* (Bennett and Klich 2003; Kaaya and Warren 2005; Lewis et al. 2005). The risks and potential health consequences associated with consuming aflatoxin-contaminated foods have been reviewed by Williams et al. (2004). Risks include severe aflatoxicosis, with symptoms including hemorrhagic necrosis of the liver, bile duct proliferation, edema, and lethargy; liver and lung cancer (the latter among workers handling contaminated grain); immunological suppression (demonstrated in animals); and nutritional interference, including interference with micronutrient nutrition (that is, vitamins A and D, iron, selenium, and zinc). On the basis of the reported role of aflatoxins on the immune system and micronutrient metabolism, Williams et al. (2004) hypothesize that aflatoxin exposure may also affect the epidemiology of many diseases and health risks in countries where the presence of toxins is uncontrolled, including the major killer diseases in Sub-Saharan Africa: HIV/AIDS and malaria.

Although aflatoxin exposure is undesirable for all individuals, children, the elderly, the pregnant, and immuno-compromised individuals are especially at risk. Turner et al. (2007) reported a strong association between maternal aflatoxin exposure during pregnancy and faltering child growth during the first year of life. Aflatoxins have been reported in human breast milk (El-Sayed, Neamat-Allah, and Soher 2000; El-Sayed, Soher, and Neamat-Allah 2002; Galvano et al. 2008), so an infant can be exposed to aflatoxins even if solely breast-fed. Aflatoxin exposure in utero and young childhood has been associated with underweight children with stunted growth (Gong et al. 2002; Turner et al. 2007). The children identified by Gong el al. (2002) as underweight and stunted were also found to have 30–40 percent higher aflatoxin levels in their blood than other children. A strong dose-response relationship was observed between aflatoxin levels in children's blood and the extent of stunting and underweight (Gong et al. 2003).

High levels of aflatoxins are documented to be present in a wide range of foods in different Sub-Saharan African countries, including raw peanuts, preharvested maize, dried yam chips, melon seeds, peanut oil, and traditionally brewed beers (WHO 2006e). When grain is used for animal feed in Sub-Saharan Africa, it is unlikely to be sorted to eliminate moldy kernels before use; therefore grain considered unfit for human consumption can be fed to animals. As a consequence, humans also may be exposed to mycotoxins through consumption of food products, such as milk from animals fed with contaminated grains. Repeated incidences of human consumption of aflatoxin-contaminated maize in Kenya and resulting aflatoxicosis cases, which have resulted in numerous illnesses and deaths, have been reported (CDC 2004b; Lewis et al. 2005).

Poor pre- and postharvest practices for foods susceptible to mold growth include late harvesting; drying on bare ground or on ground "cemented" with cow dung; and inadequate drying, packaging, and storage. These practices, all of which are common in Sub-Saharan African countries, expose foods to molds and support mold proliferation with subsequent production of mycotoxins. The predominance of such rudimentary food-harvesting and -processing practices reflects poorly developed food production and protection systems. In Sub-Saharan Africa, the food production system is largely subsistent, characteristically based on small farms run by many poor farming families or individual farmers, with low financial investment and a high dependence on nature. The farms rely on rain for growth of their crops. Postharvest handling generally consists of sun drying of produce with no control over the conditions. As a result, produce is commonly not dried to below the 10 percent moisture content necessary to prevent rampant mold spoilage.

Approaches to controlling the presence of molds and mycotoxins in foods must target the full spectrum of points at which contamination can occur, starting before harvest, so identifying likely contamination points is essential. Williams et al. (2004) reviewed several possible intervention strategies aimed at the three stages where contamination is most likely to occur—production, storage, and processing.

The key to minimizing mycotoxin contamination during food production lies in controlling the environmental factors that favor mold infestation, such as insect damage and water stress. Food production systems in Sub-Saharan Africa, however, do not lend themselves easily to preharvest control of contamination because they are mostly subsistence oriented, rely on rainfed agriculture and limited use of pest control measures, and suffer from frequent droughts and flooding. Biotechnology research to create crops that will either prevent the formation of mycotoxins by fungi or prevent or decrease fungal activity is underway and may provide future solutions to farmers who can afford them.

Mycotoxin control during storage is typically achieved using the conventional and highly effective control of maintaining storage moisture below 10 percent. Foods must be adequately dried before storage and then maintained at low moisture levels. Both of these requirements pose a major challenge in Sub-Saharan Africa, where both drying and storage facilities are frequently poor and poverty prohibits investments in better facilities.

Processing provides some opportunities to reduce mycotoxin content by dilution, decontamination, and separation or sorting. Dilution and decontamination are not practical for African conditions. Dilution requires require accumulating and mixing foods with high and low mycotoxin content and which is not feasible for small-scale farmers that produce small volumes of products. Decontamination involves using chemicals that may not be affordable to most African farmers. Sorting and separation provide the most viable solution for African countries and are currently widely practiced. The procedures involve removing grains that appear physically damaged or moldy, as well as extraneous matter such as insects and their excreta and carcasses, stones, plant remains, and soil. Sorting, as currently practiced, generally does not specifically target mycotoxin decontamination but contributes to it by removing moldy and shriveled grains. Including specific strategies for reducing mycotoxin content of the sorted product would make sorting more effective at reducing the mycotoxin content of foods. For example, a blanching step that causes an enzyme-based color change in infested peanut kernels can effectively indicate which grains should be discarded. An unfortunate consequence of both the routine and improved sorting methods is that the infested grains that are sorted out may, and indeed do, end up back in the food system (Williams et al. 2004). Possible solutions include ensuring that "sort-outs" are destroyed or applying chemical treatment to the sort-outs to detoxify the food. The latter strategy would become affordable only if the infected grains are sorted before treatment.

The following post-ingestion intervention steps have been considered as strategies to reduce the human health consequences of mycotoxin ingestion:

- Chemoprotection involves using drug therapy for humans or including additives in animal feeds to minimize the toxic effects of mycotoxins (such as aflatoxins). Like preharvest control measures, these interventions are expensive and therefore not practical for Sub-Saharan African countries.
- Enterosorption interventions involve the use of clay minerals such as hydrated sodium calcium aluminosilicates (HSCAS) to selectively bind aflatoxins and prevent their absorption in the gastrointestinal tract. Toxicological evaluations of dietary NovaSil clay in Sprague-Dawley rats supported use of the clay for dietary intervention studies in human populations at high risk for aflatoxicosis (Afriyie-Gyawu et al. 2005). Earlier studies demonstrated NovaSil to be effective for preventing aflatoxicosis in turkeys, chickens, lambs, cattle, pigs, goats, rats, and mice (reviewed by Williams et al. 2004). NovaSil, commonly used as an anti-caking agent in animal feeds, has been tested in a Sub-Saharan African country and has been reported to be safe and practical for protecting humans against aflatoxins in populations at high risk of aflatoxicosis (Afriyie-Gyawu et al. 2008).

Control of aflatoxin contamination and levels in foods presents a major challenge as well as a major opportunity for improving the safety of Sub-Saharan
African food systems and consequently human nutrition and health. Further research on and implementation of effective interventions on aflatoxin control will
ultimately reduce the burden of disease in African countries and accelerate progress toward meeting the nutrition- and health-related MDGs (UN 2001).

Physical Contaminants in Foods

Of comparatively less risk to human health is the presence of physical contaminants in foods such as such as soil, weeds, husks, stones, and pests and their excreta.
Nonetheless, a food system that tolerates the presence of physical contaminants
in foods is generally also at greater risk for the presence of chemical and biological contaminants owing to the absence of effective preventive systems for managing food safety risks. The presence of extraneous matter in food is undesirable
because it lowers the quality of the food and may lead to its rejection or devalua-
tion in the market. The financial consequences of such rejection are especially
serious for producers when international markets are involved. When producers
must strive to meet the expectations of domestic consumers with adequate financial resources to demand safe, high-quality food, the prevalence of physical contaminants in the food supply diminishes.

Interactions between Societal and Physical, Chemical, and
Microbiological Factors Affect the Safety of Available Foods

The following discussion presents factors affecting the safety of fresh fruits and
vegetables and street-vended foods to illustrate the multiple entry points for
potential hazards and the complexity of the economic, biological, and societal
issues associated with foods commonly consumed by those with limited financial
resources in Sub-Saharan Africa.

Fresh Fruits and Vegetables

Fruits and vegetables are important components of a healthy diet. Consumption
of recommended amounts of fruits and vegetables is thought to contribute to prevention of or reductions in morbidity and mortality due to noncommunicable
diseases (NCDs) such as cancer, cardiovascular diseases, obesity, type II diabetes
mellitus, micronutrient deficiencies, and respiratory diseases (FAO/WHO 2003;
FAO 2006a). Five of the 10 leading global disease burden risk factors, including

high blood pressure, high cholesterol, obesity, physical inactivity, and insufficient consumption of fruits and vegetables, are among the major risk factors associated with NCDs. NCDs are estimated to account for 59 percent of the 56.5 million deaths annually worldwide, or 45.9 percent of the global burden of disease (WHO 2009a). Dietary guidelines for good health therefore recommend a varied diet, including consumption of adequate fruits and vegetables. Presently, worldwide fruit and vegetable consumption is estimated to be only 20–50 percent of the recommended minimum (FAO 2006a). In addition to their direct health benefits, fruits and vegetables indirectly contribute to improved health for people in developing countries by raising their incomes from sales to urban markets and particularly sales to export markets in developed countries.

Relative to developing countries, promotion of fruit and vegetable consumption is more common and widespread in developed countries, where their significance to human health is well recognized and where income levels are generally sufficiently high to sustain their frequent purchase. In contrast, economic realities in Sub-Saharan Africa, where a high proportion of people live on less than one dollar a day, greatly constrain food choices. Individuals and families are primarily concerned about satisfying hunger, and considerations of a balanced diet are secondary. Diets in Sub-Saharan Africa are therefore typically high in carbohydrates, with considerably lower proportions of other food types, including fresh fruits and vegetables. Although reliable data on food consumption patterns are sparse, fruit and vegetable consumption is likely to fall below WHO's minimum recommended level of 400 grams per day, which is considered important for preventing chronic diseases and micronutrient deficiencies (excluding consumption of potatoes and other root tubers) (WHO 2003a; FAO 2006a). The high incidence of micronutrient deficiencies and generally poor health in Sub-Saharan Africa is probably at least a partial reflection of the low per capita fruit and vegetable consumption there.

Postharvest handling and storage methods for fruits and vegetables in Sub-Saharan Africa are underdeveloped and generally inadequate, in both commercial and domestic settings. Storage and handling deficiencies lead to high postharvest losses of fruits and vegetables, as well as to contamination of food products with food-borne pathogens and agrochemicals. For example, pesticides and heavy metals have been reported in Egyptian leafy vegetables (Dogheim et al. 2004). In combination with inadequate food control systems, poor production and postharvest handling technologies and marketing systems allow poor-quality and unsafe fruits and vegetables to be availed to consumers. Many fresh fruits and vegetables (such as apples, melons, and leafy greens) are highly perishable because of their high water content, coupled with their susceptibility to damage or bruising, which releases nutrients and makes them readily available to microorganisms. Spoiled or semi-spoiled fruits and vegetables are often sold cheaply and consumed by low-income earners, directly leading to food-borne illnesses. Fresh fruits and vegetables, like other raw foods, are commonly contaminated with pathogens found at their source. A wide range of pathogens and parasites have been isolated from leafy vegetables in African countries, including, but not limited to, *Salmonella* spp., *Shigella* spp., *Escherichia coli, Campylobacter, Enterobacter sakazakii, Cryptosporidium,* helminth eggs like *Ascaris lumbricoides,* and hookworms like *Ancylostoma* spp. (FAO/WHO 2008).

Families commonly cultivate vegetables in their own yards, frequently using livestock waste as a source of fertilizer. If animal manure is fresh or inadequately composted, however, it can be a direct source of contamination for the vegetables. Domestic wastewater may be used for irrigation. In urban areas, where high land pressure limits the possibility of backyard gardens, vegetables are often grown and harvested near garbage dumps or contaminated streams and sewers or by dusty roadsides where they may or may not have been intentionally cultivated.

Postharvest handling of vegetables can result in contamination from, for instance, reused packaging materials such as sacks and plastic bags or truck surfaces, where vegetables are sometimes directly placed. During transportation to markets, vegetables may be packed together with a variety of other merchandise, including live animals, whose excreta may end up on the produce. Foods also may come in contact with undesirable nonfood items (such as pesticides, detergents, or gasoline), which can contaminate produce with chemical and physical hazards. On the way to markets, vegetables are typically exposed to dust from road surfaces because they have inadequate or no covering. Upon arrival in the marketplace, vegetables are commonly exposed to unhygienic conditions, particularly when they are loaded onto the muddy or dusty surfaces of poorly constructed and maintained market stalls.

Contamination of produce can be reduced by trimming and washing foods during preparation. Access to potable water, however, is limited in Sub-Saharan Africa, with only about 53 percent of the population having access to sanitation services (WHO 2004d). As a consequence, foods are likely to be further contaminated by unhygienic washing water. Fortunately, consumption of raw vegetables (salads) is not typical in most Sub-Saharan African cultures; most vegetables are cooked before consumption. If readily consumed following preparation, cooked vegetables should have few or no pathogenic organisms remaining. Cooking will not, however, eliminate the presence of all heat-stable food-borne intoxicants (such as *Staphylococcus aureus* toxin). Therefore, mishandling of food before cooking can still result in consumer illness. In addition, re- and cross-contamination of cooked foods from dirty hands of food servers and consumers, as well as from food preparation and serving utensils, remains a real danger.

All of the risks just described apply in the case of fruits, but in addition, fruits are generally eaten in raw or semicooked forms. Drinks, particularly freshly prepared fruit juices, are commonly vended on the streets or sold in food service establishments. Fresh juices are also often recommended for vulnerable individuals such as children, the sick, and convalescents. Unfortunately, they constitute a food safety risk because of the high likelihood that the water and utensils used to prepare the juice are unhygienic and that food handlers themselves may be sources of food-borne illness.

Processing fresh produce into fresh-cut products increases the risk of bacterial growth and contamination by disrupting the natural protective exterior barrier of the produce. The release of plant cellular fluids when produce is chopped or shredded provides a nutritive medium in which pathogens, if present, are better able to survive or grow. Thus, if pathogens are present on the fruit or in the environment when the surface integrity of the fruit or vegetable is broken, bacterial growth may occur and contamination can spread. Processing of fresh produce (such as through cutting or blending) without proper sanitation procedures in the processing environment increases the potential for contamination by pathogens. Consequently, fruits and vegetables have been implicated as vehicles for foodborne illnesses and, despite the lack of reliable statistics, are judged to be major contributors to the burden of disease in developing countries, specifically because of a lack of clean water with which to grow and wash produce (FAO/WHO 2008).

In view of the dietary importance and nutrition and health benefits of consuming fruits and vegetables, coupled with the recognition of their potential to transmit food-borne illnesses, several efforts are underway worldwide to improve the availability and safety of fruits and vegetables. Resources aimed at reducing the food safety risks associated with consuming fruits and vegetables and maximizing the resulting benefits have been published (for example, FDA 1998). Consistent application of these and other measures should improve the quality, safety, availability, and affordability of fresh fruits and vegetables around the world. Other efforts include activities by WHO and FAO to provide guidelines, standards, training guides, and expert advice. A recent FAO-sponsored expert meeting evaluated microbiological hazards in fresh fruits and vegetables to identify the commodities of greatest concern as well as to provide guidance to FAO and WHO on how to address these issues (FAO/WHO 2008). Increased inclusion of fruits and vegetables in Sub-Saharan African food systems has the potential to directly and indirectly improve consumer health in the region, through both improved nutrient intake and improved incomes, which improve food security. For these benefits to be realized, however, the chemical, physical, and microbiological safety of fruits and vegetables must be ensured.

Street Foods and Substandard Food Service Establishments

Street foods are defined as ready-to-eat foods or beverages prepared and sold in the streets and other public places such as schools and workplaces. In Africa, a growing number of low-income earners live in the periurban slum areas of cities. Increasing urbanization has resulted in a growing demand for, and therefore, increased preparation, sale, and consumption of street foods in urban and semi-urban areas of low-income countries (WHO 2008b). Many people depend on street foods for their meals, both during their working hours in the city and for their evening meals, since they are affordable and can be purchased in small quantities. A study in Nairobi, Kenya, reported that non-home-prepared foods are an important source of energy and nutrients for men, women, and school-children and that energy and nutrient intakes between consumers and noncon-sumers of non-home-prepared foods are similar (van't Riet, den Hartog, and van Staveren 2002). These findings illustrate the relationships among urbanization, poverty, and the need for low-cost foods and employment, especially for women. Clearly, street foods are an important source of affordable nourishment for the urban poor. The poor hygienic conditions in which streets foods are prepared and served, however, make them a source of food-borne illnesses for the vulner-able people who depend on them (WHO 2008b).

Most street foods are prepared in the cities' back streets, with limited space, inadequate or no toilet facilities, inadequate or no proper hand-washing facilities, and inadequate or no access to potable water. Because of limited resources, the food-serving utensils such as plates and cutlery are often limited in number and must be hurriedly washed to be reused by other customers. The water used to prepare food and clean utensils is often limited in quality and quantity and is thus frequently used repeatedly to clean a large number of utensils. To remove stubborn food remnants, food stall workers often wipe plates and cutlery with overused and unhygienic cloths. Thus, there are abundant opportunities for bio-logical contamination of street foods. Further risks associated with street foods include poor hygienic practices of food handlers, limited or no enforcement of health screens and checks on food service staff, extended display of ready-to-eat foods in warmers at temperatures that enable growth of microbial contaminants, and cross-contamination of ready-to-eat foods. Many factors, therefore, affect the safety of street foods, including the environment in which they are prepared and served; the availability of water and sanitation facilities for use during food preparation, vending, and serving; the type of food and its preparation and serv-ing methods; and the vulnerability of the target group to food-borne illnesses (FAO/WHO 2005b; WHO 2008a,b).

Many studies have examined the microbiological safety of street foods, with some conflicting conclusions. Mosupye and Von Holy (1999) examined 51 ready-to-eat street foods, 18 dishwater samples, and 18 surface swab samples from six vendors in Johannesburg, South Africa. They reported very low levels of *Bacillus* spp., *Micrococcus* spp., and *Staphylococcus* spp. and did not detect pathogens such as *Campylobacter* spp., *Listeria monocytogenes, Staphylococcus aureus, Vibrio cholerae*, or *Yersinia enterocolitica*. The authors concluded that the foods analyzed in this study were of acceptable quality and safety. On the other hand, Tendekayi et al. (2008) evaluated the microbiological quality of informally street-vended foods in Harare, Zimbabwe. They tested for the presence of *Bacillus cereus* and *Salmonella* spp. in foods, *Escherichia coli* in water, and *Staphylococcus aureus* and *E. coli* on the hands of food handlers and food surfaces. The results showed that some vendors' hands were unacceptably contaminated, indicating poor hygienic practices. A comparison of surface and hand swabs taken at multiple vending sites showed that hygienic standards were particularly difficult to achieve in highly crowded markets. The need for food hygiene training for vendors and provision of appropriate infrastructure were identified as essential for improving the safety of informally vended foods in Harare. Similarly, a study on the microbial quality of street foods in Accra, Ghana, found *Shigella sonnei*, enteroaggregative *Escherichia coli*, and *Salmonella arizonae* in some food samples (Mensah et al. 2002). Another study in Gaborone, Botswana, reported the presence of *Bacillus cereus* in prepared foods (Murindamombe et al. 2005).

Clearly, information and education must be delivered to street food handlers to stimulate desirable behavioral changes, for their knowledge of safe food-handling practices can be limited (Omemu and Aderoju 2008). To address the challenges facing the street food subsector in Sub-Saharan Africa, the WHO Regional Office for Africa is developing training and advocacy materials and guidance to promote safety issues related to street and market food vending (WHO 2008b). The "Healthy Marketplaces" concept initiated by the WHO also has been promoted as an appropriate approach for food safety enhancement and education. A Healthy Food Market is a setting in which all stakeholders (including local authorities, market managers, suppliers, vendors, and other food market workers and consumers) collaborate to provide safe and nutritious food for the community (WHO 2006d). The WHO has developed a Guide to Healthy Food Markets (WHO 2006d). These materials urge all responsible parties to take local action and to apply participatory approaches to food safety efforts. Given the contributions of street and market food vending to poverty alleviation and improved food security, local action to develop healthy marketplaces should be linked with poverty reduction. Sustainable poverty reduction is an essential element in significantly improving food safety in the region (WHO 2008b).

General Conclusions and Way Forward

A high prevalence of unsafe foods, and resulting food-borne illnesses, can have severe and long-lasting consequences for human populations. For instance, children exposed to negative biological and psychosocial factors during their first five years of life may fail to attain their full developmental potential (Walker et al. 2007). Multiple risk factors, including frequent illnesses, have been associated with poor cognitive and educational performance among children five years and under in developing countries. Most of the more than 200 million children under five years of age that are estimated to be at risk of not fulfilling their developmental potential live in Asia and Sub-Saharan Africa (Grantham-McGregor et al. 2007). The cumulative loss to global human capacity associated with this risk is enormous and cannot be ignored.

In summary, the ability of food producers and processors in Sub-Saharan Africa to reliably manufacture foods that are safe for human consumption will require attention and investment in each of the following areas:

- The basic problems of water and sanitation, which are key to improving food safety, must be solved by providing the basic infrastructure for hygiene such as access to toilet and hand-washing facilities as well as to potable water for food-related businesses and for domestic use. Lack of or poor access to water and sanitation services in communities results in food-borne diseases and poor health for individuals living in those communities. For example, a direct relationship exists between water contamination and cholera outbreaks (Gundry, Wright, and Conroy 2004), which are among the most significant waterborne diseases in Sub-Saharan Africa in terms of both frequency and scale. Most of the outbreaks occur during or just after the rains. In the absence of proper sanitation systems, the associated flooding results in contamination of water sources, and consequently food, with sewage.
- It is crucial to raise public awareness of basic hygiene and food safety measures, based on internationally acceptable basic information (WHO 2006c). Food safety knowledge and skills must be transmitted to food handlers, including processors, caterers, and street food vendors. Ideally, these efforts should include effective information, education, and communication strategies on food safety risks and on how to prevent or control them.
- Food-borne illness surveillance systems must be established to collect, analyze, and share epidemiological data and to use these data as a basis for setting priorities on the most critical food-borne risks that need to be addressed in order to realize the highest impact—that is, to protect the most vulnerable individuals. Regional cooperation for improving monitoring and traceability systems to minimize the risks to human life or markets should be a central consideration.
- Food system developments must be appropriate and sustainable for the local community, region, and country.

In view of the globalization of the food system, hazards associated with the production and distribution of unsafe foods can extend beyond national borders. Therefore, to effectively control food-borne illnesses worldwide, African countries must implement food safety measures that equally safeguard the health of both domestic and export market consumers. This goal presents a major challenge because it calls for human and infrastructure requirements that are limited in the African region. A possible approach to developing a regulatory framework designed to safeguard food systems in Sub-Saharan Africa is to adopt and adapt appropriate existing international guidelines, regulations, and standards. This approach will greatly reduce the time and resources necessary to develop food safety systems where needed, while simultaneously improving product safety and acceptability both within and beyond their countries of origin. Ultimately, because the safety of foods in a given food system is a critical factor affecting public health, strategies that effectively reduce food-borne illnesses by enhancing the safety of local, national, and international food systems will yield tangible improvements in the global public health profile.

CHAPTER 9

~~~~~~~~~

Population Dynamics and Future Food Requirements in Sub-Saharan Africa

Barbara Boyle Torrey

Abstract

The inexorable growth in the Sub-Saharan African population in the next 40 years will complicate agricultural solutions developed for today's problems. Even assuming that fertility rates drop steadily, the numbers of people to feed will more than double by 2050. They will also be older than today's populations, more urban, and more demanding of their agricultural systems.

Estimates of caloric production from current agricultural harvests are similar to the biological requirements for calories of the current African population, suggesting that the problem of undernutrition in Africa today is more a function of supply wastage and poor distribution systems than of agricultural productivity. Current demographic trends, however, will increase future biological caloric requirements. The number of people in future populations will be the largest determinant of future caloric requirements, of course. But changing age structure will also have important caloric implications, even more important than the implications of changes in urbanization.

Demography is not destiny, however; too many intervening factors, such as nutrition, can change the course of population trends. Nonetheless, the momentum of demographic growth and change means that population trends will be a major factor in whether agricultural systems in Africa succeed in feeding their people adequately in the future.

Introduction

The inexorable growth in the Sub-Saharan African population in the next 40 years will complicate agricultural solutions developed for today's problems. Even assuming that fertility rates drop steadily, the numbers of people to feed will more than double by 2050. They will also be older than today's population, more urban, and more demanding of their agricultural systems.

This chapter begins with a brief discussion of the broad population changes in Africa since 1950. These changes vary by region but are impressive in aggregate. The population changes are occurring simultaneously with epidemiological change, changes in how people live, the illnesses they live with, and changes in the risk factors for their deaths. One major risk factor for death in Sub-Saharan Africa is undernutrition. Child nutrition, in particular, affects mortality at early ages and morbidity, productivity, and fertility later as the child matures. Comparisons of estimates by the Food and Agriculture Organization of the United Nations (FAO) of current food supply in Africa with what would be required to adequately nourish its current population suggests the importance of current governance and agricultural infrastructure in Africa in meeting food requirements.

This chapter will then discuss future population trends, which will be determined in part by the fertility rates of the current generation. Therefore current fertility rates will also be important in determining food requirements in the 21st century. The requirements for more food in 2050 will be determined not only by the number of people who will be alive 40 years from now, however, but also by how old they are and whether they live in urban areas where they are less active than in rural areas.

This chapter will conclude with estimates of how future population trends are likely to increase the demands on the African food system in general and the requirements for calories in particular. These estimated requirements for food are only illustrative, given the nature of the data and assumptions. But they raise a number of research and policy questions that need to be addressed today to ensure a well-nourished population in Sub-Saharan Africa in the future.

Population, Health, and Nutrition Trends from 1950 to 2005

Population

In 1950 Sub-Saharan Africa had a similar number of people as North America and a growth rate that was only slightly higher (2.1 percent compared with 1.8 percent a year). In subsequent years, however, Africa's annual population growth rate accelerated, peaking at 2.8 percent between 1980 and 1990. As a consequence today's African population is more than twice the population of North America. Eight hundred million people now live in Sub-Saharan Africa, and 43 percent of Africans are children under the age of 15 (Figure 9.1) (PRB 2007).

Three of the four major regions of Sub-Saharan Africa have had explosive population growth rates. Central Africa is growing fastest, at an average annual rate of 2.8 percent a year; West Africa is growing at 2.7 percent, and East Africa is

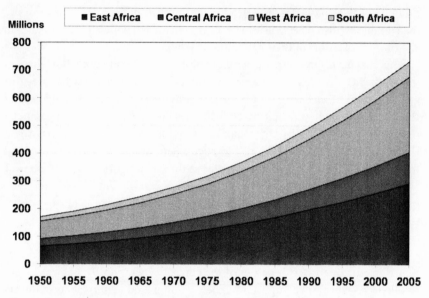

Figure 9.1   Population growth in Africa, 1950–2005
SOURCE: United Nations 2007b.

growing only slightly slower at 2.5 percent annually. Only Southern Africa, which had the smallest population to begin with in 1950, is growing at the much lower rate of 0.8 percent a year (PRB 2007). These historically rapid population growth rates are caused in large part by the substantial drops in mortality since 1950, which have not been matched by similar drops in fertility.

The quality of African demographic and health data is neither as bad as most people assume nor as good as industrial-country researchers are accustomed to using. The population estimates are based on multiple sources of data and indirect estimates, the most important of which are the decennial population censuses that are used for the sampling frames for intracensal surveys. The most important intracensual population surveys are the periodic Demographic and Health Surveys that provide more in-depth data about subsets of the population. The disadvantage of demographic data in Africa, however, is that most come from cross-sectional surveys. Therefore, only correlations among the data can be observed. Conclusions about causality must wait for the longitudinal surveys that are now beginning in selected countries.

Morbidity, Mortality, and Undernutrition

One of the leading causes of rapid population growth in Sub-Saharan Africa is the drop in death rates since 1950 and the lack of similar drops in fertility rates.[1]

After World War II almost 20 percent of all infants born in Sub-Saharan Africa died. The introduction of modern medicine, new public health measures, better nutrition, and changing child care helped cut the 1950 infant mortality rate in half by 2000. Southern Africa, which in 1950 had a much lower infant mortality rate than the rest of the continent, also halved its rate (Figure 9.2).

Rates of improvement in infant mortality have slowed, however, partly because of the effects of the HIV/AIDS epidemic. Southern Africa has been hardest hit by the epidemic (with an estimated 20 percent of the population affected) (UNAIDS 2006). In contrast, only 3 percent of the West African population is infected with the virus; 4 percent are affected in Central Africa, and 6 percent in East Africa. AIDS has increased the death rates in every country in Africa from what it would have been without AIDS and has therefore decreased population growth rates (PRB 2004). Estimated deaths from the epidemic are reflected in current and future population estimates. Despite the epidemic, the population growth rates for Sub-Saharan Africa in aggregate are still positive, although the seven most-affected countries, which are in Southern Africa, are projected to have no population growth by 2015, and they may even begin to lose population after that (United Nations 2004b, 21).[2]

The historical declines in infant mortality rates indicate fundamental improvements in the general health of the society (Mosely and Gray 1993, 69). The decline in African mortality is due largely to the decrease in infectious and parasitic diseases. Nevertheless, these diseases still caused 57 percent of all deaths in

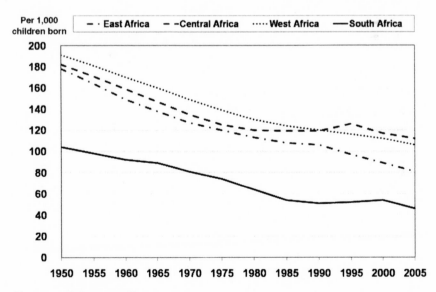

Figure 9.2   Infant mortality rates, 1950–2005
SOURCE: United Nations 2007b.

Africa in 2001, and the age group most at risk of death consists of zero- to four-year-olds (Murray and Lopez 1996, 162, Table 3B7). One of the major risk factors for these early deaths is malnutrition. In Sub-Saharan Africa malnutrition was a major risk factor for 32 percent of deaths in 1990—more than the contributions to death from other risk factors such as poor water and hygiene, unsafe sex, tobacco, and alcohol combined. Malnutrition is a major contributor to both morbidity and mortality in Africa today, causing 39 percent of the years of life lost (Murray and Lopez 1996, 312, Table 6.3). It contributes to children's weak defenses against such diseases as diarrhea, measles, malaria, and respiratory infections. In fact, if no African child zero to four years old had been underweight in 2001, total mortality would have declined 17 percent in Sub-Saharan Africa (Murray and Lopez 1996). Malnutrition, therefore, is one of the most critical issues for the future health of the continent.

Undernutrition's Effect on Population

Sub-Saharan Africa's prevalence of undernutrition is the highest in the world. In 2000 undernutrition in the total population ranged from more than 56 percent in Central Africa to 37 percent in East and Southern Africa and 15 percent in West Africa (Figure 9.3; FAO 2006c, 33, Table 1). Undernourished pregnant women are especially vulnerable to producing either low-birth-weight or malnourished infants. And infants in both categories are at much higher risk of death

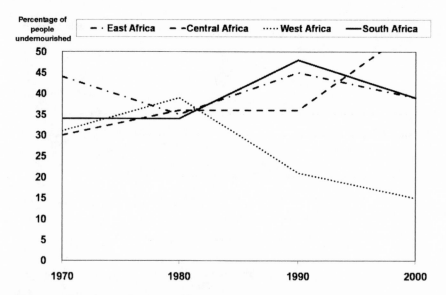

Figure 9.3   Prevalence of undernutrition, 1970–2000
SOURCE: FAOSTAT.

than infants from well-nourished mothers. Despite the high prevalence of mal-nourished mothers and low-birth-weight children, 90 percent of infants sur-vive in Africa today, but they do show the effects of undernutrition: an estimated 40 percent of African children under age five were stunted in 2005, defined as having a height lower than two standard deviations for their age (Figure 9.4; Black et al. 2008).

It is a cruel irony that infant mortality rates can decrease while the stunting of surviving children increases because there is not enough food to feed the survi-vors. Since 1986 at least eight African countries have experienced improved infant mortality but increased stunting (Benin, Burkina Faso, Guinea, Malawi, Mali, Niger, Rwanda, and Zambia) (Alva et al. 2007). Children who are stunted by age two cannot make up for their early nutritional deficit later in life. And the early nutritional deficit has other more pernicious long-term consequences that under-mine the long-term development of Africa.

To see the long-term consequences of improved nutrition, children and appro-priate control groups need to be followed for many years into adulthood. These kinds of studies are as rare as they are valuable. One of the few longitudinal stud-ies of nutritional effects is from the INCAP (Instituto de Nutrición de Centro America y Panama) study of Guatemalan babies born from 1969 to 1977 in two neighboring villages (Martorell 2005). When the INCAP longitudinal study began, 45 percent of children in the two villages were stunted, similar to the rate of stunt-ing in Africa today. For seven years villagers were given a supplement, but one

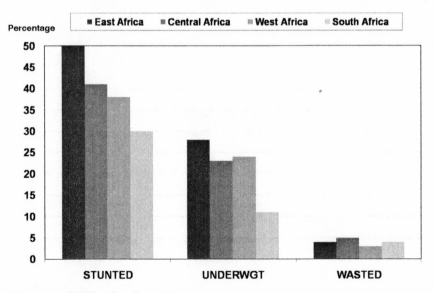

Figure 9.4   Childhood undernutrition, 2005
SOURCE: Black et al. 2008.

village received a more nutritious supplement than the other. After seven years, in the village that received the more nutritious supplement, the stunting of children under age two was half the original rate. The rate of low-birth-weight deliveries was cut in half, and infant mortality rates fell 66 percent (compared with a decrease of 24 percent in the village that received a less nutritious supplement).

The INCAP study also found that in the first two years of life the effect of the more nutritious supplement on mental development was positive but small compared with the control village. The 1988–89 follow-up, however, found that the adolescents who had had the better supplement for the first seven years of life were taller and had a higher work capacity as measured by maximal oxygen consumption. This conclusion was consistent with a historical study of Europeans in the 19th century who also suffered from malnutrition and had a high prevalence of stunting (Fogel 1994).

Other studies of the effect of nutrition on productivity in Africa suggest similar results. A study of farm output in Sierra Leone showed that increased calories had a large and highly significant effect on farm productivity. The effects were the strongest for people who began with the lowest level of daily calorie consumption (Strauss 1986).

Better nutrition, especially in early years, not only has strong positive outcomes in terms of health, mental development, and productivity, but also has an effect on the fertility of individual women. In the INCAP longitudinal study, the infant girls who had been given the most nutritious supplement had first intercourse and first births a year earlier than girls who had had the less nutritious supplement (Martorell 2005, 10). In other studies, undernourished women tended to have later menarche and were therefore fertile for a shorter period of time than well-nourished women (Zeitlin et al. 1982, 33; Frisch 2002, 31). One interesting African study of the differences between the nomadic and the agrarian !kung found that the average age of menarche is later among the nomads, whose diet was not as nutritious as that of the agrarian !kung; they also lactated longer and had longer birth intervals. The agrarian !kung were taller, heavier, fatter, and more fertile (Zeitlin et al. 1982, 70). Studies of fertility during famines also suggest that malnutrition is correlated with fewer births (Zeitlin et al. 1982, 40).

There is modest evidence for a slight increase in births at the beginning of demographic transitions. The increased fecundity (the ability to reproduce) is assumed to be caused by improvements in maternal nutritional status (Zeitlin et al. 1982, 32). In the INCAP study better nutrition did tend to increase fertility (the number of children born) of individual women, but lower education and earlier marriage were more powerful influences on higher fertility than better nutrition (Martorell 2005, 10). Better nutrition can also decrease the duration of amenorrhea, but it is likely to be for a short percentage of the total fecund life of an individual woman (Wood 1994, 522). While the effects of better nutrition on fecundity and fertility are biologically understandable at the individual level, the effects tend to be insignificant at the population level.

Ironically, although undernutrition is a major, chronic issue in Africa, the first signs of a transition to overnutrition are emerging in Africa's urban areas. The Demographic and Health Surveys have documented the trends in weight gain over time, especially for urban populations with access to subsidized and imported food. In Ghana, Kenya, and Tanzania, the number of overweight people has been increasing since the 1990s; prevalence today is now between 13 and 16 percent in these countries (Popkin 2002). Subsidized foods, especially in the urban areas, and the availability of and preference for foods with higher fat and sugar content are characteristic of the nutritional transition occurring in many countries (Popkin 2003). This nutrition transition will directly affect the health and epidemiological transitions in developing countries by creating a new set of health issues and shifting the morbidity and mortality profiles of urban populations toward noncommunicable diseases, such as strokes and heart attacks. With 40 percent of the populations of many Africa countries still undernourished, however, the challenge is to improve their nutrition without encouraging overnutrition.

Comparison of Current Food Supply and Biological Requirements for Food

Fortunately, the high prevalence and long persistence of undernutrition in Africa is not intractable. FAO estimates the dietary energy supply in terms of calories per person per day available from the estimated crops harvested by country and year (FAO 2006c, 35, Table 2). These estimates are necessarily imprecise because of the nature of the data, which are based on assumed size of the harvest for different crops and estimated number of calories each crop represents. There are many reasons why harvested calories do not represent what is available on the ground over a 12-month period. Wastage of food during both storage and transit is one important issue. But the estimate of dietary energy supply (harvested calories) is useful in judging the supply of food theoretically available in Sub-Saharan Africa.

The 2001–03 FAO estimates of dietary energy supply of calories per person per day in each country can be multiplied by the number of people in that country to estimate the gross number of calories available by country per day and then aggregated by country to provide an estimate for Sub-Saharan Africa (Table 9.1 shows that African harvests in 2001–03 produced approximately 1.421 billion calories per day). The FAO estimate of harvested calories raises the immediate question of how many daily calories in aggregate the people of Africa require to be healthy. This concept of calorie requirement is fundamentally different from food demand. Caloric requirements are based solely on biological requirements, whereas food demand is based on prices, tastes, and availability, in addition to biology.

Table 9.1 Sub-Saharan African calories available per day, 2001–03 (based on food harvested)

Country	Dietary energy supply (kcal per capita per day)	Millions of people	Total kcal per day (billions)
Angola	2,070	10.4	21.528
Benin	2,530	6.6	16.698
Botswana	2,180	1.6	3.488
Burkina Faso	2,460	12.3	30.258
Burundi	1,640	6.2	10.168
Cameroon	2,270	15.8	35.866
Central African Republic	1,940	3.6	6.984
Chad	2,160	8.7	18.792
Congo	2,150	3.5	7.525
Côte d'Ivoire	2,630	16.4	43.132
Democratic Republic of Congo	1,610	69.8	112.378
Eritrea	1,520	4.3	6.536
Ethiopia	1,860	65.9	122.574
Gabon	2,450	1.3	3.185
Gambia	2,280	1.8	4.104
Ghana	2,650	22.6	59.89
Guinea	2,420	9.3	22.506
Kenya	2,150	30.8	66.22
Lesotho	2,620	2.2	5.764
Liberia	1,940	3.2	6.208
Madagascar	2,040	16	32.64
Mali	2,220	11	24.42
Malawi	2,140	11.6	24.824
Mauritania	2,780	2.7	7.506
Mauritius	2,890	1.2	3.468
Mozambique	2,070	19.4	40.158
Namibia	2,260	1.8	4.068
Niger	2,160	10.4	22.464
Nigeria	2,700	126.6	341.82
Rwanda	2,070	7.3	15.111
Senegal	2,310	10.3	23.793
Sierra Leone	1,930	5.4	10.422
Sudan	2,260	36.1	81.586
Swaziland	2,360	1.1	2.596
Tanzania	1,960	36.2	70.952
Togo	2,320	5.2	12.064
Uganda	2,380	24	57.12
Zambia	1,930	9.8	18.914
Zimbabwe	2,010	11.4	22.914
Total		643.8	1,420.644

SOURCE: Dietary energy supply is from FAO Agricultural Produce, 2001–03. Population estimates are from the Population Reference Bureau and the United Nations.«

The caloric requirement measure used in this chapter is based on the biological requirements for a healthy individual and therefore assumes no undernutrition. It does not take into account changing demand for different kinds of food, such as more meat and imported luxuries, or deficits in micronutrients, which mean that the calories may not be efficiently consumed. Thus caloric requirements do not reflect urban populations' demand for more and different kinds of food. The estimates in this chapter do, however, reflect the differences in required calories by age (adults require more calories than children), gender (men require more than women), and activity level.

Both the FAO and the U.S. Institute of Medicine (IOM) of the U.S. National Academy of Sciences conduct periodic estimates of daily caloric requirements (FAO 2004; IOM–FNB 2005). The FAO and IOM estimates differ in the details but are similar in the aggregate. The IOM estimates (used in this chapter) are based on the biological requirements of individuals of median (U.S.) height and healthy weight associated with the median height (a body mass index of 21.5 for adult females and 22.5 for adult males). Most Americans are now heavier than this assumption would imply, but the estimates continue to be based on healthy, not current, body weights. The IOM estimates also vary for sedentary (light physical activity), moderate (1.5–3 miles of walking a day), and high activity levels (more than 3 miles of walking a day). The calculation of the average caloric requirement in Africa made in this chapter assumes that the active caloric requirement is a minimum needed for Africans in rural areas and that the moderately active caloric requirement is the minimum needed for urban populations. Few Africans have a sedentary lifestyle, and therefore the caloric requirements for sedentary activity are not used. (The appendix to this chapter has more information on the IOM-estimated caloric requirements by age, gender, and activity level.)

Applying the IOM estimated caloric requirement to the UN estimates of Sub-Saharan Africa population in 2000 disaggregated by age, gender, and urban versus rural residence results in an estimate of 1,399 billion calories needed per day for the people of Sub-Saharan Africa (Table 9.2). Therefore, a caloric requirement based on a U.S. standard for today's African population is approximately the same as the FAO's estimate of caloric supply from African agriculture (98.5 percent). These estimates, however, like the FAO estimate of calories available per day in Africa, imply a precision that is impossible given the nature of the numbers. These estimates of caloric supply and requirements are macro estimates based on multiplying aggregate data from different sources. Other problems with the calculations include the fact that the caloric requirement estimate is based on median U.S. activity levels that surely are modest compared with African levels, but no estimates have been made of African requirements. Moreover, the estimated harvested calories are greater than the availability of calories because of wastage in storage and inadequate distribution of the existing calories. For these and other

Table 9.2 Caloric requirements for Africa's future population, 2000–50

	Total population (millions of people)	Urban population (millions of people)	Population age nine and over (millions of people)	Total daily calorie requirements (billions)
	Medium population projections			
2000	679.9	222.9	465.5	1,399.1
2005	748.3	269.3	531.7	1,602.6
2010	866.9	323.4	605.0	1,809.4
2015	971.5	386.7	688.2	1,034.0
2020	1,081.0	458.4	780.8	2,273.4
2025	1,103.6	539.5	880.1	2,522.1
2030	1,308.5	630.7	984.1	2,776.0
2035	1,424.4	729.3	1,090.8	3,031.0
2040	1,539.6	836.0	1,199.4	3,283.0
2045	1,652.3	948.4	1,308.6	3,528.7
2050	1,760.7	1,065.2	1,416.6	3,764.3
% increase, 2000–50	159%	378%	204%	169%
	Low population projections			
2010	860.1	320.8	605.0	1,801.2
2015	952.2	379.0	688.2	2,008.1
2020	1,043.8	442.6	774.3	2,218.2
2025	1,135.7	513.3	861.6	2,427.1
2030	1,225.6	590.7	948.1	2,629.8
2035	1,310.7	671.1	1,034.6	2,821.3
2040	1,388.6	754.0	1,118.8	2,997.8
2045	1,458.1	836.9	1,198.1	3,155.4
2050	1,518.4	918.7	1,269.8	3,290.7
% increase, 2000–50	123%	312%	173%	135%

SOURCES: United Nations 2007b; IOM–FNB 2005.

reasons, these estimates should only be used illustratively. Still, because the estimates of calorie supply and requirements are a similar order of magnitude, it suggests that the problem of undernutrition in Africa today is less the result of too little supply than a misallocation of the caloric supply of food that is harvested.

Future Population Trends and Their Implications for Food Requirements

Sub-Saharan Africa's population, which is growing at 1.8 percent a year, will put relentless pressure on the agricultural system in the future. The momentum of past population trends will have a powerful effect in the future because the infants and children of today will be the parents of tomorrow. The size of the future generation of parents is already determined, and their fertility will determine the size of the subsequent generation.

Fertility represents the biggest uncertainty about the estimates of future populations. A demographic transition from high fertility and high mortality to lower mortality and lower fertility within a population has occurred in most countries around the world. A decline in fertility historically occurs after infant mortality rates decline, but the lag between the two declines varies widely. In Sweden death rates started to drop in 1820 because of the agricultural revolution in the 18th century, but fertility did not begin to decline until 40 years later (PRB 2004). In Mexico death rates began to drop in 1920, but fertility did not start to drop until 55 years later. In Mauritius the lag between the start of the death rate decline in 1945 and the beginning of the drop in fertility was 15 years. Africa's mortality rates began dropping 50 years ago, and fertility rates began to decline 25 years later (Figure 9.5). Fertility declines are correlated with increases in education, urbanization, age of marriage, and contraceptive use, all of which are correlated with each other (Garenne 2008). But even though education, urbanization, and age of marriage are all increasing, many African fertility rates are declining slowly and some have stalled. Each country has responded differently to drops in mortality and changes in other factors because initial conditions vary widely among African countries (Preston 1980; Teitelbaum 1975).

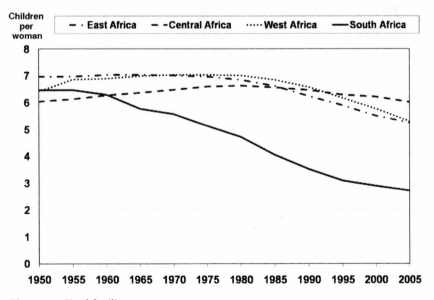

Figure 9.5   Total fertility rates, 1950–2005
SOURCE: United Nations 2007b.

One indicator of possible future decreases in fertility is the responses of African women today when they are asked about their ideal number of children—a question the Demographic and Health Surveys have been asking for years in their periodic national surveys. Because the surveys are cross-sectional, it is impossible to observe whether the ideal predicts the future number of children a particular woman will have. But patterns of responses can be correlated with other demographic characteristics to give at least suggestions about the ideal future. In the 1990s African women who had an ideal number of children lower than the current fertility in their country tended to be younger (women ages 20–24 wanted one child fewer than their mother's generation, who are 40–44), better educated (women with high school education wanted one children fewer than those with only a primary education), and more urbanized (urban women wanted one child fewer than rural women). There are many reasons why women may not reach their ideal number of children, including unwanted fertility, sex preferences, and lack of contraceptives (Bongaarts 2001). As a result, the ideal number of children a woman says she wants may foreshadow the direction of change in future fertility, but it is very imprecise in estimating the magnitude of the change (Mbake and Torrey 2007).

The UN's population projections assume that fertility rates will steadily decline from now to 2050. And the data on ideal number of children suggest that the UN assumption about the direction of change is almost certainly right over the long term. Given that fertility declines have stalled in several African countries, however, the UN assumption about steady declines in fertility is optimistic. Because of the uncertainty in the future of fertility changes, the UN has projected three different fertility scenarios that reflect high, medium, and low fertility assumptions. But even under the low fertility assumption, the future population of Africa will more than double between 2000 and 2050 (Figure 9.6). Therefore, the implications for agricultural development in the next 40 years become more complicated.

Projections of the Caloric Requirements for Future African Populations

Increasing populations inevitably translate into increasing demand for food. The International Food Policy Research Institute has developed a model that analyzes baseline and alternative scenarios for global food demand, supply, and trade (Rosegrant and Meijer 2002). Demand is defined as a function of prices, income, and population growth so it is not equivalent to the biological demand concept used in this chapter. But it is important to understand the trends such a model projects. Recent projections of the demand for food suggest that the growth in consumption of cereals in Sub-Saharan Africa will slow from 3 percent a year in the past 30 years to 2.5 percent in the next 30 years. At the same time growth in meat consumption is projected to increase from 2.6 percent a year in the past 30 years to 2.9 percent in the next 30 years (World Bank 2007b, 62). These projections

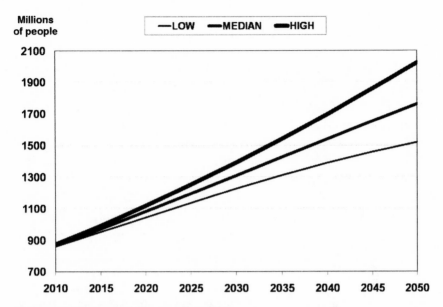

Figure 9.6   Future population growth in Africa, 2010–50
SOURCE: United Nations 2007b.

partly reflect the absolute increase in population, but decreases in rates of population growth, decreases in undernutrition, and changes in tastes from cereals to
meat. These projections assume that demand is driven by prices, markets, and
preferences, all of which are harder to predict many years into the future than
biological requirements.

As explained earlier, this chapter projects biological food demand for a well-
nourished individual. Assuming that the biological requirements for future individuals are similar to those of today, it is possible to estimate total biological
requirements by using population projections disaggregated by age, gender, and
urbanization. (The caloric requirements implicit in the UN's long-term demographic projections for Sub-Saharan Africa are shown in Table 2.) The increase
in caloric requirements is similar to the increase in population because of the net
offsetting effects of the increase in urban population and the change in the age
structure. Urban population goes from 33 percent of Sub-Saharan African population in 2000 to 60.5 percent in 2050 (under both medium and low population
growth projections). Increasing urbanization will tend to decrease the requirement for calories because urban activity levels require fewer calories than the
higher activity in rural areas. (In reality, much of the obesity in Africa occurs
in urban areas because although the activity level is lower than in rural areas,
demand for food is not.) The estimated decrease in the urban caloric requirement
per capita, however, is likely to be offset by the change in age structure by 2050.
By 2050 the population nine years old and older will grow from 68 percent of the

population to 81 percent under the medium projection. This age group requires 70 percent more calories per capita than the zero to eight age group. Although the magnitude of the change in urbanization is much larger than the change in the age structure, the caloric implications of the age structure change are much more important. Therefore, the age structure change more than offsets the decrease in the requirements for calories from urbanization. The total daily caloric requirement for a healthy Sub-Saharan population increases 98 percent between 2000 and 2030 for the median population projection; in the low population projection the increase in caloric requirements is 88 percent by 2030. A previous study, which calculated the effect of demographic changes on food requirements using the FAO instead of the IOM caloric requirements found similar results. It also examined the effects of demographic change on food requirements in Africa from 1995 to 2050 and estimated that food requirements would increase slightly more than population growth, with the effects of urbanization offsetting the increasingly older age structure (Bender and Smith 1997).

Once again, it is important to understand the biases in these calculations. Biological requirements are almost certainly an underestimate of what future populations are likely to demand. As Africa continues to urbanize, its populations are likely to eat more food rather than less, even if they do not biologically need more food, because it is available and, in many cases, subsidized. They are also likely to eat more animal products, which are calorie intensive and therefore require more calorie production than their current diets. Therefore, biological caloric needs should be considered a minimum or baseline rather than a medium projection of future food needs.

Another condition will affect the harvested supply of calories in the future but has not been reflected in the current estimates—the impact of climate change on African agriculture. Recent estimates of the effect of climate change suggest that the amount of arid and dry semi-arid areas in Africa is likely to increase between 5 and 8 percent by 2080 (Fischer et al. 2005). Thirteen African countries are likely to lose cereal-production potential by the 2080s; 10 countries are likely to gain. The net changes in cereal production potential for Sub-Saharan Africa are projected to be losses of up to 12 percent. Although the projections are based on assumptions about climate change and the future, they suggest that improving African agriculture to fully meet the demands of its population will be a moving target that will be buffeted by more than demography.

Policy Implications and Research Needs

Today Africans are largely dependent on domestic agriculture to meet their food needs, partly because of the limited tradability of the staples in their diet and partly because of the continent's high transaction costs due to inadequate infrastructure such as roads and markets (World Bank 2007b, 6). These conditions are likely to improve in the next 40 years, making it easier for African populations to satisfy their food needs from international trade. Until those improvements are made, the required food and calories will have to be supplied more by African agriculture than international trade.

As noted earlier, Sub-Saharan Africa likely grows enough food today to supply its current population with its biological caloric requirements. But the presence of so much undernutrition means that the food is not efficiently distributed either spatially or temporally, with some areas having too much food and being overnourished while other areas have too little food. The simultaneous existence of obesity in urban areas and undernutrition in rural areas within the same country illustrates this dilemma. Many people have suggested that a better marketplace for food would help solve food distribution problems in Africa. This chapter supports that suggestion. The infrastructure required for functioning markets, however, includes expensive investments such as roads and communications networks to inform farmers about prices, supplies, and weather. Although the efficacy and sequence of needed investments are beyond the scope of this chapter, research on these issues is critical to addressing current issues.

Improving current infrastructure alone, however, will not be enough to meet the challenges of a population that will more than double in size in the next 40 years. And because the population will be older, it will require disproportionately more calories. Increasing agricultural productivity will be needed to meet the caloric requirements of a growing and changing Sub-Saharan African population.

Increasing agricultural productivity will not only boost the amount of food available in Africa, but also increase labor productivity, income growth, and growth of gross domestic product (World Bank 2007b, 68). If agricultural productivity growth is larger than population growth, it may also decrease undernutrition even while the agricultural market infrastructure is improving. And it may also affect the population dynamics themselves. One recent study has suggested that increasing the use of modern crops in Africa by 50 percent will decrease the fertility rate by half a child (Conley, McCord, and Sachs 2007). The developing countries that adopted modern crops during the Green Revolution have all seen decreases in fertility as incomes of farmers rose.

Demography is not destiny. Too many intervening factors, such as nutrition, can change the course of population trends. But demography is a powerful factor interacting with health, nutrition, education, economic productivity, and other variables, influencing and being influenced by all of them. The momentum of population growth means that demography will be a major factor in whether agricultural systems in Africa succeed or fail to feed their people adequately in the future.

Appendix to Chapter 9

Table A9.1 Estimated calorie requirements (in kilocalories) for each gender and age group at different levels of physical activity

Gender	Age	Moderately active	Active
Child[a]	2–3	1,000–1,400	1,000–1,400
Female[b]	4–8	1,400–1,600	1,400–1,800
	9–13	1,600–2,000	1,800–2,200
	14–18	2,000	2,400
	19–30	2,000–2,200	2,400
	31–50	2,000	2,200
	51+	1,800	2,000–2,200
Male	4–8	1,400–1,600	1,600–2,000
	9–13	1,800–2,200	2,000–2,600
	14–18	2,400–2,800	2,800–3,200
	19–30	2,600–2,800	3,000
	31–50	2,400–2,600	2,800–3,000
	51+	2,200–2,400	2,400–2,800

SOURCE: IOM 2002, as reprinted in HHS/USDA 2005.

NOTES: Moderately active means a lifestyle that includes physical activity equivalent to walking about 1.5 to 3 miles per day at 3 to 4 miles per hour, in addition to the light physical activity associated with typical day-to-day life. Active means a lifestyle that includes physical activity equivalent to walking more than 3 miles per day at 3 to 4 miles per hour, in addition to the light physical activity associated with typical day-to-day life.

[a] Children younger than 2 have rapidly increasing calorie requirements, from 520–570 at 0–6 months to an estimated 1,200 at age 2–3. In this chapter the requirements of the 2- to 3-year-olds were applied to children who were younger, but the increased calories required for pregnant and lactating mothers was not factored into the older ages.

[b] Women who are pregnant have an increasing calorie requirement by trimester, reaching 18 percent more than nonpregnant women of the same age. Lactating women have an estimated 17 percent increase in caloric requirements. Neither was taken into account in the calculations in this chapter.

Notes

1. Data in this section come from United Nations (2007b) unless otherwise stated.

2. The seven countries with the highest AIDS rates are Botswana, Lesotho, Namibia, South Africa, Swaziland, Zambia, and Zimbabwe.

CHAPTER 10

∿∿∿∿

Income and Food Transfers to Improve
Human Health and Nutrition

Harold Alderman

Abstract

Regardless of what policies, if any, are chosen to address the real income loss and increased hunger attendant to high food prices, food policy has only a partial overlap with nutrition policy. This chapter focuses on what programs can complement—or in some cases substitute for—food-centered approaches to addressing malnutrition. These programs are often focused on women of child-bearing age and children less than two years of age. They include not only communication for behavioral change and measures to improve the quality of health systems, but also targeted cash transfers linked to use of services as well as in-kind transfers of specific foods. Their relative merits are context specific and will generally be debated. What is less debatable is that there are different approaches to different problems; addressing hunger is not the final word in a national strategy to combat malnutrition.

Introduction

One of the first major initiatives launched by Nelson Mandela after becoming president of South Africa was to establish a nationwide school meal program in August 1994. By coincidence, the announcement came while the country's nutritionists were holding a conference in Durban. The news was not greeted by congratulatory smiles. Rather, the workshop participants were generally disappointed. Why would the announcement of a full-scale food transfer program receive such a cool reaction? This chapter addresses that question, although, hopefully, the inquiry can be placed in the more constructive framework of how programs that aim to increase food consumption can complement, or be complemented by, programs to address child care and the delivery of health services.

The short answer to the question of why many nutritionists are reluctant to consider food-based programs as core interventions to address malnutrition is that they fear food programs often fail to target the "window of opportunity" between pre-pregnancy and 24 months of age. There is also a concern that governments will equate such food programs—which are often successful in addressing food insecurity and hunger (that is, at reducing poverty)—with investments in nutrition and thus fail to pursue further measures to improve child nutrition aggressively. There is substantial consensus regarding which interventions work in this capacity (Bhutta et al. 2008). Key interventions that have been proven to be cost-effective in reducing infant and child mortality, improving underweight rates, and reversing micronutrient deficiencies include

- promotion of exclusive breastfeeding;
- promotion of adequate and timely complementary feeding (at about six months of age);
- promotion of key hygiene behaviors (such as hand washing with soap);
- micronutrient interventions such as vitamin A and iron supplements for pregnant and lactating women and young children;
- presumptive treatment for malaria for pregnant women in endemic malarial regions and promotion of long-lasting insecticide-treated bednets;
- deworming in endemic parasitic areas and oral rehydration in high-diarrhea regions;
- fortification of commonly eaten foods with micronutrients (such as salt fortification with iodine) and staple foods like wheat, oil, and sugar with iron, vitamin A, and zinc.

Furthermore, birth spacing and family planning interventions, as well as strategies to address women's empowerment and gender equity, have strong impact on nutrition and on child health outcomes. It is noteworthy that many, albeit not all, of these promising interventions lie within the responsibility of the health sector and thus are not directly responsive to changes in African food systems.

It is beyond the scope of this chapter to review the extensive evidence supporting the effectiveness of these interventions. Moreover, it is likely futile to attempt to assess the relative contribution toward reducing malnutrition from such health sector responsibilities relative to those of agriculture. Rather, this chapter looks at selective interventions that complement the role of agricultural development. As an entry into the discussion, the chapter first briefly summarizes the standard model that links household decision making to nutritional outcomes to guide the choice of issues to investigate.

Households and the individuals in them are the proximate sources of demand for health and nutrition, given their preferences, predetermined assets (physical, financial, and human), and production technologies. They can be considered to maximize expected utility from the consumption of goods and leisure subject to production functions for nutrition as well as expected impacts of nutrition on productivity. These decisions also take into account current and expected prices for inputs, such as food and health care, used in the production of nutrition, many of which are also valued for their direct contribution to utility. Also key in this framework is the technology that combines these inputs in order to produce nutrition.

Clearly any change in prices or assets will influence the amounts of various inputs that are purchased. New technologies or a household's increased understanding of how to use existing technology or how to combine inputs more effectively can also lead to better health outcomes. Included in this category of effective use of inputs is time allocation. Government policies may enter directly or indirectly through a number of channels ranging from the accessibility and quality of public and private services to the functioning of capital markets for financing health or nutrition investments and the functioning of markets in which these investments are expected to have returns.

More specifically, change in food systems in African environments can potentially influence nutrition by changing the underlying production function that constrains decision making or by increasing the assets the household controls. Thus, this chapter begins with a brief discussion of the influence of income and its variability on nutrition. Programs to enhance income or reduce its variability do not have to be food-based transfers or focus on agricultural incomes. Still, a core set of interventions aimed at improving nutrition often either includes food transfers directly or is designed to influence how food and other inputs are used to produce nutrition. Thus, the chapter includes discussions of conditional transfers and of the linking of food assistance with nutritional education. The standard production model indicates that changing prices also affect nutrition. Micronutrient programs change the price of nutrients either through food-related programs or through supplementation, and these programs are therefore discussed. Finally, the chapter shows how programmatic responses to increasing food prices—often a key tool in programs addressing poverty and hunger—affect nutritional outcomes.

Responding to Income Shocks

The path from improved productivity to improved nutrition is most often mediated by income growth. Data from household surveys and cross-country comparisons confirm that income growth has a statistically significant positive impact on malnutrition rates (Haddad et al. 2003). This finding is unsurprising. What is less expected, however, is that this impact is modest even when growth is evenly distributed over a population. For example, Alderman (2007) finds that robust income growth would have a positive and statistically significant impact on malnutrition in rural Uganda, yet also estimates that with a 5 percent rate of per capita income growth—substantially higher than the average for the past decade—it would take 33 years to reduce current underweight rates by half. If per capita income growth rises to 8 percent, the number of years required to halve malnutrition drops to 14. The impact of income growth on anemia is also modest; overall anemia rates decline only half the speed that rates of underweight decline with income growth (Alderman and Linnemayr 2009).

Still, it is also clear that adverse income shocks contribute to malnutrition; the misfortune of being born in a year of low rainfall can leave a child stunted for life. For example, during droughts in Zimbabwe in the 1980s, infants zero to two years old—that is, in the period of greatest vulnerability to malnutrition—had higher malnutrition attributable to the weather shock. Studies following these children to their young adult years showed that this stunting led to fewer completed years of school, translating into a 14 percent reduction in lifetime earnings (Alderman, Hoddinott, and Kinsey 2006).

The substantial impact of such shocks can be reconciled with the moderate impact of income growth by the fact that shocks can rapidly reverse the income growth achieved over years. For many households, accumulating assets is like the child's board game, with laborious efforts to increase one's position set back in one unlucky draw (Barrett, this volume; Dercon 2005). Because drawing down a household's assets reduces its ability to earn income in the future, many households respond to an income shock by reducing human capital investments—in both health and schooling. They may do so by reallocating a limited cash budget or by changing time allocation within the household.

Safety nets are thus a key instrument in an overall nutrition strategy. Some shocks can be *prevented* by increased investment in water control and pest maintenance, often with little or no trade-off between reducing risk and raising productivity. Shocks may also be *mitigated* with improved access to insurance and credit. Additionally, households may be assisted in *coping* with shocks by public programs such as enhanced public works and transfer programs. Such programs can prevent a short-term crisis from becoming an irreversible loss.

Despite extensive research on publicly supported safety nets in developing countries, however, far more is known about how to achieve their income transfer function than about their insurance function, following either a natural disaster or an economic downturn. Ideally, a safety net would be countercyclical, increasing expenditures when income or production declines and scaling back after the crisis subsides. The capacity for such responsive safety nets, however, needs to be in place long before the shock hits. They also require contingent and flexible financing mechanisms (Alderman and Haque 2006).

Although a complete review of such safety nets goes beyond the range of this chapter, one issue central to the theme of this book is the role of food aid. The recent review of successful nutrition interventions in *The Lancet* (Bhutta et al. 2008) specifically mentions that in non-emergency situations, food aid is often counterproductive and not recommended. Conversely, there may be scope for food aid in natural disasters. For example, Yamano, Alderman, and Christiaensen (2005) show that food aid largely offset the expected increase in malnutrition attributable to harvest failure in Ethiopia. The study also observed, however, that this aid merely held the line; malnutrition rates in Ethiopia remained among the highest in Africa. Moreover, the study did not address the issue of whether an equal amount of cash assistance would have done as much or more to prevent malnutrition.[1]

It is clear that protecting incomes can protect nutrition, but can the impact of transfer programs be increased by the nature of the transfer? One way is to tie the transfer to specific activities that are likely to improve health and nutrition. This option is discussed in the section that follows. Another way is to embody the transfer by making it in-kind—that is, using food or vouchers—a type of intervention that bridges the discussion from income support to price policy.

Conditioning Food and Income Transfers to Health-Seeking Behavior

In the past decade various countries have attempted to address both equity and economic efficiency concerns with cash transfers that are linked to either health care or schooling, or both (Das, Do, and Ozler 2005). The best-known of these, Mexico's Progresa (now called Oportunidades), has been extensively evaluated, and clear evidence shows that the program improves nutrition (Rivera, Sotres-Alvarez et al. 2004; Barber and Gertler 2010).[2] The linking of transfers to health care in such conditional cash transfer (CCT) programs is conceptually similar, albeit administratively superior, to various programs that provide food assistance to families attending health centers. Indeed, in a precursor to Progresa, Mexico piloted a smart card in the state of Campeche that was validated in clinics and could be used for food purchases. Such programs, however, impose an unwelcome administrative burden on health care providers and are less well positioned to take advantage of proxy means and community-based targeting than are CCT programs. CCTs are now in virtually every country in Latin America. Mexico's program might be the most studied and one of the most favorable in terms of nutritional outcomes, but similar results showing improved health are often observed (Lagarde, Haines, and Palmer 2007).

CCTs have also been piloted and occasionally implemented on scale in lower-income countries,[3] but they are criticized as being less appropriate where the supply of services on which transfers are conditioned is weak. Additional challenges to the use of both conditions and to the targeting that most programs employ are presented in terms of human rights and thus not directly assessed in empirical terms. Other critiques, however, are based on the argument that the conditions add little; low-income households—or, according to some adherents to this view, low-income women—do not need to be advised on the best means to invest in their children. A variation of this perspective is that conditions may indeed increase investments in children and thus serve to address intergenerational equity, but this outcome is achieved at a cost in terms of monitoring that exceeds the gains.

The question of the value of adding conditions to eligibility for a transfer program is clearly tied to a theme of this chapter—what is the impact of income on nutrition and how can it be enhanced? Based solely on the evidence from many household surveys on how income affects child health, there may be little reason to expect that transfers of the size most CCTs can provide will address widespread malnutrition. Analysis of some CCT programs, however, shows that income transfers generate sizable improvements, even beyond the impact of the conditions themselves (Fernald, Gertler, and Neufeld 2008) and in programs that did not enforce conditions (Paxson and Schady 2007). The latter study, for example, shows that income had a larger impact on health indicators in the population receiving a transfer than a similar amount of income had before the transfer program. Furthermore, this change in the relationship of income and outcomes was not observed in the population that was not included in the program.

Thus, leaving aside the question of whether the monitoring of behavior itself increases the use of health clinics (and whether these clinics are themselves effective), there is evidence that these programs motivate caregivers to invest more in children. This observation is consistent with earlier studies of food stamps in the United States, which regularly showed that spending on food from the implicit income transfer embodied in food stamps was greater than that based on the equivalent income from other sources. Similarly, Aguero, Carter, and Woolard (2007) note that the income transfer in the unconditioned child support grant in South Africa, also targeted to women, has a substantial and larger-than-expected impact on nutrition, although this is true only for children whose caregivers receive the grant when the child is very young. This pattern in various countries may be due to women's increased control over resources in CCT or stamp programs. This explanation is consistent with extensive econometric evidence (Thomas 1994), although direct experimental evidence is currently lacking. The pattern may also be due to the fact that the process of receiving a transfer influences household preferences in a manner not fully accounted for in static household models. Regardless of the underlying cause, such evidence implies that the impact of income transfers can be enhanced by pairing such programs with health promotion, by using either soft or hard constraints.

Many transfer programs are designed to support household income rather than explicitly address the needs of children. Targeted supplementary feeding, however, is clearly focused on preventing the nutritional insults to children that may occur. With the increased availability of locally produced ready-to-use foods (RUFs) that are less susceptible to spoilage than traditional supplementary foods and that do not require mixing with water, this approach can be managed by community health workers. Indeed, it may be hard to separate out the intrinsic advantage of the products promoted with RUFs from the advantages of the community-based management of care. Recent studies have shown that RUFs can reduce child mortality in a cost-effective manner (Ashworth 2006; Collins et al. 2006).

This curative function is, however, only one dimension of the potential benefits of RUFs. Arguably, they can also be useful in preventing malnutrition. Yet because of the cost, the practicality of distributing RUFs to children who are not currently malnourished but have a heightened risk is still controversial (Enserink 2008). A recent study shows that preventive supplementation in the lean season in Niger can prevent wasting (Isanaka et al. 2009). Geographically and temporally targeting RUFs, whether peanut or grain and soy based, to children at risk of malnutrition finds a midway point between the well-established role for these foods in therapeutic feeding for the severely malnourished and the still-controversial use of similar products for preventing malnutrition. It is important, though, that the distribution of RUFs for children not undermine the promotion of age-appropriate exclusive breastfeeding.

Food for Education, Not Necessarily for Nutrition

School feeding is another type of program that aims at both transferring resources and enhancing investment in health and education. Although school feeding programs are often offered as a strategy to address malnutrition, their immediate impact is not child growth, but increased school attendance. The impact on attendance is conceptually similar to the expected outcome of a CCT program; the value of the food partially offsets the cost in fees or the lost labor and leisure and thus increases investments in schooling. School meals are directly conditional since one must be in school—at least for part of the day—to receive the support. Take-home rations are often used in conjunction with, or in lieu of, school meals and are generally conditioned on a minimum level of attendance in the previous month. The empirical evidence suggests that such programs have a positive impact on school participation in areas where initial indicators of school participation are low. Both in-school meal programs and take-home rations have been shown to have small but positive impacts on school attendance rates for children already enrolled in school (Adelman, Gilligan, and Lehrer 2008).

Overall, several studies of school meals show that they contribute to increased body size for school-aged children (for example, height, weight, and body mass index). Improvements are typically small, however, perhaps because the window of opportunity for child nutrition closes long before classroom education begins. Moreover, nutritionists question whether gains in weight relative to height at school age are beneficial; rapid weight gain among stunted children may increase the risk of chronic disease later in life (Victora et al. 2008). If, however, a reallocation within households of the food provided in school programs takes place— in what is often curiously and probably mistakenly termed "leakage"—it may, in fact, increase the *overall* nutritional impact of the feeding program to the degree that the reallocation is targeted toward more vulnerable members of a household. This outcome is particularly likely with take-home rations. In Burkina Faso, for example, younger siblings of beneficiaries, aged between 12 and 60 months, increased their weight-for-age by 0.38 standard deviations and the weight-for-height by 0.33 standard deviations more than the control group in a year of program operation (Kazianga, de Walque, and Alderman 2009).

Iron fortification of school meals appears to improve iron status in nearly all studies in the literature. Moreover, a combination of deworming and iron treatments proved particularly beneficial in reducing infection and improving hemoglobin concentration among South African primary school children with low-baseline iron stores compared with either treatment alone (Kruger et al. 1996).

Since short-term hunger may affect a child's attention span, a few studies have attempted to investigate the tie between hunger and classroom performance using experimental design. This impact is expected only when a child would otherwise have fasted—if a school meal substitutes for a breakfast that would otherwise be provided, it serves as an income support and incentive for attendance, but changes in cognition are less likely. Available results, however, are not conclusive regarding the impact of reducing classroom hunger, perhaps in part because controlled studies are hampered by difficulties in running experiments for an appreciable duration as well as the difficulty of encouraging parents to conform to the protocols of research design and the inability to use a placebo. Moreover, as shown in Grantham-McGregor, Chang, and Walker (1998), although feeding children improved attention in Jamaican classrooms, its impact on learning depended on the classroom organization. Additionally, because the impact of such an intervention is more likely if the snack or meal is early in the day, timing the meals appropriately can present a logistical challenge. Thus, although there is both a plausible pathway linking nutrition and education and a set of promising interventions, key questions remain on the efficacy, not to mention the efficiency, of these interventions.

Even when these studies are randomized or otherwise have proper control groups to infer causality, many of them are conducted in fairly specialized administrative environments and may lack external validity. That is, the studies do not necessarily indicate the impacts of a full-scale program; school meal programs are often plagued with irregular supply of inputs and missed meals. Moreover, the cost of successful school feeding programs ranges between US$18 (for fortified snacks) and US$50 (for meals) per child per year. Thus, a school meal program can cost more than what many countries in Africa budget for all of the other costs of education. They also cost far more than other high-priority nutrition investments. Typically, community-based nutrition programs aimed at children under 24 months of age cost about US$10 per beneficiary; child health days organized to provide vitamin A supplementation, immunizations, and deworming cost US$3 per child per year.

Nutrition Education with and without Supplements; Supplements with and without Education

In general, food supplementation has had a mixed reputation as a nutritional intervention since the publication of an extensive review in the early 1980s (Beaton and Ghassemi 1982). Nonetheless, food supplementation programs remain politically popular. Beaton and Ghassemi noted two widespread problems with supplementary feeding programs. First, the programs—frequently based on external in-kind assistance—often failed to deliver the intended amounts regularly. Second, only a portion of the food delivered went to the target age group. The so-called leakage within households should not be confused with the use of this term in studies of mistargeting of means-tested programs and misuse of transfers of various kinds. Although many supplementary feeding programs are aimed at young children—and the targeted age range when Beaton and Ghassemi undertook their review was wider than the current focus on children under 24 months— it would require a very polar case of individual, as opposed to household, budgeting to rule out direct sharing of food resources. Under less polar models of intrahousehold allocation, even with on-site feeding, the resources provided to the child would be viewed as resources indirectly available to the economic unit— that is, the household—that shares expenditures.

Given this track record, it is noteworthy that the pooled analysis of interventions published in *The Lancet* (Bhutta et al. 2008) found that in food-insecure populations—defined as those having per capita income of less than $1 a day— supplementation for complementary feeding of children under 18 months old led to a weighted average increase of 0.41 in height-for-age Z scores. The analysis looked at only seven trials in low-income settings, including Ghana and South Africa, and could not ascertain the impact on children of slightly older ages (although the projections assumed that the intervention had a positive impact up until 36 months). Preschool feeding beyond this age was not effective; furthermore, there is some evidence that such programs can lead to obesity, even in populations that exhibit chronic malnutrition. The review did not include clinical trials and thus excluded one trial in four villages in Guatemala that documents the long-term gains from food supplements, largely divorced from other services (Hoddinott et al. 2008).

Notably, the analysis of the seven studies did not distinguish the role of food provision per se from that of the education often provided in the trials. That is, although the results show the combined effects, it is not clear from the data presented whether or not education or complementary feeding alone in food-insecure populations would have an impact. The three studies reviewed by Bhutta et al. (2008), however, in which education about complementary feeding was provided to food-secure populations of Brazil, China, and Peru showed an average improvement in height-for-age Z scores of 0.25.[4]

Given the logistical and financial challenges of providing complementary feeding, it is unfortunate that this key and highly visible review was unable to uncover enough credible evidence to answer the question of the efficacy of programs that aim at behavioral change but do not provide food supplements in the low-income settings of Africa. It is beyond reasonable dispute, however, that one key intervention—breastfeeding promotion, which rarely involves food assistance—can save lives. Breastfeeding promotion combines a set of recommendations: the provision of colostrum shortly after birth, exclusive breastfeeding until the age of six months, and the continuation of breastfeeding while complementary foods are introduced (except where the mother is HIV positive). Thus, conceptually, the recommended breastfeeding promotion and education on complementary feeding overlap.

Other inferential studies indicate the importance of nutrition education in specific contexts, quite distinct from any impacts of formal schooling. For example, Christiaensen and Alderman (2004) show that the average level of maternal knowledge about malnutrition in communities is a key determinant of growth faltering in Ethiopia, even after mother's education is included in the estimates. Such studies form one basis for growth promotion programs—a widely advocated approach to promoting recommended practices for child care such as exclusive breastfeeding up to six month of life, proper supplemental feeding at the time of weaning, and the use of oral rehydration when a child has a bout of diarrhea.

To the degree that growth promotion improves nutrition, the evidence supports the view that behavioral change can have a positive result even in the absence of food transfers. Globally, however, the record of growth promotion is mixed, in part because the concept covers a broad and somewhat diverse set of activities (Ruel 1995). Often the emphasis in such programs is on weighing children or monitoring growth, interventions for which little or no effect may be expected based on global evidence (Bhutta et al. 2008). This interpretation of growth promotion is actually, however, limited and relatively ineffective (Ruel 1995). Growth promotion can provide an opportunity to impart knowledge on a face-to-face basis—hence the stress on community mobilization in many programs. Many growth promotion programs also facilitate the provision of inoculations, vitamin supplements, and deworming medicine. Still, the emphasis is on behavioral change.

Another review of growth monitoring and promotion noted that many such programs fail because measurements are often too imprecise to serve a screening function and that the motivators are not sufficiently trained to provide useful counseling (Roberfroid et al. 2005). The monitoring or screening function is arguably less essential a feature, however, than the community mobilization[5]; after all, to be effective many features of community programs such as advice on exclusive breastfeeding and the use of colostrum must occur before a child is presented for weighing. Similarly, the screening function is not relevant to caregivers' motivation for bringing their children to obtain vitamin A and deworming. Thus it may be that the community meetings and mother's groups are as important, or more so, than the weighing per se. This hypothesis is consistent with the factors contributing to the success of Thailand's community nutrition program (Tontsirin and Winichagoon 1999).

The screening function of growth promotion may even be counterproductive to the degree that it shifts attention or resources from prevention. In Haiti, Ruel et al. (2008) compared two different models of targeting food assistance to children—one that targeted underweight children aged 6–59 months and a preventive model that targeted all children aged 6–23 months. The preventative model proved more effective at reducing malnutrition. The study does not address the comparative effectiveness of supplements with and without behavioral change, however, because both groups participated in programs that communicated best practices for child care.

One of the few longitudinal studies in the peer-reviewed literature on large-scale community growth promotion found a significant difference in weight-for-age—0.4 Z score—for the treatment group in 50 parishes in eastern Uganda (Alderman 2007). This effect, however, was observed only for children less than one year of age during the approximately two years the program was running and evaluated. There was a concomitant improvement in breastfeeding and weaning practices in these communities, supporting the interpretation of the outcome as a result of behavioral change; no supplementary food was provided in these communities.

A comparison of the improvements over time in the nutritional status of cohorts of children with and without growth promotion and other health services provided by the Senegal Nutrition Enhancement Project between 2004 and 2006 confirmed that community growth promotion can reduce the proportion of underweight children (Alderman et al. 2009). Like the Uganda study, this study found that community mobilization led to increased duration of exclusive breast-feeding. Children in the program communities also were more likely to receive vitamin A supplements and deworming medicine, and their mothers had a higher probability of using of insecticide-treated bednets and receiving presumptive treatment for malaria. The evaluation of the Senegal program does not challenge the view that monitoring *alone* is not effective; what is assessed is a package of service delivery that included many measures supported in clinical trials and that was promoted by through community organizations.

Similarly, Galasso and Umapathy (2007) find evidence from Madagascar that a large-scale program that focused on behavioral change improved height-for-age in treatment populations over a five-year period compared with the control group. Although the average change in the height-for-age Z score was modest, at 0.15–0.22 depending on details of methodology, the change in the share stunted was between 5.2 and 7.5 percentage points. Like the Uganda and Senegal programs, this intervention focused on community-based service delivery and face-to-face counseling rather than the provision of food supplements. Notably, the improvements were greatest among educated mothers and in villages with relatively more infrastructure, implying complementarities between the program and its environment.

Another area where food policy, transfer programs, and behavioral change interventions may interact is with regard to maternal nutrition. The window of opportunity for nutritional improvement includes gestation; it is clear that reducing the prevalence of low birth weight can have substantial benefits. It is less clear, however, how to deliver on this potential. Folate and iron supplementation can improve birth outcomes, but effective delivery mechanisms are difficult to achieve at scale. Maternal supplements of balanced energy and protein have also been found to reduce the risk of low-birth-weight children, but the limited evidence has a number of caveats. Most noteworthy for the theme of this volume, is the fact that the most clearly documented study found the impact of a long-term program in The Gambia to be greatest during the lean season (Ceesay et al. 1997). The lean season is also the time when the workload is increased because of planting. The cost of the supplements was kept modest by the use of forti-fied biscuits that were made from peanuts and locally available rice flour and baked in village clay ovens. The protocol of having pregnant women consume the biscuits in the presence of birth attendants sets, however, a high standard for full-scale projects.

Micronutrients: Mixing Supplementation with Food-Based Approaches

Although the public health value of increasing intakes of key micronutrients is well known, the most effective policy for addressing this concern is still subject to considerable debate. Broadly speaking, strategies can be categorized in four approaches: (1) supplementation in pills, syrups, or, rarely, injections; (2) commercial or industrial (postharvest) fortification of food and occasionally water; (3) biofortification (preharvest); and (4) dietary changes including the promotion of home gardens. Commercial fortification is generally the least expensive of those approaches that have been achieved at scale, but it involves targeting only in the sense of choosing vehicles that are purchased by populations at risk; finding such food items is often a challenge in rural Africa. Biofortification—an approach that seeks to improve the nutrient content of foods through plant breeding—has the potential for wide impact without changes in consumer behavior if the crops have as great or greater yields with little difference in taste (Nestel et al. 2006). In other cases the impact will depend on a concomitant campaign to encourage consumers to shift their dietary behavior and will thus overlap with the fourth approach listed. Such dietary changes are commonly believed to be sustainable, to complement agricultural diversification, and to add to household income.

On both economic and equity grounds, a mixed course of action using all four approaches within a national strategy is often advisable. For various strategic and institutional reasons, however, few agencies promote all of these. In the case of iodine, for example, fortification is proven and clearly the most cost-effective approach. Nevertheless, supplementation (through capsules of iodized oil given orally; injections are not recommended) can complement salt fortification and be targeted to women of child-bearing age (Field, Robles, and Torero 2009). To be sure, the cost per targeted woman in a supplementation program is around 10–20 times that of reaching a woman through a well-functioning fortification strategy. Supplementation, however, can be easily targeted by age and gender, and often geographically as well, reducing costs and increasing the average benefit received. Given the benefit-cost ratio, supplementation is still a good investment if there is a population that is underserved and cannot realistically be served by fortification in the life of a project. There are no technical reasons why this approach is not advised, and indeed the World Health Organization (WHO) recommends such a nuanced strategy (WHO 2007a). One reason it is not generally promoted, however, may be a fear that it will weaken commitment to the preferred approach of universal salt iodization.

All four broad approaches to micronutrients have a role in addressing vitamin A deficiency. The evidence base on both efficacy and costs is particularly strong for vitamin A supplementation. For example, during Child Health Days in Ethiopia, a package of interventions (vitamin A, deworming, and nutrition screening) reaches more than 10 million beneficiaries nationwide at an average cost per child per round of US$0.56 (Fiedler and Chuko 2008). The cost—which includes staff and training costs—increases to US$1.04 per round per child if the measles vaccine is included. There are two rounds per year. Fiedler and Chuko estimate the cost per death averted (due to the vitamin A component) at US$228 per life saved (or US$9 per disability-adjusted life year [DALY] saved) in the variant excluding measles vaccination. This calculation is conservative and does not take into account benefits from the other components of the intervention, namely deworming and nutrition screening. The results are likely replicable in other countries with mortality rates comparable to those in Ethiopia and in an environment where primary health care is sufficiently weak that the "campaign" strategy works well.

Biofortification with vitamin A—or with its precursor beta-carotene—is one area where biofortification technology has reached farmers' fields. Low et al. (2007a) report on the introduction of orange-fleshed sweet potatoes in Mozambique and conclude that promoting this vegetable can complement other approaches and contribute to increases in vitamin A intake and serum retinol concentrations in young children. The region of intervention was one in which vitamin A supplementation was not widespread. Additional research is needed to see whether the farmers in the community continue to plant this type of sweet potato after the introductory phase is completed and whether the crop will be adopted more widely (and what extension costs will be needed to facilitate this adoption).

Only one study known to the author has directly compared the costs of supplementation, fortification, and promotion of home gardening in the same environment—in this case as a means to prevent vitamin A deficiency (Phillips et al. 1996).[6] Using various outcome measures in terms of persons or adequacy reached, the study found that sugar fortification was generally less expensive than alternatives for the same outcome in Guatemala. For example, at medium levels of fortification, the cost of achieving vitamin A adequacy for high-risk groups (that is, women and children) was half as expensive as capsule distribution and one-fourth as expensive as encouraging home gardens under various assumptions about the dropout rate following discontinuation of input subsidies. Of course, supplements address a smaller range of micronutrients (and antioxidants) than food-based approaches. This issue was not studied in the paper cited.

Fiedler et al. (2000) make a similar comparison of the costs of supplementation of vitamin A and a hypothetical fortification of wheat flour in the Philippines in order to ensure intake of at least 70 percent of recommended levels. They note that the opportunity costs of volunteers constituted 30 percent of supplementation costs whereas the capsules themselves accounted for only 3 percent of the costs. They find that supplementation cost roughly twice as much as fortification per child per year of adequate intake. Their estimate of the full cost of supplementation was approximately US$10 per year of adequacy achieved. They conclude that although fortification is more cost-effective, it would miss many of the children reached by the supplementation program. Implicitly, then, supplementation's greater coverage with higher costs points to rising marginal costs of coverage. This situation suggests a strategy that uses the less expensive fortification to reach those it can and targets supplementation to the remaining population.

Some qualifications are needed before generalizing on the relative effectiveness of fortification in these studies. In particular, fortification during processing may be effective in urbanized Latin America or in Asian economies, where processed foods have penetrated even rural markets. Yet it may not be as promising in rural Africa, where few foods undergo centralized processing suitable for fortification technology or are consumed by the majority of individuals at risk. Although particular attention has been given to the local dietary role of the food to be supplemented, technical considerations also include loss of potency during shipping and storage and the potential for discoloration that may reduce consumer acceptance. Moreover, when close substitutes are not fortified, producers may find it difficult to pass on even small increases in costs to consumers; fortification programs in both Guatemala and the Philippines have been intermittently halted because of both shortages of imported ingredients and the disinterest of producers. On the other hand, Fielder et al. (2000) found that 10 products marketed in the Philippines were fortified with vitamin A at the time of their study.

A few field trials of biofortification show the potential for farmer adoption—especially when the ability of a crop to retain zinc or iron enhances yields as well as improves the nutrient availability for consumers. Feeding trials have also shown the efficacy of crops biofortified with iron (cited in Nestel et al. 2006). Under reasonable assumptions the research and extension needed to have a wide-scale impact on micronutrients appear cost-effective. Still, the approach remains largely in the design phase; it remains to be seen whether nature—as well as human nature—is as malleable as implied in the cost-effectiveness calculations.

Moreover, with a few exceptions, studies that indicate the effectiveness of fortification or other food-based approaches use changes in consumption or changes in serum levels of vitamin A as outcome measures rather than either morbidity or mortality. Using changes in consumption is particularly problematic when assessing the promotion of gardens because plant-based sources, particularly green leafy vegetables, may be less effective for improving vitamin A status than previously assumed (Khan et al. 2007). Full cost-effectiveness estimates are also hindered by the fact that few studies of home gardens or similar food-based approaches measure nutritional status, and none reviewed by Ruel (2001) were designed to assess changes in morbidity or mortality. Moreover, many of the studies that focus on changes in intake do not contain information on programmatic costs and thus cannot be used to indicate the long-run viability of promoting gardens. To be sure, gardens can be more sustainable than supplementation or fortification, for which recurrent costs are clearly necessary. It is plausible (but not yet studied), however, that the promotion of home gardening requires regular investments in extension and, in some cases, subsidies that are essential to sustainability.

Still, the general impression from the review by Ruel (2001) of food-based strategies is that few garden programs themselves had a measurable impact on consumption, although a few did have an impact when linked with social marketing or nutrition education. For example, in her discussion of approaches to increase vitamin A, Ruel concludes, "Thus, in spite of the lack of information about the efficacy of food-based approaches, it seems likely that well-designed food-based approaches may play an important role in the control of vitamin A deficiency" (Ruel 2001, 48). She correctly points out that this lack of information occurs partly because it is far more difficult to study home gardening than supplementation. Nevertheless, the policy conclusion that can be derived from her conclusion is like the proverbial half-full or half-empty glass. One can conclude that when the body of evidence is more complete—and some encouraging projects have been published since her review—the case for home garden promotion will be more apparent. Or, one can say that the difficulty in finding strong evidence—and people have tried—leads to the conclusion that however useful as part of a livelihood strategy, home gardens will for some time remain an adjunct to an overall micronutrient strategy for many African families.

Does Influencing Food Prices Affect Nutrition?

The impact of increased agricultural production on prices depends, in part, on trade regimes. In a fully open economy prices are determined by border prices; increases in production in such an economy would raise incomes of producers but would not influence local market prices. In more isolated regions, however, the gap between the price at which a country can import and that at which exports are possible might be wide. As a consequence, price volatility within an open trade regime could be appreciable. Moreover, as shown in 2007 and 2008 when various countries banned wheat and rice exports, although trade can stabilize prices, price volatility remains a vexing problem.

From the standpoint of nutrition, price shocks both affect real income and, by shifting relative prices, influence consumers' purchasing patterns. The real income effect of rising prices is often assumed to be primarily an urban concern, although many rural residents—and often the majority of the rural poor—are net food purchasers and thus also see their incomes decline when food prices spike. Although balancing producer and consumer interests is a dilemma—and largely outside the scope of this chapter—it is relatively straightforward to calculate the first-order effects of price changes for different groups given the budget shares and net purchases frequently available in household surveys. Similarly, the impact of this real income change on nutrient consumption is often estimated, although the magnitude of the impact is still debated.

But a price change affects consumption not only through the income effect, but also through the substitution of different commodities. Determining how a change in the price of even a single food affects nutrients is difficult because consumers reallocate their budgets following a price increase, and this substitution between foods can lead to *increased* consumption of some nutrients as consumers switch to cheaper alternatives (Pitt 1983). Thomas, Lavy, and Strauss (1996) show a similar decrease in malnutrition with an increase in selected prices. Moreover, because the increase in one price will put upward pressure on the prices of close substitutes, substantial price movements for a single commodity often have appreciable second-round effects. The pathway may be quite indirect, as in Ghana in 2008, when the increase in the price of barley on the world market—reflecting both bad weather and the competition for land for oilseeds used in biofuels—led to an increase in sorghum prices as brewers shifted to local grains.

Food price subsidies can influence nutrition through substitution between commodities. Indeed, food price subsidies have the potential to affect purchases more than the equivalent resources applied to income transfers. Nevertheless, this potential has been achieved in relatively few circumstances, partly because many targeted price subsidies have a quota on the amount a consumer can purchase.[7] If a targeted household is allowed to buy a quantity of subsidized food that is less than it would have purchased before the subsidy, the program provides an income transfer but does not affect the marginal price of the subsidized food and thus does not shift purchases any more than an income transfer.[8]

Generalized, untargeted price subsidies are well known to be expensive and to create distortions to agricultural production. Moreover, they are generally regressive. Because the subsidy is per unit purchased, with the exception of a "self-targeted" inferior good—that is, a commodity for which consumption decreases as income rises—a well-off household will receive more of the subsidy in absolute per capita terms than a low-income family. The subsidy for an income-inelastic commodity such as grains will still be a larger *share* of the income of poorer households whereas subsidies for goods like meat and often oilseeds will actually be a larger share of the income of well-off households and will also be larger in absolute terms.

Unfortunately, few commodities in Africa are both self-targeted and a significant share of the budget of the poor—a necessary condition for a subsidy to contribute appreciably to real income. Yellow maize may be one such commodity in much of East and Southern Africa, although governments often are reluctant to distribute yellow maize for drought relief because globally its main use is for animal feed. Drèze and Sen (1989), however, cite an example of the distribution of yellow maize during a drought in Kenya in 1985 in which self-targeting eased the burden on community leaders by reducing pressure to allocate assistance equally. The suitability of yellow maize for safety nets in this circumstance may reflect both consumer preferences about types of maize and the possibility that the stigma from using a safety net rises with income, thus providing a degree of implicit self-targeting in transparent community targeting. Alderman and del Ninno (1999) also report that white maize is consumed primarily by the poor in South Africa, so an exemption of value-added tax on maize was progressive.[9] It had only a small impact on nutrient consumption, however, because as consumers increased their maize consumption, they decreased their bread consumption.

One way to increase the impact of a price subsidy on nutrition is to link it with education. One study designed to ascertain the synergy of consumer nutrition education and price policy randomized price subsidies, education, and their overlap in villages in the Philippines. This study found that the subsidies with education had a greater impact than the subsidy alone but that the education by itself had little effect (Garcia and Pinstrup-Andersen 1987).

The difficulties of finding self-targeting commodities as well as the challenges of administering selective price subsidies provide practical reinforcement to welfare economists' theoretical argument that consumers benefit more from a cash transfer than from an equivalent price support. This perspective parallels the related view presented by Sen (1981a) that famines are as much about loss of earning power as about food unavailability. Thus, during famine—with the exception of rapid-onset disasters that destroy market infrastructure, such as earthquakes and cyclones—income support is preferred to food support.

Sen's argument in favor in income support concerns both market functioning and administrative burden. In the case of food price increases that erode the incomes of the poor, the administrative concerns tie in with fiscal realities. Even if, as various projections of climate change anticipate, food prices increase in many agroecological zones, price supports will need to be selective if they are to be sustainable. This conclusion is both a budgetary issue and a reflection of the fact projected climate trends vary spatially and temporally. The duration of the expected price increase is central to determining the appropriate response. Typically the start-up costs of a targeted program such as a CCT are appreciable. Thus, administrative costs may dominate in the initial year and then decline as a share of the program (Caldes, Coady, and Maluccio 2006). Because few African countries had income support or public works programs large enough for a national poverty alleviation program when global prices began their recent rise, these initial costs may not be justified to address a short-term price spike but may have a rationale as part of a long-run strategy.

Notes

1. For a complete review of issues around food aid, see Barrett and Maxwell (2005).

2. These conditional transfer programs differ from safety nets designed to address shocks in terms of both the infrastructure for delivery and the targeting mechanism

3. The evaluations completed in such settings deal primarily with schooling or occasionally food consumption. Latin America still produces the bulk of CCT studies that report on nutritional outcomes.

4. A similar review covering more studies (Dewey and Adu Afarwuah 2008) but with substantial overlap with Bhutta et al. (2008) comes to a similar conclusion that education about complementary feeding can have a favorable impact even with no transfer. That review, however, includes only one setting—Bangladesh—that is likely food insecure (the study does not make this classification). This review also finds that education complemented food delivery and vice versa, based on studies from Bangladesh and India.

5. Indeed, a comprehensive review of growth promotion reaches this conclusion (Ashworth, Shrimpton, and Jamil 2008, 110). A key message in this review is that "to be effective in reducing child malnutrition and mortality, growth monitoring must be accompanied by community-based health and nutrition interventions."

6. Others compare two of the three. Karim et al. (2005) conclude that supplements are less expensive means of increasing micronutrient intakes than food-based approaches.

7. In the absence of a quota, the subsidized good is likely to be purchased for resale.

8. Such a program also risks setting up a two-tier price system and thus creates incentives for back-door sales in which dealers sell grain that is meant to be subsidized at the higher open market prices.

9. A tax exemption is conceptually similar to a subsidy. Although not generally targeted, across-the-board removals of tariffs and levies have been used widely in response to the recent steep rise in food prices. They have a particular advantage in that they can be implemented quickly.

CHAPTER 11

The Impact of Poor Health and Nutrition on Labor Productivity,
Poverty, and Economic Growth in Sub-Saharan Africa

David E. Sahn

Abstract

This chapter reviews the theoretical, conceptual, and empirical literature that links health to economic prosperity. It concludes that by raising the productivity of the workforce, good health will help transform the African food system into a modern sector that contributes to economic growth and poverty alleviation. This conclusion is reached despite formidable econometric challenges in verifying causation. Problems such as missing variable bias and unobserved heterogeneity have limited the reliability of research in this area. Although much of the discussion in the chapter focuses on private returns to improvements in health and nutrition, it also highlights the need to better quantify the potential externalities and spillovers that result from policies designed to improve health and nutrition. Likewise, particular attention is given to gender dimensions of vulnerability to health shocks.

Introduction

It is well recognized that health status is the end product of the process of economic growth. Receiving less attention, however, is that economic development and prosperity are, in large measure, determined by the quality of human resources. More specifically, the productivity of workers is directly influenced by the health and nutritional well-being of the population. That the physical and mental health of workers is essential to economic growth is a concept that dates back to perhaps the most notable economics treatise ever written: Adam Smith's *The Wealth of Nations*, which first appeared in 1776. In that influential work, Smith discusses how sickness and hunger can be expected to reduce worker productivity (Smith 1960). Smith was not alone in recognizing the link between disease and economic productivity, as evidenced by the early work of Chadwick (1842), who argued that poor sanitary conditions were contributing to economic losses.

Despite this early recognition of the link between economic growth and the physical well-being of workers, most of the literature on the returns to investing in human capital has focused on the impact of education on productivity, largely in the form of models of wage determination. Far less attention has been given to testing the hypothesis that healthier individuals are more productive, despite the pioneering development of efficiency wage theories of the labor market, initially formulated by Leibenstein (1957) and Mazumdar (1959), and subsequently expanded upon by Mirrlees (1976), Bliss and Stern (1978a, b), and others. This largely theoretical body of evidence examines the role of health and nutrition in terms of labor market outcomes. It has, however, been subjected to considerably less empirical investigation than, for example, the role of education in wages and labor market participation. Nonetheless, this relationship of health and nutrition to labor productivity, especially at low levels of economic development, is of great importance to workers and their families.

One reason for highlighting the relationship between health and productivity is that poor health and nutrition not only limit a worker's productivity and earning power, but also contribute to a cycle of poverty and poor health and human capital outcomes across generations. Lower productivity of workers can directly lead to a poverty trap whereby reduced output of mothers and fathers due to poor health and nutrition leads to poverty, and a subsequent worsening of health and nutritional outcomes, for their children. These poor health outcomes will, in turn, contribute to lower productivity for the children as they grow up. A number of mechanisms can contribute to such a downward spiral. First, poor health and nutrition of parents can contribute to children's leaving school to substitute for sick parents, further exacerbating this downward cycle of poor health and economic stagnation. That is, adverse health events not only reduce the number of hours workers can supply to the labor market and the productivity of their work, but may also mean that child labor will be substituted, potentially lowering children's educational attainment and their own future productivity. Parental illness or death not only limits productivity in the labor market, but also affects parents' ability to care for children, greatly increasing the risk that adverse health events will have long-lasting consequences (Strong 1998). Expectations of a short life span also reduce saving, and thus investment in physical capital. The challenging data and empirical demands of exploring intergenerational impacts of poor health and nutrition, however, have limited the availability of evidence on these relationships.

Second, disease and early mortality among children have adverse effects over time. The prospect of disease reduces parents' incentives to invest in the education of their children, as these factors lower the returns to schooling. Similarly, malnutrition and disease among children contribute to delayed entry into school and reduce their cognitive functioning and ability to learn, thus diminishing the quality of human capital and subsequent earnings when the child enters the labor market.

Although the relationship between health, nutrition, and productivity is of general interest, it is nowhere more pressing than in Africa, and more specifically, in rural areas where agriculture dominates as a source of income and employment. There are several reasons for this. First, the productivity effects of health and nutrition problems will necessarily be greatest in populations with more serious health problems. In Africa, not only are health indicators worse than in the rest of the world (Sahn and Younger 2010), but health and well-being in rural areas lag far behind that in urban areas (Sahn and Stifel 2003). The productivity consequences of poor health are furthermore expected to be worse in areas where hard physical labor is the critical input. Again, this is a characteristic of rural Africa, where there is virtually no formal wage labor, and most work is directly or indirectly related to agriculture and relies on strength and stamina.

Additionally, other features of the rural agricultural economy in Africa make the effects of health and nutrition on labor market outcomes particularly pronounced. Among these is the importance of own production and self-provisioning. Under such circumstances, reduced levels of output—owing to, say, temporary ailments and disease—can contribute to large consumption shortfalls, an outcome less likely in more market-oriented economies. At the same time, the propensity for market failures, such as in credit markets, contributes to inefficiencies due to underinvestment in health and agricultural capital. These conditions leave much of Africa's rural poor caught in a low-level equilibrium of self-provisioning that, combined with a failure to be engaged in commercialized agriculture, reduces the promise for escaping poverty. Reinforcing this low-level equilibrium are binding constraints in the time available to devote to the production of health, home production (such as care of children), and farm production. Thus shocks, whether they are health related or other exogenous shocks such as pests or adverse weather conditions, jointly have an adverse affect health and agriculture.

The link between health and productivity is particularly important for women. This situation reflects, first and foremost, women's predominant role in the production of food crops in Africa. Second, women have special vulnerabilities related to reproductive health, including the burden of child bearing, as well as social norms and behaviors that have resulted in women's bearing the brunt of HIV/AIDS in Africa. And third, women have a set of unique responsibilities in the home, particularly in terms of child care. Health and nutrition shocks to women adversely affect not only their productive role in the labor market, but their joint production role of caring for and attending to their children.

The remainder of this chapter will concentrate on discussing the theoretical, conceptual, and empirical literature that links health to economic prosperity. The main intent is to show that good health will promote transformation of the African food system into a modern sector that will contribute to economic growth and poverty alleviation by being a source of low-cost wage goods and a more productive workforce.

Poor Health and Low Productivity in Africa: Historical Trends

Concern over the relationship between health and productivity in Africa is motivated by disconcerting realities. Health and nutritional well-being in Africa lags far behind that in other regions of the world, and the geographical disparities are growing. Table 11.1 shows the share of underweight preschool children—an important indicator of the general health and nutritional status of children. Children who fall below standardized norms are deprived of a combination of needed nutrients and afflicted by disease, conditions that together impede normal growth and weight gain (Beaton et al. 1990; WHO 1983). In the most recent year for which data are available, 2005, nearly 30 percent of the children were underweight in Sub-Saharan Africa. Although the percentage is actually lower than in South Asia, the share of underweight children in Africa has not declined over the past three decades as it did in South Asia between 1975 and 2005.

Infant mortality statistics are similarly sobering (Table 11.2). During the 1960s, there were 154 deaths per 1,000 live births in Africa, and infant mortality rates (IMRs) were similarly high in the Middle East, South Asia, and East Asia. Yet East Asia, and to a lesser extent other regions, witnessed a marked decline in infant mortality over the next couple of decades, whereas Africa and South Asia did

Table 11.1 Prevalence of underweight preschool children (0–60 months) in developing countries, 1975–2005 (%)

Region	1975	1980	1985	1990	1995	2000	2005
Sub-Saharan Africa	31.4	26.2	26.7	27.3	27.9	28.5	29.1
Middle East and North Africa	19.8	17.5	16.4	15.6	14.8	14.0	13.2
Latin America and the Caribbean	19.3	14.2	12.2	10.2	8.3	6.3	4.3
South Asia	67.7	58.1	54.5	50.9	47.3	43.6	40.0
East Asia	43.6	43.5	39.9	36.2	32.6	28.9	25.3

SOURCE: ACC/SCN 2000. Data for 1975 are from ACC/SCN 1987.

Table 11.2 Infant mortality rate in developing countries, 1960–2005 (deaths before age one per 1,000 live births)

Region	1960	1970	1980	1990	2001	2005
Sub-Saharan Africa	154	145	120	112	107	101
Middle East and North Africa	154	128	91	59	47	43
Latin America and the Caribbean	105	86	61	43	28	26
South Asia	146	130	115	89	70	63
East Asia	133	84	55	43	33	26
Eastern Europe and Former Soviet Union	76	68	55	44	30	29

SOURCE: UNICEF 2007b, http://www.childinfo.org/areas/childmortality/infantdata.php.

not. By 1990, the IMR in Sub-Saharan Africa was substantially higher than in any other region. The tepid rate of improvement in Africa continued through 2005.

Life expectancy figures paint a similarly discouraging picture (Table 11.3). In 1960, life expectancy in Africa was 40 years, not dramatically different from other regions of the developing world and Eastern Europe. The 1960s and 1970s witnessed rapid improvements in life expectancies in other regions, but not in Africa. By 1990, life expectancy in Africa had reached only 50 years, in contrast to 58 years in South Asia, the second-worst region. Most sobering, however, is that life expectancy in Africa has fallen back down to 1975 levels, largely because of AIDS-related deaths. Even in South Asia, life expectancy is now 64 years, the next-lowest number to Sub-Saharan Africa's life expectancy of 46 years.

Table 11.3 Life expectancy in developing countries, 1960–2005

Region	1960[a]	1965[a]	1970	1975[a]	1980[a]	1985[a]	1990	1995[a]	2001	2005
Sub-Saharan Africa	40	42	44	46	48	49	50	50	48	46
Middle East and North Africa	46	48	52	54	57	57	63	64	67	69
Latin America and the Caribbean	54	57	60	60	62	64	68	70	70	72
South Asia	46	49	48	58	60	60	58	65	62	64
East Asia	46	49	58	58	60	60	66	65	69	71
Eastern Europe and Former Soviet Union			66				68		69	67

[a] WRI 2009.
SOURCE: UNICEF, *State of the world's children 1998* to *2007*.

THE IMPACT OF POOR HEALTH AND NUTRITION

Given these discouraging figures on health, it comes as no surprise that eco-nomic well-being in general, and worker productivity specifically (for example, output per worker), is lower in Sub-Saharan Africa than in any other region of the world. Table 11.4 shows that the share of people falling below the poverty line has changed little in Africa, while declining markedly in other regions, especially East Asia. The most recent data from 2005 show that purchasing power parity–adjusted productivity in Africa is US$4,935 compared with US$7,531 for South Asia, the next-lowest region (Table 11.5). Output per worker in Africa is less than half that in East Asia and around one-quarter of that in Latin America. Similarly, agricultural productivity is lower in Africa than in any other region—US$337 per worker in 2001–2003, compared with US$393 in the next-lowest region, South Asia. Like health indicators, productivity growth in Africa over the past decade has lagged behind other regions of the world as well. Thus, Africa is also falling further and further behind in this area.

Of course, the bleak results for health and poverty in Africa are not independ-ent of one another. Figure 11.1 shows the strength of the relationship between gross domestic product (GDP) per capita and life expectancy. Virtually all the countries with low GDP and low life expectancy are in Africa.[1] Although the economist's instinct is to infer some degree of causality in terms of the impact of income on health, this relationship may in fact work partially in the opposite direction. A combination of greater physical and mental abilities of workers may result in both increased productivity and labor supply.[2]

Theoretical Framework

It is useful to formalize the process by which an individual's health is expected to affect productivity and economic output, giving particular emphasis to indi-viduals engaged in agriculture, whether they are engaged in home production,

Table 11.4 Estimated share of people below the $1-a-day poverty line (%)

Region	1981	1990	1999	2004
Sub-Saharan Africa	42.24	46.77	45.94	41.09
Middle East and North Africa	5.08	2.33	2.08	1.47
Latin America and the Caribbean	10.77	10.19	9.62	8.64
South Asia	49.57	43.05	35.04	30.84
East Asia	57.73	29.84	15.40	9.05
Eastern Europe and Central Asia	0.70	0.47	3.60	0.95

SOURCE: World Bank, PovcalNet, http://iresearch.worldbank.org/PovcalNet/jsp/index.jsp.

Table 11.5 World and regional estimates of productivity (output per worker, constant 2000 US$ at PPP)

Region	1996	2002	2003	2004	2005	2006
World	15,824	17,626	18,019	18,613	19,150	19,834
Developed economies and European Union	52,876	58,642	59,588	60,749	61,759	62,952
Central and Southeastern Europe (non-EU) and Commonwealth of Independent States	11,787	14,215	15,281	16,148	17,088	18,121
East Asia	6,347	9,345	9,965	10,745	11,552	12,591
Southeast Asia and the Pacific	8,068	8,202	8,520	8,860	9,067	9,419
South Asia	5,418	6,353	6,662	7,111	7,531	7,998
Latin America and the Caribbean	17,652	17,337	17,228	17,758	18,250	18,908
North Africa	12,967	13,962	14,174	14,159	14,292	14,751
Sub-Saharan Africa	4,490	4,618	4,677	4,806	4,935	5,062
Middle East	22,130	20,990	21,273	21,119	21,630	21,910

NOTE: PPP = purchasing power parity. Estimates for 2006 are preliminary.
SOURCE: International Labour Organization Global Employment Trends Model.

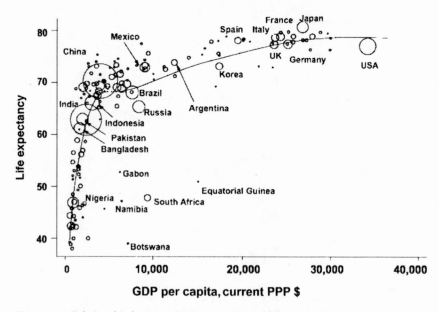

Figure 11.1   Relationship between GDP per capita and life expectancy, 2000
SOURCE: Deaton 2006.

cash-cropping, or agricultural wage labor. The basic economic framework used here is the standard neoclassical approach to utility maximization at the household level. This framework assumes the unitary model of decision making, where the household is treated as a single decision-making unit.[3] This assumption greatly simplifies the exposition and as such is widely relied upon in the literature. I will, however, discuss the implications of relaxing this assumption along the way and instead relying on intrahousehold bargaining models in which preferences differ among household members.

Examining the impact of health and nutrition on agricultural productivity and earnings poses two major challenges: the first is defining and measuring health and nutritional status, and the second is the simultaneity of the health and earnings relation. To begin to sort these issues out, I initially use the model of Behrman and Deolalikar (1988), which is a household-farm production model consistent with those presented by Singh, Squire, and Strauss (1986), in which the household engages in agricultural production as well as the production of health, nutrition, productivity, and children. This model is discussed in great detail in the literature,[4] and I therefore discuss it only briefly here, focusing on two equations that arise from this utility maximization process. Specifically, as initially discussed by Grossman (1972), current health status is a function of the previous period's health stock; nutrient availability; nonfood consumption goods, including shelter and living environment; the consumption of curative and preventative health services; the time devoted to the maintenance of health; and the years of schooling. The availability of nutrients, of course, has much to do with the time spent in home production on the family farm, as well as other choices that the household makes, such as the time allocated to processing and preparing food. The skill and education level of various household members also indirectly affect the availability of nutrients.

This straightforward conceptual model shows how the production of health and nutrients are inextricably connected among farm households. In rural Africa, however, there is the additional complexity that labor market productivity and agricultural production are jointly determined by household consumption decisions. Thus, the impact of health and nutrition on productivity are of particular interest here. More specifically, an individual's wage is expected to be affected by malnutrition and illness that result from shortfalls in nutrient intake. Thus, the wage cannot be treated as exogenously determined by wages prevailing in the local labor markets, as would be the case in a nonagricultural setting with little or no malnutrition and where labor markets function effectively.

In combination, the functional relationships highlighted imply, first, that it is important to distinguish health inputs from the stock of health. Anthropometric measures, for example, represent health outcomes, as do other clinical and biochemical outcomes, such as measures of hemoglobin and C-reactive protein (CRP) and new low-cost HIV-testing techniques for measuring sero-status. In contrast, nutrient intake, risk behaviors such as alcohol consumption and smoking, and health-seeking behaviors such as curative care and vaccinations are inputs into health. Exploring the link that joins health and nutritional status to productivity involves focusing on health outcomes, not inputs. By implication, much of the research that examines the impact of nutrient intake on productivity is less compelling, although it could be argued that nutrient intake captures short-run or current nutritional status.

Another problem in examining the impact of nutrient consumption on productivity is that the available data on nutrient consumption are characterized by considerable measurement error. Moreover, the measurement errors associated with such methods are likely not random. Likewise, since nutrient consumption is usually measured at the household level, analysts generally make the unsupportable assumption that nutrients are distributed, relative to need, equally within the household.

Alternative techniques exist for measuring intake at the individual level, such as the 24-hour recall or the actual weight of the food consumed by each household member before consumption. Here too, other problems arise, despite the improved accuracy of such approaches. Most obvious is the expense of such efforts. Furthermore, while these methods provide a short-term measure of nutrient consumption, intertemporal variation is likely to be large and thus would require expensive repeated visits to the household to obtain an accurate picture of nutrient intake. Such an approach is generally not feasible. Such intrusive procedures are also likely to influence household and individual behaviors, thus making them less than accurate.

These considerations therefore commend reliance on other health and nutrition outcomes, such as height or body mass index (BMI), relative to productivity. Height for adults is clearly a long-term, cumulative measure of health that captures investments made during early childhood. These investments include inputs ranging from nutrient intake to vaccinations and sanitation. Height is likely to be of importance in activities requiring strength. Similarly, body mass is expected to be associated with higher maximum physical work capacity, and thus greater productivity in strenuous tasks.

Although much of the literature on the impact of health on productivity relies on standardized heights and weights, the fact remains that health, like poverty, is multidimensional. Although anthropometric indicators are good measures of general health status, a plethora of other health indicators could be considered, such as biomarkers like hemoglobin. Similarly, there are a range of other possible health outcome measures, ranging from self-reported illness to measures of activities of daily living (ADLs). In contrast to the case for anthropometric indicators, however, it cannot be assumed that the measurement errors are random. And it is likely that measurement errors are systematically related to health-seeking behavior and other risky behaviors that are likely correlated with labor market and productivity outcomes. Making matters worse is that the correlation across the range of possible health outcomes, even measured at the individual level, is often quite low. Thus, unlike research on the impact of education on productivity, where schooling is relatively easy to measure and where errors are more likely to be uncorrelated with labor market outcomes, research on health is impeded by the multidimensionality of health and its measurement.

At a statistical level, modeling the impact of health on productivity also raises many challenges. First and perhaps foremost is that individuals have important unobservable features that affect healthiness but cannot be measured and are thus omitted from the health production function. The same set of unobservables—innate ability, for example—may also simultaneously affect success in the labor market. Heterogeneity may even bias the estimates of the impact of height on earnings: this result will occur if height is correlated with unmeasured human capital investments and general background early in life that directly affect labor market productivity. Many of these childhood investments, however, are likely to be health-related, so a positive correlation of height and labor incomes, if not indicating actual returns to stature or strength, may still indicate returns to improved health. For example, labor market performance may be influenced by better nutrition or the absence of illness in early childhood that lead to, along with greater height, better mental development and improved overall health in adulthood.

Similarly, reverse causality, from labor income to health, is expected to the extent that individuals living in households with higher earnings can purchase more food, more health care, and other health-producing goods and services. This situation, along with the correlation, between unobservables and both health outcomes and labor market activity, will bias the estimation of the impact of health on productivity, labor supply, and related outcomes such as wages and earnings.

The use of instrumental variables is commended to derive the causal effects of health on productivity. The requirements are quite simple in concept: variables that affect health but that have no direct influence on labor market outcomes. Food prices, community characteristics such as the health environment or medical care availability, nonlabor income, assets of the household, and household size or composition have been widely applied, although all have their limitations. For example, community infrastructure itself may be endogenous (Rosenzweig and Wolpin 1988); there is the concern that wealth is systematically correlated with measurement error in health. Likewise, in a dynamic model, wealth and asset accumulation are largely choices and thus are endogenous (Strauss and Thomas 1998). Additionally, there is the concern that they are weak instruments, being weakly correlated with the health outcomes that they are trying to predict. An alternative to instrumental variable approaches is to rely on panel data sets and the use of fixed effects estimators.

Finally, as referred to at the beginning of this section, the model presented relies essentially on the standard neoclassical approach to utility maximization at the household level. Although the unitary model of household decision making is well suited to many applications, there are also compelling reasons to consider bargaining models of intrahousehold decision making (Chiappori 1988, 1992; Ulph 1988; Lundberg and Pollack 1993). There are several different forms of intra-household bargaining models, differing in terms of the level of complexity of assumed interactions. The Nash cooperative bargaining model is the most common (McElroy 1990; McElroy and Horney 1990). The underlying premise of these models—that preferences among different household members are not uniform, implying that each member will seek to allocate resources over which they have control to the goods they most prefer—holds considerable appeal. Perhaps the most important insight relative to the focus on this chapter that could be gained from such models is how investments in health and related labor market decisions are dependent on the distribution of resources in the household, not just the aggregate household resources. The difficulty that arises is that identification of these models usually necessitates having information on resources controlled by each family member. In practice, this information is extremely difficult to obtain. Although various applications have made use of individual asset ownership (Hoddinott and Haddad 1995) or nonearned income (Sahn and Gerstle 2004; Thomas 1990, 1993) to identify demand behavior and health production functions that allow for hetereogeneity in preferences, there is a lack of successful applications of either cooperative or noncooperative game theory to the examination of the impact of individual health status on labor outcomes (Strauss and Thomas 1998). Considerable insight could come from understanding how power relations within the household will jointly affect health and labor outcomes of different individuals, especially in terms of agricultural productivity, which is generally measured for plots owned (and often operated) by the household. Quite simply, a household's productivity in agriculture may not appear to be affected by an individual's being ill or malnourished, but that does not necessarily mean that the productivity of the household member is left unaffected by their illness. Instead, farm profits could be maintained through the clever substitution of labor—for example, young girls may shift into agricultural work or mothers may reduce their time engaged in home production activities.

Empirical Evidence

The empirical evidence that links health outcomes to productivity can be broadly categorized into two groups. The first is the macroeconomic literature that shows that countries with healthier workers tend to be more productive and achieve better economic outcomes and that within countries, as health status improves, workers' earnings and productivity improve commensurately. The microeconomic evidence, in contrast, focuses on trying to link the productivity of individuals, as measured in terms of earnings, wages, and labor supply, to their specific health status.

Macroeconomic Evidence

Economic historians have put forth persuasive arguments that there is a causal aspect to the relationship between health and economic productivity: that is, that economic growth and related increases in productivity have resulted from improvements in nutrition and health. Among the seminal work in this area are the papers by Robert Fogel (1991, 1994, 2000), who showed how inadequacies in diet contributed to disease and early mortality and greatly limited the possibility for productive work in 18th-century England and France. Not only were large numbers of potential workers unable to participate in the labor force because of nutrient deficits, but the output of those able to work was significantly reduced. In fact, estimates suggest that nearly 30 percent of Britain's per capita growth between 1780 and the middle of the 20th century was attributable to improvements in nutrition (WHO 2002a).

More recent studies have also suggested that health matters for economic growth and productivity. For example, Barro (1997) estimates that an increase in life expectancy of 10 percent will lead to an increase in economic growth of 0.4 percent a year. His work is broadly consistent with the results of others showing that health-induced increases in productivity play an important role in determining the world distribution of income (Arora 1999; Bloom and Sachs 1998; Gallup, Sachs, and Mellinger 1999). A more recent study of Bloom, Canning, and Sevilla (2004) relies on estimating a production function, with life expectancy used as a covariate to capture health, as well as other control variables such as education, physical capital, and worker experience. They find a large effect—that a one-year increase in life expectancy at the country level results in a 4 percent increase in output. Part of this increase may in fact be explained by the "demographic dividend," whereby improvements in health services bring about a decline in mortality and fertility falls only after a considerable lag (see Torrey, chapter 9). For a short period of time, this demographic shift leads to an increase in the dependency ratio, shortly followed by a large decline in the dependency ratio and a bulge in the working-age population relative to the rest of the population. This shift contributes to the demographic dividend that Bloom and Canning (2000) have estimated to last for nearly 50 years in East Asia.

The temporary demographic dividend raises the interesting question of whether there are threshold effects. There are good reasons to believe that health improvements have diminishing marginal returns. In another recent study, Bhargava et al.

(2001) show that a 1 percent increase in adult survival rates (ASRs) leads to a 0.05 percent increase in the GDP growth rate in poor countries. They also found a threshold where the impact of health on economic growth disappeared. Similar threshold effects were reported by Jamison, Lau, and Wang (2004), who found that although there was an average contribution of 0.23 percent per year from better health to the income growth rate between 1965 and 1990, this was greater for countries with lower ASRs.

Another recent paper explores the extent to which the health status of populations explains variations in income among countries (Weil 2005). Also using ASRs to measure health, Weil reports that if health status were equalized across countries, the variance of log GDP per worker would be reduced by 9.9 percent. The results also suggest that eliminating health gaps would reduce disparities in country-level mean incomes. But overall, the results show relatively small effects of poor health on economic development compared with other studies that rely on cross-country regressions.

A number of cross-country and macroeconomic analyses focus on the high productivity losses resulting from specific diseases. Much of this is summarized by the WHO Commission on Macroeconomics and Health (WHO 2001), which focuses on the macroeconomic implications of various diseases such as tuberculosis (TB), malaria, and HIV/AIDS. For example, estimates are that the economic costs of TB to the poor are around US$12 billion (WHO 2001). More recently, however, much of the attention on the macroeconomic impacts has focused on HIV/AIDS. Early work, such as the paper by Bloom and Mahal (1997), observed little impact on economic growth. This optimism was in fact consistent with a Solow-type growth framework where the impact of disease on growth was mitigated by a drop in the supply of labor relative to capital, which in turn increases the productivity of labor (Glick 2007). Young (2007) further posits a low impact of HIV/AIDS on growth through a process of the epidemic contributing to reduced fertility and a decline in the dependency ratio, which subsequently leads to increases in per capita consumption as well as savings. The assumption is that these increases will not only lead to increased investment, but also provide the resources to provide health and related support for those suffering from AIDS.

These optimistic assessments have given way to more sobering estimates. For example, Arndt and Lewis (2000) estimate that GDP will fall by 17 percent, and per capita incomes by 8 percent, between 1997 and 2010 as a result of the AIDS epidemic in South Africa. Bell, Devarajan, and Gersbach (2006) also discuss the possibly devastating effects of HIV/AIDS if the epidemic in Southern Africa continues unchecked. Although such estimates are informative, the challenges of arriving at actual details of the impact of these communicable diseases on economic growth are clearly daunting. They obviously depend on the economic structure of each country, the relative importance of agriculture, whether land or labor is a greater constraint to growth, and the existence of economic and social infrastructure. Likewise, the extent to which interventions such as the provision of antiretroviral therapy are available has an enormous impact on such estimates. Nonetheless, it is indisputable that diseases such as malaria and HIV are concentrated in the poorest regions of the world, particularly in Sub-Saharan Africa, and they often afflict countries and individuals least able to cope. But perhaps most compelling is that the costs of prevention, treatment, or both are undoubtedly far less than the exorbitant economic costs associated with such diseases.

Microeconomic Evidence

Although the cross-country evidence is persuasive that improvements in health and nutrition are strongly correlated with productivity across time and countries, microeconomic studies have focused on assessing causation in such a relationship at the level of individuals, rather than using average values where the unit of observation is countries. Here again, distinguishing causation from correlation is a challenge. The correlation between health and wages of individuals has been well established with household survey data (Strauss and Thomas 1998), but moving beyond this finding has proven far more challenging. For example, healthier workers may also be better educated. Likewise, healthier workers may have parents who made choices that not only contributed to their better health, but also instilled a greater sense of work ethic and effort. Thus, caution is once again required before making any causal argument.

Several microeconomic papers make a serious attempt to overcome the econometric problems inherent in examining such a relationship. Much of the body of evidence is comprehensively reviewed by Strauss and Thomas (1998). Broadly speaking, it is possible to distinguish between the non-experimental evidence, largely the domain of economists, and the experimental evidence, which has been undertaken by economists, nutritionists, and other public health researchers.

The non-experimental papers rely heavily on anthropometric indicators as general measures of health and nutritional status. Height, in particular, is often employed as an indicator of well-being. Of course, height captures conditions and investments both *in utero* and during early childhood, especially before the age of three years. Nonetheless, many studies from developing countries offer compelling evidence of productivity effects associated with greater stature (Haddad and Bouis 1991; Thomas and Strauss 1997; Glick and Sahn 1997).[5]

Another widely used anthropometric indicator is the body mass index, and the results have led to similar conclusions about the loss of productivity associated with leanness (Glick and Sahn 1997). Similarly, Strauss (1986) has examined the effects of nutrient intakes on labor market outcomes and estimated a farm production function for Sierra Leone. He finds that calories per adult equivalent have significant positive effects on the marginal product of agricultural labor. Sahn and Alderman (1988) instrument per capita household calories using prices, and the results from Sri Lanka show that higher per capita calorie consumption has a positive effect on market wages for rural men but not women.[6]

Other studies of nutrient consumption rely on individual 24-hour recalls and the measuring of food prepared or consumed in the household. Here, the evidence is more mixed. Deolalikar (1988) studies the impact of individual calorie consumption on agricultural production functions and wage equations. Employing fixed effects to control for individual heterogeneity, results show that calorie consumption has no impact on the marginal product of agricultural labor or on agricultural wage rates. Interestingly, he does find that weight-for-height—a measure of leanness—affects these outcomes, consistent with the findings of Glick and Sahn. Behrman and Deolalikar's study on rural India (1989) finds some interesting seasonal effects: calories have a greater impact on productivity in the peak season for men, but weight-for-height is more important in the preharvest season when work is less demanding. And Haddad and Bouis's (1991) study on agricultural workers from the Philippines finds that individual calorie intake from 24-hour recall has no significant impact on productivity, whereas BMI has significant effects on earnings.

A number of papers have examined the impact of days of illness on productivity. As already mentioned, such self-reported measures not only tend to involve considerable measurement error, but also are likely not to be random. Better-educated persons presumably are more likely to report being ill. For example, Murrugarra and Valdivia (2000) find that each extra day of illness in Peru contributes to a 1 percent decline in hourly earnings among male wage workers and a 3 percent decline among the self-employed. For females, the comparable figure is 2 percent among the self-employed. Overall, however, a general picture of reduced labor supply in response to illness emerges, although the impacts on productivity are more mixed.[7] This result perhaps reflects the fact that such studies are examining agricultural productivity, and as mentioned, agriculture provides considerable latitude for substitution of labor, either with other family members or hired labor.

Recently, a great deal of attention has been accorded to examining the microeconomic impact of HIV/AIDS on productivity, as well as the macroeconomic impact. Glick (2007) provides a comprehensive review of this issue, noting numerous studies that focus on the impact of AIDS illness and death on household incomes and expenditures, largely mediated through declines in labor supply, decreases in farm production, and the burdens associated with spending on health care and funerals. There is troubling evidence that these economic stresses often lead to household dissolution (Hosegood et al. 2004; Mushati et al. 2003) and, of course, a dramatic increase in orphanage, which is shown to have significant deleterious economic and social consequences (Evans and Miguel 2004; Case and Ardington 2005; Beegle, De Weerdt, and Dercon 2005).

Evidence also suggests that declines in labor availability due to illness lead households to change cropping patterns and cultivation practices. Yamano and Jayne (2004) show that although Kenyan households afflicted by AIDS protect land under food cultivation, land devoted to cash crop production declines. Barnett et al. (1995) report a similar finding for Uganda. Other studies, however, have not found such changes in labor supply (Beegle 2003).

The research just described relies on non-experimental evidence, largely from cross-sectional surveys, although it increasingly takes advantage of panel data sets, which are generally superior to cross-sectional data for examining the economic effects of poor health and nutrition. But a recent review by Meyerhoefer and Sahn (2006) suggests that new and compelling evidence on the links between health and productivity comes from experiments designed to isolate the impact of health on productivity and labor market outcomes. Much of that research has looked at the impact of iron deficiency, widely prevalent throughout the developing world, particularly in South and Southeast Asia. As noted by Haas and Brownlie (2001), several studies have demonstrated a causal effect of iron deficiency on reduced work capacity, in turn suggesting a link to earnings. The plethora of experimental results on the impact of iron deficiency on work capacity and productivity[8] is bolstered by extensive biological evidence on iron's essential role in oxidative energy production. Iron-deficiency anemia affects physical activity through two main pathways. As hemoglobin levels decline, the maximum amount of oxygen the body can use (aerobic capacity) declines. As iron stores are depleted, the amount of oxygen available to muscles declines, reducing endurance and causing the heart to work harder for the same activity. Iron deficiency is also associated with, among other things, greater susceptibility to disease, fatigue, and reduced cognitive development.

Of particular interest is the Work and Iron Status Evaluation (WISE), an experimental study that examines the immediate and longer-term impact of providing iron supplements to older adults in central Java, Indonesia (Thomas et al. 2006). Findings show that those receiving iron-deficiency treatments are better off in terms of physical health, psycho-social health, and economic success. Relative to similar controls, treated subjects are more likely to be working, lose less work time to illness, are more energetic, and are more able to conduct physically arduous activities. About half of the male workers in the study are self-employed (primarily as rice farmers), and the other half are paid a time wage. There is no evidence that treatment affected hours of work for time-wage workers or the self-employed. Among males who earned a time wage, there is no evidence of changes in productivity as indicated by their hourly earnings. Of course, if their wages are set by an employer, workers may not reap the benefits of greater productivity, as self-employed workers do. Males who were iron deficient and self-employed at baseline reported around 20 percent higher hourly earnings after six months of supplementation relative to similar controls. Because their hours of work underwent no change, this increase translates into 20 percent higher income from labor. Wage workers who received the treatment reduced the amount of time spent sleeping by around 40 minutes and reallocated all of this time toward leisure. Self-employed workers made no such adjustments.

Iron deficiency thus appears to have a causal impact on work capacity and energy needed to complete tasks. The self-employed who benefited from the treatment allocated the additional energy to their fields, worked harder, produced more, and earned more per hour of work. In contrast, wage workers were able to channel the greater energy to reduced sleep and more time allocated to leisure. After 12 months of supplementation, some of the treated iron-deficient males who were working for a time wage at baseline had shifted to self-employment or taken up an additional job. Although the study demonstrates that iron deficiency has a causal impact on time allocation and economic productivity, it also highlights the importance of including behavioral responses to the experiment itself in assessing the impact of the treatment. Furthermore, it reinforces that work and productivity gains depend not only on improved health, but also on the individual's incentives. If agricultural and related economic policies are not right, the increased ability and potential output from nutrition and health interventions and policies may be directed to leisure (for example, more time on the soccer field) instead of to output-enhancing work.

Experimental evidence on other forms of disease and other measures of nutritional deficiency is far less available than evidence on iron status. Noteworthy among them is the work of Dow et al. (1997), who exploit variation in the price of health care to examine the short-run impact on health and labor market outcomes. They report that higher prices for health care reduce health status and that this in turns spills over to lower labor supply, and in some instances, wages.

Although much of the evidence cited focuses on the direct impacts of illness and nutrition on labor supply, productivity, and economic outcomes, a large body of evidence also addresses the indirect effects of health on economic outcomes across the life span. This research takes two major forms. The first concerns the impact of health on productivity as mediated through education and cognitive achievement. This literature is quite large, but only the more recent studies deal effectively with the econometric challenge that unobserved child- and household-specific factors may jointly affect schooling outcomes and nutritional status. Among the early seminal works that effectively address this methodological problem is the study by Glewwe and Jacoby (1995) for Ghana. They find compelling evidence that early childhood malnutrition, rather than alternative explanations such as credit constraints, explain delayed enrollments. More important, their calculations show that over the course of a lifetime, early childhood malnutrition imposes large costs in terms of lost potential earnings. Similarly, Alderman et al. (2001) employ a dynamic model using data from rural Pakistan to show that the impact of health and nutrition on school enrollment is three times greater than naïve estimates that take the health and nutrition of children of children as exogenous to household choices. One important implication is that the economic impact of health and nutrition, as found in most of the early literature, is likely to be underreported. Another recent study also shows strong evidence from the Philippines that children's performance in school is enhanced by better nutritional status, both because of earlier entry and, more important, because better-nourished children display greater learning productivity per year of schooling (Glewwe, Jacoby, and King 2001). Likewise, work by Alderman, Hoddinott, and Kinsey (2006) substantiates the impact of preschool nutrition on education in Zimbabwe and offers firm support for the hypothesis that early childhood malnutrition causes delayed enrollment. Further support for these findings comes from the work of developmental psychologists showing cognitive deficits associated with malnutrition and related health problems (Grantham-McGregor, Fernald, and Sethuraman 1999a, b; Pollitt and Amante 1984; Pollitt 1993).

One problem that plagues all of this work is the paucity of longitudinal studies that span birth, years in school, and later economic activity in the labor market. Moreover, of the longitudinal studies available, none of them are from Africa. A recent paper on the long-term economic impact of early childhood malnutrition in Guatemala by Hoddinott et al. (2008) is nonetheless interesting in terms of its potential implications for Africa. The authors report that early childhood food supplements increased schooling and improved test score outcomes. Interestingly, the improved educational outcomes for both men and women translated into economic gains only for men. Plausible explanations for such an anomaly revolve around the structure of the labor market and social norms that may limit women's economic roles and opportunities.

The second strain of literature that addresses the indirect or longer-term impact of health on economic outcomes is the research on the effects of health *in utero* or of newborns on productivity over the life span. For example, Behrman and Rosenzweig (2004) present compelling evidence that raising birth weights will contribute to better labor market outcomes, particularly among low birth-weight babies. Specifically, they report that if the birth weight of low birth-weight babies in the United States were to be increased to the mean, their lifetime earnings would increase by 26 percent. But perhaps of greatest interest are other examples of well-designed studies that have focused on the fetal period and yielded persuasive evidence on the intergenerational transmission of health and well-being (Eriksson, Bratsberg, and Raaum 2005; Barker et al. 2005; Doblhammer and Vaupel 2001). The "Barker hypothesis" suggests that maternal health and nutrition can affect fetal development, and specifically adaptations in organ development that will increase the perinatal survival probabilities. Barker (1994) and Victora et al. (2008), among others, argue that over the long term such adaptations produce a range of health problems that afflict the child as she grows into adulthood. Perhaps most prominent among these problems is the prospect of fetal nutritional deprivation leading to what is often referred to as the "thrifty phenotype." The *in utero* stress may lead to irreversible and potentially adverse metabolic and endocrine adaptations that contribute to a higher risk of obesity, diabetes, and heart disease in later life (Hales and Barker 1992; Godfrey and Barker 2000).

The challenge of relating fetal health to lower productivity later in life is formidable, requiring instruments that explain fetal health, but not health as mediated by choices and decisions that parents (and their child) make during the life course of their offspring. Some recent papers take on this challenge. For example, Alderman, Hoddinott, and Kinsey (2006) use weather or civil disturbances as instruments for *in utero* health. Almond (2006) similarly employs the impact of disease outbreaks (the 1918 flu epidemic in the United States) on pregnant women to identify fetal stress. He shows that these prenatal events lead to substantial impacts on the economic well-being of the child during adolescence.

A final point is that the impact of health on productivity may show important gender differences. This point is of particular importance in Africa's food system, where there are gender-differentiated roles and where women bear a disproportionate responsibility for food production, marketing, and preparation. Furthermore, in addition to sharing men's concerns about the morbidity and mortality associated with disease, women have other health and related vulnerabilities that revolve around their reproductive roles before, during, and after pregnancy. Adverse health events not only may reduce the number of hours that women can work in the labor market and the productivity of their work, but may lead to a substitution with child labor, which will in turn lower children's educational attainment and future productivity. Maternal morbidity and mortality may also adversely affect home production and caring for children. Indeed, there is every reason to expect that the same type of deleterious effect of poor maternal health and mortality on work performance outside the household will occur with respect to traditional household roles and responsibilities. Mothers who suffer from maternal morbidity—not to mention mortality—are also less productive at home and less able to take care of their newborn or older children. For example, the inability to breastfeed may have negative consequences for child nutrition. Sick and malnourished women will also be less likely to provide appropriate nurturing, prepare food, ensure a safe and sanitary living environment, or even take the child for appropriate postnatal care. As intimated earlier, loss of productivity in this sphere is particularly worrisome because it lasts beyond the contemporaneous loss of income and earnings, possibly adversely affecting outcomes later in life and reducing the future productivity of children, thus creating an intergenerational poverty trap.

Research in this area is far more limited, although some interesting work by Bhargava (1997) finds that the low incomes and high prices that reduced nutrient intake contributed to additional time resting and sleeping, at the expense of both household and agricultural work. Interestingly, however, it appears that sick women continue to spend time working in agriculture, whereas work in the home is relegated to other members. This finding implies that the illness of mothers poses a higher level of risk for children, especially if this pattern occurs during lactation and weaning, than it does for labor market outcomes.

Discussion

This chapter has focused on the relationship between health and nutrition and the productivity of workers and economic outcomes. Whereas most other chapters in this book focus on the impacts of the food system on health and other measures of well-being, this chapter has addressed the extent of reverse causality, running from health to economic performance and productivity. There is compelling theoretical and empirical evidence that health matters and that the benefits of improved health and nutrition will accrue largely to the poor. It seems abundantly clear that policies targeting health and nutrition interventions to the poor will have externalities that promote pro-poor growth, largely mediated by the food system, where the poor are widely employed and to which needy households, including those living in urban areas, allocate most of their budgets.

This chapter has also highlighted the gender dimensions of vulnerability to health shocks. The risks faced by women, particularly of reproductive age, differ systematically from those faced by men, and they include issues of health and violence, often of a sexual nature (Narayan et al. 2000; Narayan, Narayan-Parker, and Walton 2000; Smith, Barrett, and Box 2001). Policy-oriented research that identifies vulnerability in a gender-sensitive fashion and focuses on women's reproductive health experiences and subsequent roles as caregivers is needed. Of special note are the downside risks of negative shocks associated with childbirth and women's deleterious health-related events that contribute to a poverty trap. In other words, maternal death or severe maternal morbidity represents an additional risk that can induce an intergenerational cycle of crisis and deprivation, especially given women's joint roles as food producers, food marketers, food preparers, and child care providers.

The dynamic element of health shocks, however, is not limited to women. Household members, including men, may be able to mitigate the consequences of health shocks on farm output or earnings, in part through complex adjustments in intrahousehold time allocation, such as substituting child labor for that of sick parents. Doing so, however, may impose severe long-term costs that are transmitted across generations through, for example, reduced investments in education. Likewise, illness and shorter expected life spans will reduce savings and subsequent investments in physical capital. The need for more attention to the dynamic processes over an individual's lifetime productivity, as well that of successive generations, is thus an important point that emerges from this review. A better understanding is also needed of when, during the life course, health investments will have the biggest payoff.

Although much of the discussion in this chapter has focused on private returns to improvements in health and nutrition, the potential externalities and spillovers might also contribute to large social rates of return from policies designed to improve health and nutrition. For example, broad benefits of preventing and treating infectious diseases may accrue to the nonpoor as well. Similarly, investing in health and nutrition can be justified by the fact that market failures (such as in credit and insurance markets) and imperfect information may contribute to lower than optimal levels of investment in health, thus impeding economic growth. Unfortunately, there is a paucity of research on the externalities and related efficiency gains of improving health and nutrition; the focus of the existing literature is primarily on private benefits and returns. This area of research is certainly ripe for further study.

Despite the compelling evidence in this review, far less attention has been accorded to the link between health and productivity than to other well-studied relationships, such as the returns to education. In summarizing what is known, it is difficult to do much better than to quote Strauss and Thomas, whose general conclusion is that "some dimensions of health status and some health inputs do affect labor supply and productivity" (Strauss and Thomas 1998, 798). A few important factors explain why this relationship has not been studied as extensively and why the variance in the results is so large.

First, measuring and defining health and nutrition are difficult tasks. The multiple dimensions of health make it far more complex to examine this relationship than to examine, for example, the impact of years of schooling or educational attainment on labor market outcomes. Similarly, the impact of various dimensions of health on productivity is conditioned by the nature of work to be done, and in particular the extent to which it is intensive in cognitive skills, strength, stamina, and other related characteristics. There is evidence that, for example, health indicators such as stature and body mass might be especially important determinants of productivity among those engaged in hard physical labor. But as labor markets evolve and the nature of work changes, the links between different aspects of healthiness and productivity in different occupations also evolves. For example, a better understanding of the impacts of health and nutrition on cognitive skill attainment and learning, as opposed to increased strength and endurance, is recommended.

Furthermore, although evidence may suggest that adult survival rates or life expectancy may be significant parameters in cross-country regression, a range of underlying factors may affect these outcomes, from smoking behaviors to accidents to infectious diseases to issues related to the demographic transition. Knowing the relative importance of these factors and their differential contribution to lost productivities would be quite useful.

This situation, of course, highlights the fact that much remains to be learned in terms of measuring and understanding health status, as well as understanding threshold effects that indicate which health measures affect which productivities. Although much progress has been made in the literature on multidimensional poverty measurement, the same does not apply to multidimensional health, including the physical and mental dimensions of health.

Inevitably, the types of challenges noted, such as the need to better understand transmission mechanisms between health and productivity, focus attention on the need for more and better microeconomic evidence. The task of verifying causation, however, presents formidable econometric challenges. Problems such as missing variable bias and unobserved heterogeneity have limited the reliability of research in this area. Efforts to overcome these problems have a mixed record. On the one hand, reliance on instrumental variables has been plagued by weak and questionable instruments, highlighting the potential role of experimental studies. Yet randomized control and treatment studies are difficult to operationalize. Practical issues impede these efforts, such as the difficulty of ensuring compliance with randomization procedures and limiting spillovers and externalities in which untreated individuals (or communities) are affected by the treatment. These problems represent an important threat to the internal validity of randomized trials. Troubling ethical issues often also limit the scope for such experiments, as do the costs associated with these efforts. And then, of course, there are the issues of external validity. Extrapolating to a broader population from experiments conducted on a small group of communities and individuals is difficult, especially when experiments focus on mean impacts, rather than mechanisms and differential impact according to the differing circumstances and characteristics of the individuals, households, and communities.

Despite the fact that the extant literature does not allow for clear conclusions about the magnitude of different measures of health on different types of productivities and thus poverty (or for that matter, the causation from poverty to health), the evidence in this chapter does have important implications for thinking about the central theme of this book, the Millennium Development Goals (MDGs). One extreme view, as discussed and rejected in Reddy and Heuty (2005), is that if economic and material poverty are eliminated, all the other MDGs will follow. This perspective, while naïve, has some foundation based on the notion that incomes are instrumental to improving the nonmaterial standard of living. The income-focused view fails to take into account, however, that it is possible to improve health outcomes without large increases in material living standards and that improvements in health will lead to increased productivity, more investment, and economic growth. Furthermore, health and nutrition are intrinsically important measures of well-being, regardless of their impact on productivity and relationship with incomes. That is, an individual's utility function includes both consumption of goods and health status, and it is important to be just as concerned with nonmaterial measures of human development as incomes.

Finally, findings of significant productivity effects from improvements in health and nutrition naturally lead to a recommendation of targeted policies and interventions to improve health and nutritional status. Where and how to intervene, however, are far from clear. For example, there is a case for iron supplementation to address the reasonably well-understood productivity losses associated with anemia. If iron deficiencies were successfully reduced, however, would other binding constraints hold back the poor and limit the potential productivity gains? These constraints could be in the form of other nutritional deficits or other inputs into the agricultural production function. Moreover, is supplementation, in fact, the correct public policy response? If the price of adding some iron-rich foods to the diet is indeed trivial and substantially less than the returns in terms of increased productivity, why have those individuals with iron deficits not acted in their own self-interest? This question is not purely hypothetical. Low hemoglobin and other nutritional deficits, for example, are only weakly linked to income status. In other words, a large share of individuals with iron deficits come from households that are not at the bottom end of the income distribution. So if the constraints on increasing iron intake or utilization are primarily a matter of information or knowledge, perhaps that is the correct point of departure for intervention.

Another reason for caution in proposing policy guidance is that breaking the cycle of poor health, reduced productivity, and subsequent economic losses may in large part require answers that are not direct health and nutrition interventions, but improvements in the functioning of other markets, such as credit and related insurance markets. Considerable evidence shows that just as poor rural households are unable to insure against crop loss, incomplete insurance markets prevent them from coping with health shocks, particularly extreme ones. Once again, therefore, defining appropriate solutions inevitably focuses attention on the complexities of the constraints that jointly hold back the poor from being swept up into the virtuous circle of improved health and poverty reduction.

Notes

1. A similar relationship holds between GDP and malnutrition (Haddad et al. 2003).

2. There are also secular trends in this relationship over time. More specifically, as shown by Deaton (2006), this curve has tended to shift upward over the years, commensurate with improvements in health care knowledge and technology.

3. The unitary model implies that either all household members share the same preference structure or the household head is a dictator that imposes his or her will on the family unit. These assumptions are surely violated in some situations.

4. See, for example, Meyerhoefer and Sahn (2006).

5. There is also evidence from the historical literature that height affected the price of slaves, presumably reflecting the expected productivity gains associated with greater stature (Margo and Steckel 1982).

6. Strauss and Thomas (1998) point out the limitations of relying on household calorie intake as these papers do.

7. See, for example, Schultz and Tansel (1997) and Pitt and Rosenzweig (1986).

8. See, for example, Li et al. (1994), Edgerton et al. (1979), and Basta et al. (1979).

CHAPTER 12

~~~~~~~

Food Systems and the Escape from Poverty and Ill-Health Traps in Sub-Saharan Africa

Christopher B. Barrett

Abstract

Millennium Development Goal 1 is to halve extreme poverty ($1 a day per person) and hunger. Progress toward this goal has been excellent at the global level, led by China and India, but woefully insufficient in Sub-Saharan Africa. In Africa, a disproportionate share of the extreme poor are ultra-poor, surviving on less than $0.50 a day per person, a condition that appears both stubbornly persistent and closely associated with widespread severe malnutrition—"ultra-hunger"— and ill health. Indeed, ill health, malnutrition, and ultra-poverty are mutually reinforcing states that add to the challenge of addressing any one of them on its own and make integrated strategies essential. Food systems are a natural locus for such strategies because agriculture is the primary employment sector for the ultra-poor and because food consumes a large share of the expenditures of the ultra-poor. The causal mechanisms underpinning the poverty trap in which ultra-poor, unhealthy, and undernourished rural Africans too often find themselves remain only partially understood but are clearly rooted in the food system that guides their production, exchange, consumption, and investment behaviors. Four key principles to guide interventions in improving food systems emerge clearly. But there remains only limited empirical evidence to guide detailed design and implementation of strategies to develop African food systems so as to break the lock of poverty and ill-health traps.

Introduction

The Millennium Declaration of September 2000, adopted by the 189 member states of the United Nations, renewed the vigor of the global community's commitment to improving living conditions throughout the world. The very first Millennium Development Goal (MDG) is to halve, by 2015, the proportion of people living in extreme poverty and suffering from hunger. This chapter focuses on that objective and its relation to food systems—the human-managed biophysical systems that are involved in the production, distribution, and consumption of food—especially in Sub-Saharan Africa.

The bold but attainable goal enshrined in MDG 1 seems likely to be met at global scale if the trend from 1980 continues (Figure 12.1). The decreases in the share of the population living under the poverty line were led by dramatic improvements in India and, especially, China. Yet achieving the MDG still leaves an unacceptably large number of people in extreme poverty. Moreover, in key parts of the world, notably Sub-Saharan Africa, progress has been virtually nonexistent. But although serious work remains to be done, especially in Sub-Saharan Africa, the experience of the past quarter century should remind us of the remarkable progress that is possible. There is reason for hope.

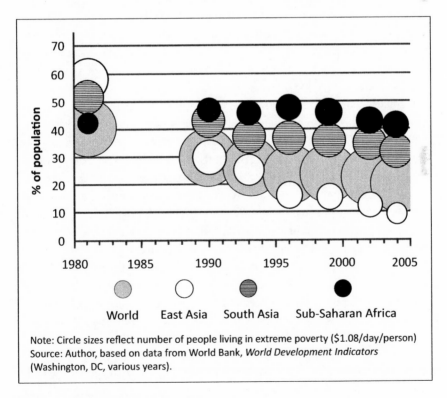

Note: Circle sizes reflect number of people living in extreme poverty ($1.08/day/person)
Source: Author, based on data from World Bank, *World Development Indicators* (Washington, DC, various years).

Figure 12.1 Extreme poverty, 1981–2004
SOURCE: Author, based on data from the World Bank, *World development indicators* (Washington, DC, various years).
NOTE: Bubble sizes reflect number of people living in extreme poverty ($1.08/day/person).

Poverty and hunger go together in MDG 1 because extreme income poverty goes hand-in-hand with poor nutritional status, with mutually reinforcing causation. This close relationship between poverty and malnutrition is reflected in hunger or micronutrient undernutrition statistics that show no significant progress in Sub-Saharan Africa in the past 20 years, just as negligible progress in reducing income poverty has occurred there. Thus the likelihood of meeting the first MDG in Sub-Saharan Africa is discouragingly low.

Of perhaps greatest concern, recent research finds that the ultra-poor—those living on less than $0.54 per capita per day, half the amount considered to indicate extreme poverty—are disproportionately concentrated in Sub-Saharan Africa (Ahmed et al. 2007). In 2004 Sub-Saharan Africa was home to only 31 percent of those living below the dollar-a-day poverty line worldwide but 76 percent of the world's ultra-poor (Figure 12.2). Furthermore, progress among the ultra-poor has been far slower than among the extreme poor. Twenty-nine million more Africans were living in ultra-poverty in 2004 than in 1990. Although extreme poverty is an overwhelmingly Asian phenomenon, ultra-poverty is primarily an African condition. This situation may well help account for the relatively poor performance of Sub-Saharan Africa in achieving poverty reduction overall. It is the only region where a plurality of the poor in 1990 were ultra-poor. Poverty reduction is easier where the poor are nearer the poverty line, as was especially true in Asia and Latin America, relative to Sub-Saharan Africa.

Similarly, ultra-hunger, defined as consumption of less than 1,600 calories a day per capita, is alarmingly high in Sub-Saharan Africa, far greater than in any other region of the world. Thus the deepest poverty and the most severe hunger are proving the most intractable. Poor nutrition combines with high prevalence of infectious disease (such as HIV/AIDS, malaria, and tuberculosis) to create widespread ill health that reinforces ultra-poverty in a way that poses serious humanitarian and development challenges for Sub-Saharan Africa.

Growing recognition of the unsettling multidimensional challenge of ultra-poverty and ill health has rekindled long-dormant interest in poverty traps. The idea is an old one, reflected in prominent development theories of the 1940s and 1950s that tried to explain the geographic clustering of poverty in the world (Rosenstein-Rodan 1943; Nurkse 1953; Myrdal 1957; Hirschman 1958). The essence of a poverty trap is that there exists a low-level equilibrium level of well-being in which individuals, households, communities, nations, or even multinational regions appear caught unnecessarily. Small adjustments are insufficient to move people, communities, or nations out of those equilibria sustainably. Systems must change, major positive shocks must occur, or both. And in the absence of systemic change, recurring adverse shocks will only drive more people into the trap. The sorts of health shocks that remain distressingly commonplace in Sub-Saharan Africa can, along with population growth, help explain the growth of ultra-poverty

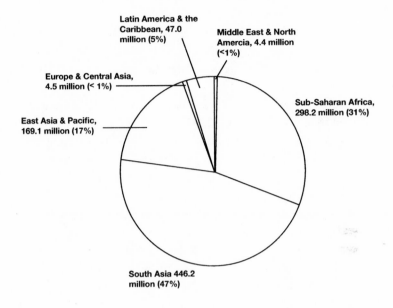

Extreme poor in 2004: 969 million

Latin America & the Caribbean, 47.0 million (5%)

Middle East & North Amercia, 4.4 million (<1%)

Europe & Central Asia, 4.5 million (< 1%)

Sub-Saharan Africa, 298.2 million (31%)

East Asia & Pacific, 169.1 million (17%)

South Asia 446.2 million (47%)

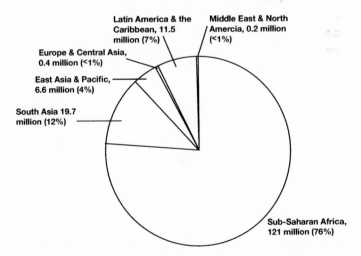

Ultra poor in 2004: 162 million

Latin America & the Caribbean, 11.5 million (7%)

Middle East & North Amercia, 0.2 million (<1%)

Europe & Central Asia, 0.4 million (<1%)

East Asia & Pacific, 6.6 million (4%)

South Asia 19.7 million (12%)

Sub-Saharan Africa, 121 million (76%)

Figure 12.2 Extreme and ultra poverty, 2004

NOTE: The extreme poor are those living on less than $1 a day per capita; the ultra-poor are those living on less than $0.50 a day per capita   or more precisely, $1.08 and $0.54, respectively.

SOURCE: Ahmed et al. 2007. Reproduced with permission from the International Food Policy Research Institute, www.ifpri.org.

in the region. This chapter therefore focuses on the basic nature of the apparent ultra-poverty/ultra-hunger/ill-health trap in Sub-Saharan Africa, the importance of risk, and the need for systemic change, starting with food systems.

The Poverty/Ill-Health Trap

A poverty trap is "any self-reinforcing mechanism which causes poverty to persist" (Azariadis and Stachurski 2007, 33). This definition can include single-equilibrium systems where the unique equilibrium is at a low level of well-being or systems characterized by multiple dynamic equilibria, at least one of which involves an unacceptably low standard of living. The poverty trap idea remains a conjecture—albeit a compelling one—because finding irrefutable empirical evidence that poverty traps really exist remains a difficult challenge for researchers. This difficulty arises both because of a paucity of high-quality longitudinal data on households and individuals in low-income countries and because of disagreements among technical experts over how best to test the hypothesis that some people might be caught in a poverty trap.[1] Although it is important to attack that epistemological question through basic research in the social sciences, the core empirical fact of widespread ultra-poverty, ultra-hunger, and ill health that has proved largely intractable to recent interventions remains, regardless of the academic dispute. And much is already known that can usefully inform policy even as the intellectual struggle to understand the etiology of Sub-Saharan Africa's apparent poverty trap continues.

At the most basic level, it is well understood that ill health, malnutrition, and ultra-poverty are mutually reinforcing states. The links are multidirectional. Low real incomes are the primary cause of chronic and acute hunger, as a vast literature spawned by Amartya Sen (1981b) emphasizes. Even when food availability is adequate—which is not the case in large portions of Sub-Saharan Africa today—low incomes impede access to sufficient and appropriate food to maintain a healthy lifestyle. But causality runs the other way as well. WHO (2002b) reports that undernutrition, including micronutrient deficiencies, is the leading risk factor for disease and death worldwide, accounting for more than half the disease burden in low-income countries. As further discussed in the previous chapter, undernutrition also impedes cognitive and physical development, thereby depressing educational attainment and adult earnings.

Disease, in turn, impedes the uptake of scarce nutrients, aggravating hunger and micronutrient malnutrition problems and hurting labor productivity and earnings. Indeed, recent research suggests that major health shocks are perhaps the leading cause of collapse into long-term poverty (Gertler and Gruber 2002; Barrett et al. 2006; Krishna 2007). And a large literature amply demonstrates the corollary that improved nutrition and health status increases individuals' current and lifetime productivity, thereby increasing incomes and assets and contributing to poverty reduction (Dasgupta 1997; Schultz 1997; Strauss and Thomas 1998; and chapter 11 of this book). And, of course, poverty depresses demand for health care, hygiene, and other inputs into good health, so that poverty is a cause as well as a consequence of ill health. Furthermore, since much health care provision is a public good funded by tax revenues, areas of concentrated ultra-poverty commonly cannot afford the physical infrastructure or professional staffing necessary to ensure an adequate, high-quality supply of preventive and curative health care. This relationship between the public finance problems associated with health care provision and the dynamics that lead to individual- and household-level poverty and ill-health traps is a classic example of spillovers between micro- and meso-scale phenomena that lead to what Barrett and Swallow (2006) term "fractal poverty traps," meaning patterns that are replicated at multiple scales of analysis. The reinforcing feedback among poverty, ill health, and hunger—manifestat all levels of analysis in contemporary Africa—is clear and important. It is a central characteristic of the ultra-poverty/ill-health trap apparent in Sub-Saharan Africa today.

Two other key things about poverty traps are well understood and merit brief review. First, initial conditions matter. This fact applies not just to nutritional and health status (for instance, low-birth-weight babies typically have retarded cognitive and physical development, with long-term economic and health consequences), but far more broadly. Those who possess the means to invest are commonly better able and more willing to secure credit, access to complementary resources, political favors, or whatever else it might take to induce investment, whether in new production technologies, new marketing relationships, education and health care for children, productive new assets, or improvements to the natural resource base on which future earnings depend. Such investment is the engine for exiting long-term poverty and hunger.

In thinking about initial conditions for the ultra-poor in Sub-Saharan Africa, it is extremely important to keep in mind that they are especially likely to live in rural areas. Poverty remains a disproportionately rural phenomenon worldwide. But this phenomenon is especially pronounced among the ultra-poor; the average percentage difference between rural and urban poverty incidence is roughly 400 percent for the ultra-poor, more than twice as large a gap as for those living on $0.51–$1.00 a day per person (Ahmed et al. 2007). Rural people depend heavily on the natural resource base for their livelihoods as farmers, fishers, forest product gatherers, herders, and workers. And in much of Sub-Saharan Africa, soil fertility and water access are especially poor and, in many places, deteriorating. Furthermore, the physical and institutional infrastructure to support commerce, innovation, and value addition are commonly rudimentary or absent. For example, in 1999 (the most recent year for which comparable data are available), only 12.1 percent of the roads in Sub-Saharan Africa were paved, compared with 36.3 percent worldwide and even 30.8 percent in South Asia (World Bank 2007a). These areas have been disfavored by both nature and states, creating an immediat disadvantage for rural Africans' productivity and investment incentives.

The second key thing that is known about poverty traps is the importance of risk. Even transitory shocks can have persistent effects by casting people into a downward spiral into destitution from which they do not recover or by keeping them from growing their way out of persistent poverty by regularly knocking them backward as they struggle to climb out of the trap, a real-world Sisyphean tragedy (Dercon 1998; McPeak and Barrett 2001; Dercon 2005; Carter and Barrett 2006; Santos and Barrett 2006; Carter et al. 2007; Krishna 2007).

People's response to shocks—both ex post and ex ante—can likewise trap them in poverty. Risk can have two distinct, crucial effects in systems characterized by poverty traps. First, ex ante efforts to reduce risk exposure can dampen accumulation—either voluntarily or through credit rationing—thereby creating a low-level equilibrium. Second, the ex post consequences of a shock—both the shock's direct biophysical effects or those due to coping strategies taken in response to the shock—can knock vulnerable people back into a poverty trap.

The ultra-poor who disproportionately inhabit rural Sub-Saharan Africa are especially risk-exposed. Conflict and associated complex emergencies are perhaps the most shocking source of risk borne by rural Africans. But even where peace reigns, weather-related risks disproportionately affect rural peoples and the agriculture sector through drought and flooding, the effects of which are compounded by less reliable physical and institutional infrastructure for responding to shocks. These patterns are aggravated by spatial inequality in the coverage and effectiveness of public and veterinary health systems, which strongly favor richer areas. Overall, people in low-income countries are four times more likely to die as a result of natural disaster, and costs per disaster as a share of gross domestic product (GDP) are considerably higher in developing than in the countries of the Organization for Economic Cooperation and Development (Gaiha and Thapa 2006). Poorer rural areas appear far more vulnerable to disasters than are wealthier and more urban areas. Moreover, at the household level, evidence from drought in Ethiopia indicates that the medium-term effects of shocks vary by initial wealth, with poorer households feeling the adverse effects more acutely and for a longer period (Carter et al. 2007).

The most serious and commonplace catastrophic risk faced by the African rural poor, however, is ill health. As already mentioned, health shocks are the single most common explanation people offer for how previously nonpoor families collapsed into persistent poverty. Those in or at risk of falling into poverty traps face a range of health challenges: maintaining an adequate diet; avoiding injuries most commonly associated with manual labor, which is the mainstay of the poor; and staving off diseases commonly associated with unreliable water supplies, exposure to animal and human waste, and other standard hardships of poor communities. Furthermore, the ultra-poor are concentrated in an employment sector that is especially risky. The International Labour Organization (ILO 2000) reports that the agricultural sector is the most hazardous to human health worldwide, accounting for a majority of work-related mortality because of, for example, exposure to animals, chemicals, plants, and weather; use of hazardous tools and machinery; and long working hours under physically challenging conditions.

The ultra-poverty/ill-health trap that seems to characterize so much of rural Sub-Saharan Africa today is thus intimately caught up with (1) the interrelationship between hunger, ill health, and low productivity, manifest in low incomes, (2) poor initial conditions associated with health and nutrition, especially early in childhood, but also with the state of infrastructure and the natural resource base on which rural livelihoods disproportionately depend, and (3) risk exposure, which is especially severe in rural areas and in agriculture. So what bridges these central characteristics, and thus where should one focus in responding to the imperative for action to address widespread ultra-poverty, ultra-hunger, and ill health? The closely coupled nature of ill health, hunger, and poverty problems add substantially to the challenge of addressing any one of them on its own and thereby make integrated strategies essential. Food systems are the natural locus for developing an integrated strategy for addressing hunger, ill health, and poverty jointly.

Food Systems Improvements as the Core of a Sensible Strategy

As several recent studies make clear, agriculture is the lead sector for reduction of poverty and hunger, especially in Sub-Saharan Africa (Christiaensen and Demery 2007; Diao et al. 2007; World Bank 2007b). Real GDP growth from agriculture is 2.7 times more effective in reducing the extreme poverty headcount in the poorest quarter of countries, including most of Sub-Saharan Africa, than is growth in nonagricultural sectors (Christiaensen and Demery 2007). And the focus must fall squarely on stimulating a smallholder food productivity revolution.

The reasons are straightforward. First, agriculture is the primary employment sector for the poor. A supermajority of Africa's ultra-poor are small farmers who grow food, at least part time. Since earnings are determined by the productivity of one's asset holdings and labor is the primary asset of the poor, their earnings in food agriculture are fundamental to their well-being. Rural Africans are disproportionately ultra-poor because their labor productivity is so low. Boosting the productivity of the labor, land, livestock, and other assets controlled by the poor must be at the center of any strategy for breaking out of the ultra-poverty/ hunger trap.

Second, although most of the ultra-poor are employed in agriculture, their productivity is so low that they typically do not produce enough to feed their families, forcing them to depend on nonfarm earnings to supplement farming to pay for their net purchases of food. As Barrett (2008) documents, across a wide array of staple grain commodities, countries, and years, multiple data sets consistently show that a small minority of food crop producers are net (or even gross) sellers of these commodities (Table 12.1). Within that minority, sales are heavily concentrated among just a few of the larger farmers. Because most smallholders are actually net buyers of the basic foods they produce, productivity gains not only have favorable real output effects on their well-being, but any induced declines in real food prices caused by aggregate supply expansion also benefit them.

Table 12.1 Participation in the staple foodgrains market in East and Southern Africa

Country	Crop	Year	% of producers who sell in the market
Ethiopia	Maize and teff	1996	25 [n]
	Barley	1999–2000	10 [g]
	Maize		23 [g]
	Sorghum		11 [g]
	Teff		20 [g]
	Wheat		12 [g]
Kenya	Maize	1997	29 [n]
		1998	34 [n]
		1999	39 [n]
		2000	30 [n]
Madagascar	Rice	1990	32 [g]
		2001	25 [n]
Mozambique	Basic food	1996–97	14 [g]
	Maize	2001–02	30 [g]
	Maize	2005	16 [g]
	Rice	2002	43 [n]
Rwanda	Beans	1986–87	22 [n]
	Sorghum		24 [n]
Somalia	Maize	1986–87	39 [n]
Tanzania	Food	2003	33 [n]
Zambia	Maize	2000	26 [n]
Zimbabwe	Maize	1984–85	45 [n]
	Grains	1996	27 [g]

SOURCE: Reproduced from Barrett 2008.
NOTE: g = gross; n = net.

Meanwhile, food overwhelmingly makes up the largest share of the budgets of the ultra-poor—whether or not they farm. The ultra-poor routinely spend 65–80 percent of total household expenditures on food (Ahmed et al. 2007). Since the budget share reflects the instantaneous elasticity of welfare with respect to prices, this fact signals that supply expansion that reduces real food prices is to be welcomed because it has a dramatic effect on the ultra-poor. [2] This point is, of course, consistent with the longstanding observation that the bulk of the poverty reduction benefits of the Green Revolution in Asia (and to a lesser extent, in Latin America) came about through the increased consumer surplus accruing to poor food buyers, not from income gains to farmers.

Both the ultra-poor's sectoral affiliation as agricultural producers and workers and the heavy concentration of their expenditures on foods point toward food systems as the nexus where interventions are most likely to bear substantial fruit. These effects are reinforced by the strong backward and forward linkages from agriculture to secondary and tertiary sectors in the economy.

Minten and Barrett (2008) provide strong empirical evidence that better agricultural performance—as proxied by higher rice yields in their analysis of Madagascar—is strongly correlated with higher real wages, improved rice profitability, and lower real consumer prices for the staple food. A doubling of rice yields in this setting leads to an average 38 percent reduction in the share of food-insecure households in the community, shortens the average hungry period by 1.7 months (or one-third), and increases real unskilled wages in the lean season (during planting and growing) by 89 percent because of both lower real rice prices and increased demand for unskilled labor by wealthier farmers. Thus greater food crop productivity reduces extreme poverty for all the major subpopulations of the poor—net rice buyers, net rice sellers, and unskilled workers—with the gains accruing disproportionately to the poorest: workers and poor net food buyers.

Such findings are not surprising given that improvements in food systems have been the foundation of poverty reduction and modern economic growth throughout history. All past cases of rapid, widespread progress out of poverty have been causally associated with the transformation of food systems, from 18th- and 19th-century Europe and North America to late 20th-century East Asia. Striking increases in agricultural productivity, improvements in food safety, and markedly reduced costs of food distribution improved the quantity, quality, and variety of food available at lower prices. These food system advances permitted historically unprecedented growth in incomes, life expectancy, and population; decreased the risk of chronic or acute malnutrition; and enabled increased investment in education and nonagricultural activities in today's advanced economies (Fogel 1994, 2004; Johnson 1997; Maddison 2001). In Asia, rapid increases in crop yields have been major drivers of historically unprecedented declines in poverty. By contrast, in Sub-Saharan Africa, staple grain yields have remained stagnant at roughly one ton per hectare for the past two decades or so, and headcount poverty measures have remained similarly stuck at 40–50 percent of the population.

The "food problem" was Schultz's (1953) label for the observation that until communities and countries made scientific and institutional advances to reliably meet their subsistence food needs through improved production, processing, and trade, few could begin the process of modern economic growth. This view has been largely echoed in a vast subsequent social science literature (Boserup 1965; Geertz 1966; Diamond 1997; Timmer 2002; Gollin, Parente, and Rogerson 2007). Growth in agricultural productivity directly accounts for a disproportionately large share of economic growth and poverty reduction in a range of rapidly growing developing countries over the past several decades (Ravallion and Datt 1996; Gollin, Parente, and Rogerson 2002). Much of this effect arises from agricultural linkages to nonagricultural sectors, including to human nutrition and improved natural resources management.

Are food systems the only thing that matter? Absolutely not. But they are hugely important and have been seriously underemphasized over the past decade or two as international assistance for agriculture has lagged and rural institutions and public goods and services have been dismantled. Complementary efforts in health systems, information systems, peacemaking, and other areas are also important. But ultimately, it is difficult to envision, based on the historical or current empirical evidence, any substantial progress in freeing Sub-Saharan Africa from its apparent ultra-poverty/hunger/ill-health trap without significant advances in the continent's food systems.

Key Principles for Targeting within Sub-Saharan African Food Systems

So where are the entry points within food systems for helping unlock the ultra-poverty/hunger/ill-health trap in which so much of rural Sub-Saharan Africa finds itself? Food productivity gains are, as one would expect, strongly and positively associated with the adoption of improved agricultural production technologies, the stock of productive assets (such as soil quality and livestock) under farmers' control, access to supporting services (such as agricultural extension), the availability of irrigation, and market access.[3] The latter four variables have both direct and indirect effects—through induced technology adoption—on crop yields in rural Sub-Saharan Africa. These policy levers are perhaps the most potent for improving agricultural productivity so as to reduce poverty and food insecurity.

But it is important to guard against excessive generalization. The binding constraints to progress vary from country to country and often from place to place within individual countries. There is no substitute for careful contextualization and empirical validation of specific policy ideas. Nonetheless, several key principles can be clearly identified from a growing mass of evidence. They are listed here in order of importance.

Principle 1: Build and Protect Household-Level Productive Asset Endowments

Given production technologies and the market and nonmarket institutions that value what a household produces, earnings depend directly on the stock of productive assets to which a household has access. Such assets include not only privately owned assets such as human capital, land, livestock, or financial savings, but also common property or public goods such as roads or irrigation infrastructure. The most basic pathway out of poverty is to accumulate productive assets. In a poverty trap, however, investment is low because the incentives to invest are poor and thus meager asset holdings emerge as a low-level equilibrium.[4] Changing this condition is a first-order imperative.

In some cases, assets must be provided to poor people who are simply unable to reserve any of their negligible income for investment. Examples include feeding programs for destitute subpopulations facing emergencies and free education for children. In most settings, however, the key is to change investment incentives. In some cases, this approach requires firming up the institutions that ensure secure access to private property—such as rules of resource tenure and police protection against property crime. Often, it requires investing in complementary inputs—"crowding in" investment, whether in key infrastructure (such as roads, electrification, and water) or in human capital through education and health programming, especially for pregnant women and children three years of age and younger. In other cases, it requires resolving financial market failures—both in credit and in insurance—to enable people to borrow against future expected earnings and to shield their investment from transitory shocks that might otherwise imperil them. Indeed, an oft-overlooked element of changing incentives for asset accumulation concerns the provision of safety nets. Informal social arrangements commonly provide some measure of insurance against shocks for those who are reasonably well integrated into local social networks (Vanderpuye-Orgle and Barrett 2009). But many people appear to fall through the holes in social safety nets in rural Africa. Moreover, these safety nets necessarily cannot handle major, covariate shocks that simultaneously challenge most or all members of a social network. In such cases public or external private safety nets, such as employment guarantee schemes, post-drought herd restocking, and emergency food and cash assistance programs, must play a role. Indeed, recent theoretical work suggests that productive safety nets may be the highest-return policy instruments available in economies characterized by poverty traps (Barrett, Carter, and Ikegami 2007).

One asset of special concern in rural Sub-Saharan Africa today is soil fertility. The land is the main nonhuman asset to which the poor have access. It is degrading rapidly in much of Sub-Saharan Africa, contributing mightily to the apparent poverty trap in which many rural Africans presently find themselves. Recent estimates show that the region faces what a recent study refers to as "an escalating soil fertility crisis" (Morris et al. 2007, 18); the region lost 4.4 million tons of nitrogen, 0.5 million tons of phosphorus, and 3 million tons of potassium between 1980 and 2004, costing the continent more than US$4 billion worth of soil nutrients per year (IFDC 2006). Declining soil fertility is also aggravating the problem of parasitic weeds in the *Striga* spp., which cause more than US$7 billion in yield losses and affect more than 100 million farmers annually in Sub-Saharan Africa (CIMMYT 2007). Shrinking landholdings due to subdivision, continuous cropping, insecure land tenure, and unaffordable fertilizer have resulted in severe soil degradation, lower crop productivity and incomes, malnutrition, and vulnerability to ill health. Without effective interventions to increase soil productivity and cropping system diversity, many farmers and their families are unable to produce enough food to feed their families or to earn adequate incomes. They then resort to destructive, but perfectly rational, exploitation of the surrounding natural resource base, such as cutting down trees to make charcoal or clearing the river and stream banks' protective vegetation to grow vegetables. Although the importance of soil nutrients to poverty reduction and overall economic development in Sub-Saharan Africa was emphasized by the June 2006 international fertilizer summit in Abuja, Nigeria, attended by many African heads of state and governments (IFDC 2006), a systems-level understanding of this growing crisis and of appropriate interventions remains distressingly scarce. In this setting, poverty reduction depends on improving understanding of the economic, social, and biological aspects of food systems as a precursor for identifying sustainable and adoptable solutions that will enable and encourage Sub-Saharan African farmers to build and protect their stock of natural capital in the soil.

Principle 2: Improve the Productivity of the Poor's Current Asset Holdings

Increasing the returns to the assets held by the poor is the second core principle that must underpin strategies to improve African food systems. Returns to assets can be improved both through technological improvements to the physical productivity of food production and postharvest processing systems and through advances in marketing systems that squeeze out costs from distribution channels and improve the economic returns farmers enjoy per unit of output grown while simultaneously holding down food prices for net buyers.

This is the second principle because adoption of improved technologies and participation in more remunerative marketing channels commonly depend in large measure on households' asset endowments. The literature shows that land holdings, livestock ownership, credit access, or other measures of wealth have a consistently strong positive relationship with adoption of improved technologies or natural resources management practices or participation in higher-value-added markets. This finding underscores how important asset endowment effects are to understanding patterns of productivity growth in food systems. Ultra-poor farmers commonly lack the assets to produce marketable surpluses and therefore cannot afford new technologies nor reap the considerable gains attainable from market-based exchange. This situation limits their ability to accumulate (or borrow) assets, reinforcing the initial condition and generating a low-level dynamic equilibrium (Carter and Barrett 2006). Making improved markets and technologies available is important, but limited uptake is to be expected in the absence of adequate endowments to take good advantage of these new opportunities.

The returns to research on improved agricultural technologies have always been and remain high. The World Bank (2007b) estimates the average rate of return on agricultural research in Sub-Saharan Africa at roughly 35 percent a year, far higher than returns on financial assets in virtually all countries in the region. Yet agricultural research remains severely underfunded on the continent. Although 75 percent of the extremely poor live in rural areas and are at least partly employed in agriculture, only 4 percent of global overseas development assistance (ODA) goes to agriculture (down from 10 percent in 1990), and only 4 percent of public expenditures in Sub-Saharan Africa are directed to agriculture (World Bank 2007b). And those figures heavily overstate the resources devoted to agricultural research and institutional development because they include the administrative costs of ministries of agriculture, which account for the overwhelming majority of such funds. Without a substantial reallocation of ODA and public resources in the direction of agricultural research, productivity growth in African food systems and thus progress in the fight against poverty, ill health, and hunger will be slow at best.

Meanwhile, the productivity problems of ultra-poor smallholders are magnified by relatively poor integration into national and global markets and by rapid changes overtaking agrifood supply chains in the low-income world. Rapid concentration worldwide in both upstream input (such as seed and fertilizer) and downstream food wholesale and retail industries threatens the future of small farms worldwide (Reardon et al. 2003). Remarkably little is known about who is able to participate in modern agrifood marketing channels, under what terms, and with what effects. Nor is much known about which interventions—for example, creation or expansion of farmer cooperatives, provision of infrastructure, improved monitoring and enforcement of grades, standards, and contracts—favorably affect poor rural residents' capacity to take advantage of new marketing channels, whether as suppliers, consumers, or workers. These are key research areas because improving the incidence and terms of market participation by the rural poor is such an important principle for food system interventions.

Principle 3: Improve Risk Management Options for the Ultra-Poor

Risk is a key impediment to investment in building up stocks of productive assets and to uptake of new technologies or participation in emerging marketing channels. Thus it is closely related to the preceding two principles. But this is where an added, tragic dimension enters: even if an ultra-poor household does make all the sacrifices necessary to invest in building up productive assets, to adopt all the best technologies, and to participate in the most remunerative marketing channels, it can all be wiped away in an instant. Catastrophic shocks—due to drought, flooding, disease, injury, conflict, crime, price fluctuations, or other risks—are distressingly common, and relatively little of this risk exposure is insured, formally or informally. Improving risk management is thus central to the task of breaking rural Sub-Saharan Africa out of the ultra-poverty/hunger trap.

Improving risk management raises three big challenges. The first is the multidimensionality of the serious risks faced by the rural ultra-poor in Sub-Saharan Africa. Price volatility is significant and leaves both producers and consumers vulnerable to sharp seasonal swings in markets. Add to this the fact that more than 95 percent of agricultural land in the region is rainfed and particularly vulnerable to climate shocks. Pests and diseases also cause massive crop and livestock losses in much of Sub-Saharan Africa. And violent conflict has been a major burden on rural Africans, aggravating routine but pervasive insecurity of property rights resulting from weak tenurial institutions and poor police protection. Furthermore, Africa is the only continent where infectious diseases cause more deaths than noncommunicable illnesses, underscoring the severity of covariate human health risks that are especially difficult to manage.

Second, risk exposure tends also to be inversely related to standards of living, with the poorest bearing the greatest uninsured risks. For example, as soil quality declines, a parallel decline in crop vigor makes plants more susceptible to abiotic and biotic stresses; soil-borne pests and diseases appear to especially thrive under these conditions. Mycotoxins, such as aflatoxin, provide another example of an insidious threat that is particularly pronounced in poorer areas and among people who have less access to proper storage technologies and to food distribution systems with reliable food safety controls. Aflatoxin is immunosuppressive, growth-retardant, and carcinogenic at lower concentrations and lethal at higher concentrations. Ill-nourished animals, like ill-nourished humans, have compromised immune function and are less productive and more susceptible to disease than their adequately fed counterparts. Meanwhile crime rates are commonly higher in poorer and more remote regions (Fafchamps and Moser 2003).

Third, the most relevant risks faced by different subpopulations are highly context specific. The most serious risks borne by the rural poor vary markedly across space and time, even among seemingly homogeneous populations (Doss,

McPeak, and Barrett 2008). Wealthy households owning large herds or enjoying high-paying salaried employment may bear considerable animal disease and unemployment risk, whereas poorer neighbors face relatively greater likelihood of contracting a serious disease or facing a disastrous staple food price spike. Few options are available for managing the risks from multiple hazards, especially in rural areas.

Effective risk management therefore involves two distinct threads: risk reduction to dampen ex ante risk exposure and risk transfer to diffuse the impacts ex post of unavoidable shocks that occur. The primary means of risk reduction for the ultra-poor involve improvements to crop and livestock production systems, through improved cultivars (animal, human, and plant), disease control, water management systems, and opportunities to build diversified portfolios of activities offering weakly correlated returns. Real progress is taking place in this arena. For example, improved maize cultivars that tolerate drought are coming online now, helping maize farmers in stress-prone areas of Southern Africa. New varieties of rice that survive flooding are being tested, and the New Rices for Africa (NERICAs) have demonstrated a remarkable capacity to combine higher yields with resistance to local abiotic and biotic stresses in West and Central Africa. Meso-level institutions associated with establishing and maintaining law and order and with control of infectious diseases are critical as well. Unfortunately, progress in these areas has been slower.

In high-income countries, financial systems and highly integrated markets provide the central means of risk transfer. The underdeveloped state of African rural financial systems and the spatially segmented nature of many rural food markets sharply limit risk transfer opportunities. Instead, there has been excessive dependence on external assistance in the form of emergency food aid relief and other instruments. But advances in food aid programming (Barrett and Maxwell 2005) and in the design of index-based risk finance instruments (Barnett, Barrett, and Skees 2008) show great promise for rapid progress in this area in the coming decade.

Principle 4: Facilitate Favorable Transitions out of Agriculture

The final principle is necessarily ironic. Because agricultural productivity growth naturally stimulates relative contraction in the agricultural sector, relative to secondary and tertiary sectors, efforts to improve food systems must be accompanied by measures to help foster deliberate migration into nonfarm livelihoods. Clearly, this migration must be of the demand-pull variety, not driven by catastrophic loss of agricultural assets. But in all past cases of successful agriculture-led growth, falling real food prices and stimulus to nonagricultural labor demand have consistently fostered such agricultural and rural transformation (Timmer 2002).

The key here is to help the current generation of adults improve their on-farm productivity so that they can invest in the health, nutrition, and education of their children, thereby equipping the next generation with the human capital necessary to leave agriculture if and when the opportunity presents itself. In particular, and most appropriate to the current focus on the ultra-poor of rural Africa, this approach underscores the especially high returns in adulthood to investments in disadvantaged children very early in life. Studies such as Heckman (2006) and Behrman et al. (2007) provide strong evidence in support of the hypothesis that early childhood health (including prenatal and neonatal health), nutrition, and educational interventions have a sizable effect on adult cognitive and physical performance and thus on earnings. Hoddinott et al. (2008) provide strong evidence that improved nutrition early in childhood led to significantly higher wages and total earnings among rural Guatemalans. Although there is no similar empirical evidence base from Africa—an important research gap waiting to be filled—the logic and moral imperative of these results carries over directly. We know that early childhood investments in readying the next generation for a transition out of agriculture is essential for breaking out of the ultra-poverty/ultra-hunger/ill-health trap in the long run.

Conclusions

Given the poor past performance of food systems in Sub-Saharan Africa and the region's discouraging trends in poverty and hunger, especially ultra-poverty and ultra-hunger, one might be inclined to think that there is no hope for agriculture-led poverty reduction. Yet there is real reason for hope in Sub-Saharan Africa. Real agricultural output growth rates are accelerating, nearly doubling from the 1980s rate so that per capita food output is growing again (Figure 12.3). More important, this agricultural growth contributes directly to falling rural poverty rates in countries enjoying increased agricultural productivity (such as Ghana).

Moreover, there is reason for optimism thanks to bold new initiatives such as the joint Gates-Rockefeller Alliance for a Green Revolution in Africa and the prospect of renewed attention to agriculture in Africa, as reflected in the World Bank's dedication of its flagship *World Development Report* to the topic for the first time in a quarter century. Yield gaps—the difference between realized output and agronomic potential—remain significant in Sub-Saharan Africa, so the opportunities to achieve significant gains in short order are very real. And although aid to agriculture for Sub-Saharan Africa declined by roughly half from the late 1980s through 2002, it is now slowly turning around. Private investment in the region is likewise picking up, with important innovations throughout food systems, from development of improved crop varieties and fertilizers to the introduction of modern agrifood supply chain management systems. Although there is no guarantee that these emerging opportunities will benefit the rural ultra-poor, such opportunities are necessary (albeit not sufficient) for progress. The prospects for agriculture-led reduction in poverty, ill health, and hunger in Sub-Saharan Africa are real.

This is good news because the apparent ultra-poverty/ultra-hunger/ill-health trap in rural Sub-Saharan Africa implies that intervention is essential if people are to escape and avoid persistent poverty. Recognizing the need for some sort of intervention is the easy part, however. Although intervention is valuable, indeed essential, and the four key principles identified earlier provide clear direction, there remains only limited empirical evidence to guide detailed design and implementation of strategies to develop African food systems so as to break the lock of poverty and hunger traps.

The structural adjustment era of economic reforms in the 1980s and 1990s focused on reaping static efficiency gains from removing policies that distorted resource allocation. Unfortunately, policy design in that era was based on empirically flawed assumptions and the structural adjustment approach largely failed to stimulate either macro-level economic growth and balance of payments stability or reduction of poverty, ill health, or hunger in Sub-Saharan Africa. The focus of the policymaking and donor communities has thankfully shifted over the past decade from static concerns about "getting prices right" to dynamic concerns about incentives to innovate, invest, and grow out of poverty over time—that is,

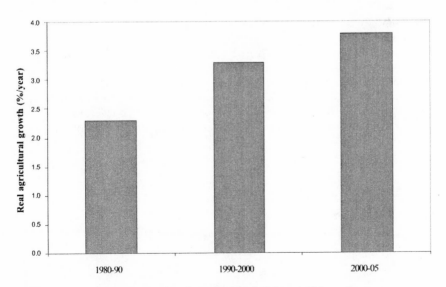

Figure 12.3 Accelerating agricultural growth in Sub-Saharan Africa, 1980–2005
SOURCE: World Bank, *World development indicators,* various years.

to finding "pathways from poverty." Today, growing attention is focusing instead on how best to stimulate investment incentives, productivity growth, risk management, and productive transitions out of agriculture. These broad foci are appropriate and reasonably well grounded in both theory and empirical evidence.

But just as the empirical and theoretical evidence base was relatively thin at the outset of the structural adjustment era, so too current knowledge about the dynamics of reducing poverty, ill health, and hunger remains disturbingly limited in several key areas. It is important to proceed with caution and remain vigilant about rigorously investigating the premises that underpin policy designs and re-evaluating policies as the evidence base grows and sheds new light on what works best under which conditions.

Notes

Ashley Dean provided excellent research assistance. Per Pinstrup-Andersen and an anonymous reviewer provided helpful comments. Any remaining errors are entirely my own.

1. See Azariadis and Stachurski (2007) and Carter and Barrett (2006) for discussion of the technical issues and empirical disagreements in the literature.

2. At the time of writing, Africa still feels the effects of the world face rapid food price increases of 2007–08 owing primarily to strong growth in demand for food crops both for improving diets in rapidly growing Asian economies and for biofuel production in high-income countries. The humanitarian concerns associated with these price rises reflect the fact that the overwhelming majority of the poor are net food buyers, although many observers continue to overlook the fact that this characteristic applies to most small farmers as well. Prices are rising because demand growth is far outpacing supply expansion, underscoring the point that accelerating productivity growth in food agriculture is critical to the well-being of the poor.

3. See, for example, Minten and Barrett (2008) for empirical evidence on these points.

4. Migratory pastoralism offers a clear example and strong recent evidence of poverty traps: herd sizes below a threshold level induce herd loss (due to involuntary sedentarization) whereas herd sizes above that threshold tend to lead to herd growth by taking advantage of spatiotemporal variation in water and forage availability. Lybbert et al. (2004) and Barrett et al. (2006) offer detailed evidence from Ethiopia and Kenya, respectively.

CHAPTER 13

Strengthening the Role of Women in the Food Systems of
Sub-Saharan Africa to Achieve Nutrition and Health Goals

Laura K. Cramer and Speciosa K. Wandira

Abstract

Women play an enormous role in agriculture and food systems in Sub-Saharan
Africa but endure countless obstacles to increased production and income generation through farming. Achieving food and nutrition security in the region will
require substantial increases in food production, processing, and storage, tasks
that fall mainly to female farmers. It is not enough to label Sub-Saharan African
women the key to food security for the region. To truly enable them to serve
in this capacity, they must be given the power to do so: through land and water
rights, increased education, access to credit, and the full range of capabilities
needed to fulfill such a role. Passing legislation for land tenure reform, ensuring
access to education, and prioritizing the other activities described in this chapter
will require enormous fortitude on the part of African governments, the private
sector, and international bodies. Off-farm opportunities that do not entail legislation in the short term but give better returns in terms of labor, capital, and
time inputs should be pursued. Those policies that promote women's productivity, capacity building, and access to health and education are essential to making
achievement of nutrition and health goals across the region possible.

Introduction

Women make up 70 percent of the agricultural workers in many countries of Sub-
Saharan Africa, contribute 60–80 percent of the labor that produces subsistence
food crops (Dao 2004), and account for 80 percent of food processing (Markwei
et al. 2008). Despite these significant contributions to agricultural output, women

have traditionally received minimal attention from local government agricultural extension services and have benefited least from innovations that reduce labor and boost value addition. Low technology inputs have resulted in low levels of productivity, poor participation in markets, and poor returns on their investments.

Researchers and development professionals have begun to recognize the large role that women play in agriculture in Sub-Saharan Africa and have begun seeing African women as vital to food security. Effort and resources have thus been directed toward helping women achieve this goal. Although studies of women's roles in food systems ably describe what they do currently, many agricultural projects intended to aid women still fail to take context-specific gender norms into account (Quisumbing and Pandolfelli 2008). Researchers have posited that despite improvements in building women's capabilities, gender gaps in entitlements to natural and physical capital—the resources that women can command through available legal means—continue to exist (Quisumbing and Meinzen-Dick 2001). These gaps in property rights present a hurdle in helping women boost agricultural productivity.

Another broad obstacle to helping strengthen the role of women in meeting the goals of food and nutrition security is the low level of communication between most research in agriculture and health. The Millennium Development Goals (MDGs) and other international protocols and instruments that shape countries' agriculture and health policies and agendas attest to this deficiency. None of them speaks to women's health and productivity as jointly necessary conditions for achieving the MDGs. The "empowerment" of women has been equated with the shaking off of cultural and traditional roles that have kept women engaged in household activities, including food production and processing. The trend then is for educated women to gravitate away from agricultural professions and practice, thus denying African food systems "modern" women farmers to serve as role models for the less educated.

Furthermore, it is necessary, but by no means sufficient, to meet food security and nutrition goals through agriculture. Strengthening the role of women in food systems requires a view beyond just agricultural production. It is not enough to simply grow more food—food must also be processed, transported, and marketed. In addition to supporting women as farmers, policies and programs should enable women to be key players along the entire supply chain from commodity to product. To this end, women should be given the same opportunities for capacity building in entrepreneurship as men.

Because of the complexity of food systems, it is important to commit adequate resources for empirical research into the range of women's agricultural activities to better inform policy. Achieving the MDGs—in particular improving nutrition and health—will require thinking outside the box and forging and nurturing new paradigms and partnerships. Agriculture and health development professionals must collaborate in the new research agenda and carry it through to implementation. New questions must be raised about human capability at present and in the future. Asking what men do that contributes to food security is pertinent because agricultural activities are often joint endeavors between males and females. Attention should be paid to the men of Africa to specifically identify their role at the household level. What is their health status? If it is better than women's health status, then why is their life expectancy lower than that of women? Is it true that access to land, legal protection, and education is a preserve of the men, and are these things synonymous with emancipation? Endless surveys, studies, and reports have all claimed for at least the past 20 years that women are the key to food security in Africa. If this reality is well understood, why has progress been so slow? Why are malnutrition rates in most places not falling quickly enough to meet the targets? One approach to tackling these issues is the method of positive deviance—identifying those individuals that are doing well and replicating their successful strategies among others. The research that is being done must be translated into action.

African men must also play a role in achieving the food security and nutrition goals for the continent. It is not enough to publish literature on how men do not spend as much of their income on food for their families as women or to document the inequalities in land titles and fertilizer use. Instead, it is important to go beyond these findings to formulate action. How can men play a role in food security and nutrition? It is essential to take a second look at the context in which both women and men carry out their roles in food systems and examine whether an enduring vision of women as the key to food security is a viable one.

Women in Sub-Saharan Africa supply their labor and produce food in economies that have a high degree of self-sufficiency at the household and community level. Poor infrastructure often denies these economies markets for exchange of knowledge, goods, and services. In addition, social institutions and support structures inhibit entrepreneurship and growth. Lending institutions, for example, hesitate to provide credit facilities to female farmers, who often lack collateral to secure the debt. How then is it possible to catalyze women's participation in the transformation of Sub-Saharan Africa's agriculture into interlinked markets, information flows, and social institutions to achieve nutrition and health goals? The first two sections of this chapter will examine the major obstacles, both agriculture and health related, facing Sub-Saharan Africa's female farmers—for example, a lack of appropriate extension services. The third and final section will suggest possible policies aimed at overcoming these hurdles, such as specially trained female extension agents. As in any complex situation, the intricacies of the food systems in Sub-Saharan Africa will not allow for a silver bullet solution. Interventions in individual countries and even in regions within countries will need to be tailored to the specific context. When appropriate policies and interventions

are formulated based on careful examination of the context in which female agri-
culturalists operate, it will be possible to improve the ability of women to make
the sustainable contributions needed to achieve nutrition and health goals in Sub-
Saharan Africa.

Farming and Food Systems in Africa: Obstacles Faced by Women

The InterAcademy Council report *Realizing the Promise and Potential of African
Agriculture* (IAC 2004) noted that the near-stagnant economies in parts of Africa
reflect, to a large extent, stagnant agriculture. Producers face many burdens: natural resource constraints, hostile weather conditions, pests and diseases, environmental degradation, and war and conflict. Moreover, a single continent-wide
solution will not work: the report identifies 17 distinct farming systems across
Africa and calls for regional strategies to boost agricultural productivity. This
diversity of farming systems prohibits the introduction of a single intervention,
as in Asia, where the rice-wheat cultivation system allowed for a rapid increase in
food production during the Green Revolution of the 1960s. The IAC identified
four African farming systems as having the most potential for improving nutrition and agricultural productivity: maize-mixed system, cereal/root crop-mixed
system, irrigated system, and tree crop–based system. These systems all involve
multiple crops and livestock species, making research complex and dissemination
difficult. The diversity of systems and crops also means that measuring agricultural improvement will not be as easy in Africa as it was in Asia during the Green
Revolution.

Beyond the general difficulty of stimulating Sub-Saharan African agriculture
because of the complexity and diversity of farming systems throughout the region,
catalyzing women to play a larger role in food security presents further difficulties. Women face the same agricultural challenges as men in terms of pests, crop
and livestock diseases, and weather phenomena such as drought. In addition, they
face a unique set of hurdles to agricultural growth that stem from their gender
(Figure 13.1).

Property rights, especially land tenure rights and water use rights, are key factors in agricultural productivity and yet are an area of inequality between women
and men in Sub-Saharan Africa. Few women own property directly; most women
are assigned land use rights through their husbands, and these rights may be in
jeopardy if the marriage ends with divorce or death of the husband (World Bank
2001). Additional customary laws further discriminate against women: in Kenya,
for example, married women do not inherit from their parents, women who are
not married inherit less than their brothers, married women with sons may only
hold their husbands' property in trust for their sons, and women with no children

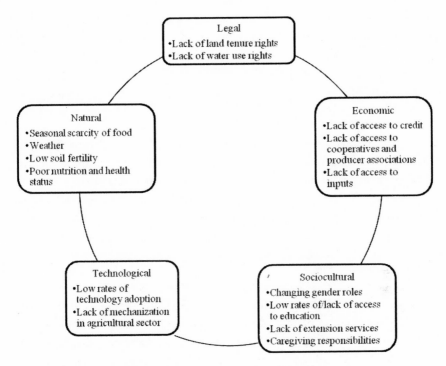

Figure 13.1   Women's obstacles to achieving agricultural growth
SOURCE: Author.

or only daughters are unlikely to inherit from their husbands (Ellis et al. 2007). In countries where land ownership is a precondition for the use of water, women who do not have title to their land may be restricted from gaining access to irrigation (United Nations 2004a). Without control over productive resources, such as land and water, women's agricultural productivity can suffer.

These legal barriers to agricultural productivity lead to economic barriers as well. Lack of land ownership prevents many women from being able to obtain credit that could be used to purchase agricultural inputs, such as improved seed, fertilizer, or crop protection products, for increased production. Financial institutions that require collateral for credit are unwilling to make loans to women who do not have title to their land (Doss 2001). Lack of land ownership can also be a hurdle in obtaining membership in cooperatives and producer associations that could help women produce and market their crops (Ellis et al. 2007). Operating individually makes it difficult for women to get access to markets. Although the farming systems of Africa are far removed from more technologically advanced systems around the world, the food systems of Africa are not isolated from global players. Food production has increasingly become market oriented. Even at the local level, increasing urbanization is producing markets with new food safety regulations and consumer demands for consistency in quantity and quality, greater convenience, and more differentiation of products. Emerging commercial farmers are becoming a threat to small producers, many of whom are women, because the size of their operations enables them to integrate their operations, exercise quality control, brand their products, and earn profits on mere turnover where small farmers require higher prices to break even (Delgado, Narrod, and Tiongco 2003).

In addition, many small farmers, especially women, have traditionally depended on unpaid labor, provided mainly by children. Children in many countries are now benefiting from government-sponsored universal primary education—a positive development. The lowered availability of children for agricultural work, however, has increased the burden on women for food production. Women may have fewer resources to hire outside paid laborers for agricultural tasks, another economic barrier to productivity (Doss 1999).

In addition to the legal and economic obstacles faced by women farmers, sociocultural obstacles stand in the way of increased agricultural production. The changes taking place within societies are altering some traditional roles and in certain cases adding responsibilities to women's workloads that did not exist before. In a farm-based economy, most people live on or near a farm. Self-sufficiency is the norm, with households consuming their own produced food with little local technology input. In locations where men migrate to cities to find work, women are left behind to take on tasks that would normally have been performed by men.

Societal roles are changing in some ways, but some traditional cultural obstacles still make it difficult for women to achieve agricultural gains. One such disadvantage to African women is the lack of animal draft power to aid in agriculture. In some regions it is taboo for women to work with cattle (IFAD 1998). Even in some societies where such taboos are absent, the use of animals for plowing and weeding is reserved for men because of social norms. Women are able to use donkeys, but they do not provide as much power as oxen. Obtaining plows or cultivators is difficult because of the expense, and many are too heavy or large to be practical for women (IFAD 1998).

Low levels of education among females also contribute to low agricultural productivity. According to one source, "four years of school boosts a farmer's annual productivity by an average of 9 percent" (Population Council 2005). Yet in Sub-Saharan Africa girls' primary school attendance is only 60 percent and secondary school attendance is 22 percent (UNICEF 2008a). Women have not traditionally been targeted by agricultural extension either (Quisumbing et al. 1995). Manuh (1998) reports that female farmers in Sub-Saharan African receive only 5 percent of agricultural extension services, perhaps because 83 percent of Sub-Saharan African extension officers are men. These men may not be allowed, because of cultural norms, to speak to women or may choose to visit male farmers instead of females (Markwei et al. 2008). It was once thought that male heads of household receiving agricultural extension services would pass information to females, but this assumption has been found to be false. In Burkina Faso a survey of women found that 40 percent had some knowledge of modern agricultural production methods. Most women who had such knowledge had learned it from a friend or relative, approximately one-third had received their knowledge from the extension service, and husbands were the source of knowledge for only 1 percent of the group (World Bank 1995). Because men and women grow different crops, even when extension knowledge is passed from husbands to wives, it may not be applicable to women's cropping activities. In many areas men grow cash crops and women grow subsistence crops. The traditional explanation given for this division is that men are responsible for providing cash income and women are responsible for providing food for the household (Doss 1999). Doss acknowledges the difficulty of determining why women grow lower-value subsistence crops: they may have different preferences, or they may have limited access to land, credit, information, and inputs. The tendency to grow subsistence crops leads to a further lack of attention from extension agents, who typically focus on commercial production. Such exclusion of women farmers from agricultural extension services hinders their ability to learn improved techniques and methods that could help increase their yields and move closer to the goal of food security.

Another sociocultural concern that impedes women's agricultural productivity is their role as caregivers. Time spent caring for children, the elderly, and the sick is time taken away from agricultural activities. This caregiving time becomes an increasing burden as HIV/AIDS takes its toll on societies. Not only do women become caregivers for the sick, but they also find themselves taking care of orphans who are added to their households as adults fall victim to the disease (Shapouri and Rosen 2001). If women become infected, the disease directly affects their ability to participate in agricultural labor.

Women farmers also face technological hurdles to meeting food security goals through improved agricultural productivity. In some cases, sociocultural traditions play a role in these technological hurdles. A study conducted by the International Fund for Agricultural Development (IFAD) and published in 1998 collected information from five countries using focus group discussions with men and women. *Agricultural Implements Used by Women Farmers in Africa* found that the hand hoe is still the most widely used tool for cultivating crops. "Uganda may be an extreme case, but in 1997, it was estimated that almost 90 percent of the farmers in that country used only hand tools and human labour to work their lands, and that animal-draught power and tractors were used on only 8 percent and 2 percent, respectively, of the cultivated land" (IFAD 1998, 4). Women's own attitudes can be part of this obstacle. The IFAD study reported that weeding in particular was expected to be difficult and painful. "In the majority of countries reviewed, it was generally felt that to work standing upright with a long-handled tool was a sign of laziness" (IFAD 1998, 6). In cases where women do want to increase the use of agricultural mechanization, they may lack access to better methods. Increased farm power, through draft animals or tractors, allows for cultivation of more land, but this technology is often out of reach for female farmers because of cost or cultural traditions (Bishop-Sambrook 2005).

Natural conditions such as seasonality, drought, and low soil fertility, as well as poor nutritional and health status, influence women's ability to meet food security goals as well. Studies have shown that women in Sub-Saharan Africa spend more time per day on agricultural tasks than men (Kes and Swaminathan 2006). Both women and men farmers face the seasonality of agricultural tasks and food availability, but during the times that women must expend the most energy in the fields, food for meeting their caloric requirements is often scarce. Although African women do not face the same bias in intrahousehold food allocation as in South Asia (where men and boys are often served the most and best food), their energy expenditure may be higher than men's during the time of year when food availability is lowest. Both women and men experience seasonal weight loss during the lean season, which affects their health and nutrition. If women are pregnant, the health and nutrition of the fetus—and the future health of the baby once it is born—are also affected (Holmboe-Ottesen, Mascarenhas, and Wandel 1988). In addition, women and men farm separate plots in most of Sub-Saharan Africa (Quisumbing et al. 1995) and are often responsible for different crops (Doss 1999). The plots assigned to women may be smaller, of poorer quality, and more widely dispersed than those farmed by men. The poorer quality of women's plots leads to higher labor requirements and lower yields (Saito 1994). If they are granted marginalized land without access to irrigation, women may also be more sensitive to weather conditions such as drought. If the land is on a steep slope, erosion may be an issue. These natural obstacles, combined with the legal, economic, sociocultural, and technological aspects, inhibit the ability of women to play an increased role in agriculture and food security in Sub-Saharan Africa.

Food Security, Nutrition, and Health among Women in Africa

Food security, nutrition, and health are inextricably linked. Without adequate food, one's health suffers. When one's health suffers, one's ability to produce or procure sufficient food is weakened. Health as defined by the World Health Organization is "a state of complete physical, mental and social well-being and not merely the absence of disease or infirmity" (WHO 2006b, 1). This is a welcome deviation from the traditional concept of health policy as synonymous with medical care policy. Internationally, however, there is no specific instrument or protocol targeting women's health. MDG 5 aims to improve maternal health by reducing the maternal mortality ratio by three-quarters, but it ignores the health of women who do not or cannot bear children. Achieving MDG 6—combating HIV/AIDS, malaria, and other diseases—would directly and indirectly improve the lives of the women by reducing not only their disease burden, but also the need for them to serve as caregivers for those who fall ill with these diseases.

Though inextricable, agriculture and health interact through different pathways. People, the natural environment, and agricultural inputs and products together produce food, fiber, and medicinal plants essential for nutrition and health. Low agricultural productivity is linked to malnutrition and disease among agricultural workers. When farmers are sick or malnourished, they are not able to work as well as if they were healthy, and they consequently experience decreased yields (IFPRI 2008). Exposure to different experiences throughout life affects and modifies risks of disease. Not only have influences on risk been found to be cumulative, but they can also modify the biological system's response to subsequent assaults. Of the factors that influence disease causation, human genes are the ones likely to express themselves through the immune system. A mother's inadequate diet has been documented to affect a child's immune programming. For example, cardiovascular disease in adults has been linked to intrauterine undernutrition (Barker et al. 1993). Research in West Africa has documented a relationship between risks of adult mortality, particularly from infectious diseases, and nutrition early in life. In this study, morbidity was found to be higher among young adults born in a season of scarcity (Moore et al. 1999).

Whereas Sub-Saharan Africa accounts for 13 percent of the population in the developing world, its contribution to the population of undernourished people is 25 percent, with one-third suffering from chronic hunger. Nutrition is the foundation for good health, and therefore nutrition, in addition to employment and growth of gross domestic product (GDP), should be a main goal of the food system. Unfortunately, many developing countries have failed to internalize this goal. Institutionally, nutrition policies tend to "float," with neither home nor concrete implementation plans. Part of the confusion stems from the controversy over nutrition programs. According to Cohen (2007), the World Bank emphasizes nutrition interventions that focus on children under two years old while deemphasizing school feeding programs that may also bring benefits. Although some progress continues to be registered in the production of staple foods, the gains are continuously offset by population increases, as well as by poor people's continued consumption of too much energy-rich but nutrient-poor food. It is therefore important to recognize that agriculture and food systems are not only economically important, but also fundamental to achieving nutrition and health goals.

In terms of health, while Africa's labor force continues to be assaulted by traditional infectious diseases like malaria, diarrhea, and tuberculosis, it also confronts newer threats like HIV/AIDS and SARS (Philipose 2007). Noncommunicable diseases like diabetes, cancer, and cardiovascular disease are on the rise as well (Moeti 2008). High rates of urbanization in African countries mean more people are moving to cities, where they often adopt sedentary lifestyles and consume highly processed, unhealthy foods. People also change their diets as their incomes increase. The "nutrition transition" occurring not only on the African continent but in developing countries around the world includes consumption of higher-fat diets and less physical activity, resulting in increasing rates of obesity (Popkin and Gordon-Larsen 2004). Obesity is well known to be a factor in the development of the noncommunicable diseases mentioned, and a healthy food system can play a role in lessening these silent killers.

As noted by Gillespie in chapter 5, a discussion of agriculture, nutrition, and health is not complete without an acknowledgment of the impact of HIV/AIDS on all three. In a household affected by HIV, food production may fall by as much as 60 percent when a woman must devote time to caring for a sick individual (Oxfam International and Save the Children 2002). HIV also affects food production because its victims—of whom the majority are women aged 15 to 50, the most productive group in society—sometimes die before being able to pass on their agricultural knowledge to the younger generation (Rosegrant et al. 2005). It follows that a drop in food production negatively affects the nutrition and health of all members of the household. The MDG target of halting and reversing the spread of HIV is crucial to aiding agricultural development and strengthening food systems in Sub-Saharan Africa.

Improving the health of women in Sub-Saharan Africa is a key component in boosting productivity in the agricultural sector and in general. Less time lost to illness and to caring for sick family members can free women's time for economically productive activities as well as much-needed and deserved leisure time. Improvements in health could help raise life expectancy for African women. Currently, life expectancy at birth for women in the African region as defined by the WHO is 52 years, compared with the second-lowest figure of 65 years in Southeast Asia and the highest life expectancy at birth of 78 years in the Americas and Europe, and it is not rising. Since 1990, women's life expectancy at birth has improved in all regions except Africa, where it has remained steady (WHO 2008d). Overall life expectancy in Africa for men and women born in 2002 would be 54 years, but the impact of HIV/AIDS alone has lowered that figure by over 6 years to just 47 (WHO 2006a).

Among the many challenges to improving health in Africa are HIV/AIDS, tuberculosis, and malaria. Sub-Saharan Africa, home to two-thirds of all people living with HIV, suffered three-quarters of the world's AIDS deaths in 2007 (UNAIDS 2008). Women account for two-thirds of new HIV infections in Sub-Saharan Africa (UNFPA 2008b). Infection with HIV can lead to co-infection with tuberculosis (TB), which is among the top causes of death for people living with HIV. Up to 77 percent of TB patients in some parts of Africa are also HIV positive. "Co-infection is now influencing the gender distribution of TB in many African countries. As HIV prevalence among young African women rises, they are also increasingly bearing the burden of TB" (Global Fund 2005, 24).

Pregnant women are more susceptible to malaria infection because pregnancy reduces their immunity. Malaria infection can lead to anemia, which then increases the risk of miscarriage, stillbirth, premature delivery, low birth weight, and maternal mortality (Roll Back Malaria Partnership 2006). Prevalence of iron-deficiency anemia among pregnant and nonpregnant women is highest in Africa at 57.1 percent and 47.5 percent, respectively, compared with global averages of 41.8 percent in pregnant women and 30.2 percent in nonpregnant women (WHO 2008e).

Another health concern for women in Africa is female genital mutilation or cutting. Also sometimes referred to as female circumcision, this practice takes place in certain countries of Sub-Saharan Africa and can lead to various complications over a woman's lifetime, including recurrent bladder and urinary tract infections and prolonged and obstructed labor during childbirth (UNFPA 2008a).

Because of unmet needs for family planning and contraception, rates of unsafe abortion are high among women in Africa. In 2003, the incidence rate for unsafe abortion in Sub-Saharan Africa was 31 per 1,000 women aged 15–44 years, compared with a world average of 14 per 1,000. Unsafe abortion accounted for 14 percent of all maternal deaths in the region in 2003 (WHO 2007b). Pregnancies carried to term can also be dangerous. The chance that a woman in an industrialized country will die in pregnancy or delivery is 1 in 2,800. In developing countries, the chance is 1 in 61, and in Sub-Saharan Africa, the chance is 1 in 16 (Roll Back Malaria Partnership 2006).

Other lesser-known health problems include acute respiratory infections and parasite infections. Cooking on indoor stoves using biomass such as wood or dung leads creates indoor air pollution, which causes pneumonia, chronic respiratory disease, and lung cancer (WHO 2005b). Women in Africa do much of the cooking for the family and can spend many hours per day breathing in smoke while tending to the cooking fire. Parasites such as hookworm and schistosomiasis are also a health burden for women in Africa and often contribute to anemia (Bates, McKew, and Sarkinfada 2007). Hotez et al. (2006) report that women and children are more susceptible than men to anemia from hookworm and schistosomiasis. Research from the U.S. Centers for Disease Control and Prevention indicates that parasitic worms may also play a role in HIV infection. The urinary form of schistosomiasis, which in some parts of Africa affects up to half of women, damages the lining of the vagina, reducing a women's first defence against HIV infection (*New Scientist* 2008).

Noncommunicable diseases (such as stroke, cancer, heart disease, and diabetes) along with mental health and injuries also affect women in Sub-Saharan Africa. These diseases—once referred to as "Western diseases" but now growing in developing countries—are causing Africa's health systems to struggle under a double burden of high morbidity and mortality from infectious diseases and the increasing needs of people with chronic, noncommunicable conditions (WHO 2006a). These noncommunicable diseases can be mitigated by improving nutrition and fostering healthy food systems.

Priorities for Policy

Given the diversity in circumstances between regions and countries in Sub-Saharan Africa, it is nearly impossible to make a single set of recommendations that is applicable in all cases for strengthening the role of women in the food system. The policy interventions discussed in this section are presented as a toolkit of options to be evaluated depending on the situation in a particular country or even a specific area within a country. Figure 13.2 presents general areas to be

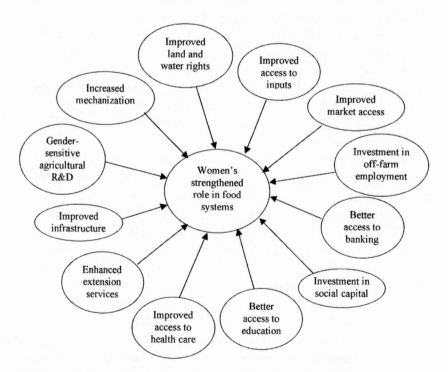

Figure 13.2   Policy options for strengthening women's role in food systems
SOURCE: Author.

addressed to help maximize women's abilities to play a larger role in achieving food and nutrition security. These are just some ways in which obstacles to women's increased agricultural productivity can be removed. Facilitating the increased production of food, whether it is accomplished through better access to credit, extension services aimed at women, increased primary schooling for girls, or any of the other means identified will help meet food security and nutrition goals.

To overcome the legal obstacles mentioned earlier, governments should address inequalities in property rights between men and women. Providing female farmers with the right to hold individual or joint land titles can help protect them in cases of divorce or their husbands' death. In some cultures, assets held by a household are stripped from the widow by the husband's relatives after his death, leaving the widow landless. Ensuring property rights can also help provide rights to water use where land ownership is a prerequisite to water access. In some countries where these rights have already been made into law, cultural practices override the legal protections. To help women understand what rights they have, legal literacy campaigns should be implemented to educate women. If women are aware of their rights, they will be better able to claim them. Training community-based paralegals in inheritance law and promoting the creation of holographic (handwritten) wills are some of the ways in which women's property rights can be strengthened (Quisumbing and Pandofelli 2008). It will not be easy to overcome persistent patriarchal cultural inheritance practices in some places. Another hurdle to women's ability to obtain land titles in some countries will be their lack of identification cards (Quisumbing and Pandofelli 2008). These impediments should not be a reason to ignore this vital aspect of women's agricultural productivity.

Another key area to address to help women increase their agricultural productivity is access to inputs, such as fertilizer and improved seed. Some measures would benefit all farmers, such as increasing the number of input retailers in rural areas to reduce the distance traveled to obtain supplies. This important measure does not, however, in itself address the underlying issue of women's ability to purchase needed inputs. Other activities could be aimed specifically at women, such as targeting fertilizer vouchers to female-headed households or helping women's groups make collective purchases of inputs. Such targeted interventions can have a more focused impact in areas where inputs are available but women are unable to obtain them owing to economic constraints.

Making it possible for women to play a larger role in food systems requires more than simply boosting yields. A household can consume only so much increased production; the surplus must reach the market and be sold. Improving women's access to markets is thus critical. In areas where the cost of permits to sell within the market area is prohibitive for women, efforts should be made to include them by, for instance, reducing fees. Where women cannot reach markets with their goods because they lack economies of scale, face time constraints, or confront other barriers, encouraging membership in producers' associations and cooperatives can open up possibilities. Such membership groups can help build capacity in market analysis and can enter into contract-farming arrangements, if available (Quisumbing and Pandofelli 2008).

Beyond strengthening the role of women in direct food production, policies should also prioritize strategies that help women move into off-farm jobs. The food system, viewed along a value chain, contains many entry points at which women can become involved and have impact. Providing women with opportunities to improve their skills in agribusiness management, marketing, supply chains, and other areas can have multiple benefits in the short and medium term. This approach can help reduce conflicts over land by opening opportunities to off-farm employment. Additionally, longer-term effects include shifting the agribusiness environment in Africa from one of commodities to one of products. The increasing rate of urbanization in Africa is a sign that local food markets are growing. Young urban professionals constitute a growing market for washed and cut vegetables that are ready to cook. Helping women add value in the food system strengthens the system as a whole. Governments can play a role in this arena by encouraging and creating incentives for education—particularly in the areas of agribusiness, finance, and management—for women and girls. The financial sector can encourage small and medium enterprises among women by extending credit for agriculture-related ventures. Nongovernmental organizations (NGOs) can assist in training and network formation for women entrepreneurs. A vision of Africa's future agricultural system must extend beyond subsistence production and low-input technologies to a system where women play roles in bringing African agribusiness into the 21st century along all points of the value chain.

Mobilizing women to strengthen their roles in the food systems of Sub-Saharan Africa must also include better access to banking services—not only credit, but also other financial services such as savings accounts and insurance. Extending banking services to women to protect their savings can minimize problems encountered after the death of a husband. Also, women's access to credit will help facilitate access to fertilizers and other inputs so they can maximize the productivity of their land. The renewed interest in African agriculture in recent years is leading to new credit schemes for smallholder farmers, such as the Kilimo Biashara initiative in Kenya through Equity Bank in collaboration with the Alliance for a Green Revolution in Africa, the International Fund for Agricultural Development, and the Government of Kenya. Efforts to reach women specifically through this credit fund and others can help promote increased productivity.

Beyond the technical aspects of strengthening women's roles in food systems, investment in social capital is also critical. Working with groups helps empower women and increase their control of assets (Quisumbing and Pandofelli 2008). In working with groups, implementers should bear in mind that not all groups are homogeneous. Within groups, members will differ in wealth, age, and status. Caution should be taken not to allow more powerful women to control groups and exclude poorer women (Quisumbing, Meinzen-Dick, and Smith 2004). Affirmative action policy is imperative for both women and men. Inequality between men and women is unacceptable, but inequality between women and women and between men and men should not be tolerated either. Class inequalities are another source of hunger, poor nutrition, and poor health and should not be overlooked in the effort to overcome gender inequities (Michael et al. 2001; Kawachi and Berkman 2000; Berkman and Glass 2000; Zinn 2001).

Beyond technical production issues and economic improvements, it is important to consider human capital. A country's most important resource is its people, but people in numbers are not enough if they are not healthy and educated. According to Quisumbing and Meinzen-Dick (2001, 1), "improving women's education is probably the single most important policy instrument to increase agricultural productivity and reduce poverty." Keeping girls in school past the primary level could have tremendous effects on agriculture, health, and nutrition. An essential part of furthering girls' education is the provision of adequate sanitation facilities at schools so that girls can continue to attend school during menstruation. If such facilities are not available, girls will often skip school during the days they menstruate or even drop out completely (Sommer 2009). Latrines that provide privacy and water for washing can help keep girls in school longer after the onset of puberty, an important aspect of achieving food and nutrition goals. Also related to the concept of human capital is access to health care. Programs that train community-based health care providers can improve the provision of health services in rural areas where travel to the nearest clinic may be difficult.

A discussion about boosting women's roles in food systems would not be complete without consideration of enhanced extension services. Targeted extension campaigns can help increase women's agricultural productivity. In one instance in Kenya, a nationwide information campaign aimed at women led to a 28 percent increase in the yield of corn, 80 percent for beans, and 84 percent for potatoes (FAO n.d.). In areas where it is feasible, women's adoption of high-value crops should be encouraged. This approach may encounter resistance from men in cultures where women do not traditionally participate in growing or marketing cash crops. Women themselves may be reluctant to switch to new crops because of the risk of moving away from staple crops. Male extension agents should be trained to meet the needs of female farmers, such as in postharvest techniques and care of animals. Female extension agents should be hired and trained as well, especially in areas where it is not culturally appropriate for male extension agents to talk with women farmers. Female extension agents need culturally appropriate modes of transport so they can effectively reach rural areas.

There are technological and physical considerations to helping women play stronger roles in food systems. Ensuring that women can make use of existing irrigation supplies and are not excluded because of lack of land title or other means is one step. Water supply systems should be designed for mixed use in both agricultural and domestic areas. Reducing the amount of time needed to gather water can lessen women's and girls' time burdens and improve health through better sanitation. Another way of reducing time burdens is to create energy infrastructure that can reduce time spent collecting fuel (Quisumbing, Meinzen-Dick, and Smith 2004).

Overcoming the technological obstacle of low adoption rates of improved seed varieties will be partially addressed by facilitating women's access to credit and extension services, but another piece of the equation is gender-sensitive agricultural research and development. Plant breeders in agricultural research services should take women's preferences, such as taste and processing qualities, into account when developing new varieties (Quisumbing, Meinzen-Dick, and Smith 2004). Involving women in on-farm trials can help create buy-in and build capacity for experimentation and problem solving. Attempts at increasing mechanization need to be gender sensitive as well, taking into account women's time allocation, physical stature, and availability of resources. Any technologies that are introduced should be culturally appropriate and labor-saving (Quisumbing and Pandofelli 2008).

The policy options enumerated here will not all be appropriate for every situation. Policy makers must tailor interventions and programs to the specific context in which they operate. Follow-through on initiatives is also important. To achieve progress, policy makers will need to set goals, reach expected outcomes, and devise exit strategies (where appropriate), while avoiding fragmented or stand-alone programs. Legal education in the absence of literacy training, or health education without accompanying agricultural extension, for example, can be wasted investments. Coordination among and collective implementation by stakeholders can boost the effectiveness of actions taken toward achieving nutrition and health goals.

Priorities for Research

Although it is tempting to state that enough is known about women and the African food system to focus entirely on implementing action plans, unanswered questions remain. What are the most effective ways of catalyzing women's roles? How are gender roles in agricultural systems changing? How can men positively affect food and nutrition security? Empirical work in all disciplines, is needed to document the shifting scenarios of intrahousehold relations that are crucial for good nutrition and the health status of communities. The factors that enable positive deviants to survive in the midst of failure may hold the key to success and should be examined. It is also important to examine the barriers to making needed improvements to women's power and how those barriers can be broken.

Women's role in the food system and in nutrition is undisputed. Yet despite previous efforts to support their role, food insecurity, malnutrition, and poverty are widespread in Sub-Saharan Africa. Why has knowledge not translated into action? The diverse farming systems, varied cultures, and changing societal norms of Sub-Saharan Africa require a web of efforts in research, policy, and implementation to strengthen the role of women in food systems.

More attention must also go to the food security and nutrition agenda for women themselves. Sub-Saharan Africa's health priorities for women are linked to reproduction (WHO/UNAIDS 2003; International Women's Health Coalition 2008; Fabiani et al. 2001). Almost all research on women's health is linked to perinatal programs with minimum health care packages revolving around maternal health and immunization (Global Fund 2005; NEPAD 2003; Oxfam International 2001). But it is unethical to expect women to take on extra burdens related to production when, for example, their anemia matters only when they are pregnant. Why should pastoral women continue to toil for others when they get no tetanus vaccine while clearing cattle enclosures of dung—the habitat for tetanus bacilli? Who cares for those with mental illness, those with arthritis, and the childless?

It is not enough to enact new policies; they must be continually monitored so that impact can be assessed and adjustments made if necessary. For example, the implications of legal reform for women's land access and ownership should be evaluated. Any attempt to diversify the crops that women grow should be accompanied by modeling of expected yields and analysis of market opportunities. Universities are well placed to collaborate in these efforts and to improve the information available on both the macro and micro levels within economics and a host of other disciplines.

Another high-priority area for research is the linkage between women's health and agricultural productivity. Some studies speak to the relationship between HIV/AIDS, malaria, and agriculture, and others stress how the death of a male head of household affects food production (Apt 2001), but there is little information on how women's health status affects agriculture and food security. A related area of investigation that could inform policies and actions is the concept of poverty traps. Understanding the factors that keep women from escaping poverty can help elucidate the reasons why past interventions have not been successful.

Research is also needed to explore ways in which the time and labor burdens of women farmers can be reduced. How can technology be employed to boost productivity? Can engineers design a lighter-weight plow that will allow for easier land preparation by women? What is the best way to raise women's adoption of improved seed varieties? In the midst of the HIV/AIDS epidemic, research on the impact of coping strategies and the loss of agricultural knowledge is crucial. How will information be passed to future farmers if generations are dying before the knowledge is passed on?

Given the changing demographics of Sub-Saharan Africa, there are at least two priority areas for research. First, continued evaluations of changing gender roles are essential. Any efforts to help women play stronger roles in food and nutrition security should take into account the many roles women play and the varied constraints on their time and labor. Second, the reality of the nutrition transition and rising rates of obesity in developing countries should not be overlooked. Research into food systems that achieve optimal health and nutrition without crossing into overnutrition is a new but critical field. Continued dedication to high-quality research is critical to finding the right pathways through which women can help meet food and nutrition security goals for Sub-Saharan Africa.

CHAPTER 14

Bridging the Gap: Linking Agriculture and Health
to Achieve the Millennium Development Goals

Joachim von Braun, Marie T. Ruel, and Stuart Gillespie

Abstract

Three-quarters of the world's poor live in rural areas of the developing world, and the large majority of them rely on agriculture for their livelihoods and food security. Agriculture is thus a key instrument for achieving the first Millennium Development Goal (MDG 1)—eradicating extreme poverty and hunger through increased food availability and access and greater income.

Agriculture is also linked—directly or indirectly—to all other MDGs, and in particular to the goals related to maternal and child health, nutrition and survival, and HIV/AIDS and other illnesses (MDGs 4, 5, and 6). Achieving these goals is in turn essential for boosting agricultural performance and productivity and eradicating poverty.

As a unified set of global poverty reduction goals—both supranational and suprasectoral—the MDGs provide an opportunity for overcoming sectoral divides and for designing and implementing collaborative approaches. In this context, they represent an opportunity to forge effective links between agriculture and health.

This chapter argues that the MDG concept—while clear on goals—is unclear on how to link goals to instruments and on how to promote synergies between goals, and it requires greater emphasis on context, policy, and governance. The framework for linking agriculture and health in ways that alleviate poverty and hunger is missing, and so is the set of instruments to effectively exploit the synergies between agriculture and health and to achieve joint policy formulation.

This chapter discusses research gaps and recommendations on how the MDGs could be used more effectively to enhance synergies between agriculture and health. It also proposes institutional arrangements to foster synergies between health and agriculture that could help overcome the deficiencies mentioned.

Introduction

In September 2000, heads of state adopted the Millennium Declaration confirming their countries' commitment to achieving the Millennium Development Goals (MDGs), a set of eight targets for addressing the many dimensions of extreme poverty—from income poverty, hunger, and health to education, environment, and gender.

The central MDG is the first one: MDG 1, which aims at "eradicating poverty and hunger." Although the MDGs do not establish a hierarchy of goals (and subgoals), most of the other goals in fact act as subgoals to MDG 1. Poverty and hunger eradication are goals as well as instruments for well-being, and they are closely linked to each other. Poverty reduction and agricultural growth have a close relationship in many developing countries, because most of the poor rely on agriculture for their livelihoods. Similarly, improved nutrition and health are also linked with agriculture. Hence, fostering positive linkages between agriculture and health will enhance progress toward meeting MDG 1 in addition to helping achieve several of the other goals.

Agriculture is the primary source of livelihoods for the majority of the world's poor, who in turn are the most vulnerable to ill health. Agricultural policy and practice affect human health, and health in turn affects agricultural productivity and output. Agriculture supports health by providing food, fiber, medicinal plants, and materials for shelter for the world's population. In rural communities, it contributes to livelihoods and food security and provides income that can be spent on health care and prevention. Successful health policies in turn benefit agriculture by protecting the labor force from days (and income) lost to illness, chronic disabilities, or mortality. In this sense, antiretroviral therapy for HIV/AIDS is not only a life-saving approach, but also a labor-saving technology. Agriculture is particularly important to achieving the first MDG—eradicating extreme poverty and hunger—because it can contribute to increased food availability and access and greater income. Agriculture is also linked directly or indirectly to several other goals, especially the health and survival goals—that is, the goals to reduce child mortality, improve maternal health, and combat HIV/AIDS, malaria, and other diseases (MDGs 4, 5, and 6). Thus, good health and productive agriculture are linked, and both are essential for poverty reduction and are key instruments for achieving the MDGs.

In spite of these obvious linkages, the agriculture and health sectors have typically failed to work together in developing joint policy. In the context of the MDGs, enormous potential exists for intersectoral work. Indeed, several of the goals are directly relevant to both agriculture and health, and countries are expected to address the eight goals, which span several sectors, simultaneously as a complete set. But has the opportunity to actively engage in intersectoral work to achieve the MDGs been taken up?

This chapter argues that the agriculture and health sectors have until recently not seen each other as key partners in achieving either their own sectoral goals or national MDGs. Some of this neglect may stem from a lack of basic awareness of the links in problems and potential solutions, and some from policy conflicts or other obstacles. The chapter highlights that this neglect may also be due to the fact that the MDG process is missing not only a framework for linking political change, economic policy, and public investments, but also a set of instruments to effectively exploit the potential synergies between agriculture and health. The chapter also identifies research gaps and provides recommendations on how the MDGs could be used more effectively to enhance synergies between agriculture and health. Finally, it proposes a set of actions for institutional arrangements that could foster synergies between health and agriculture and help overcome some of these missed opportunities.

Poverty, Ultra-Poverty, and Hunger

At a global scale, notable progress has been made in reducing poverty. Between 1990 and 2004, the proportion of people living on less than US$1 a day declined from 29 to 18 percent (Chen and Ravallion 2007). At this rate, the MDG poverty target will be met by 2015. Yet in many parts of the developing world, poverty remains severe and persistent. Three-quarters of the world's poor live in rural areas, particularly in Africa and Asia (Ravallion, Chen, and Sangraula 2007), and depend on agriculture as the primary source of their livelihoods.

Rapid economic growth has failed to reach extremely poor people, especially in environments of high inequality and poor governance. The disparity in earnings and income-generating opportunities has increased, with incomes of the poorest falling farther below the absolute poverty line and below national averages. More than 160 million people in the developing world are ultra-poor—that is, they live on less than $0.50 a day—and three-quarters of them are concentrated in Sub-Saharan Africa (Figure 14.1 and Barrett, chapter 12). The share and the number of the ultra-poor have decreased more slowly than those of the poor who live on US$1 a day. In Sub-Saharan Africa and Latin America, the proportion of the ultra-poor has actually increased since the early 1990s (Figure 14.2).

The characteristics of persistently poor people are often different from those who have been able to escape poverty. The ultra-poor (1) tend to live in remote rural areas, located farthest from roads, markets, schools, and health services; (2) often face exclusion because of their ethnicity, gender, or disability; and (3) tend to have few assets, less education, and less access to credit (Ahmed et al. 2007). This complex picture of poverty and ultra-poverty requires an equally complex policy response and effective policy instruments.

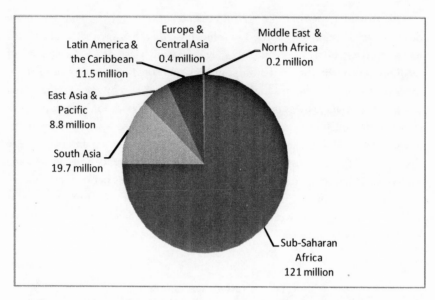

Figure 14.1 Number of ultra-poor people living on less than $0.50 a day, 2004
SOURCE: Ahmed et al. 2007. Reproduced with permission from the International Food Policy
Research Institute, www.ifpri.org.

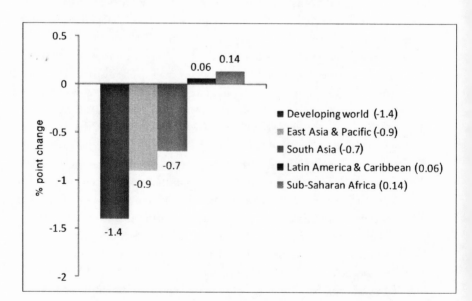

Figure 14.2 Change in the proportion of the ultra-poor in different regions, 1990–2004
SOURCE: Ahmed et al. 2007. Reproduced with permission from the International Food Policy
Research Institute, www.ifpri.org.

IFPRI has developed a Global Hunger Index (GHI), which captures three of the measurable MDG targets: the proportion of people who are calorie deficient, the prevalence of underweight in children under five (both targets for MDG 1), and the under-five mortality rate (target for MDG 4) (Wiesmann, Weingärtner, and Schöninger 2006). The GHI scores were used to rank 97 developing countries and 21 countries in transition. In addition, a progress indicator was developed to examine the performance of 91 developing countries in reducing their score in line with the MDGs and to discuss the track record of major regions and selected countries (Wiesmann et al. 2007). Only two regions of the world—Latin America and the Caribbean, and East Asia and the Pacific—are on track to reach the three MDG targets related to hunger and child mortality. According to the GHI, most countries will not reach these targets if progress persists at current rates. The Democratic Republic of the Congo and Burundi experienced the greatest set-backs in reducing the GHI to meet the MDGs, followed by Swaziland, Liberia, and North Korea. At the other extreme, countries like Cuba, Kuwait, Fiji, and Uruguay are most on track for achieving these three MDG targets.

Progress in health improvement has shown some positive trends, yet new risks are arising from infectious diseases such as avian influenza. A quarter of a century ago, AIDS was one such emerging disease—a long-wave crisis that continues to have devastating consequences. In the developing world, one out of every four children under five is underweight for his or her age (UNICEF 2008a). Child mal-nutrition has serious and irreversible consequences for health in both the short and the long term (Victora et al. 2008) and contributes to 35–53 percent of child deaths due to infections such as diarrhea, pneumonia, malaria, and measles (Black et al. 2008; Pelletier et al. 1995; Caulfield et al. 2004).

The Millennium Development Goals and a Brief History of Intersectoral Action

Although the notion of intersectoral action was implicit in the design of the first wave of applied nutrition programs in the 1960s (such as in India, Indonesia, and Thailand), it reached prominence within the health sector in 1978 with the World Health Organization (WHO)/United Nations Children's Fund (UNICEF) Alma Ata Declaration. The primary health-care model that emerged at the time explic-itly stated the need for "a comprehensive health strategy that not only provided health services but also addressed the underlying social, economic, and political causes of poor health" (WHO Commission on Social Determinants of Health 2005, 11). Bos (2006), however, points out that the intersectoral aspect of this goal has remained elusive and has often met strong resistance from within the health sector itself.

In the 1980s, conferences related to intersectoral action (IA) and the Ottawa Charter for Health Promotion further underscored the need to work between sectors to realize health gains. WHO notes, "A formal commitment to IA became part of many countries' official health policy frameworks in the 1980s. However, the track record of actual results from national implementation of IA was feeble. . . . IA to address social and environmental health determinants generally proved, in practice, to be the weakest component of the strategies associated with Health for All" (WHO 2005 Commission on Social Determinants of Health, 15).

Beyond the health sector, the importance of intersectoral action was historically promoted by the sustainable development movement—indeed, the 1987 Report of the World Commission on Environment and Development made intersectoral action a cornerstone of sustainability. Yet at this time, as noted by Lipton and de Kadt (1988), health (and population) considerations played little part in governments' decisions about agricultural policy.

The relationship between development policies as a whole—including agricultural policies—and the health status of communities was clearly articulated in the 1991 WHO publication *The Impact of Development Policies on Health*. The focus of this discussion was, however, unidirectional—that is, it looked only at the extent to which development policies affect health (Bos 2006). The bi-directionality of the linkages between agriculture and health policies started to be acknowledged in the context of the worsening AIDS epidemic in Sub-Saharan Africa during the late 1990s.

In 1997 a WHO conference spelled out the rationale for intersectoral action for health and emphasized the need to view the health sector as one of a number of intersectoral players (WHO 1997). It called for new systems of governance to manage partnerships and alliances and new roles and responsibilities. But the ultimate goal was, again, sectoral—intersectoral action was only intended to better achieve health outcomes.[1]

It was not until 2000 that a major high-level stimulus for mutually beneficial intersectoral collaboration emerged with the Millennium Declaration. The pillars of the declaration were the eight MDGs, each with quantified targets:

1. eradicate extreme poverty and hunger;
2. achieve universal primary education;
3. promote gender equality and empower women;
4. reduce child mortality;
5. improve maternal health;
6. combat HIV/AIDS, malaria, and other diseases;
7. ensure environmental sustainability; and
8. develop a global partnership for development.

As global goals, the MDGs provide a unique opportunity to overcome sectoral divides and to design and implement collaborative approaches. In this context, they represent an opportunity to forge more effective links between agriculture and health to achieve positive outcomes *across* different sectors. But there are also limitations that need to be overcome in order to unleash this potential.

Limitations of the MDGs in Fostering Intersectoral Action

The MDGs are relevant in the sense that they guide the planning and implementation of different development efforts. Their usefulness is limited, however, unless they are combined with a policy framework, strategy, and implementation plans (Sachs 2005; von Braun 2005). Although they offer a shared vision of what is needed, they provide no common articulation of how to get there—and especially how to address the goals as a whole rather than through separated actions.

The following limitations center on MDG 1, but they are also relevant for most other MDGs:

1. There is a lack of effective policy instruments. Economic theory emphasizes that achieving goals depends on the use of as many different instruments as possible (Tinbergen 1952). Pursuing each goal independently may result in an inefficient instrument portfolio. In the context of MDG 1, both the number and types of strategies essential for achieving the goal remain ambiguous.
2. A great deal of emphasis is placed on the first component of MDG 1 (halving the prevalence of poverty by 2015), but not on the second (halving the prevalence of hunger by 2015).
3. The monitoring process is poorly defined and lacks transparency, which raises questions about the measurement of progress. It is unclear whether the process is carried out honestly or independently, and discrepancies in results raise doubts about the reliability of the estimation methods and findings (Keyzer and van Wesenbeeck 2007).
4. Monitoring also focuses on average change, which hides important information on changes in inequality and poverty gaps. The fact that the issue of inequity is not appropriately addressed in achieving (and monitoring) the goals also raises an ethical issue. In Sub-Saharan Africa and Latin America, the share of people living on less than $0.50 a day has actually increased in recent decades (Ahmed et al. 2007), and it is perfectly conceivable that progress may be made toward MDG 1 while ultra-poverty continues to rise.
5. The MDGs are unrealistic and unachievable; cost assessments of aid needed to achieve the MDGs suggest that they are unachievable in the context of

past financial assistance and likely levels in the coming years (Devarajan, Miller, and Swanson 2002; Keyzer and van Wesenbeeck 2007). It is also important to note that while the MDGs were formally established in 2000, reductions in various MDG indexes are calculated from the year 1990. Reducing poverty by one-half from 1990 to 2015 depends on growth over the full 25 years. Nearly half of that growth would need to have occurred in the decade before the signing of the Millennium Declaration; countries with little to no growth in that period are unlikely to achieve it in the 15 years from 2000 to 2015.

6. Finally, partners and countries are not accountable to the needs of the poorest and hungry and to improving the delivery of public services in order to achieve MDG 1. Accountability also tends to be defined by individual goals, not the whole set of MDGs. Different sectors and development agencies tend to claim one or two goals as "on their watch" while largely ignoring the rest.

The MDGs: An Opportunity for Synergistic Policy Linking Agriculture and Health

Table 14.1 identifies some areas where greater synergies between agriculture and health could help achieve the MDGs.

Sustainable progress on the MDGs is dependent on an effective strategy that serves all the goals in an integrated manner. To this end, a comprehensive development approach is relevant (von Braun, Swaminathan, and Rosegrant 2004). In the context of the MDGs, collaborative research and action between the agriculture and health sectors is important because (1) agriculture is important for most of the MDGs, (2) health is important for most of the MDGs, and (3) positive synergies link agricultural and health policy, programming, and research that would benefit both sectors and the MDGs as a whole.

In addition, the case can be made that nutrition (which itself is a pivotal interface between agriculture and health) is important for most of the MDGs (Gillespie and Haddad 2003; World Bank 2006).

Agriculture Is Related to Most of the MDGs

Because agriculture is central to poverty reduction (see, for example, Ravallion and Datt 2002), higher agricultural productivity is a critical component in successfully meeting the MDGs. Although the linkage with agriculture is particularly strong for the first goal (MDG 1—halving hunger and poverty by 2015), all MDGs have direct or indirect linkages with agriculture (Rosegrant et al. 2006). By increasing

Table 14.1 Agriculture and health linkages in the MDGs

MDG	Rationale for synergistic policy development
Goal 1. Eradicate extreme poverty and hunger.	• Better health is linked to a reduction in poverty and in turn helps sustain the natural resource base for agriculture. • The security of agricultural livelihoods depends on the health of those engaged in agriculture; adults who are ill themselves or must care for sick children are less productive. • Ill-health conditions that may be related to agricultural production systems generate high health costs relative to the income of the rural and periurban poor. • Different agricultural production systems have different impacts on health, nutrition, and well-being. • Households can use income from agricultural production for improved access to health products and services. • Some agriculture-associated infections affect nutrient absorption and people's nutritional status.
Goal 2. Achieve universal primary education.	• Where members of rural communities are healthy, there is less demand on children to participate in agricultural production and school absenteeism is reduced.
Goal 3. Promote gender equality and empower women.	• Promotion of gender equality in agricultural production systems can help focus attention on gender-specific vulnerability to health risks related to specific agricultural tasks.
Goal 4. Reduce child mortality.	• Improved environmental management, fewer episodes of illness associated with agroecosystems, and better nutrition lead to healthy physical and mental growth of children and an important decline in childhood illness and under-five mortality.
Goal 5. Improve maternal health.	• Better maternal health and nutrition increase the chances of a healthy pregnancy and the ability to engage in agricultural activities. • Occupational health policies can target pregnant women working in agriculture for additional protection.
Goal 6. Combat HIV/AIDS, malaria, and other diseases.	• Environmental management practices in agriculture and the combination of integrated pest management and integrated vector management contribute to a reduction in malaria transmission risk. • Ensuring rural communities a proper livelihood from agriculture reduces risky sexual behavior as a source of additional income and thus reduces risk of HIV/AIDS and other sexually transmitted diseases. • Less pressure by infections on the immune system of HIV/AIDS sufferers enhances their potential in agricultural production.
Goal 7. Ensure environmental sustainability.	• Sustainable use of water resources, balanced for domestic and agricultural use, supports healthy communities. • Using wastewater, excreta, and graywater as valuable resources addresses issues of health protection and of water scarcity in agriculture. • Careful use of chemical inputs in agriculture contributes to health protection by avoiding contamination of surface and groundwater.
Goal 8. Develop a global partnership for development.	• Intersectoral partnerships between agriculture and health can act on rationales for synergistic policy development. • Impact assessment procedures by national governments and bilateral and multilateral agencies will enhance the health potential of agricultural development projects.

SOURCE: Bos 2006.

food availability that translates into better health and nutrition, generating income for farmers, and improving purchasing power and asset levels of the poor, agricultural growth contributes to MDG 1 (Rosegrant et al. 2006; World Bank/IFPRI 2007). Higher demand for agricultural products and for rural nonfarm labor can also help poor households increase their incomes. If they can achieve higher economic returns, farmers may diversify production into higher-value crops that would provide positive spillover effects for the entire economy (von Braun, Swaminathan, and Rosegrant 2004).

Agriculture is also linked to MDG 2, on universal education. A more dynamic agricultural sector will change households' assessment of the economic returns to educating children compared with the returns to keeping children out of school to work in household agricultural enterprises. Rising agricultural productivity resulting from the use of hired labor or labor-saving agricultural technologies will enable farmers to send their children to school. Agriculture-led economic growth could also free up more public resources to invest in education. In addition, it could create nonfarm jobs for skilled labor in the agroindustrial sector— as the agricultural sector expands, farmers grow more high-value products, and the specialized production and marketing requirements of these products increase the demand for skilled labor (von Braun, Swaminathan, and Rosegrant 2004).

Agriculture contributes to MDG 3 through the economic empowerment of women farmers. Women's "time poverty" is a major obstacle to gender equality. Because most women in developing countries depend on agriculture, improvements in agricultural technology will reduce their work hours and give them the opportunity to be employed in the nonagricultural sector (von Braun, Swaminathan, and Rosegrant 2004).

Maternal and child malnutrition, widespread in rural areas, are the underlying cause of 3.5 million deaths, 35 percent of the disease burden in children less than five years old, and 11 percent of total global disability-adjusted life years (DALYs) lost (Black et al. 2008). Agriculture can contribute to reducing child mortality (MDG 4) by increasing the diversity of food production and making more resources available to prevent and manage childhood illnesses. Agriculture can help improve maternal health (MDG 5) through more diversified food production, more micronutrient-dense food staples (such as through biofortification), and overall higher-quality diets (von Braun, Swaminathan, and Rosegrant 2004; Bouis 2002). Rising incomes from agriculture can also translate to reduced time burdens on women, which in turn may improve women's quality of life, health, and well-being.

Agriculture helps to combat HIV and AIDS, malaria, and other diseases (MDG 6) directly through better nutrition and indirectly by providing additional income that can be devoted to health services. Successful agriculture can eliminate the need for people to migrate to find work and thus eliminate a key driver of enhanced HIV risk. Agricultural practices can be both causes of, and important solutions to, environmental degradation (MDG 7). More productive agricultural technologies allow the withdrawal of agriculture from marginal, sensitive environments. Profitable agricultural systems can also ease population pressures in urban slums (von Braun, Swaminathan, and Rosegrant 2004). The competition over land for food and biofuels and the recent soaring prices of food and fuel now present a whole set of new challenges for the achievement of both MDG 7 and MDG 1. Von Braun states, "Only in the presence of appropriate economic, trade, science, and social policies will biofuels contribute to energy security without jeopardizing food security of the poor" (von Braun 2007a, 8). Finally, this chapter—in its call for intersectoral research and action on agriculture-health links—supports MDG 8, which advocates a global partnership for development.

Health Is Related to Most of the MDGs

Health and optimal nutrition are fundamental to people's productivity and well-being. Nutrition is directly affected by food intake and health and is in turn a direct determinant of people's health and survival. Some of the MDGs are directly related to health—specifically MDGs 4, 5, and 6—whereas several others can be supported (or hindered) by good (or bad) health or nutrition.

MDG 1 has two components, both related to health and nutrition. It is clear that hunger, one element of the goal, is inextricably linked to nutrition. Hunger is strongly correlated with a variety of underlying factors, including low food production, availability, and access; lack of mothers' education; and lack of access to safe water and sanitation and to health facilities. Poverty is also linked to poor nutrition and illness and premature death. For individuals to be productive, they must be healthy enough to work. Disease and malnutrition both decrease productivity (Gillespie and Haddad 2003).

Health and nutritional status also have a major impact on MDG 2. Malnourished children are less likely to enroll in school, and those that do, enroll later (Adelman, Gilligan, and Lehrer 2008). In addition, lack of sufficient calories or micronutrients has a negative impact on cognitive abilities and attention span (Whaley et al. 2003; van Stuijvenberg et al. 1999), thereby reducing school performance, grade achievement, and future economic productivity (Hoddinott et al. 2008).

Gender discrimination (MDG 3) often has strong and irreversible impacts on health and nutrition. Women living with gender inequality usually have limited decision-making power over issues that affect their own and their children's health and nutrition. Small mothers who suffered malnutrition during early childhood are more likely to deliver small babies, who in turn are at increased risk of malnutrition, poor health, and death during childhood. If they survive, these children are likely to have impaired development, perform poorly in school, and have lower economic productivity in adulthood (Hoddinott et al. 2008). Gender discrimination thus fuels the intergenerational transmission of malnutrition, poor health, and poverty; erodes human capital formation; and slows down a country's economic development.

MDG 7 has great implications for health and nutrition. Burning solid fuels in enclosed kitchens is often toxic, but other fuel options are more expensive, so the poor continue degrading natural resources and their own health status out of necessity. The rapid rise in biofuels has contributed to reduced food availability, rising food prices, and consequent stress on nutrition security, especially for households that are net food consumers (von Braun et al. 2008). In addition, the availability of safe drinking water and sanitation has both environmental and health implications, as both are clearly linked to diarrheal and other diseases.

The Need for a Multisectoral MDG Implementation Framework

The Millennium Declaration emphasizes the need for collaboration among governments, international organizations, and civil society organizations throughout the world in order to alleviate global poverty. Yet concrete action to achieve the goals is mostly addressed within a single sector, and the need for multisectoral work is largely overlooked.

Recommendations to guide governments in meeting the MDGs were developed through the establishment of 12 task forces. In general, the reports issues by these task forces largely missed possible synergies of multisectoral plans. For instance, the Child and Maternal Health Task Force focused on Goals 4 and 5, the most obvious links. The recommendations emphasize the need to strengthen health systems and the delivery and coverage of health services but do not mention the potential role of agricultural policies in reducing maternal and child morbidity and mortality or the importance of maternal and child health for achieving several of the other goals.

The Hunger Task Force report, on the other hand, includes a discussion of the importance of linking agriculture and health to eradicate extreme poverty and hunger. It specifically recommends promoting "integrated policy approach(es) to hunger reduction" and policies linking nutritional and agricultural interventions in each country, as agriculture, health, and hunger are inseparable in most developing-country contexts. A discussion of how to implement these integrated policy approaches, however, is lacking, and the report fails to discuss how to overcome some of the serious challenges involved in multisectoral policy making.

The task force reports propose the use of poverty reduction strategy papers (PRSPs) to create national plans in line with the attainment of the MDGs. The MDGs are seen as recommended policy targets within the PRSPs, with poor

countries developing a plan to achieve them by 2015 and rich countries supporting these plans through policy assistance and financial backing. The documents
emphasize a set of needed actions, such as reform of country governance, improvement of core infrastructure, human capital development, attention to gender
inequality, and increasing donor support. The PRSP process could have provided
a framework for multisectoral planning and action, but in most cases proposed
actions defaulted to conventional sectoral lines. A WHO analysis (WHO 2004b)
of a number of PRSPs, for example, revealed that they had led to little investment
in health-relevant cross-cutting areas (such as the provision of safe drinking water
and adequate sanitation). Most of the investments in health remained within the
confines of the health sector and focused on strengthening health services.

The UN report *Investing in Development: A Practical Plan to Achieve the Millennium Development Goals* (Sachs 2005) recognizes that most interventions will
have effects on several goals. It acknowledges that achieving the MDGs will
require ambitious, simultaneous action in many sectors. It does not, however,
acknowledge the benefits of—and the need for—policies that are developed with
multisectoral actions and impacts in mind. It also fails to recognize the unintended
potentially negative impacts that may result from single-sector policy making.

The lack of communication between agriculture and health observed in the
context of the MDGs is clearly not a new phenomenon. Agriculture and health
policies and programs tend to remain locked in sectoral silos, and seldom are they
integrated or coordinated. Agricultural policies address natural resource management, farmers' livelihoods, food security, and food safety, whereas public health
policies tend to revolve around the provision of prevention and curative care
within clinic-based health systems. Agriculture is driven by an economic development rationale, while health aims to maximize human development. Agriculture is productive; health is concerned with reproduction. These fundamentally
different societal functions have kept the sectors apart. Incentives are thus skewed
toward competition over limited resources rather than toward collaboration.

Even where policies and plans explicitly invoke intersectoral action, their implementation tends to default to the comfort zone of sectoral systems and procedures. Progress indicators for the MDGs are tracked by different United Nations
agencies presenting additional barriers to intersectoral (in this case, interagency)
action. For example, Gavian, Galaty, and Kombe (2006) found an upswing in the
number of countries with comprehensive, multisectoral national AIDS strategies but also noted that implementation lags behind. In 2004, the World Bank's
Multi-country AIDS Program (MAP) Interim Review described a "somewhat half-
hearted" introduction into many ministries, with "cookie-cutter" sectoral plans
for responding to HIV tending to ignore the local context and line ministries
adopting workplace action plans yet failing to consider programs for their con-
stituencies and failing to submit fundable proposals and work plans.

A Conceptual Framework of Agriculture-Health Linkages

This section describes the role that research can play in fostering intersectoral collaboration between the agriculture and health sectors. It starts with the presentation of a conceptual framework, which highlights the multiple linkages between agriculture and health (Hawkes and Ruel 2006a) and the importance of looking at the bi-directionality of these linkages, in Figure 14.3. The framework shows that agriculture and health interact through people, the natural environment, and food and other outputs: poor agricultural producers and their families are particularly vulnerable to malnutrition and poor health; agricultural systems interact with the environment, in turn affecting human health; and agriculture produces foods, fibers, and plants with medicinal properties essential for human life, health, and culture. The core nodes in the agricultural supply chain—agricultural producers, agricultural systems, and agricultural outputs—are shown along the top of the framework. At the bottom are some of the most important health challenges affecting the poor in developing countries: undernutrition, malaria and other water-associated vector-borne diseases, HIV/AIDS, foodborne diseases, diet-related chronic diseases, and a range of occupational health hazards. In the middle are the most critical intermediary processes linking agriculture and health in both directions: the labor process, environmental change, income generation, and access to food, water, land, and health-related services. As shown on the left side of the figure, these interactions are all influenced by policies, policy processes, and governance.

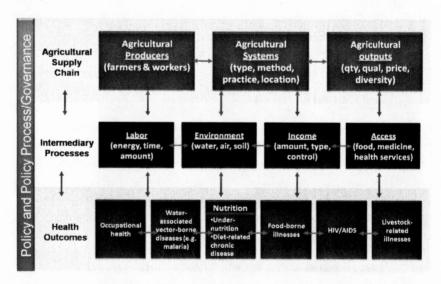

Figure 14.3   A conceptual framework of the linkages between agriculture and health
SOURCE: Hawkes and Ruel 2006a.

In sum, the process of agricultural production and the outputs it generates can contribute to both good and poor health, among producers as well as in the wider population. Agriculture is fundamental for good health through the production of the world's food, fiber, materials for shelter, and, in some systems, medicinal plants. Yet agriculture is also associated with many of the world's major health problems, including undernutrition, malaria, HIV/AIDS, foodborne diseases, diet-related chronic diseases, and a range of occupational health hazards. Agriculture can contribute to both the spread and alleviation of these health conditions. In the other direction, the occurrence of these health conditions has tremendous implications for agriculture. In the general population, the prevalence of malnutrition and disease influences market demand for agricultural products. For example, chronically undernourished populations have lower caloric needs, whereas certain disease patterns may increase the demand for specific medicinal plants. In the agricultural population, workers in poor health are less able to work, a situation that cuts productivity and income, perpetuates a downward spiral into ill health and poverty, and further jeopardizes food security and economic development for the wider population.

Toward Implementation and Action:
The Agriculture and Health Research Platform

The Consultative Group on International Agricultural Research (CGIAR), recognizing the potential benefits of cooperation in research, policy making, and practice between the two sectors, has created the Agriculture and Health Research Platform to facilitate this cooperation. In particular, the platform aims to improve coordination on health-related research, create productive partnerships with the health sector, and thus maximize the impact of research and policy innovation on pro-poor agricultural development. The International Food Policy Research Institute (IFPRI) coordinates the work of the platform in partnership with other organizations, including the WHO.

Setting priorities for research on agriculture and health requires a unified framework to avoid "ad hoc-ism." Two complementary options may best be pursued in parallel: one framework could focus on lives saved and livelihoods improved (mortality, morbidity, DALYs); another framework could focus on economic productivity, growth, and returns to investment (expected benefit-cost ratios, human productivity, lifetime earnings). In view of the different positions of health and agriculture in society and the economy, a dual framework approach that includes both of these concepts may be helpful for generating an informed policy discourse on priority setting.

The Platform's research is intended to focus on mitigating the negative effects of agricultural activities while maximizing opportunities for agriculture to benefit health, and better health to benefit agriculture.[2] The platform has—on a preliminary basis—identified five research priorities that would benefit from greater intersectoral collaboration:

1. *Nutrition, diet, and health:* Food quantity and food quality are the primary linkages between agriculture, nutrition, and health (Box 1). A lack of energy is generally an issue only in highly food-insecure areas, whereas micronutrient malnutrition is much more widespread and pervasive. While problems of insufficient and poor-quality food persist, changes in the global environment are creating emerging nutritional issues such as the "nutrition transition"—a process by which globalization, urbanization, and changes in lifestyle are linked to excess caloric intake, poor-quality diets, and low physical activity that lead to rapid rises in obesity and chronic diseases even among the poor in developing countries. The main challenge for agriculture-health-nutrition is thus to adapt to the changing environment, address the double burden of under- and overnutrition, and maintain adequate food supply while increasing the production of low-cost high-quality foods to improve diet quality among the poor (Hawkes and Ruel 2006b). Research on biofortification—or the process of breeding micronutrient-rich staple crops—is particularly relevant in this context (Bouis 2002). As further discussed by Herforth in chapter 7, agricultural biodiversity, and its linkages with dietary diversity for better nutrition, is another important area of research on agriculture and nutrition linkages.

Box 1: Successful agriculture and health collaboration:
Agriculture and nutrition

The linkages between agriculture and nutrition are particularly strong and direct for agricultural producers (farmers or laborers), largely through the intermediary processes of income, food access, and labor. Agriculture influences the amount, type, stability, distribution, and control of income, and these factors have important implications for the nutrition of agricultural households. The labor supplied by agricultural households also influences nutritional status by affecting energy expenditure and the time available for child care and food preparation. Agriculture also affects the nutrition of consumers. Nutrition is influenced by the quantity of food available, its quality and diversity, its price, and how it is distributed. These characteristics of the food supply are in turn influenced by agriculture and the policies that govern it. The quality of foods and their micronutrient content have particularly important implications for micronutrient deficiencies. Agricultural policies can create incentives or disincentives for the production of different foods and in turn determine their prices, thus affecting the environment in which people make choices about the foods they eat (Hawkes and Ruel 2006b; World Bank/IFPRI 2007).

Experience over past decades has shown that agriculture can make positive contributions to good nutrition. An example is the work of Helen Keller International (HKI) on homestead food production in four Asian countries. The program aimed at improving the nutritional status of vulnerable members of low-income households in Bangladesh, Cambodia, Nepal, and the Philippines through the promotion of small-scale production and consumption of micronutrient-rich crops and small animals. HKI, through its networks of more than 250 local nongovernmental organizations (NGOs) and local government offices in health and agriculture, successfully scaled up the program, which currently covers 1 million households (Spahn 2008). Positive impacts of the program have been documented: households are producing and consuming more micronutrient-rich foods; they are earning increased incomes from the sale of high-value products; and mothers, infants, and children have better micronutrient intakes and (HKI/Asia-Pacific 2001).

Biofortification—the process of breeding food crops that are rich in essential micronutrients—is another agricultural strategy with proven benefits for health and nutrition. Orange-fleshed sweet potato (rich in vitamin A), for instance, represents a successful agriculture and health partnership that has had well-documented impacts on the vitamin A intake and status of young children in Mozambique (Low et al. 2005, 2007a, b).

2. *Food safety and growing complexity in food supply chains:* The increased complexity of agricultural production and food supply chains has introduced new risks of food contamination; millions of adults and children suffer from the ill-health effects of foodborne diseases. In developing countries, diarrhea from foodborne and water-associated diseases kills an estimated 2 million people annually and is predominantly linked to the lack of access to safe water, inadequate sanitation, and poor hygiene, particularly among the rural poor. Capacity for prevention and control is limited, but an integrated water management approach for agricultural and domestic needs holds potential. Zoonoses are another major food safety issue (see priority 4). Effective, equitable, intersectoral collaboration on research and action to prevent and control animal-borne and foodborne microbial zoonotic diseases should be prioritized. Adjusting food production and agricultural

practices is key to reducing the risk of diarrheal diseases and zoonoses. Other important research areas here include understanding the impacts of— and developing policies to address—globalization, the rise in importance of supermarkets, the changes in food demand, and the impacts of the Green Revolution on human and animal health. Another important area of research is the impact of food safety standards on the ability of small farmers in developing countries to sell their products across borders and the consequences for their livelihoods, incomes, and the health and nutrition of their family members.

3. *Water-associated disease and water management.* The linkages between agriculture, water, health, and disease are fundamental to the disease burden on rural communities. Land and animals need water, aquaculture depends on water, and families need water for consumption and for hygiene. Agriculture, water, and health interact through multiple pathways—some beneficial (for example, irrigation increases agricultural productivity) and others detrimental (for example, irrigation water may increase malaria). And the relationships are often bi-directional (Box 2). The health risks of agricultural use of wastewater, which is increasingly used in periurban agriculture, need to be given careful consideration. Research needs in this area include acquiring new knowledge about the interactions between agriculture, water, and health; developing joint thinking and efforts to disseminate and apply this knowledge more widely and effectively; and carrying out specific case studies of integrated applicable solutions that can be brought to scale.

Box 2: Successful agriculture and health collaboration:
Irrigation and malaria control

Every year an estimated 300–500 million people get sick from malaria, and more than 1 million die from it, many of them children (Hay et al. 2004). Characteristics of agricultural production systems, such as crop rotation, the presence of livestock, and the proximity of villages to fields and water sources, affect malarial risk. In particular, irrigation, if not carefully planned, can create conditions that favor parasitic vectors and facilitate disease transmission (Mutero et al. 2005). In Ethiopia researchers found malaria prevalence to be higher in those villages close to government-promoted micro dams (Amacher et al. 2004).

Irrigation brings higher agricultural yields and incomes but can heighten the risk of malarial transmission, thus decreasing agricultural productivity (Keiser et al. 2005). In the first half of the 20th century, malaria was the leading public health problem in Italy, much as in many developing countries today. Absences resulting from illness and death were common during the agricultural season, leaving millions of hectares of Italy's most fertile land fallow (Snowden 2006). In the developing world malaria continues to have serious negative impacts on productivity. One study of farmers engaged in intensive vegetable production in Côte d'Ivoire showed that malaria sufferers produced about half the yields and half the incomes that healthy farmers did (Girardin et al. 2004).

Successful partnerships between agriculture and health have allowed implementation of preventive measures to control malaria while modifying or manipulating agricultural water systems. For example, in the early 1900s, better maintenance of and improvements to irrigation and drainage systems reduced malaria cases by more than half in Egypt, India, and Indonesia (Keiser et al. 2005). A case study in India in 1940–41 showed that intermittent irrigation of rice fields reduced malaria contraction from 48 percent to 4 percent. Today, many options are available to mitigate the negative effects of irrigation while maintaining agricultural productivity. They include providing location-specific knowledge of drainage techniques, intermittently wetting and drying rice fields, alternating rice with a dryland crop, and using livestock as "bait" for mosquitoes (van der Hoek et al. 2003; Mutero et al. 2005).

4. *Zoonotic diseases (such as avian influenza) and livelihoods.* Zoonotic diseases represent a major risk to human health and security today and in the future (80 percent of new diseases in the past century have been zoonotic). Though people everywhere would be at risk if there were a major epidemic outbreak, 90 percent of casualties would be in developing countries. Linkages from wild animals to food animals to humans are one pathway of zoonotic diseases, with avian influenza being the most recent example. Addressing this risk requires understanding the pathways of zoonotic disease transmission and building the capacity to deal with them. Tasks include conducting anthropological research on zoonotic diseases, building capacity to quickly identify the pathogen causing an outbreak, and working with producers and market agents to help control livestock diseases. To guide the design and targeting of compensation schemes, it is also important to evaluate the impact of avian influenza and related control measures on producer household livelihoods, consumption patterns, diet quality, and nutrition. Avian influenza outbreaks represent a unique opportunity to conduct intersectoral research linked to action. Such opportunities should not be missed, and lessons learned from successful intersectoral collaboration on this complex issue should be carefully documented to highlight both the challenges and the benefits of such approaches.

5. *HIV and AIDS and agriculture.* The livelihoods of most people affected by HIV and AIDS globally depend on agriculture, which in turn is being significantly undermined by the disease in many developing countries. The interactions between HIV and AIDS and agriculture are bi-directional. AIDS affects agriculture—households struggling to respond to illness and death experience decreased agricultural productivity and reduced income. But agriculture also affects HIV risk—if agriculture fails to provide a livelihood, people may migrate to find work or resort to riskier behavior, increasing their exposure to HIV. As discussed in Box 1, significant opportunities are available for making agricultural policy more HIV-responsive and thus for furthering both health and agricultural goals. Some of the main research issues concern how to operationalize intersectoral responses to the known links between HIV and agriculture.

Adopting agriculture as the starting point may lead to a focus on increasing the health benefits of agricultural production—that is, by generating safe, productive work, income, and nutrition—while minimizing the potential harm caused by agriculture through, for example, waterborne diseases, zoonoses, mycotoxins, highly hazardous pesticides, landscape destruction, and climate change. Examples of successful partnerships that address some of the linkages between health and agriculture are provided in Box 3.

Box 3: Successful agriculture and health collaboration:
Agriculture and HIV/AIDS response

In 2006 an estimated 39.5 million people in the world were living with HIV, and an estimated 2.9 million people died from AIDS (UNAIDS 2006). The majority of people affected by HIV and AIDS depend on agriculture, and their livelihoods are undermined by the disease in many countries. Illness and death from HIV and AIDS reduce agricultural earnings and productivity. A 1997 study of worker productivity in a Kenya tea estate found the average daily output of HIV-positive workers to be 23 percent less than that of healthy workers in the same fields (Fox et al. 2004). A study of rural households in Mozambique showed that a household that suffered an adult male illness or death likely to be HIV-related experienced a significant reduction in food production relative to other categories of households. This loss of food production represents a major shock for households that rely on subsistence production and are often already far below their recommended food intake.

AIDS also reduces the capacity of the agricultural civil service. Between 1996 and 2000 in Kenya, 58 percent of all deaths of staff in the Ministry of Agriculture were AIDS-related. Mozambique's Ministry of Agriculture projects that it may lose 20–24 percent of its staff to AIDS from 2004 to 2010. Lower agricultural earnings and productivity can also increase the risk of contracting HIV. Facing insecure livelihoods, some household members migrate to find work or engage in transactional sex. Many studies show a significant correlation between HIV prevalence and migration, suggesting that mobility increases the probability of risky behavior (Gillespie and Kadiyala 2005a).

There is tremendous scope for agricultural policy to become more HIV-responsive and further both health and agricultural goals. Promoting labor-saving technologies and crops is one way to address lost labor resulting from AIDS-related mortality in agriculture. But for poorer smallholder households, the main constraints on livelihoods may be land and cash rather than labor. So cash transfers to help them hire labor, more secure land tenure for women, and expanded agricultural extension programs to include women and orphans could have a greater impact on welfare (Jayne, Pingali, and Villarreal 2006).

To overcome the lack of land and labor often facing AIDS-affected households, the Livelihoods Recovery through Agriculture Programme, implemented in Lesotho in 2002 by CARE and the Ministry of Agriculture, promotes producing crops with high nutritional content on small plots of land close to the home. Of the participants, 53 percent reported that they had stabilized or increased their food production (Abbot et al. 2005). Another program in Mozambique provides orphans and vulnerable children in high HIV-prevalence areas with crucial farming and life skills as well as nutritious daily meals. Similar programs are being tested in Kenya, Namibia, Swaziland, and Zimbabwe (Gillespie 2006).

Bringing the Agriculture and Health Sectors Together

To create holistic, systems-based approaches to plant, animal, and human health, truly collaborative, multisectoral, and interdisciplinary approaches are necessary. But promoting cooperation in research and policy between two different sectors is challenging—sectoral barriers that provide disincentives to collaboration need to be overcome, and challenges in transdisciplinary analyses and communications must be confronted. Intersectoral cooperation is a mechanism, a matter of practice, not an end in itself. It requires an enabling policy environment, effective institutional arrangements, and the capacity of individuals to engage in an intersectoral dialogue. It relies on evidence generated by multidisciplinary research from credible sources.

Challenges in achieving intersectoral collaboration include

- *the prevailing vertical orientation* of funding, budget control, organizational/sectoral planning, monitoring, and accountability;
- *ignorance of intersectoral issues,* with no one sector willing to take responsibility or advocate effectively;
- *differences in paradigms,* worldviews, mindsets, and professional language;
- *competing priorities,* incentives (such as promotion criteria), and decision-making processes;
- *complex processes of engagement;* and
- *capacity constraints,* including rapid turnover of staff (technical, managerial, and political) that impedes the formation of the kinds of relationships and partnerships necessary to bridge institutional divides across sectors (Bryce et al. 2008).

Regarding the issue of capacity, another long-term challenge is to ensure appropriate training of researchers and professionals at universities and other institutions. Students are often funneled into their respective disciplines without much exposure to peers, faculty, and professionals in other departments who share similar research interests but have a different professional language or view a common issue from a different perspective. Training institutions need to re-cruit students from a wider range of disciplines and create opportunities for stu-dents to collaborate with other disciplines. This spirit of collaborative research, and perhaps more important, the professional and personal connections estab-lished between individuals across disciplines, will likely carry into future research and catalyze collaboration. The importance of individuals, and the relationships between individuals, in influencing the research and policy process at all scales should not be underestimated. These relationships are important for many, if not all, of the success factors described below.

These challenges—and ways of confronting them—are researchable issues in themselves. Ultimately, there is a need to better understand how to promote a shared understanding that translates into integrated implementation of interven-tions for greater impact (World Bank/IFPRI 2007). A well-structured framework for implementing MDGs could provide an excellent tool for integrating sectors in practice, and this framework would also need to be tested by research.

Success factors in intersectoral collaboration include

- *early inclusive engagement* with relevant partners;
- *an identified need to work together* to achieve goals, whether sectoral or global;
- *shared objectives* of collaboration;
- *opportunities*[3] for intersectoral collaboration and approaches to surmount barriers;

- *innovative systems of communication* between disciplinary domains based on clear agreements on common goals, shared values and principles, clearly understood rules of engagement, common notions of validity of knowledge and evidence, and appropriate tools for communication;
- *capacity* (human, economic, organizational, institutional, and knowledge resources) and incentives for development professionals to think and act intersectorally, whether in research, programming, policymaking, or funding for new initiatives;
- *models, tools, and mechanisms* for working together;
- *jointly agreed and compatible monitoring and evaluation* plans and mechanisms, linked to jointly held accountability;
- *stable teams* with time to develop;
- *an enabling policy environment* involving good connectivity with intersectoral bodies; and
- *synthesis and prompt dissemination* of intersectoral research findings, experiences, and impact.

How can national policy frameworks be oriented to promote synergies between agriculture and health? The following approaches, drawn in particular from Bos (2006) and Bryce et al. (2008), are promising:

- Governments can formulate policies that create incentives for intersectoral collaboration that benefits the national good over and above strict sectoral division. Such incentivized policies would have to emanate from the highest policymaking level, such as the prime minister's office, and have the support of the ministry of finance (which would allocate financial resources for proposed intersectoral actions).
- Such incentives (financial or otherwise) would need to apply at the local levels where implementation occurs. Because key decisions about priorities and resource allocation are often made at subnational levels, local as well as national capacity to develop contextually appropriate interventions will need to be strengthened.
- Bisectoral or multisectoral policy reviews could be undertaken, aimed at harmonizing existing policies, identifying opportunities for reciprocal action to address each other's concerns, and formulating new policies that support the concept of intersectoral collaboration. Bos (2006) provides the example of countries with increasing water scarcity formulating policies for its optimal use in agriculture and simultaneously ensuring that this resource is used in ways that protect the health of agricultural producers, their families, and the consumers of products cultivated with wastewater. Such reviews could also identify perverse policies—that is, sectoral policies that contradict

and counteract each other. Gillespie and Kadiyala (2005a) describe the application of an HIV lens to agricultural policy to ensure that agricultural policies do not inadvertently provide the conditions for more rapid spread of HIV infection or reduce households' options for responding to the impacts of AIDS (for example, agricultural diversification is associated with resilience and a strengthened ability to respond to AIDS).

• Health impact assessments could be undertaken (implemented in parallel and in consultation with environmental impact assessment) to ensure that the health impacts of any new agricultural development project or new agricultural policy are considered in a timely fashion and that a public health management plan incorporates intersectoral action. This approach also requires bilateral and multilateral development agencies to review their decision-making criteria for projects ahead of time and adopt policies that ensure that health safeguards are incorporated.

Conclusions

The MDGs offer new opportunities for more comprehensive approaches to im-proving human well-being. To realize these potentials, it is important to stop singling out individual MDGs and instead to start recognizing the linkages among them and their functional relationships and interdependence. Strategic use and strengthening of the linkages between agriculture and health offer particularly strong opportunities for achieving poverty reduction and health goals in many low-income countries. Exploiting these opportunities requires a new initiative for evidence-based and research-intensive action across the agriculture and health sectors, allied with effective communications, capacity strengthening, and social mobilization.

Notes

We gratefully acknowledge comments and contributions by Corinna Hawkes, Rajul Pandya-Lorch, Tolulope Olofinbiyi, Bella Nestorova, Noora-Lisa Aberman, and Teunis van Rheenen (all at the International Food Policy Research Institute); Robert Bos (World Health Orga-nization); and two anonymous reviewers.

1. The definition of intersectoral action for health was "a recognized relationship between part or parts of the health sector with part or parts of another sector which has been formed to take action on an issue to achieve health outcomes (or intermediate health outcomes) in a way that is more effective, efficient, or sustainable than could be achieved by the health sector acting alone" (WHO 1997, 3).

2. There are many ways to define problems that require intersectoral research and action. Problem definitions may be place-based (that is, location-specific), or they may be

targeted to a disease, a population subgroup, or a livelihood system. Each of these entry points brings with it a particular conceptual base; related assumptions, vocabulary, and measurement approaches; a set of institutional actors; and commonly used policy instruments. It is also important to emphasize that the disease orientation adopted here is purely a starting point—one that should permit a complementary livelihoods perspective and an exploration of the ways in which different health and agriculture conditions overlap and intersect to affect people's livelihoods in different ways. Many countries have used strategies focusing on a specific disease, risk factor, or groups of risk factors. Dahlgren and Whitehead note that disease-specific approaches focus on the downstream factors in the causal chain, but they acknowledge that "sometimes, a coordinated systematic approach that focuses on a specific disease is effective in mobilizing public action" (2006, 101). Common risks associated with this approach include duplication of effort and a narrow focus on downstream effects.

3. Opportunities for research may emerge where the landscape is changing in ways that preclude business as usual. For example, when internally displaced people return home, agricultural livelihood systems may have to be completely restructured, and this restructuring can be done in a health-conscious manner. Patterns of climate change may result in reduced precipitation, and where water management for irrigation must be adapted to new realities of scarcity, it can also take on board considerations of health impact and opportunities.

REFERENCES

Abate, T., A. van Huis, and J. K. O. Ampofo. 2000. Pest management strategies in traditional agriculture: An African perspective. *Annual Review of Entomology* 4: 631–59.

Abbot, J., M. Lenka, P. J. Lerotholi, M. Mahao, and S.Mokhamaleli. 2005. From condoms to cabbages: Rethinking agricultural interventions to mitigate the impacts of HIV/AIDS in Lesotho. Paper prepared for the International Conference on HIV/AIDS and Food and Nutrition Security, April 14–16, Durban, South Africa.

ACC/SCN (Administrative Committee on Coordination/Subcommittee on Nutrition). 1987. *First report on the world nutrition situation.* Geneva.

———. 2000. *Fourth report on the world nutrition situation.* Geneva: ACC/SCN in collaboration with the International Food Policy Research Institute.

Adato, M., and L. Bassett. 2008. What is the potential of cash transfers to strengthen families affected by HIV and AIDS? RENEWAL and the Joint Learning Initiative on Children and AIDS working paper. www.ifpri.org/renewal.

Adato, M., A. Ahmed, and F. Lund. 2004. *Linking safety nets, social protection, and poverty reduction: Directions for Africa.* 2020 Africa Conference Brief 12. Washington, DC: International Food Policy Research Institute.

Adelman, S., D. O. Gilligan, and K. Lehrer. 2008. *How effective are food for education programs? A critical assessment of the evidence from developing countries.* Food Policy Review 9. Washington, DC: International Food Policy Research Institute.

Adom, K. K., M. E. Sorrells , and R. H. Liu. 2005. Phytochemicals and antioxidant activity of milled fractions of different wheat varieties. *Journal of Agricultural and Food Chemistry* 53 (6): 2297–2306.

Afiriyie-Gyawu, E., J. Mackie, B. Dash, M. Wiles, J. Taylor, H. Huebner, L. Tang, H. Guan, J.-S. Wang, and T. Phillips. 2005. Chronic toxicological evaluation of dietary NovaSil clay in Sprague-Dawley rats. *Food Additives and Contaminants* 22 (3): 259–69.

Afiriyie-Gyawu, E., N.-A. Ankrah, H. J. Huebner, M. Ofosuhene, J. Kumi, N. M. Johnson, L. Tang, L. Xu, P. E. Jolly, W. O. Ellis, D. Ofori-Adjei, J. H. Williams, J.-S. Wang, and T. D. Phillips. 2008. NovaSil clay intervention in Ghanaians at high risk for aflatoxicosis. I. Study design and clinical outcomes. *Food Additives and Contaminants* 25 (1): 76–87.

African Studies Center. N.d. Intensified maize cultivation enhances malaria transmission in western Ethiopia. African Studies Center, Boston University; Harvard School of Public Health, Harvard University; Ethiopian Ministry of Health/World Health Organization; Ethiopian Institute for Agricultural Research. http://www.bu.edu/africa/resources/psae/Malaria1.pdf.

Aguero, J., M. R. Carter, and I. Woolard. 2007. *The impact of unconditional cash transfers on nutrition: The South African child support grant.* Working Paper 39. Brasilia: International Policy Centre.

Ahmed, A. U., R. V. Hill, L. C. Smith, D. M. Wiesmann, and T. Frankenberger. 2007. *The world's most deprived: Characteristics and causes of extreme poverty and hunger.* Washington, DC: International Food Policy Research Institute.

AIARD (Association for International Agriculture and Rural Development). 2003. The agriculture, nutrition, and HIV/AIDS connections in developing countries. Paper prepared for the U.S. Agency for International Development (USAID). http://pdf .usaid.gov/pdf_docs/PNACW456.pdf.

Ainsworth, M., and I. Semali. 1998. Who is most likely to die of AIDS? Socioeconomic correlates of adult deaths in Kagera Region, Tanzania. In *Confronting AIDS: Evidence from the developing world,* ed. M. Ainsworth, L. Fransen, and M. Over. Brussels: European Commission.

Aksoy, S., M. Berriman, N. Hall, M. Hattori, W. Hide, and M. J. Lehane. 2005. A case for a *Glossina* genome project. *Trends in Parasitology* 21 (3): 107–11.

Alderman, H. 2007. Improving nutrition through community growth promotion: Longitudinal study of the nutrition and early child development program in Uganda. *World Development* 35 (8): 1376–89.

Alderman, H., and C. del Ninno. 1999. Poverty issues for zero rating VAT in South Africa. *Journal of African Economies* 8 (2): 182–208.

Alderman, H., and T. Haque. 2006. Countercyclical safety nets for the poor and vulnerable. *Food Policy* 34 (4): 372–83.

Alderman, H., and S. Linnemayr. 2009. Anemia in low-income countries is unlikely to be addressed by economic development without additional programs. *Food and Nutrition Bulletin* 30 (3): 265–70.

Alderman, H., J. Hoddinott, and B. Kinsey. 2006. Long-term consequences of early childhood malnutrition. *Oxford Economic Papers* 58 (3): 450–74.

Alderman, H., J. R. Behrman, V. Lavy, and R. Menon. 2001. Child health and school enrollment: A longitudinal analysis. *Journal of Human Resources* 36 (1): 185–205.

Alderman, H., B. Ndiaye, S. Linnemayr, A. Ka, C. Rokx, K. Dieng, and M. Mulder-Sibanda. 2009. Effectiveness of a community-based intervention to improve nutrition in young children in Senegal: A difference in difference analysis. *Public Health Nutrition* 12 (5): 667–73.

Allison, E. H., and J. A. Seeley. 2004. HIV and AIDS among fisherfolk: A threat to "responsible fisheries"? *Fish and Fisheries* 5 (3): 215–34.

Almond, D. 2006. Is the 1918 influenza pandemic over? Long-term effects of in utero influenza exposure in the post-1940 U.S. population. *Journal of Political Economy* 114 (4): 672–712.

Alonso, P., J. Sacarlal, J. J. Aponte, et al. 2004. Efficacy of the RTS,S/AS02A vaccine against *Plasmodium falciparum* infection and disease in young African children: Randomized controlled trial. *Lancet* 364 (9443): 1411–20.

Altieri, M., P. Rosset, and L. A. Thrupp. 2001. The potential of agroecology to combat hunger in the developing world. In P. Pinstrup-Andersen and R. Pandya-Lorch, eds., *The unfinished agenda: Perspectives on overcoming hunger, poverty, and environmental degradation.* Washington, DC: International Food Policy Research Institute.

Alva, S., E. Kleinau, K. Rowan, and C. Teller. 2007. A growing gap between malnutrition and mortality among children in Sub-Saharan Africa. Photocopy, Population Reference Bureau, Washington, DC.

Amacher, G. S., L. Ersado, W. F. Hyde, and D. Grebner. 2004. Disease, microdams, and natural resources in Tigray, Ethiopia: Impacts on productivity and labor supplies. *Journal of Development Studies* 40 (6): 122–45.

Amin, D. N., S. G. Kamita, G. M. Muluvi, J. Machuka, B. D. Hammock, and E. O. Osir. 2006. Glossina proteolytic lectin does not require a carbohydrate moiety for enzymatic or trypanosome-transforming activities. *Journal of Medical Entomology* 43 (2): 301–08.

Anderson, R. M., R. M. May, M. C. Boily, G. P. Garnett, and J. T. Rowley. 1991. The spread of HIV-1 in Africa: Sexual contact patterns and the predicted demographic-impact of AIDS. *Nature* 352 (6336): 581–89.

Antle, J., D. Cole, and C. Crissman. 1998. Further evidence on pesticides, productivity, and farmer health: Potato production in Ecuador. *Agricultural Economics* 18 (2): 199–207.

Apt, N. A. 2001. Rapid urbanization and living arrangements of older persons in Africa. Background paper for *United Nations Population Bulletin*, Special Issue nos. 42/43. http://www.un.org/esa/population/publications/bulletin42_43/apt.pdf.

Arndt, C., and J. D. Lewis. 2000. The macro-implications of HIV/AIDS in South Africa: A preliminary assessment. *South African Journal of Economics* 68 (5): 380–84.

Arora, S. 1999. Health and long-term economic growth: A multi-country study. Ph.D. diss., Ohio State University.

Ashworth, A. 2006. Efficacy and effectiveness of community-based treatment of severe malnutrition. *Food and Nutrition Bulletin* 27(Supplement 3): S24–48.

Ashworth, A., R. Shrimpton, and K. Jamil. 2008. Growth monitoring and promotion: Review of evidence of impact. *Maternal and Child Nutrition* 4 (S1): 86–117.

Auvert, B., A. Buvé, B. Ferry, M. Caraël, L. Morison, E. Lagarde, N. J. Robinson, M. Kahindo, J. Chege, N. Rutenberg, R. Musonda, M. Laourou, and E. Akam. 2001. Ecological and individual level analysis of risk factors for HIV infection in four urban populations in Sub-Saharan Africa with different levels of HIV infection. *AIDS* 15 (Supplement 4): 15–30.

Ayalew, G. 2006. Comparison of yield loss on cabbage from diamondback moth, *Plutella xylostella* L. (Lepidoptera: Plutellidae) using two insecticides. *Crop Protection* 25 (9): 915–19.

Ayalew, G., and C. K. P. O. Ogol. 2006. Occurrence of the diamondback moth (*Plutella xylostella* L.) and its parasitoids in Ethiopia: Influence of geographical region and agronomic traits. *Journal of Applied Entomology* 130 (6–7): 343–48.

Azariadis, C., and J. Stachurski. 2007. Poverty traps. In P. Aghion and S. Durlauf, eds. *Handbook of economic growth*, Vol. 1b. Amsterdam: Elsevier.

Azziz-Baumgartner E., K. Lindblade, K. Gieseker, H. Schurz-Rogers, S. Kieszak, H. Njapau, R. Schleicher, L. McCoy, A. Misore, K. DeCock, C. Rubin, L. Slutsker, and the Aflatoxin Investigative Group. 2005. Case-control study of an acute aflatoxicosis outbreak, Kenya, 2004. *Environmental Health Perspectives* 113 (12): 1779–83.

Bailes, E., F. Gao, F. Bibollet-Ruche, V. Courgnaud, M. Peeters, P. A. Marx, B. H. Hahn, and P. M. Sharp. 2003. Hybrid origin of SIV in chimpanzees. *Science* 300 (5626), 1713.

Bannon, I., and P. Collier. 2003. *Natural resources and violent conflict: Options and actions.* Washington, DC: World Bank.

Baoua, I. 2007. Personal communication. Institut National de Recherche Agronomique du Niger (INRAN), Niamey, Niger.

Barber, S. L. and P. J. Gertler. 2010. Empowering women: How Mexico's conditional cash transfer programme raised prenatal care quality and birth weight. *Journal of Development Effectiveness* 2(1): 51–73.

Barker, D. J. P. 1994. *Mothers, babies, and disease in later life.* London: BMJ Publishing.

Barker, D. J., and P. D. Gluckman, K. M. Godfrey, J. E. Harding, J. A. Owens, and J. S. Robinson. 1993. Fetal nutrition and cardiovascular disease in adult life. *Lancet* 341 (8850): 938–41.

Barker, D. J. P., C. Osmond, T. J. Forsén, E. Kajantie, and J. G. Eriksson. 2005. Trajectories of growth among children who later develop coronary heart disease or its risk factors. *New England Journal of Medicine* 353 (17): 1802–09.

Barnett, B. J., C. B. Barrett, and J. R. Skees. 2008. Poverty traps and index-based risk transfer products. *World Development* 36 (10): 1766–85.

Barnett, T., J. Tumushabe, G. B. Bantebya, R. Ssebuliba, J. Ngasongwa, D. Kapinga, M. Ndelike, M. Drinkwater, G. Mitti, and M. Haslwimmer. 1995. The social and economic impact of HIV/AIDS on farming systems and livelihoods in rural Africa: Some experience and lessons from Uganda, Tanzania, and Zambia. *Journal of International Development* 7 (1): 163–76.

Bärnighausen, T., V. Hosegood, I. M. Timaeus, and M. L. Newell. 2007. The socioeconomic determinants of HIV incidence: Evidence from a longitudinal, population-based study in rural South Africa. *AIDS* 21 (Supplement 7): S29–S38.

Barrett, C. B. 2008. Smallholder market participation: Concepts and evidence from Eastern and Southern Africa. *Food Policy* 33 (4): 299–317.

Barrett, C. B., and D. G. Maxwell. 2005. *Food aid after fifty years: Recasting its role.* London: Routledge.

Barrett, C. B., and B. M. Swallow. 2006. Fractal poverty traps. *World Development* 34 (1): 1–15.

Barrett, C. B., M. R. Carter, and M. Ikegami. 2007. *Poverty traps and social protection.* World Bank Social Protection Discussion Paper No. 0804. Washington, DC.

Barrett, C. B., P. P. Marenya, J. McPeak, B. Minten, F. Murithi, W. Oluoch-Kosura, F. Place, J. C. Randrianarisoa, J. Rasambainarivo, and J. Wangila. 2006. Welfare dynamics in rural Kenya and Madagascar. *Journal of Development Studies* 42 (2): 248–77.

Barro, R. 1997. *Determinants of economic growth: A cross-country empirical study.* Cambridge, MA: MIT Press.

Baruch, D. I., B. Pasloski, H. B. Singh, X. Bi, X. C. Ma, M. Feldman, T. F. Taraschi, and R. J. Howard. 1995. Cloning the *P. falciparum* gene encoding PfEMP1, malarial variant antigens and adherence receptor on the surface of parasitized human erythrocytes. *Cell* 82 (1): 77–87.

Basta, S. S., D. Soekirman, D. Karyadi, and N. S. Scrimshaw. 1979. Iron deficiency anemia and the productivity of adult males in Indonesia. *American Journal of Clinical Nutrition* 32 (4): 916–25.

Bates, I., S. McKew, and F. Sarkinfada. 2007. Anaemia: A useful indicator of neglected disease burden and control. *PLoS Medicine* 4 (8): 1285–90.

Baum, M. K., and G. Shor-Posner. 1998. Micronutrient status in relationship to mortality in HIV-1 disease. *Nutrition Reviews* 56 (1): S135–39.

BBC. 2008. Food crisis looms in East Africa. http://news.bbc.co.uk/2/hi/africa/7520286.stm (accessed July 30).

Beaton, G., and H. Ghassemi. 1982. Supplementary feeding programs for young children in developing countries. *American Journal of Clinical Nutrition* 35 (4): 864–916.

Beaton, G. H., A. Kelly, J. Kevany, R. Martorell, and J. Mason. 1990. Appropriate uses of anthropometric indices in children: A report based on an ACC/SCN workshop. ACC/SCN State-of-the-Art Series, Nutrition Policy Discussion Paper No. 7. New York: United Nations Administrative Committee on Coordination/Subcommittee on Nutrition.

Beck, A. M., and N. M. Myers. 1996. Health enhancement and companion animal ownership. *Annual Review of Public Health* 17 (1996): 247–57.

Beegle, K. 2003. *Labor effects of adult mortality in Tanzanian households.* World Bank Policy Research Working Paper 3062. Washington, DC: World Bank.

Beegle, K., and B. Ozler. 2007. *Young women, rich(er) men, and the spread of HIV.* Washington, DC: World Bank.

Beegle, K., J. De Weerdt, and S. Dercon. 2005. Orphanhood and the long-run impact on children. Photocopy, World Bank Economic Development Institute and Oxford University, Washington, DC, and Oxford, UK.

Behrman, J. R., and A. B. Deolalikar. 1988. Health and nutrition. In H. Chenery and T. N. Srinivasan, eds., *Handbook of development economics*, Vol. 1. Amsterdam: North-Holland Press.

————. 1989. Seasonal demands for nutrient intakes and health status in rural South India. In D. E. Sahn, ed., *Seasonal variability in third world agriculture: The consequences for food security.* Baltimore, MD: Johns Hopkins University Press.

Behrman, J. R., and M. R. Rosenzweig. 2004. Returns to birthweight. *Review of Economics and Statistics* 86 (2): 586–601.

Behrman, J. R., J. Hoddinott, J. A. Maluccio, E. Soler-Hampejsek, E. L. Behrman, R. Martorell, M. Ramirez-Zea, and A. D. Stein. 2007. What determines adult cognitive skills? Impacts of pre-schooling, schooling, and post-schooling experiences in Guatemala. Photocopy, International Food Policy Research Institute, Washington, DC.

Beisel, W. R. 1996. Nutrition and immune function: Overview. *Journal of Nutrition* 126 (10 Supplement): 2611S–15S.

Bell, C., S. Devarajan, and H. Gersbach 2006. The long-run economic costs of AIDS: Theory and an application to South Africa. *World Bank Economic Review* 20 (1): 55–89.

Bellamy, R., C. Ruwende, T. Corrah, K. P. W. J. McAdam, H. C. Whittle, and A. V. S. Hill. 1998. Variations in the NRAMP1 gene and susceptibility to tuberculosis in West Africans. *New England Journal of Medicine* 338 (10): 640–644.

Bender, W., and M. Smith. 1997. Population, food, and nutrition. *Population Bulletin* 51 (4): 13.

Bennett, J. W., and M. Klich. 2003. Mycotoxins. *Clinical Microbiology Reviews* 16 (3): 497–516.

Bentley, J., and G. Thiele. 1999. Bibliography of farmer knowledge and management of crop disease. *Agriculture and Human Values* 16 (1): 75–81.

Beran, D., and J. S. Yudkin. 2006. Diabetes care in sub-Saharan Africa. *Lancet* 386 (9548): 1689–95.

Berg, A. 1987. *Malnutrition: What can be done? Lessons from World Bank experience.* Baltimore, MD: Johns Hopkins University Press.

Berg, A., and R. J. Muscat. 1973. *The nutrition factor: Its role in national development.* Washington, DC: Brookings Institution.

Berkman, L., and T. Glass. 2000. Social integration, social networks, social support, and health. In L. Berkman and I. Kawachi, eds., *Social epidemiology.* New York: Oxford University Press.

Berner, D. K, J. G. Kling, and B. B. Singh. 1995. *Striga* research and control: A perspective from Africa. *Plant Disease* 79 (7): 652–60.

Betran, F. J., T. Isakeit, and G. Odvody. 2002. Aflatoxin accumulation of white and yellow maize inbreds in diallel crosses. *Crop Science* 42 (6): 1894–1901.

Bezner Kerr, R. 2008. Farming for health: Social dimensions of improving child nutrition with smallholder farmers in Malawi. Seminar given in the Field of Nutrition seminar series in the Division of Nutritional Sciences, Cornell University, March 13.

Bezner Kerr, R., S. Snapp, M. Chirwa, L. Shumba, and R. Msachi. 2007. Participatory research on legume diversification with Malawian smallholder farmers for improved human nutrition and soil fertility. *Experimental Agriculture* 43 (4): 437.

Bhargava, A. 1997. Nutritional status and the allocation of time in Rwandese households. *Journal of Econometrics* 77 (1): 277–95.

Bhargava, A., D. T. Jamison, L. J. Lau, and C. J. L. Murray. 2001. Modeling the effects of health on economic growth. *Journal of Health Economics* 20 (3): 423–40.

Bhutta, Z., T. Ahmad, R. Black, S. Cousens, K. Dewey, E. Giugliani, B. A. Haider, B. Kirkwood, S. S. Morris, H. P. S. Sachdev, and M. Shekar for the Maternal and Child Undernutrition Study Group. 2008. What works: Interventions for maternal and child undernutrition and survival. *Lancet* 371 (9610): 417–40.

Binswanger, H., S. Gillespie, and S. Kadiyala. 2006. Scaling up multi-sectoral approaches to combating HIV/AIDS: What have we learnt and what should be done? In S. Gillespie, ed., *AIDS, poverty, and hunger: Challenges and responses*. Washington DC: International Food Policy Research Institute.

Bishop-Sambrook, C. 2003. *Labor constraints and the impact of HIV/AIDS on rural livelihoods in Bondo and Busia Districts Western Kenya*. Rome: International Fund for Agricultural Development (IFAD)/Food and Agriculture Organization of the United Nations (FAO).

———. 2005. *Contribution of farm power to smallholder livelihoods in Sub-Saharan Africa*. Rome: Food and Agriculture Organization of the United Nations.

Black, R. E., L. H. Allen, Z. A. Bhutta, L. E. Caulfield, M. de Onis, M. Ezzati, C. Mathers, and J. Rivera for the Maternal and Child Undernutrition Study Group. 2008. Maternal and child undernutrition: Global and regional exposures and health consequences. *Lancet* 371 (9608): 243–60.

Bliss, C., and N. Stern. 1978a. Production, wages, nutrition: Part I: The theory. *Journal of Development Economics* 5 (4): 331–62.

———. 1978b. Production, wages, nutrition: Part II: Some observations. *Journal of Development Economics* 5 (4): 362–398.

Bloom, D., and D. Canning. 2000. The health and wealth of nations. *Science* 287 (18): 1207–09.

Bloom, D. E., and A. S. Mahal. 1997. Does the AIDS epidemic threaten economic growth? *Journal of Econometrics* 77 (1): 105–24.

Bloom, D., and J. Sachs. 1998. Geography, demography, and economic growth in Africa. *Brookings Papers on Economic Activity* 2: 207–295.

Bloom, D. E., D. Canning, and J. Sevilla. 2004. The effect of health on economic growth: A production function approach. *World Development* 32 (1): 1–13.

Blössner, M., and M. de Onis. 2005. *Malnutrition: Quantifying the impact at national and local levels*. Geneva: World Health Organization.

Boerma, J. T., S. Gregson, C. Nyamukapa, and M. Urassa. 2003. Understanding the uneven spread of HIV within Africa: Comparative study of biologic, behavioral, and contextual factors in rural populations in Tanzania and Zimbabwe. *Sexually Transmitted Diseases* 30 (10): 779–87.

Bongaarts, J. 2001. Fertility and reproductive preferences in post-transitional societies. In R. Bulatao and J. Casterline, eds., *Global fertility transition*. New York: Population Council.

Boothroyd, J. C. 1985. Antigenic variation in African trypanosomes. *Annual Review of Microbiology* 39 (1985): 475–502.

Borgemeister, C., A. Chabi-Olaye, C. Nolte, F. Schulthess, R. Ndemah, and M. Setamou. 2005. Role of habitat management technologies in the management of cereal stem and cob borers in sub-Saharan Africa. International Symposium on Biological Control of Arthropods, Davos, Switzerland, September 12–16. http://www.cabi-bioscience.ch/ISBCA-DAVOS-2005/s04/Borgemeister_Abstract_Talk.pdf.

Borst, P. 1986. Discontinuous transcription and antigenic variation in trypanosomes. *Annual Review of Biochemistry* 55 (1986): 701–32.

Bos, R. 2006. Opportunities for improving the synergies between agriculture and health. In C. Hawkes and M. T. Ruel, eds., *Understanding the links between agriculture and health*. 2020 Vision Focus 13, No. 16. Washington, DC: International Food Policy Research Institute.

Boserup, E. 1965. *The conditions of agricultural growth: The economics of agrarian change under population pressure*. Chicago: Aldine.

Bouis, H. 2002. Plant breeding: A new tool for fighting micronutrient malnutrition. *Journal of Nutrition* 132 (3): 491S–94S.

Bowen, A., H. Ma, J. Ou, W. Billhimer, T. Long, E. Mintz, R. M. Hoekstra, and S. Luby. 2007. A cluster-randomized controlled trial evaluating the effect of a handwashing-promotion program in Chinese primary schools. *American Journal of Tropical Medicine and Hygiene* 76 (6): 1166–73.

Brabin, B. J. 1991. *The risks and severity of malaria in pregnant women*. World Health Organization Applied Field Research in Malaria Reports No. 1. Geneva: WHO.

Brush, S. B., and H. R. Perales. 2007. A maize landscape: Ethnicity and agro-biodiversity in Chiapas. *Agriculture, Ecosystems and Environment* 121 (3): 211–21.

Brussaard, L., P. C. de Ruiter, and G. C. Brown. 2007. Soil biodiversity for agricultural sustainability. *Agriculture, Ecosystems and Environment* 121 (3): 233–44.

Bryce, J., D. Coitinho, I. Darnton-Hill, D. Pelletier, and P. Pinstrup-Andersen. 2008. Maternal and child undernutrition: Effective action at national level. *Lancet* 371 (9611): 510–26.

Bryceson, D., and J. Fonseca. 2006. An enduring or dying peasantry: Interactive impact of famine and HIV/AIDS in rural Malawi. In S. R. Gillespie, ed., *AIDS, poverty, and hunger: Challenges and responses*. Washington DC: International Food Policy Research Institute.

Burlingame, B. 2000. Wild nutrition. *Journal of Food Composition and Analysis* 13 (2): 99–100.

Bushamuka, V. N., S. de Pee, A. Talukder, L. Kiess, D. Panagides, A. Taher, and M. Bloem. 2005. Impact of a homestead gardening program on household food security and empowerment of women in Bangladesh. *Food and Nutrition Bulletin* 26 (1): 17–25.

Buvé, A., E. Lagarde, M. Carael, N. Rutenberg, B. Ferry, J. R. Glynn, M. Laourou, E. Akam, J. Chege, and T. Sukwat for the Study Group on Heterogeneity of HIV Epidemics in African Cities. 2001. Interpreting sexual behavior data: Validity issues in the multicentre study on factors determining the differential spread of HIV in four African cities. *AIDS* 15 (Supplement 4): S117–26.

Byron, E., S. R. Gillespie, and P. Hamazakaza. 2006. Local perceptions of risk and HIV prevention in southern Zambia. RENEWAL (Regional Network on AIDS, Livelihoods, and Food Security) Working Paper. Washington, DC: International Food Policy Research Institute. www.ifpri.org/renewal/renewalpub.asp.

Byron, E., S. Gillespie, and M. Nangami. 2008. Integrating nutrition security with treatment of people living with HIV: Lessons being learned in Kenya. *Food and Nutrition Bulletin* 29 (2): 87–97.

CABI (CAB International). 2004. *Crop protection compendium*. 2004 edition. Wallingford, UK.

Caldes, N., D. Coady, and J. Maluccio. 2006. The cost of poverty alleviation transfer programs: A comparative analysis of three programs. *World Development* 34 (5): 818–37.

Calis, J. C. J., K. S. Phiri, E. B. Faragher, B. J. Brabin, I. Bates, L. E. Cuevas, R. J. de Haan, A I. Phiri, P. Malange, M. Khoka, P. J. M. Hulshof, L. van Lieshout, M. G. H. M. Beld, Y. Y. Teo, K. A. Rockett, A. Richardson, D. P. Kwiatkowski, M. E. Molyneux, M. B. van Hensbroek. 2008. Severe anemia in Malawian children. *New England Journal of Medicine* 358 (9): 888–99.

Carter, M. R., and C. B. Barrett. 2006. The economics of poverty traps and persistent poverty: An asset-based approach. *Journal of Development Studies* 42 (2): 178–99.

Carter, M. R., P. D. Little, T. Mogues, and W. Negatu. 2007. Poverty traps and natural disasters in Ethiopia and Honduras. *World Development* 35 (5): 835–56.

Case, A., and C. Ardington. 2005. The impact of paternal death on school enrollment and achievement: Longitudinal evidence from South Africa. Paper presented at the International Union of the Scientific Study of Population Seminar on Interactions between Poverty and HIV/AIDS, Cape Town, South Africa, December.

Cassman, K. G. 1999. Ecological intensification of cereal production systems: Yield potential, soil quality, and precision agriculture. *Proceedings of the National Academy of Sciences of the United States of America* 96 (11): 5952–59.

Castleman, T., E. Seumo-Fosso, and B. Cogill. 2004. *Food and nutrition implications of antiretroviral therapy in resource limited settings.* FANTA (Food and Nutrition Technical Assistance) Technical Note No. 7. Washington, DC: Academy for Educational Development.

Caswell, J., and C. F. Bach. 2007. Food safety standards in rich and poor countries. In P. Pinstrup-Andersen and P. Sandøe, eds., *Ethics, hunger, and globalization: In search of appropriate policies.* Dordrecht, the Netherlands: Springer.

Caulfield, L. E., M. de Onis, M. Blössner, and R. E. Black. 2004. Undernutrition as an underlying cause of child deaths associated with diarrhea, pneumonia, malaria, and measles. *American Journal of Clinical Nutrition* 80 (1): 193–98.

CDC (Centers for Disease Control and Prevention). 1995. Reptile-associated salmonellosis—selected states, 1994–1995. *Morbidity and Mortality Weekly Report* 44 (17): 347–50.

———. 2004a. Diagnosis and management of foodborne illnesses: A primer for physicians and other health care professionals. *Morbidity and Mortality Weekly Report* 53 (RR04): 1–33. http://www.cdc.gov/mmwr/preview/mmwrhtml/rr5304a1.htm (accessed August 4, 2009).

———. 2004b. Outbreak of aflatoxin poisoning: Eastern and Central Provinces, Kenya, January–July, 2004. *Morbidity and Mortality Weekly Report* 53 (34): 790–93. http://www.cdc.gov/mmwr/preview/mmwrhtml/mm5334a4.htm (accessed August 4, 2009).

Ceesay, S. M., A. M. Prentice, T. J. Cole, R. Ford, E. Poskitt, L. T. Weaver, and R. G. Whitehead. 1997. Effects on birth weight and perinatal mortality of maternal dietary supplements in rural Gambia: 5 year randomised controlled trial. *British Medical Journal* 315 (7111): 786–90.

Chadwick, E. 1842. *Report on the sanitary conditions of the laboring population of Great Britain, 1842.* Edited with an introduction by M. W. Flinn. Edinburgh: Edinburgh at the University Press, 1965.

Chaisson, R. E., and N. A. Martinson. 2008. Tuberculosis in Africa: Combating an HIV-driven crisis. *New England Journal of Medicine* 358 (11): 1089–92.

Chakravarty, I. 2000. Food-based strategies to control vitamin A deficiency. *Food and Nutrition Bulletin* 21 (2): 135–43.

Chapoto, A., and T. Jayne. 2006. Socio-economic characteristics of individuals afflicted by AIDS-related prime-age mortality in Zambia. In S. R. Gillespie, ed., *AIDS, poverty, and hunger: Challenges and responses.* Washington DC: International Food Policy Research Institute.

Chapoto, A., T. S Jayne and N. Mason. 2007. Security of widows' access to land in the era of HIV/AIDS: Panel survey evidence from Zambia. Policy Synthesis No. 22. Food Security Research Project – Zambia, Ministry of Agriculture and Cooperatives, Agricultural Consultative Forum, and Michigan State University, Lusaka, Zambia. http://aec.msu.edu/fs2/zambia/ps22.pdf.

Chen, S., and M. Ravallion. 2007. *Absolute poverty measures for the developing world, 1981–2004.* Policy Research Working Paper No. 4211. Washington, DC: World Bank.

Chiappori, P. A. 1988. Rational household supply. *Econometrica* 56 (1): 63–90.

———. 1992. Collective labor supply and welfare. *Journal of Political Economy* 100 (3): 437–467.

Chinyamunyamu, B. 2007. Personal communication. National Smallholder Farmers' Association of Malawi (NASFAM), Lilongwe, Malawi.

Chivian, E., and A. Bernstein, eds. 2008. *Sustaining life: How human health depends on biodiversity.* New York: Oxford University Press.

Christiaensen, L., and H. Alderman. 2004. Child malnutrition in Ethiopia: Can maternal knowledge augment the role of income? *Economic Development and Cultural Change* 52 (2): 287–312.

Christiaensen, L., and L. Demery. 2007. *Down to earth: Agriculture and poverty reduction in Africa.* Washington, DC: World Bank.

CIMMYT (International Maize and Wheat Improvement Center). 2007. *Striga weed control with herbicide-treated maize seed.* Mexico City.

Clay, J. 2004. *World agriculture and the environment: A commodity by commodity guide to impacts and practices.* Washington, DC: Island Press.

Cliff, A., P. Haggett, and M. Smallman-Raynor. 1993. *Measles: A historical geography of a major human viral disease.* Oxford: Blackwell.

Cline, W. R. 2007. *Global warming and agriculture: Impact estimates by country.* Washington, DC: Center for Global Development and Peterson Institute for International Economics.

Clutton-Brock, J. 1981. *Domesticated animals from early times.* London: Heinemann and British Museum of Natural History.

Cockburn, A. 1977. Where did our infectious diseases come from? The evolution of infectious disease. In Ciba Foundation Symposium 49 (new series), *Health and disease in tribal societies.* New York: Elsevier/Excerpta Medica/North-Holland.

Coelli, T. J., and D. S. P. Rao. 2005. Total factor productivity growth in agriculture: A Malmquist index analysis of 93 countries, 1980–2000. *Agricultural Economics* 32 (S1): 115–34.

Cohen, M. J. 2007. *Food security: Vulnerability despite abundance.* Coping with Crisis Working Paper Series. New York: International Peace Academy.

Cohen, M. J., C. Tirado, N.-L. Aberman, and B. Thompson. 2008. Impact of climate change and bioenergy on nutrition. Washington, DC, and Rome: International Food Policy Research Institute (IFPRI) and Food and Agriculture Organization of the United Nations (FAO).

Collins, S., K. Sadler, N. Dent, T. Khara, S. Guerrero, M. Myatt, M. Saboya, and A. Walsh. 2006. Key issues in the success of community-based management of severe malnutrition. *Food and Nutrition Bulletin* 27 (Supplement 3): S49–82.

Conley, D., G. C. McCord, and J. D. Sachs. 2007. Africa's lagging demographic transition: Evidence from exogenous impacts of malaria ecology and agricultural technology. NBER Working Paper Series 12892. Cambridge, MA: National Bureau of Economic Research.

Connolly, M. 2003. *Study of practices implemented to mitigate the impact of HIV/AIDS at farm household level in six African countries.* Paper presented at the workshop "Mitigation of HIV/AIDS impacts through agricultural and rural development," Human Sciences Research Council, May 27–29, Pretoria, South Africa.

Cos, P., N. Hermans, T. De Bruyne, S. Apers, J. B. Sindambiwe, M. Witvrouw, E. De Clercq, D. Vanden Berghe, L. Pieters and A. J. Vlietinck. 2002. Antiviral activity of Rwandan medicinal plants against human immunodeficiency virus type-1 (HIV-1). *Phytomedicine* 9 (1): 62–68.

Crameri, A., J. Marfurt, K. Mugittu, et al. 2007. Rapid microarray-based method for monitoring of all currently known single-nucleotide polymorphisms associated with parasite resistance to antimalaria drugs. *Journal of Clinical Microbiology* 45 (11): 3685–91.

Crompton, D. W. T. 1999. How much human helminthiasis is there in the world? *Journal of Parasitology* 85 (3): 397–403.

———. 2000. The public health importance of hookworm disease. *Parasitology* 121 (Supplement): S39–S50.

Crush, J., B. Frayne, and M. Grant. 2006. Linking migration, HIV/AIDS, and urban food security in Southern and Eastern Africa. RENEWAL Working Paper. Washington DC: International Food Policy Research Institute. www.ifpri.org/renewal/renewal pub.asp.

Curtis, V., and S. Cairncross. 2003. Effect of washing hands with soap on diarrhoea risk in the community: A systematic review. *Lancet Infectious Disease* 3: 275–81.

Curtis, V., S. Cairncross, and R. Yonli. 2000. Domestic hygiene and diarrhoea: Pinpointing the problem. *Tropical Medicine and International Health* 5 (1): 22–32.

Dahlgren, G., and M. Whitehead. 2006. *Leveling up (Part 2): A discussion paper on European strategies for tackling social inequities in health.* Studies on Social and Economic Determinants of Population Health No. 3. Copenhagen: WHO Regional Office for Europe.

Dao, M. Q. 2004. Rural poverty in developing countries: An empirical analysis. *Journal of Economic Studies* 31 (6): 500–08.

Das, J., Q.-T. Do, and B. Ozler. 2005. Reassessing conditional cash transfer programs. *World Bank Research Observer* 20 (1): 57–80.

Dasgupta, P. 1997. Nutritional status, the capacity for work, and poverty traps. *Journal of Econometrics* 77 (1): 5–37.

Deaton, A. 2006. Global patterns of income and health: Facts, interpretations, and policies. United Nations University World Institute for Development Economics Research (UNU-WIDER), Helsinki, Finland. http://www.wider.unu.edu/publications/annual-lectures/en_GB/AL10/.

De Groote, H., C. Bett, J. O. Okuro, M. Odendo, L. Mose, and E. Wekesa. 2001. Direct estimation of maize crop losses due to stemborers in Kenya: Preliminary results from 2000 and 2001. Paper presented at Seventh Eastern and Southern Africa Regional Maize Conference, February 11–15.

Delgado, C. L., C. A. Narrod, and M. M. Tiongco. 2003. *Project on livestock industrialization: Trade and social-health-environment impacts in developing countries.* Rome: Food and Agriculture Organization of the United Nations. http://www.fao.org/WAIR DOCS/LEAD/X6170E/X6170E00.HTM.

de Menezes Toledo Florêncio, T. M., H. da Silva Ferreira, A. P. Tojal de França, J. C. Cavalcante, and A. L. Sawaya. 2001. Obesity and undernutrition in a very-low-income population in the city of Maceió, northeastern Brazil. *British Journal of Nutrition* 86 (2): 277–83.

Deolalikar, A. B. 1988. Nutrition and labour productivity in agriculture: Estimates for rural South India. *Review of Economics and Statistics* 70 (3): 406–13.

Dercon, S. 1998. Wealth, risk, and activity choice: Cattle in western Tanzania. *Journal of Development Economics* 55 (1): 1–42.

———, ed. 2005. *Insurance against poverty.* Oxford: Oxford University Press.

Devarajan, S., M. J. Miller, and E. V. Swanson. 2002. *Goals for development: History, prospects, and costs.* Policy Research Working Paper. Washington, DC: World Bank.

Devine, G. J., and M. J. Furlong. 2007. Insecticide use: Contexts and ecological consequences. *Agriculture and Human Values* 24 (3): 281–306.

DeVries, H. R., S. M. Maxwell, and R. G. Hendrickse. 1990. Aflatoxin excretion in children with kwashiorkor or marasmic kwashiorkor: A clinical investigation. *Mycopathologia* 110 (1): 1–9.

De Waal, A. 2006. *AIDS and power.* London: Zed Books.

De Walque, D., J. S. Nakiyingi-Miiro, J. Busingye, and J. A. Whitworth. 2005. Changing association between schooling levels and HIV-1 infection over 11 years in a rural population cohort in south-west Uganda. *Tropical Medicine and International Health* 10 (10): 993–1001.

Dewey, K., and S. Adu-Afarwuah. 2008. Systematic review of the efficacy and effectiveness of complementary feeding interventions in developing countries. *Maternal and Child Nutrition* 4 (S1): 24–85.

de Wit, M., and J. Stankiewicz. 2006. Changes in surface water supply across Africa with predicted climate change. *Science* 311 (5769): 1917–21.

Diamond, J. 1997. *Guns, germs, and steel: The fates of human societies.* New York: W.W. Norton.

Diao, X., P. Hazell, D. Resnick, and J. Thurlow. 2007. *The role of agriculture in development: Implications for Sub-Saharan Africa.* Washington, DC: International Food Policy Research Institute.

Dixon, J., A. Gulliver, and D. Gibbon. 2001. *Farming systems and poverty.* Rome and Washington, DC: Food and Agriculture Organization of the United Nations (FAO) and World Bank.

Doblhammer, G., and J. W. Vaupel. 2001. Lifespan depends on month of birth. *Proceedings of the National Academy of Sciences* 98 (5): 2934–39.

Dogheim, S. M., E. M. M. Ashraf, S. A. G. Alla, M. A. Khorshid, and S. M. Fahmy. 2004. Pesticides and heavy metals levels in Egyptian leafy vegetables and some aromatic medicinal plants. *Food Additives and Contaminants* 21 (4): 323–30.

Donovan, C., and L. Bailey. 2005. Understanding Rwandan agricultural households' strategies to deal with prime age illness and death: A propensity score matching approach. In S. R. Gillespie, ed., *AIDS, poverty, and hunger: Challenges and responses.* Washington, DC: International Food Policy Research Institute.

Dore, M. P., M. Bilotta, D. Vaira, A. Manca, G. Massarelli, G. Leandro, A. Atzei, G. Pisanu, D. Y. Graham, and G. Realdi. 1999. High prevalence of *Helicobacter pylori* infection in shepherds. *Digestive Diseases and Sciences* 44 (6): 1161–64.

Dorward, A., and I. Mwale. 2006. Labour market and wage impacts of HIV/AIDS in rural Malawi. In S. R. Gillespie, ed., *AIDS, poverty, and hunger: Challenges and responses.* Washington DC: International Food Policy Research Institute.

Doss, C. 1999. *Twenty-five years of research on women farmers in Africa: Implications for agricultural research institutions, with an annotated bibliography.* CIMMYT Economics Program Paper No. 99-02. Mexico City: International Wheat and Maize Improvement Center (CIMMYT).

———. 2001. Designing agricultural technology for African women farmers: Lessons from 25 years of experience. *World Development* 29 (12): 2075–92.

Doss, C. R., J. G. McPeak, and C. B. Barrett. 2008. Interpersonal, intertemporal, and spatial variation in risk perceptions: Evidence from East Africa. *World Development* 36 (8): 1453–68.

Dow, W., P. Gertler, R.-F. Schoeni, J. Strauss, and D. Thomas. 1997. Health care prices, health, and labor outcomes: Experimental evidence. Labor and Population Working Paper Series 97-01. Santa Monica, CA: Rand.

Drechsel, P., D. Kunze; and F. Penning de Vries. 2001. Soil nutrient depletion and population growth in Sub-Saharan Africa: A Malthusian nexus? *Population and Environment* 22 (4): 411–23.

Drewnowski, A., and N. Darmon. 2005. The economics of obesity: Dietary energy density and energy cost. *American Journal of Clinical Nutrition* 82 (1 Supplement): 265S–73S.

Drewnowski, A., and B. M. Popkin. 1997. The nutrition transition: New trends in the global diet. *Nutrition Review* 55 (2): 31–43.

Dreyfuss, M. L., R. Stolzfus, J. S. Shrestha, E. K. Pradhan, S. C. LeClerq, S. K. Khatry, S. R. Shrestha, J. Katz, M. Albonico, and K. P. West, Jr. 2000. Hookworms, malaria, and vitamin A deficiency contribute to anemia and iron deficiency among pregnant women in the plains of Nepal. *Journal of Nutrition* 130 (10): 2527–36.

Drèze, J., and A. Sen. 1989. *Hunger and public action.* Oxford: Clarendon Press.

Drimie, S., and D. Mullins. 2006. Mainstreaming HIV and AIDS into livelihoods and food security programmes: The experience of CARE Malawi. In S. R. Gillespie, ed., *AIDS, poverty, and hunger: Challenges and responses.* Washington DC: International Food Policy Research Institute.

Drinkwater, M., M. McEwan, and F. Samuels. 2006. *The effects of HIV/AIDS on agricultural production systems in Zambia: A restudy 1993–2005.* Analytical report, CARE-RENEWAL study. http://www.ifpri.org/renewal/pdf/Zambia_AR.pdf.

Dubos, R., and J. Dubos. 1952. *The white plague: Tuberculosis, man, and society.* New Brunswick, NJ: Rutgers University Press (reprinted in 1996).

Du Guerny, J. 2004. *Meeting the HIV/AIDS challenge to food security: The role of labor-saving technologies in farm-households.* New York: United Nations Development Programme.

Edgerton, V. R., G. W. Gardner, Y. Ohira, K. A. Gunawardena, and B. Senewiratne. 1979. Iron-deficiency anemia and its effect on worker productivity and activity patterns. *British Medical Journal* 2 (6204): 1546–49.

Egal, S., A. Hounsa, Y. Y. Gong, P. C. Turner, C. P. Wild, A. J. Hall, K. Hell, and K. F. Cardwell. 2005. Dietary exposure to aflatoxin from maize and groundnut in young children from Benin and Togo, West Africa. *International Journal of Food Microbiology* 104 (2): 215–24.

Egge, K., and S. Strasser. 2006. Measuring the effect of targeted food assistance on beneficiaries with chronic illness: Lessons learned from the literature and the field. In S. R. Gillespie, ed., *AIDS, poverty, and hunger: Challenges and responses.* Washington DC: International Food Policy Research Institute.

Ellis, A., J. Cutura, N. Dione, I Gillson, C. Manuel, and J. Thongori. 2007. *Gender and economic growth in Kenya: Unleashing the power of women.* Washington, DC: World Bank.

El-Sayed, A. M. A., A. A. Neamat-Allah, and E. S. Soher. 2000. Situation of mycotoxins in milk, dairy products, and human milk in Egypt. *Mycotoxin Research* 16 (2): 91–100.

El-Sayed, A. M. A., E. A. Soher, and A. A. Neamat-Allah. 2002. Human exposure to mycotoxins in Egypt. *Mycotoxin Research* 18 (1): 23–30.

El-Sayed, N. M., P. J. Myler, G. Blandin, et al. 2005. Comparative genomics of trypanosomatid parasitic protozoa. *Science* 309 (5733): 404–09.

Elufioye, T. O., and J. M. Agbedahunsi. 2004. Antimalarial activities of *Tithonia diversifolia* (Asteraceae) and *Crossopteryx febrifuga* (Rubiaceae) on mice in vivo. *Journal of Ethnopharmacology* 93 (2–3): 167–712004.

Englberger, L., W. Aalbersberg, P. Ravi, E. Bonnin, G. C. Marks, M. H. Fitzgerald, and J. Elymore. 2003. Further analyses on Micronesian banana, taro, breadfruit and other foods for provitamin A carotenoids and minerals. *Journal of Food Composition and Analysis* 16 (2): 219–36.

Englebert, P., and J. Ron. 2004. Primary commodities and war: Congo-Brazzaville's ambivalent resource curse. *Comparative Politics* 37 (1): 61–81.

Enserink, M. 2008. The peanut butter debate. *Science* 322 (5898): 36–38.

Eriksson, T., B. Bratsberg, and O. Raaum. 2005. Earnings persistence across generations: Transmission through health? Department of Economics, Oslo University. Memorandum.

Espinosa de los Monteros, L. E., J. C. Galán, M. Gutiérrez, S. Samper, J. F. García Marín, C. Martín, L. Domínguez, L. de Rafael, F. Baquero, E. Gómez-Mampaso, and J. Blázquez. 1998. Allele-specific PCR method based on *pncA* and *oxyR* sequences for distinguishing *Mycobacterium bovis* from *Mycobacterium tuberculosis*: Intraspecific *M. bovis pncA* sequence polymorphism. *Journal of Clinical Microbiology* 36 (1): 239–42.

Esquinas-Alcazar, J. T. 1993. Plant genetic resources. In M. D. Hayward, N. O. Bosemark, and I. Romagosa, eds., *Plant breeding: Principles and prospects.* Cambridge, MA: Chapman and Hall.

Evans, D., and E. Miguel. 2004. Orphans and schooling in Africa: A longitudinal analysis. Photocopy, Harvard University and University of California, Berkeley.

Faber, M., C. M. Smuts, and A. J. S. Benade. 1999. Dietary intake of primary school children in relation to food production in a rural area in KwaZulu-Natal, South Africa. *International Journal of Food Sciences and Nutrition* 50 (1): 57–64.

Faber, M., S. Venter, M. A. Phungula, and A. J. Benade. 2001. An integrated primary health-care and provitamin A household food production program: Impact on food-consumption patterns. *Food and Nutrition Bulletin* 22 (4): 370–75.

Fabiani, M., S. Accorsi, M. Lukwiya, T. Rosolen, E. O. Ayella, P. A. Onek, and S. Declich. 2001. Trend in HIV-1 prevalence in an antenatal clinic in North Uganda and adjusted rates for the general female population. *AIDS* 15 (1): 97–103.

Fafchamps, M., and C. Moser. 2003. Crime, isolation, and law enforcement. *Journal of African Economies* 12 (4): 625–71.

FAO (Food and Agriculture Organization of the United Nations). N.d. *Gender and food security: Education, extension, and communication.* http://www.fao.org/gender/en/educ-e.htm

———. 1994. *What has AIDS to do with agriculture?* Rome.

———. 1996a. *Report of the World Food Summit, Rome, 13–17 November 1996.* WFS 96/REP, Part One. Rome. http://www.fao.org/docrep/003/w3548e/w3548e00.htm (accessed August 4, 2009).

———. 1996b. *Rome Declaration on World Food Security and World Food Summit Plan of Action.* Rome.

———. 1999. FAO warns of the dangerous legacy of obsolete pesticides. Press release, May 24. http://www.fao.org/waicent/ois/press_ne/presseng/1999/pren9931.htm.

———. 2000. *The state of food insecurity in the world 2000.* Rome.

———. 2003a. *FAO methodology for the measurement of food deprivation.* Rome: FAO Statistics Division.

———. 2003b. *Progress report on implementation of the plan of action for the pan-African tsetse and trypanosomiasis eradication campaign.* Conference, November 29–December 10, Rome. http://www.fao.org/DOCREP/MEETING/007/J0088e.HTM.

———. 2004. *Human energy requirements: Report of a Joint FAO/WHO/UNU expert consultation.* FAO Food and Nutrition Technical Report Series 1. Rome. http://www.fao.org/docrep/007/y5686e/y5686e00.HTM.

————. 2005. FAOSTAT–Agriculture. http://faostat.fao.org/faostat/collections?subset=agriculture.

————. 2006a. More fruits and vegetables. FAO Spotlight. http://www.fao.org/ag/magazine/0606sp2.htm (accessed August 4, 2009).

————. 2006b. *State of food and agriculture: Food aid for food security?* Rome.

————. 2006c. *State of food insecurity in the world, 2006.* Rome.

————. 2006d. *World's agriculture towards 2030/2050.* Interim report. Rome.

————. 2007a. *Assessment of the world food security situation.* CFS: 2007/2. Rome.

————. 2007b. *Guidelines for measuring household and individual dietary diversity.* Rome: FAO with support from the EC/FAO Food Security Information for Action Programme and the Food and Nutrition Technical Assistance (FANTA) Project. http://www.foodsec.org/tools_nut.htm.

————. 2007c. Monitoring progress since the World Food Summit. http://www.fao.org/monitoringprogress/index_en.html (accessed October).

————. 2008a. The number of hungry people rises to 963 million. Press release, December 9. http://www.fao.org/news/story/en/item/8836/.

————. 2008b. *The state of food insecurity in the world 2008.* Rome.

————. 2009a. FAOSTAT. http://faostat.fao.org (accessed September 27).

————. 2009b. *The state of food insecurity in the world 2009.* Rome.

————. 2009c. *World food situation.* http://www.fao.org/worldfoodsituation/ (accessed June 14).

FAO/WHO (Food and Agriculture Organization of the United Nations/World Health Organization). 2002. *Assuring food safety and quality: Guidelines for strengthening national food control systems.* http://www.who.int/foodsafety/publications/capacity/en/Englsih_Guidelines_Food_control.pdf (accessed August 4, 2009).

————. 2003. *Diet, nutrition, and the prevention of chronic diseases.* WHO Technical Report Series 916. http://www.fao.org/DOCREP/005/AC911E/AC911E00.HTM (accessed August 4, 2009).

————. 2004a. Developing and maintaining food safety control systems for Africa: Current status and prospects for change. Conference Room Document 32. Prepared by WHO Regional Office for Africa for Second FAO/WHO Global Forum of Food Safety Regulators, Bangkok, Thailand, October 12–14. http://www.fao.org/docrep/meeting/008/ae144e/ae144e00.htm (accessed August 4, 2009).

————. 2004b. *FAO/WHO guidance to governments on application of HACCP in small and/or less developed businesses.* FAO Food and Nutrition Paper 86. ftp://ftp.fao.org/docrep/fao/009/a0799e/a0799e00.pdf (accessed August 4, 2009).

————. 2005a. FAO/WHO Regional Conference on Food Safety for Africa. Final report. Harare, Zimbabwe, October 3–6. ftp://ftp.fao.org/docrep/fao/meeting/010/a0215e/a0215e00.pdf (accessed August 4, 2009).

————. 2005b. Improving street food vending in South Africa: Achievements and lessons learned. Conference Room Document 14. Prepared by the International Union of Microbiological Societies, International Committee on Food Microbiology and Hygiene (IUMS–ICFMH), and South Africa for the FAO/WHO Regional Conference on Food Safety in Africa, Harare, Zimbabwe, October 3–6. ftp://ftp.fao.org/docrep/fao/meeting/009/af077e.pdf (accessed August 4, 2009).

————. 2006. *Food safety risk analysis: A guide for national food control authorities.* FAO Food and Nutrition Paper 87. ftp://ftp.fao.org/docrep/fao/009/a0822e/a0822e00.pdf (accessed August 4, 2009).

————. 2008. *Microbiological hazards in fresh fruits and vegetables.* Microbiological Risk Assessment Series. http://www.who.int/foodsafety/publications/micro/MRA_Fruit Veges.pdf (accessed August 4, 2009).

Fawzi, W. 2003. Micronutrients and human immunodeficiency virus type 1 disease progression among adults and children. *Clinical Infectious Diseases* 37 (Supplement 2): S112–16.

FDA (U.S. Food and Drug Administration). 1998. *Guidance for industry: Guide to minimize microbial food safety hazards for fresh fruits and vegetables.* http://www.fda.gov/Food/GuidanceComplianceRegulatoryInformation/GuidanceDocuments/ProduceandPlanProducts/ucm064574.htm (accessed August 4, 2009).

Fernald, L., P. Gertler, and L. Neufeld. 2008. Role of cash in conditional cash transfer programs for child health, growth, and development: An analysis of Mexico's Oportunidades. *Lancet* 371 (9615): 828–37.

Fiedler, J. L., and T. Chuko. 2008. The cost of Child Health Days: A case study of Ethiopia's Enhanced Outreach Strategy (EOS). *Health Policy and Planning* 23 (4): 222–33.

Fiedler, J., D. Dado, H. Maglalang, N. Juban, M. Capistrano, and M. Magpantay. 2000. Cost analysis as a vitamin A program design and evaluation tool: A case study of the Philippines. *Social Science and Medicine* 51 (2): 223–42.

Field, E., O. Robles, and M. Torero. 2009. Iodine deficiency and schooling attainment in Tanzania. *American Economic Journal: Applied Economics* 1(4): 140–169.

Filteau, S. M., and A. M. Tomkins. 1994. Micronutrients and tropical infections. *Transactions of the Royal Society of Tropical Medicine and Hygiene* 88 (1): 1–3.

Finckh, M. R. 2008. Integration of breeding and technology into diversification strategies for disease control in modern agriculture. *European Journal of Plant Pathology* 121 (3): 399–409.

Finckh, M. R., E. S. Gacek, H. Goyeau, C. Lannou, U. Merz, C. C. Mundt, L. Munk, J. Nadziak, A. C. Newton, C. de Vallavielle-Pope, and M. S. Wolfe. 2000. Cereal variety and species mixtures in practice, with emphasis on disease resistance. *Agronomie* 20 (7): 813–37.

Fischer, G., M. Shah, F. N. Tubiello, and H. van Velhuizen. 2005. Socio-economic and climate change impacts on agriculture: An integrated assessment, 1990–2080. *Philosophical Transactions of the Royal Society Biological Sciences* 360 (1463): 2067–83.

Fleck, A. 1989. Clinical and nutritional aspects of change in acute phase proteins during inflammation. *Proceedings of the Nutrition Society* 48 (3): 347–54.

Fogel, R. W. 1991. *New sources and new techniques for the study of secular trends in nutritional status, health, mortality, and the process of aging.* Working Paper Series on Historical Factors and Long Run Growth No. 26. Cambridge, MA: National Bureau of Economic Research.

———. 1994. Economic growth, population theory, and physiology: The bearing of the long-term processes on making of economic policy. *American Economic Review* 84 (3): 369–95.

———. 2000. *The fourth great awakening and the future of egalitarianism.* Chicago: University of Chicago Press.

———. 2004. *The escape from hunger and premature death, 1700-2100: Europe, America, and the Third World.* New York: Cambridge University Press.

Fondong, V. N., J. M. Thresh, and S. Zok. 2002. Spatial and temporal spread of cassava mosaic virus disease in cassava grown alone and when intercropped with maize and/or cowpea. *Journal of Phytopathology* 150 (7): 365–74.

Fox, M. P., S. Rosen, W. B. MacLeod, M. Wasunna, M. Bii, G. Foglia, and J. L. Simon. 2004. The impact of HIV/AIDS on labour productivity in Kenya. *Tropical Medicine and International Health* 9 (3): 318–24.

Fresno, M., M. Kopf, and L. Rivas. 1997. Cytokines and infectious diseases. *Immunology Today* 18 (2): 56–58.

Frieden, T. R., T. R. Sterling, S. S. Munsiff, C. J. Watt, and C. Dye. 2003. Tuberculosis. *Lancet* 362 (9387): 887–99.

Friis, H., S. Gillespie, and S. Filteau. 2008. Nutrition and HIV. In K. Heggenhougen and S. Quah, eds., *International encyclopedia of public health.* Vol. 4. San Diego: Academic Press.

Frisch, R. E. 2002. *Female fertility and the body fat connection.* Chicago: University of Chicago Press.

Frison, E. A., I. F. Smith, T. Johns, J. Cherfas, and P. B. Eyzaguirre. 2006. Agricultural biodiversity, nutrition, and health: Making a difference to hunger and nutrition in the developing world. *Food and Nutrition Bulletin* 27 (2): 167–79.

Gacheru, E., and M. R. Rao. 2001. Managing *Striga* infestation on maize using organic and inorganic nutrient sources in western Kenya. *International Journal of Pest Management* 47 (3): 233–39.

Gaiha, R., and G. Thapa. 2006. Natural disasters, vulnerability, and mortalities: A cross-country analysis. Working paper. International Fund for Agricultural Development, Rome.

Galasso, E., and N. Umapathy. 2007. Improving nutritional status through behavioral change: Lessons from Madagascar. Photocopy, World Bank, Washington, DC.

Gallup, J. L., J. D. Sachs, and A. D. Mellinger. 1999. Geography and economic development. *International Regional Science Review* 22 (2): 179–232.

Galvano, F., A. Pietri, T. Bertuzzi, L. Gagliardi, S. Ciotti, S. Luisi, M. Bognanno, L. La Fauci, A. M. Lacopino, F. Nigro, G. Li Volti, L. Vanella, G. Giammanco, G. L. Tina., and D. Gazzolo. 2008. Maternal dietary habits and mycotoxin occurrence in human mature milk. *Molecular Nutrition and Food Research* 52 (4): 496–501.

Galvin, S. R., and M. S. Cohen. 2004. The role of sexually transmitted diseases in HIV transmission. *Nature Reviews Microbiology* 2 (1): 33–42.

Garcia, M., and P. Pinstrup-Andersen. 1987. *The pilot food price subsidy scheme in the Philippines: Its impact on income, food consumption, and nutritional status.* Research Report 61. Washington, DC: International Food Policy Research Institute.

Gardner, M. J., et al. 2002. Genome sequence of the human malaria parasite *Plasmodium falciparum. Nature* 419 (6906): 498–511.

Garenne, M. M. 2008. *Fertility changes in Sub-Saharan Africa.* DHS Comparative Reports No. 18. Calverton, MD: Macro International.

Gari, J. A., and M. Villarreal. 2002. *Agricultural sector responses to HIV/AIDS: Agrobiodiversity and indigenous knowledge.* Rome: Food and Agriculture Organization of the United Nations.

Garner, P., and B. Brabin. 1994. A review of randomized controlled trials of routine antimalarial drug prophylaxis during pregnancy in endemic malarious areas. *Bulletin of the World Health Organization* 72 (1): 89–99.

Gavian, S., D. Galaty, and G. Kombe. 2006. Multisectoral HIV/AIDS approaches in Africa: How are they evolving? In S. Gillespie, ed., *AIDS, poverty, and hunger: Challenges and responses.* Washington, DC: International Food Policy Research Institute.

Geertz, C. 1966. *Agricultural involution: The process of ecological change in Indonesia.* Berkeley: University of California Press.

Gertler, P., and J. Gruber. 2002. Insuring consumption against illness. *American Economic Review* 92 (1): 51–70.

Gethi, J. 2009. Personal communication. Kenyan Agricultural Research Institute.

Gethi, J. G., and M. E. Smith. 2004. Genetic responses of single crosses of maize to *Striga hermonthica* (Del.) Benth and *Striga asiatica* (L.) Kuntze. *Crop Science* 44 (6): 2068–77.

Gibbons, A. 2007. Food for thought: Did the first cooked meals help fuel the dramatic evolutionary expansion of the human brain? *Science* 316 (5831): 1558–60.

———. 2008. Tuberculosis jumped from humans to cows, not vice versa [electronic version]. *Science* 320 (5876): 608.

Gifford-Gonzalez, D. 2000. Animal disease challenges to the emergence of pastoralism in Sub-Saharan Africa. *African Archaeological Review* 17 (3): 95–139.

Gikonyo, N. K., A. Hassanali, P. G. N. Njagi, and R. K. Saini. 2003. Responses of *Glossina morsitans morsitans* to blends of electroantennographically active compounds in the odours of its preferred (buffalo and ox) and un-preferred (waterbuck) hosts in a two-choice wind tunnel. *Journal of Chemical Ecology* 29 (10): 2331–45.

Gillespie, S. R. 1989. Potential impact of AIDS on farming systems: A case study from Rwanda. *Land Use Policy* 6 (4): 301–12.

———, ed. 2006. *AIDS, poverty, and hunger: Challenges and responses.* Washington DC: International Food Policy Research Institute.

———. 2008. Food prices and the AIDS response: How are they linked and what can be done? RENEWAL (Regional Network on AIDS, Livelihoods, and Food Security) Brief 1. Washington, DC: International Food Policy Research Institute. http://www .ifpri.org/renewal/renewalpub.asp.

Gillespie, S., and L. Haddad. 2003. The relationship between nutrition and the Millennium Development Goals: A strategic review of the scope for DfID's influencing role. International Food Policy Research Institute, Washington, DC.

Gillespie, S. R., and S. Kadiyala. 2005a. *HIV/AIDS and food and nutrition security: From evidence to action.* Food Policy Review 7. Washington, DC: International Food Policy Research Institute.

———. 2005b. HIV/AIDS and food and nutrition security: Interactions and response. *American Journal of Agricultural Economics* 87 (5): 1282–88.

Gillespie, S. R., S. Kadiyala, and R. Greener. 2007. Is poverty or wealth driving HIV transmission? *AIDS* 21 (7 Supplement): S5–S16.

Girardin, O., D. Dao, B. G. Koudou, C. Essé, G. Cissé, T. Yao, E. K. N'Goran, A. B. Tschannen, G. Bordmann, B. Lehmann, C. Nsabimana, J. Keiser, G. F. Killen, B. H. Singer, M. Tanner, and J. Utzinger. 2004. Opportunities and limiting factors of intensive vegetable farming in malaria endemic Côte d'Ivoire. *Acta Tropica* 89 (2): 109–23.

Githeko, A. K., J. M. Ayisi, P. Odada, F. K. Atieli, B. A. Ndenga, J. I. Githure, and G. Yan. 2006. Topography and malaria transmission heterogeneity in western Kenya highlands: Prospects for focal vector control. *Malaria Journal* 5:107.

Gladwin, C. H., J. S. Peterson, D. Phiri, and R. Uttaro. 2002. Agroforestry adoption decisions, structural adjustment and gender in Africa. In C. B. Barrett, F. Place, and A. A. Aboud, eds., *Natural resource management in African agriculture: Understanding and improving current practices.* New York: CABI.

Glass, R. 2006. New hope for defeating rotavirus. *Scientific American* 294 (4): 46–55.

Glewwe, P., and H. G. Jacoby. 1995. An economic analysis of delayed primary school enrollment in a low-income country: The role of early childhood nutrition. *Review of Economics and Statistics* 77 (1): 156–69.

Glewwe, P., H. Jacoby, and E. King. 2001. Early childhood nutrition and academic achievement: A longitudinal analysis. *Journal of Public Economics* 81 (3): 345–68.

Glick, P. 2007. Reproductive health and behavior, HIV/AIDS, and poverty in Africa. Cornell Food and Nutrition Policy Program Working Paper No. 219. Ithaca, NY: Cornell University. http://www.cfnpp.cornell.edu/images/wp219.pdf.

Glick, P., and D. E. Sahn. 1997. Gender and education impacts on employment and earnings in West Africa: Evidence from Guinea. *Economic Development and Cultural Change* 45 (4): 793–823.

Global Coalition of Women and AIDS. 2007. *Economic security for women fights AIDS.* Issue No. 3. Geneva. http://womenandaids.org.

Global Fund (Global Fund to Fight AIDS, Tuberculosis, and Malaria). 2005. *HIV/AIDS, tuberculosis, amd malaria: The status and impact of the three diseases.* Geneva.

Godfrey, K. M., and D. J. P. Barker. 2000. Fetal nutrition and adult disease. *American Journal of Clinical Nutrition* 71 (5): 1344S–52S.

Gollin, D., S. Parente, and R. Rogerson. 2002. The role of agriculture in development. *American Economic Review* 92 (2):160–64.

———. 2007. The food problem and the evolution of international income levels. *Journal of Monetary Economics* 54 (4): 1230–55.

Gomes, J., O. L. Lloyd, and D. M. Revitt. 1999. The influence of personal protection, environmental hygiene, and exposure to pesticides on the health of immigrant farm workers in a desert country. *International Archives of Occupational and Environmental Health* 72 (1): 40–45.

Gong, Y. Y., K. Cardwell, A. Hounsa, S. Egal, P. C. Turner, A. J. Hall, and C. P. Wild. 2002. Dietary aflatoxin exposure and impaired growth in young children from Benin and Togo: A cross sectional study. *British Medical Journal* 325 (7354): 20–21.

Gong, Y. Y., S. Egal, A. Hounsa, P. C. Turner, A. J. Hall, K. F. Cardwell, and C. P. Wild. 2003. Determinants of aflatoxin exposure in young children from Benin and Togo, West Africa: The critical role of weaning. *International Journal of Epidemiology* 32 (4): 556–62.

Gourama, H., and L. B. Bullerman. 1995. *Aspergillus flavus* and *Aspergillus parasiticus*: Aflatoxigenic fungi of concern in foods and feed: A review. *Journal of Food Protection* 58 (12): 1395–1404.

Government of Rwanda, Ministry of Agriculture and Animal Resources. 2008. *Agriculture sector overview.* http://www.minagri.gov.rw/ (accessed July 30).

Graham, R. D., R. M. Welch, D. A. Saunders, I. Ortiz-Monasterio, H. E. Bouis, M. Bonierbale, S. de Han, G. Burgos, G. Thiele, R. Liria, C. A. Meisner, S. E. Beebe, M. J. Potts, M. Kadian, P. R. Hobbs, R. K. Gupta, and S. Twomlow. 2007. Nutritious subsistence food systems. *Advances in Agronomy* 92: 1–74.

Grantham-McGregor, S. M., S. Chang, and S. P. Walker. 1998. Evaluation of school feeding programs: Some Jamaican examples. *American Journal of Clinical Nutrition* 67 (4): 785S–89S.

Grantham-McGregor, S., L. Fernald, and K. Sethuraman. 1999a. Effects of health and nutrition on cognitive and behavioural development in children in the first three years of life. Part 1: Low birthweight, breastfeeding, and protein-energy malnutrition. *Food and Nutrition Bulletin* 20 (1): 53–75.

———. 1999b. Effects of health and nutrition on cognitive and behavioural development in children in the first three years of life. Part 2: Infections and micronutrient deficiencies: Iodine, iron, and zinc. *Food and Nutrition Bulletin* 20 (1): 76–99.

Grantham-McGregor, S., Y. B. Cheung, S. Cueto, P. Glewwe, L. Richter, and B. Strupp. 2007. Developmental potential in the first 5 years for children in developing countries. *Lancet* 369 (9555): 60–70.

Gregson, S., G. P. Garnett, C. A. Nyamukapa, T. B. Hallett, J. J. Lewis, P. R. Mason, S. K. Chandiwana, and R. M. Anderson. 2006. HIV decline associated with behaviour change in eastern Zimbabwe. *Science* 311(5761): 664–66.

Gressel, J., A. Hanafi, G. Head, W. Marasas, A. B. Obilana, J. Ochanda, T. Souissi, and G. Tzotzos. 2004. Major heretofore intractable biotic constraints to African food security that may be amenable to novel biotechnological solutions. *Crop Protection* 23 (8): 661–89.

Grimble, R. F. 1994. Malnutrition and the immune response. *Transactions of the Royal Society of Tropical Medicine and Hygiene* 88 (6): 615–19.

Grisley, W. 1997. Crop-pest yield loss: A diagnostic study in the Kenya highlands. *International Journal of Pest Management* 43 (2): 137–42.

Grivetti, L. E., and B. M. Ogle. 2000. Value of traditional foods in meeting macro- and micronutrient needs: The wild plant connection. *Nutrition Research Reviews* 13 (1): 31–46.

Grossman, M. 1972. On the concept of health capital and the demand for health. *Journal of Political Economy* 80 (2): 223–55.

Gruhn, P., F. Goletti, and M. Yudelman. 2000. *Integrated nutrient management, soil fertility, and sustainable agriculture: Current issues and future challenges.* 2020 Vision Discussion Paper 32. Washington, DC: International Food Policy Research Institute (IFPRI).

Gundry, S., J. Wright, and R. Conroy. 2004. A systematic review of the health outcomes related to household water quality in developing countries. *Journal of Water and Health* 2 (1): 1–13.

Haas, J. D., and T. Brownlie IV. 2001. Iron deficiency and reduced work capacity: A critical review of the research to determine a causal relationship. *Journal of Nutrition* 131 (Supplement): 676S–90S.

Haas, J., E. J. Martinez, S. Murdoch, E. Conlisk, J. A. Rivera, and R. Martorell. 1995. Nutritional supplementation during the preschool pears and physical work capacity in adolescent and young adult Guatemalans. *Journal of Nutrition* 125 (4 Supplement): 1078S–89S.

Haddad, L., and H. Bouis. 1991. The impact of nutritional status on agricultural productivity: Wage evidence from the Philippines. *Oxford Bulletin of Economics and Statistics* 53 (1): 45–68.

Haddad, L., H. Alderman, S. Appleton, L. Song, and Y. Yohannes. 2003. Reducing child malnutrition: How far does income growth take us? *World Bank Economic Review* 17 (1): 107–31.

Hales, C. N., and D. J. Barker. 1992. Type 2 (non-insulin-dependent) diabetes mellitus: The thrifty phenotype hypothesis. *Diabetologia* 35 (7): 595–601.

Hall, A., G. Hewitt, V. Tuffrey, and N. de Silva. 2008. A review and meta-analysis of the impact of intestinal worms on child growth and nutrition. *Maternal and Child Nutrition* 4 (Supplement 1): 118–236.

Hallman, K. 2004. *Socioeconomic disadvantage and unsafe sexual behaviors among young women and men in South Africa.* Policy Research Division Working Paper No. 190. New York: Population Council.

Hanotte, O., D. G. Bradley, J. W. Ochieng, Y. Verjee, E. W. Hill, and J. E. Rege. 2002. African pastoralism: Genetic imprints of origins and migrations. *Science* 296 (5566): 336–39.

Hare, R. 1967. The antiquity of diseases caused by bacteria and viruses: A review of the problem from a bacteriologist's point of view. In D. Brothwell and A. T. Sandison, eds., *Diseases in antiquity.* Springfield, IL: Charles C. Thomas.

Hargreaves, J. R., and J. R. Glynn. 2002. Educational attainment and HIV-1 infection in developing countries: A systematic review. *Tropical Medicine and International Health* 7 (6): 489–98.

Hargreaves, J. R., C. P. Bonell, L. A. Morison, J. C. Kim, G. Phetla, J. D. H. Porter, C. Watts, and P. M. Pronyk. 2007. Explaining continued high HIV prevalence in South Africa: Socioeconomic factors, HIV incidence, and sexual behaviour change among a rural cohort, 2001–2004. *AIDS* 21 (7): S39–S48.

Hargreaves, J. R., C. P. Bonell, T. Boler, D. Boccia, I. Birdthistle, A. Fletcher, P. M. Pronyk, and J. R. Glynn. 2008. Systematic review exploring time trends in the association between educational attainment and risk of HIV infection in sub-Saharan Africa. *AIDS* 22 (3): 403–14.

Harjes, C. E., T. R. Rocheford, L. Bai, T. P. Brutnell, C. B. Kandianis, S. G. Sowinski, A. E. Stapleton, R. Vallabhaneni, M. Williams, E. T. Wurtzel, J. Yan, and E. S. Buckler. 2008. Natural genetic variation in lycopene epsilon cyclase tapped for maize biofortification. *Science* 319 (5861): 330–33.

Hart, T. 2005. *Local innovations using traditional vegetables to improve soil quality.* Indigenous Knowledge (IK) Notes No. 79. Washington, DC: World Bank.

Hartikainen, H. 2005. Biogeochemistry of selenium and its impact on food chain quality and human health. *Journal of Trace Elements in Medicine and Biology* 18 (4): 309–18.

HarvestPlus. 2009. About HarvestPlus. http://www.harvestplus.org/content/about-harvest plus.

Hawkes, C., and M. Ruel. 2006a. The links between agriculture and health: An intersectoral opportunity to improve the health and livelihoods of the poor. *Bulletin of the World Health Organization* 84 (12): 984–90.

———. 2006b. Agriculture and nutrition linkages: Old lessons and new paradigms. In C. Hawkes and M. T. Ruel, eds., *Understanding the links between agriculture and health.* 2020 Vision Focus 13, No. 4. Washington, DC: International Food Policy Research Institute.

Hay, S. I., C. A. Guerra, A. J. Tatem, A. M. Noor, and R. W. Snow. 2004. The global distribution and population at risk of malaria: Past, present, and future. *Lancet Infectious Diseases* 4 (6): 327–36.

Health in Your Hands. 2009. Global handwashing day October 15. http://www.globalhand washingday.org/ (accessed August 4).

Heckman, J. 2006. Skill formation and the economics of investing in disadvantaged children. *Science* 312 (5782): 1900–02.

Hedberg, C. W., M. J. David, K. E. White, K. L. MacDonald, and M. T. Osterholm. 1993. Role of egg consumption in sporadic *Salmonella enteritidis* and *Salmonella typhimurium* infections in Minnesota. *Journal of Infectious Diseases* 167: 107–11.

Henao, J., and C. Baanante. 2001. Nutrient depletion in the agricultural soils of Africa. In P. Pinstrup-Andersen and R. Pandya-Lorch, eds., *The unfinished agenda: Perspectives on overcoming hunger, poverty, and environmental degradation.* Washington, DC: International Food Policy Research Institute.

Hendrickse, R. G. 1997. Of sick turkeys, kwashiorkor, malaria, perinatal mortality, heroin addicts, and food poisoning: Research on the influence of aflatoxins on child health in the tropics. *Annals of Tropical Medicine and Parasitology* 91 (7): 787–93.

Henry, S. H., F. X. Bosch, T. C. Troxell, and P. M. Bolger. 1999. Reducing liver cancer: Global control of aflatoxin. *Science* 286 (5499): 2453–54.

Herforth A. 2009. Food security, nutrition, and health in Costa Rica's indigenous populations. In P. Pinstrup-Andersen and F. Cheng, eds., *Case studies in food policy for developing countries,* Vol. 1: *Policies for health, nutrition, food consumption, and poverty.* Ithaca, NY: Cornell University Press.

Herforth, A. 2010. Promotion of traditional African vegetables in Kenya and Tanzania: A case study of an intervention representing emerging imperatives in global nutrition. Ph.D. dissertation, Cornell University.

Hernandez-Valladares, M., P. Rihet, O. K. ole-MoiYoi, and F. A. Iraqi. 2004. Mapping of a new quantitative trait locus for resistance to malaria in mice by a comparative approach of human chromosome 5q31- q33. *Immunogenetics* 56 (2): 115–17.

Herren, H. R., and P. Neuenschwander. 1991. Biological control of cassava pests in Africa. *Annual Review of Entomology* 36: 257–83.

Herrman, T. 2002. *Mycotoxins in feed grains and ingredients.* MF 2061. Kansas State University Agricultural Experiment Station and Cooperative Extension Service.

HHS/USDA (U.S. Department of Health and Human Services/U.S. Department of Agriculture). 2005. *Dietary guidelines for Americans.* Washington, DC.

Hijmans, R. J., G. A. Forbes, and T. S. Walker. 2000. Estimating the global severity of potato late blight with GIS-linked disease forecast models. *Plant Pathology* 49 (6): 697–705.

Hill, A., J. Elvin, A. C. Willis, M. Aidoo, C. E. M. Allsopp, F. M. Gotch, X. Ming Gao, M. Takiguchis, B. M. Greenwood, A. R. M. Townsend, A. J. McMichael, and H. C. Whittle. 1992. Molecular analysis of the association of HLA – B53 and the resistance to severe malaria. *Nature* 360 (6403): 434–39.

Hirschman, A. 1958. *The strategy of economic development.* New Haven: Yale University Press.

HKI (Helen Keller International). 2003. Integration of animal husbandry into home gardening programs to increase vitamin A intake from foods: Bangladesh, Cambodia, and Nepal. *Asia-Pacific Special Issue Bulletin.* Jakarta.

HKI (Helen Keller International)/Asia-Pacific. 2001. *Homestead food production: A strategy to combat malnutrition and poverty.* Jakarta, Indonesia.

Hoberg, E. P., N. L. Alkire, A. de Queiroz, and A. Jones. 2001. Out of Africa: Origins of the *Taenia* tapeworms in humans. *Proceedings of the Royal Society of London, Series B* 268 (1469): 781–87.

Hoddinott, J., and L. Haddad. 1995. Does female income share influence household expenditures? Evidence from Côte d'Ivoire. *Oxford Bulletin of Economics and Statistics* 57 (1): 77–96.

Hoddinott, J., and Y. Yohannes. 2002. *Dietary diversity as a food security indicator.* Washington DC: Food and Nutrition Technical Assistance (FANTA).

Hoddinott, J., J. A. Maluccio, J. R. Behrman, R. Flores, and R. Martorell. 2008. Effect of a nutrition intervention during early childhood on economic productivity in Guatemalan adults. *Lancet* 371 (9610): 411–16.

Hoffman, S. L., C. C. Campbell, and N. J. White. 2006. Malaria. In R. Guerrant, D. Walker, and P. Weller, eds., *Tropical infectious diseases: Principles, pathogens, and practice,* Vol. 2. 2nd ed. Philadelphia: Churchill Livingstone.

Holmboe-Ottesen, G., O. Mascarenhas, and M. Wandel. 1988. Women's role in food production and nutrition: Implications for their quality of life. *Food and Nutrition Bulletin* 10 (3): 8–15.

Horrocks, P., R. Pinches, Z. Christodoulou, S. A. Kyes, and C. I. Newbold. 2004. Variable *var* transition rates underlie antigenic variation in malaria. *Proceedings of the National Academy of Sciences* 101 (30): 11129–34.

Horton, S., and J. Ross. 2003. The economics of iron deficiency. *Food Policy* 28 (1): 51S–75S.

Hosegood, V., N. McGrath, K. Herbst, and I. M. Timæus. 2004. The impact of adult mortality on household dissolution and migration in rural South Africa. *AIDS* 18 (11): 1585–90.

Hotez, P. J., D. H. Molyneux, A. Fenwick, E. Ottesen, S. Ehrlich Sachs, and J. D. Sachs. 2006. Incorporating a rapid-impact package for neglected tropical diseases with programs for HIV/AIDS, tuberculosis, and malaria. *PLoS Medicine* 3 (5): e102. doi:10.1371/journal.pmed.0030102.

Hotz, C., and K. Brown, ed. 2004. Assessment of the risk of zinc deficiency in populations and options for its control. *Food and Nutrition Bulletin* 25 (1): 194–95.

Huan, N. H., L. V. Thiet, H. V. Chien, and K. L. Heong. 2005. Farmers' participatory evaluation of reducing pesticides, fertilizers, and seed rates in rice farming in the Mekong
Delta, Vietnam. *Crop Protection* 24 (5): 457–64.

Hutin, Y. J. F., A. M. Hauri, and G. L. Armstrong. 2003. Use of injections in healthcare settings worldwide, 2000: Literature review and regional estimates. *British Medical
Journal* 327 (7423): 1075

IAC (InterAcademy Council). 2004. *Realizing the promise and potential of African agriculture.* Amsterdam, the Netherlands.

IDF (International Diabetes Federation). 2006. The Diabetes Declaration and Strategy for
Africa. http://www.idf.org/webdata/docs/Diabetes%20Declaration%20&%20Strate
gy%20for%20Africa_full.pdf (accessed October 27, 2009).

IFAD (International Fund for Agricultural Development). 1998. *Agricultural implements
used by women farmers in Africa.* Rome. http://www.ifad.org/pub/other/!ifadafr.pdf.
————. 2008. Growing demand on agriculture and rising prices of commodities: An
opportunity for smallholders in low-income, agricultural-based countries? Paper
prepared for the round table organized during the 31st session of IFAD's Governing
Council, February 14. Rome: Trade and Markets and Agricultural Development
Economics Divisions of the FAO.

IFDC (International Fertilizer Development Center). 2006. *IFDC Report* 31, 1.

IFPRI (International Food Policy Research Institute). 2008. *Agriculture and health:
Addressing the vital links.* Washington, DC. http://www.ifpri.org/sites/default/files/
publications/aghealthbro.pdf.

IITA (International Institute of Tropical Agriculture). 2002. Child labor in the cocoa sector
of West Africa: A synthesis of findings in Cameroon, Côte d'Ivoire, Ghana, and Nigeria. www.globalexchange.org/campaigns/fairtrade/cocoa/IITACocoaResearch.pdf.

Ikerra, S. T., E. Semu, and J. P. Mrema. 2006. Combining *Tithonia diversifolia* and minjingu
phosphate rock for improvement of P availability and maize grain yields on a
chromic acrisol in Morogoro, Tanzania. *Nutrient Cycling in Agroecosystems* 76 (2–3):
249–60.

ILO (International Labour Organization). 2000. *Safety and health in agriculture.* International Labour Conference, 88th Session, Geneva. Report VI (1). Geneva.

International Society for Infectious Diseases. 2004. Avian influenza, human—East Asia.
ProMED-mail, January 29.

International Women's Health Coalition. 2008. *Women and HIV/AIDS.* New York. http://
www.iwhc.org/resources/hivaidsfactsheet.cfm.

IOM (Institute of Medicine of the National Academies). 2002. *Dietary reference intakes for
energy, carbohydrate, fiber, fat, fatty acids, cholesterol, protein, and amino acids.* Washington, DC: National Academies Press.

IOM–FNB (Institute of Medicine–Food and Nutrition Board). 2005. *Dietary reference
intakes for energy, carbohydrate, fiber, fat, fatty acids, cholesterol, protein, and amino
acids.* Washington, DC: National Academies Press.

IPCC (Intergovernmental Panel on Climate Change). 2001. *Climate change 2001: Synthesis
report: A Contribution of Working Groups I, II, and III to the Third Assessment Report
of the Intergovernmental Panel on Climate Change,* R. T. Watson and Core Writing
Team, eds. New York: Cambridge University Press.

Irungu, C. 2007. *Analysis of markets for African leafy vegetables within Nairobi and its envi-
rons and implications for on-farm conservation of biodiversity.* Rome: Global Facili-
tation Unit for Underutilized Species.

Isanaka, S., N. Nombela, A. Djibo, M. Poupard, D. Van Beckhoven, V. Gaboulaud, P. J.
Guerin, and R. F. Grais. 2009. Effect of preventive supplementation with ready-to-use

therapeutic food on the nutritional status, mortality, and morbidity of children aged 6 to 60 months in Niger: A cluster randomized trial. *Journal of the American Medical Association* 301 (3): 277–85.

Ismail, M. R., J. Ordi, C. Menendez, P. Ventura, J. Aponte, E. Kahigwa, R. Hirt, A. Cardesa, and P. Alonso. 2000. Placental pathology in malaria: A histological, immunohisto-chemical, and quantitative study. *Human Pathology* 31 (1): 85–93.

Isubikalu, P., J. M. Erbaugh, A. R. Semana, and E. Adipala. 1999. Influence of farmer pro-duction goals on cowpea pest management in eastern Uganda: Implications for developing IPM programmes. *African Crop Science Journal* 7 (4): 539–48.

———. 2000. The influence of farmer perception on pesticide usage for management of cowpea field pests in eastern Uganda. *African Crop Science Journal* 8 (3): 317–25.

Jacob, B. G., E. Muturi, P. Halbig, J. Mwangangi, R. K. Wanjogu, E. Mpanga, J. Funes, J. Shilulu, J. Githure, J. L. Regens, and R. J. Novak. 2007. Environmental abundance of Anopheles (*Diptera:Culicidae*) larval habitats on landcover change sites in Karima Village, Mwea Rice Scheme, Kenya. *American Journal of Tropical Medicine and Hygiene* 76 (1): 73–80.

Jamison, D. T., L. J. Lau, and J. Wang. 2004. Health's contribution to economic growth in an environment of partially endogenous technical progress. Working Paper No. 10. Disease Control Priorities Project, Bethesda, MD: Fogarty International Center, National Institutes of Health. http://www.dcp2.org/file/25/wp10.pdf.

Jayne, T., P. Pingali, and M. Villarreal. 2006. HIV/AIDS and the agricultural sector in East-ern and Southern Africa: Anticipating the consequences. In S. R. Gillespie, ed., *AIDS, poverty, and hunger: Challenges and responses.* Washington, DC: International Food Policy Research Institute.

Jayne, T., A. Chapoto, E. Byron, M. Ndiyoi, P. Hamazakaza, S. Kadiyala, and S. Gillespie. 2006. Community-level impacts of AIDS-related mortality: Panel survey evidence from Zambia. *Review of Agricultural Economics* 28 (3): 440–57.

Jayne, T. S., M. Villarreal, P. Pingali, and G. Hemrich. 2006. HIV/AIDS and the agricul-tural sector in Eastern and Southern Africa: Anticipating the consequences. In S. R. Gillespie, ed., *AIDS, poverty, and hunger: Challenges and responses.* Washington DC: International Food Policy Research Institute.

Jayne, T. S., T. Yamano, M. T. Weber, D. Tschirley, R. Benfica, A. Chapoto, and B. Zulu. 2003. Smallholder income and land distribution in Africa: Implications for poverty reduc-tion strategies. *Food Policy* 28 (3): 253–75.

Jiang, Y., P. E. Jolly, W. O. Ellis, J.-S. Wang, T. D. Phillips, and J. H. Williams. 2005. Aflatoxin B1 albumin adduct levels and cellular immune status in Ghanaians. *International Immunology* 17 (6): 807–14.

Johns, T., and P. B. Eyzaguirre. 2006. Linking biodiversity, diet, and health in policy and practice. *Proceedings of the Nutrition Society* 65 (2): 182–89.

Johns, T., and P. Maundu. 2006. Forest biodiversity, nutrition, and population health in market-oriented food systems. *Unasylva* 57 (224): 34–40.

Johns, T., and B. Sthapit. 2004. Biocultural diversity in the sustainability of developing-country food systems. *Food and Nutrition Bulletin* 25 (2): 143–55.

Johnson, D. G. 1997. Agriculture and the wealth of nations. *American Economic Review* 87 (2): 1–12.

Kaaya, N. A., and H. L. Warren. 2005. A review of past and present research on aflatoxin in Uganda. *African Journal of Food Agriculture and Nutrition and Development* 5 (1): 1–18.

Kabambe, V. H., and H. Mloza-Banda. 2000. Options for management of witch weeds in cereals for smallholder farmers in Malawi. In J. M. Ritchie, ed., *Integrated crop management research in Malawi: Developing technologies with farmers.* Chatham, UK: Natural Resources Institute.

Kanampiu, F. K., V. Kabambe, C. Massawe, L. Jasi, D. Friesen, J. K. Ransom, and J. Gressel. 2003. Multi-site, multi-season field tests demonstrate that herbicide seed-coating herbicide-resistance maize controls *Striga* spp. and increases yield in several African countries. *Crop Protection* 22 (5): 697–706.

Karim, R., G. Desplats, T. Schaetzel, A. Herforth, F. Ahmed, Q. Salamatullah, M. Shahjahan, M. Akhtaruzzaman, and J. Levinson. 2005. Seeking optimal means to address micronutrient deficiencies in food supplements: A case study from the Bangladesh Integrated Nutrition Project. *Journal of Health, Population, and Nutrition* 23 (4): 369–76.

Kawachi, I., and L. Berkman. 2000. Social cohesion, social capital, and health. In L. Berkman and I. Kawachi, eds., *Social epidemiology.* New York: Oxford University Press.

Kazianga, H., D. de Walque, and H. Alderman. 2009. Educational and health impact of two school feeding schemes: Evidence from a randomized trial in rural Burkina Faso. World Bank Policy Research Working Paper 4976. World Bank, Washington, DC.

Keiser, J., M. Caldas De Castro, M. F. Maltese, R. Bos, M. Tanner, B. H. Singer, and J. Utzinger. 2005. Effect of irrigation and large dams on the burden of malaria on a global and regional scale. *American Journal of Tropical Medicine and Hygiene* 72 (4): 392–406.

Kenmore, P. K. 1991. Indonesia's integrated pest management: A model for Asia. Report on Food and Agriculture Organization of the United Nations (FAO) intercountry programme for integrated pest control in rice in South and Southeast Asia, Manila, Philippines.

Kes, A., and H. Swaminathan. 2006. Gender and time poverty in Sub-Saharan Africa.I In *Gender, time use, and poverty in Sub-Saharan Africa.* World Bank Working Paper No. 73. Washington, DC: World Bank.

Kessel, A. S., I. A. Gillespie, S. J. O'Brien, et al. 2001. General outbreaks of infectious intestinal disease linked with poultry, England and Wales, 1992–1999. *Communicable Disease and Public Health* 4 (3): 171–77.

Keyzer, M., and L. van Wesenbeeck. 2007. *The Millennium Development Goals: How realistic are they?* 2020 Focus Brief on the World's Poor and Hungry People. Washington, DC: International Food Policy Research Institute.

Khan, N., C. West, S. de Pee, D. Bosch, H. D. Phuong, P. J. M. Hulshof, H. H. Khoi, H. Verhoef, and J. G. A. J. Hautvast. 2007. The contribution of plant foods to the vitamin A supply of lactating women in Vietnam: A randomized controlled trial. *American Journal of Clinical Nutrition* 85 (4): 1112–20.

Khan, Z. R., A. Hassanali, W. Overholt, T. M. Khamis, A. M. Hooper, J. A. Pickett, L. J. Wadhams, and C. M. Woodcock. 2002. Control of witchweed *Striga hermonthica* by intercropping with *Desmodium* spp., and the mechanism defined as allelopathic. *Journal of Chemical Ecology* 28 (9): 1871–85.

Kibata, G. N. 1996. Diamondback moth, *Plutella xylostella* L. (Lepidoptera: Yponomeutidae), a problem pest of brassicae crops in Kenya. In G. Farrell and G. N. Kibata, eds., *Proceedings of the First Biennial Crop Protection Conference, 27–28 March 1996, Nairobi, Kenya.* Nairobi: Kenya Agricultural Research Institute.

Kimetu, J., J. Lehmann, S. Ngoze, D. Mugendi, J. Kinyangi, S. Riha, L. Verchot, J. Recha, and A. Pell. 2008. Reversibility of soil productivity decline with organic matter of differing quality along a degradation gradient. *Ecosystems* 11 (5): 726–39.

Kissling, E., E. H. Allison, J. A. Seeley, S. Russell, M. Bachmann, S. D. Musgrave, and S. Heck. 2005. Fisherfolk are among groups most at risk of HIV: Cross-country analysis of prevalence and numbers infected. *AIDS* 19 (17): 1939–46.

Koona, P., and S. Dorn. 2005. Extracts from *Tephrosia vogelii* for the protection of stored legume seeds against damage by three bruchid species. *Annals of Applied Biology* 147 (1): 43–48.

Kooy, R. F. 1991. *Cellular differentiation and genetic aspects of the trypanosome life cycle.* The Hague, Netherlands: CIP-Gegevens Kononklijke Bibliotheek.

Kosek, M., C. Bern, and R. L. Guerrant. 2003. The global burden of diarrhoeal disease, as estimated from studies published between 1992 and 2000. *Bulletin of the World Health Organization* 81 (3): 197–204.

Kosek, M., R. E. Black, and G. T. Keusch. 2006. Nutrition and micronutrients in tropical infectious diseases. In R. Guerrant, D. Walker, and P. Weller, eds., *Tropical infectious diseases: Principles, pathogens, and practice,* Vol. 1. 2nd ed. Philadelphia: Churchill Livingstone.

Krishna, A. 2007. For reducing poverty faster: Target reasons before people. *World Development* 35 (11): 1947–60.

Kröpelin, S., D. Verschuren, A.-M. Lézine, H. Eggermont, C. Cocquyt, P. Francus, J.-P. Cazet, M. Fagot, B. Rumes, J. M. Russell, F. Darius, D. J. Conley, M. Schuster, H. von Suchodoletz, and D. R. Engstrom. 2008. Climate-driven ecosystem succession in the Sahara: The past 6000 years. *Science* 320 (5877): 765–68.

Kruger, M., C. J. Badenhorst, E. P. G. Mansvelt, J. A. Laubscher, and A. J. Spinnler Benadé. 1996. Effects of iron fortification in a school feeding scheme and anthelmintic therapy on the iron status and growth of six- to eight-year-old schoolchildren. *Food and Nutrition Bulletin* 17 (1): 11–21.

Kuhnlein, H. V., and O. Receveur. 2007. Local cultural animal food contributes high levels of nutrients for Arctic Canadian indigenous adults and children. Journal of Nutrition 137 (4): 1110–14.

Kuntashula, E., G. Sileshi, P. L. Mafongoya, and J. Banda. 2006. Farmer participatory evaluation of the potential for organic vegetable production in the wetlands of Zambia. *Outlook on Agriculture* 35 (4): 299–305.

Lagarde, E., M. Schim, C. Enel, B. Holmgren, R. Dray-Spira, G. Pison, et al. 2003. Mobility and the spread of human immunodeficiency virus into rural areas of West Africa. *International Journal of Epidemiology* 32 (5): 744–52.

Lagarde, M., A. Haines, and N. Palmer. 2007. Conditional cash transfers for improving uptake of health interventions in low- and middle-income countries: A systematic review. *Journal of the American Medical Association* 298 (16): 1900–10.

Lagoke, S. T. O., V. Parkinson, and R. M. Agunbiade. 1991. Parasitic weeds and control methods in Africa. In S. K. Kim, ed., *Combating Striga in Africa.* Proceedings of an International Workshop organized by International Institute of Tropical Agriculture (IITA), International Crops Research Institute for the Semi-Arid Tropics (ICRISAT), and International Development Research Centre (IDRC). Ibadan, Nigeria: IITA.

Lal, R. 1995. Erosion-crop productivity relationships for soils of Africa. *Soil Science Society of America Journal* 59 (3): 661–67.

———. 2007. Anthropogenic influences on world soils and implications to global food security. *Advances in Agronomy* 93: 69–93.

Lambden, J., O. Receveur, and H. V. Kuhnlein. 2007. Traditional food attributes must be included in studies of food security in the Canadian Arctic. *International Journal of Circumpolar Health* 66 (4): 308–19.

Lamptey, P., M. Wigley, D. Carr, and Y. Collymore. 2002. Facing the HIV/AIDS pandemic. *Population Bulletin* 57, no. 3. Washington, DC: Population Reference Bureau.

Leibenstein, H. A. 1957. *Economic backwardness and economic growth.* New York: Wiley.

Lewis, O. 1976. Five families: Mexican case studies in the culture of poverty. New York: Basic Books.

Lewis, L., M. Onsongo, H. Njapau, H. Schurz Rogers, G. Luber, S. Kieszak, J. Nyamongo, L. Backer, A. Dahiye, A. Misore, K. DeCock, C. Rubin, and the Kenya Aflatoxicosis Investigation Group. 2005. Aflatoxin contamination of commercial maize products during an outbreak of acute aflatoxicosis in eastern and central Kenya. *Environmental Health Perspectives* 113 (12): 1763–67.

Lewis, W. J., J. C. vanLenteren, S. C. Phatak, and J. H. Tumlinson. 1997. A total system approach to sustainable pest management. *Proceedings of the National Academy of Sciences of the United States of America* 94 (23): 12243–48.

Li, R., X. Chen, H. Yan, P. Deurenberg, L. Garby, and J. G. Hautvast. 1994. Functional consequences of iron supplementation in iron-deficient female cotton workers in Beijing, China. *American Journal of Clinical Nutrition* 59 (4): 908–13.

Lipton, M., and E. de Kadt. 1988. *Agriculture-health linkages.* Geneva: World Health Organization.

Liu, J., T. Dietz, S. R. Carpenter, M. Alberti, C. Folke, E. Moran, A. N. Pell, P. Deadman, T. Kratz, J. Lubchenco, E. Ostrom, Z. Ouyang, W. Provencher, C. L. Redman, S. H. Schneider, and W. W. Taylor. 2007. Complexity of coupled human and natural systems. *Science* 317 (5844): 1513–16.

Liu, R. H., M. V. Eberhardt, and C. Y. Lee. 2001. Antioxidant and antiproliferative activities of selected New York apple cultivars. *New York Fruit Quarterly* 9 (2): 15–17.

Loevinsohn, M. E., and S. R. Gillespie. 2003. HIV/AIDS, food security and rural livelihoods: Understanding and responding. RENEWAL (Regional Network on AIDS, Livelihoods, and Food Security) Working Paper No. 2/IFPRI (International Food Policy Research Institute) Discussion Paper No. 157. Washington, DC: RENEWAL/IFPRI.

Loevinsohn, M., and A. Rola. 1998. Linking research and policy on natural resource management: The case of pesticides and pest management in the Philippines. In S. Tabor and D. Faber, eds., *Closing the loop: From research on natural resources to policy change.* Policy Management Report No. 8. Maastricht: European Centre for Policy Management.

Löhr, B. 2001. Towards biocontrol-based IPM for the diamondback moth in eastern and southern Africa. Paper presented at Fourth International Workshop on the Management of Diamondback Moth and Other Crucifer Pests, November 26–29, Melbourne.

London, L., S. De Grosbois, C. Wesseling, S. Kisting, H. A. Rother, and D. Mergler. 2002. Pesticide usage and health consequences for women in developing countries: Out of sight, out of mind? *International Journal of Occupational and Environmental Health* 8 (1): 46–59.

Lopez, A. D., C. D. Mathers, M. Ezzati, D. T. Jamison, and C. J. L. Murray. 2006. Global and regional burden of disease and risk factors, 2001: Systematic analysis of population health data. *Lancet* 367 (9524): 1747–57.

Lopman, B., J. Lewis, C. Nyamukapa, P. Mushati, S. Chandiwana, and S. Gregson. 2007. HIV incidence and poverty in Manicaland, Zimbabwe: Is HIV becoming a disease of the poor? *AIDS* 21 (7): S57–S66.

Low, J., M. Arimond, N. Osman, A. K. Osei, F. Zano, B. Cunguara, M. Selemane, D. Abdullah, and D. Tschirley. 2005. *Towards sustainable nutrition improvement in rural Mozambique: Addressing macro- and micro-nutrient malnutrition through new cultivars and new behaviors: Key findings.* East Lansing, MI, USA: Michigan State University Press. http://aec.msu.edu/fs2/tsni/index.htm (accessed November 1, 2007).

Low, J., M. Arimond, N. Osman, B. Cunguara, F. Zano, and D. Tschirley. 2007a. A food-based approach introducing orange-fleshed sweet potatoes increased vitamin A intake and serum retinol concentrations among young children in rural Mozambique. *Journal of Nutrition* 137 (5): 1320–27.

———. 2007b. Ensuring supply and creating demand for a biofortified crop with a visible trait: Lessons learned from the introduction of orange-fleshed sweet potato in drought-prone areas of Mozambique. *Food and Nutrition Bulletin* 28 (Supplement 2): S258–70.

Lozoff, B. 2007. Iron deficiency and child development. *Food and Nutrition Bulletin* 28 (4 Supplement): S560–71.

Luke, N. 2005. Confronting the "sugar daddy" stereotype: Age and economic asymmetries and risky sexual behavior in urban Kenya. *International Family Planning Perspectives* 31 (1): 6–14.

Luke, T. C., and S. L. Hoffman. 2003. Rationale and plans for developing a non-replicating, metabolically active, attenuated *Plasmodium falciparum* sporozoites vaccine. *Journal of Experimental Biology* 206 (21): 3803–08.

Lundberg, S. J., and R. A. Pollack. 1993. Separate-spheres bargaining and the marriage market. *Journal of Political Economy* 101 (6): 988–1010.

Lybbert, T. J., C. B. Barrett, S. Desta, and D. L. Coppock. 2004. Stochastic wealth dynamics and risk management among a poor population. *Economic Journal* 114 (498): 750–77.

Maberly, G. F., F. L. Trowbridge, R. Yip, K. M. Sullivan, and C. E. West. 1994. Programs against micronutrient malnutrition: Ending hidden hunger. *Annual Review of Public Health* 15: 277–301.

Macharia, I., B. Löhr, and H. De Groote. 2005. Assessing the potential impact of biological control of *Plutella xylostella* (diamondback moth) in cabbage production in Kenya. *Crop Protection* 24 (11): 981–89.

MacLeod, C. L., ed. 1988. *Parasitic infections in pregnancy and the newborn*. New York: Oxford University Press.

Maddison, A. 2001. The world economy: A millennial perspective. Development Centre Seminars. Paris: Organisation for Economic Co-operation and Development.

Mafongaya, P. L., A. Bationo, J. Kihara, and B. S. Waswa. 2006. Appropriate technologies to replenish soil fertility in southern Africa. *Nutrient Cycling in Agroecosystems* 76 (2–3): 137–51.

Mahdi, S. 2005. Promising health and food security. *Pambazuka News,* January 20. http://www.pambazuka.org/en/issue/190#cat_2.

Makombe, R. 2005. *Update on tuberculosis control in Africa.* Addis Ababa, Ethiopia: African Union.

Mangili, A., D. H. Murman, A. M. Zampini, and C. A. Wanke. 2006. Nutrition and HIV infection: Review of weight loss and wasting in the era of highly active antiretroviral therapy from the nutrition and healthy living cohort. *Clinical Infectious Diseases* 42 (6): 836–42.

Manuh, T. 1998. Women in Africa's development: Overcoming obstacles, pushing for progress. *Africa Recovery Briefing Paper.* New York: United Nations. http://www.un.org/ecosocdev/geninfo/afrec/bpaper/maineng.htm.

Margo, R. A., and R. H. Steckel. 1982. The height of American slaves: New evidence on slave nutrition and health. *Social Science History* 6 (4): 516–38.

Margulis, L., and K. V. Schwartz. 2001. *Five kingdoms: An illustrated guide to the phyla of life on earth.* New York: W. H. Freeman.

Markwei, C., L. Ndlovu, E. Robinson, and E. Shah. 2008. *International assessment of agricultural knowledge, science, and technology for development, Sub-Saharan Africa: Summary for decision makers.* Washington, DC: Island Press for International Assessment of Agricultural Knowledge, Science, and Technology for Development (IAASTD).

Marriott, E. 2002. *Plague: A story of science, rivalry, and a scourge that won't go away.* New York: Henry Holt.

Martens, W. J. M., L. W. Niessen, J. Rotmans, T. H. Jetten, and A. J. McMichael. 1995. Potential impact of global climate change on malaria risk. *Environmental Health Perspectives* 103 (5): 458–64.

Martorell, R. 1995. Results and implications of the INCAP follow-up study. *Journal of Nutrition* 125 (4 Supplement): 1127S–1138S.

———. 2005. The policy and program implications of research on the long-term consequences of early childhood nutrition: Lessons from the INCAP follow-up. In W. B. Freire, ed., *Nutrition and an active life: From knowledge to action.* Washington, DC: Pan American Health Organization.

Masanjala, W. H. 2006. HIV/AIDS, household expenditure, and consumption dynamics in Malawi. In S. R. Gillespie, ed., *AIDS, poverty, and hunger: Challenges and responses.* Washington DC: International Food Policy Research Institute.

Mashali, A., D. L. Suarez, H. Nabhan, and R. Rabindra. 2005. Integrated management for sustainable use of salt-affected soils. *FAO Soils Bulletin.* Rome.

Matthews G., T. Wiles, and P. Baleguel. 2003. A survey of pesticide application in Cameroon. *Crop Protection* 22 (5): 707–14.

Maxwell, D., C. Levin, and J. Csete. 1998. Does urban agriculture help prevent malnutrition? Evidence from Kampala. Food Consumption and Nutrition Division Discussion Paper 45. Washington, DC: International Food Policy Research Institute.

Maxwell, S., and T. Frankenberger. 1992. *Household food security: Concepts, indicators, measurements: A technical review.* Rome: International Fund for Agricultural Development/ United Nations Children's Fund.

Mazumdar, D. 1959. The marginal productivity theory of wages and disguised unemployment. *Review of Economic Studies* 26 (3): 190–97.

Mbake, C., and B. B. Torrey. 2007. Testing reality: Ideal number of children vs. real total fertility rates in Sub-Saharan Africa. Photocopy, private consultant and Population Reference Bureau.

McElroy, M. B. 1990. The empirical content of Nash-bargained household behavior. *Journal of Human Resources* 25 (4): 559–83.

McElroy, M. B., and M. J. Horney. 1990. Nash-bargained household decisions: Reply. *International Economic Review* 31 (1): 237–42.

McGregor, I. A., M. E. Wilson, and W. Z. Billewicz. 1983. Malaria infection of the placenta in The Gambia, West Africa: Its incidence and relationship to stillbirth, birth weight, and placental weight. *Transactions of the Royal Society of Tropical Medicine and Hygiene* 77 (2): 232–44.

McKnight Foundation CCRP (Collaborative Crop Research Program). 2009. Insect pest management. http://mcknight.ccrp.cornell.edu/projects/WAF_IPM/insect_pest_pr oject.html.

McPeak, J. G., and C. B. Barrett. 2001. Differential risk exposure and stochastic poverty traps among East African pastoralists. *American Journal of Agricultural Economics* 83 (3): 674–79.

Mead, P. S., L. Slutsker, V. Dietz, L. F. McCaig, J. S. Bresee, C. Shapiro, P. M. Griffin, and R. V. Tauxe. 1999. Food-related illness and death in the United States. *Emerging Infectious Disease* 5 (5): 607–25

Medilinks. 2008. Causes of African mortality (WHO estimates, 1999). http://medilinkz. org/healthtopics/statistics/Causes%20of%20mortality%20in%20Africa.htm (accessed June 17).

Mehlum, H., K. O. Moene, and R. Torvik. 2006. Cursed by resources or institutions? *The World Economy* 29 (8): 1117–31.

Mendez, M. A., C. A. Monteiro, and B. M. Popkin. 2005. Overweight exceeds underweight among women in most developing countries. *American Journal of Clinical Nutrition* 81 (3): 714–21.

Menendez, C., J. Ordi, M. R. Ismail, P. J. Ventura, J. J. Aponte, E. Kahigwa, F. Font, and P. L. Alonso. 2000. The impact of placental malaria on gestational age and birth weight. *Journal of Infectious Diseases* 181 (5): 1740–45.

Mensah, P., D. Yeboah-Manu, K. Owusu-Darko, and A. Ablordey. 2002. Street foods in Accra, Ghana: How safe are they? *Bulletin of the World Health Organization* 80 (7): 546–54.

Meyerhoefer, C., and D. E. Sahn. 2006. The relationship between poverty and maternal morbidity and mortality in Sub-Saharan Africa. Cornell Food and Nutrition Working Paper No. 213. Cornell University, Ithaca, NY.

MI (The Micronutrient Initiative), UNICEF (United Nations Children's Fund), GAIN (Global Alliance for Improved Nutrition), NEPAD (New Partnership for Africa's Development), and DBSA (Development Bank of Southern Africa). 2004. *Vitamin and mineral deficiency: A partnership drive to end hidden hunger in Sub-Saharan Africa.* New York.

Michael, Y. L., L. F. Berkman, G. A. Colditz, and I. Kawachi. 2001. Living arrangements, social integration, and change in functional health status. *American Journal of Epidemiology* 153 (2): 123–31.

Millennium Ecosystem Assessment. 2005a. *Ecosystems and human well-being: Health synthesis.* Geneva: World Health Organization.

———. 2005b. *Ecosystems and human well-being: Biodiversity synthesis.* Washington, DC: World Resources Institute.

Miller, S. I., E. L. Hohmann, and D. A. Pegues. 1995. *Salmonella* (including *Salmonella typhi*). In G. L. Mandell, J. E. Bennett, and R. Dolin, eds., *Principles and practice of infectious diseases*, Vol. 2. 4th ed. New York: Churchill Livingstone.

Minja, E. M., T. G. Shanower, J. M. Songa, J. M. Ong'aro, W. T. Kawonga, P. J. Mviha, F. A. Myaka, S. Slumpa, H. Okurut-Akol, and C. Opiyo. 1999. Studies of pigeonpea insect pests and their management in Kenya, Malawi, Tanzania and Uganda. *African Crop Science Journal* 7 (1): 59–69.

Minten, B., and C. B. Barrett. 2008. Agricultural technology, productivity, and poverty in Madagascar. *World Development* 36 (5): 797–822.

Mirle, C. 2006. Predicting the effects of crop-based agricultural programs in household-level consumption in rural Bangladesh: The case of the Northwest Crop Diversification Program in Aditmari Upazilla, Northwest Bangladesh. Ph.D. dissertation, Tufts University.

Mirrlees, J. A. 1976. A pure theory of underdeveloped economies. In L. Reynolds, ed., *Agriculture in development theory.* New Haven, CT: Yale University.

Mishra, V., S. B. Assche, R. Greener, M. Vaessen, R. Hong, P. D. Ghys, J. T. Boerma, A. Van Assche, S. Khan, and S. Rutstein. 2007. HIV infection does not disproportionately affect the poorer in Sub-Saharan Africa. *AIDS* 21 (7): S17–S29.

Moeti, M. 2008. Noncommunicable diseases: An overview of Africa's new silent killers. *African Health Monitor* 8 (1): 2.

Molyneux, D. H., and R. W. Ashford. 1983. *The biology of trypanosoma and leishmania, parasites of man and domestic animals.* London: Taylor and Francis.

Moore, S. E., T. J. Cole, A. C. Collinson, E. Poskitt, I. A. McGregor, and A. M. Prentice. 1999. Prenatal or early postnatal events predict infectious deaths in young adulthood in rural Africa. *International Journal of Epidemiology* 28 (6): 1088–95.

Morris, M., V. A. Kelly, R. J. Kopicki, and D. Byerlee. 2007. *Fertilizer use in African agriculture: Lessons learned and good practice guidelines.* Washington, DC: World Bank.

Morris, S. S., B. Cogill, and R. Uauy, for the Maternal and Child Undernutrition Study Group. 2008. Effective international action against undernutrition: Why has it proven so difficult and what can be done to accelerate progress? *Lancet* 371 (9612): 608–21.

Morse, S. S. 1995. Factors in the emergence of infectious diseases. *Emerging Infectious Diseases* 1 (1): 7–15.

Mosely, W. H., and R. Gray. 1993. Childhood precursors of adult morbidity and mortality in developing countries. In J. N. Gribble and S. H. Preston, eds., *The epidemiological transition.* Washington, DC: National Academies Press.

Mostad, S. B., J. K. Kreiss, A. J. Ryncarz, K. Mandaliya, N. B. Choha, J. Ndinya-Achola, J. J. Bwayo, and L. Corey. 2000. Cervical shedding of herpes simplex virus in human immunodeficiency virus-infected women: Effects of hormonal contraception, pregnancy, and vitamin A deficiency. *Journal of Acquired Immune Deficiency Syndrome* 181 (1): 58–63.

Mosupye, F. M., and A. von Holy. 1999. Microbiological quality and safety of ready-to-eat street-vended foods in Johannesburg, South Africa. *Journal of Food Protection* 62 (11): 1278–84.

Msachi, R., L. Dakishoni, R. Bezner Kerr. 2009. Soils, food and healthy communities: working towards food sovereignty in Malawi. *The Journal of Peasant Studies* 36 (3): 712–17.

Murindamombe, G. Y., E. K. Collison, S. F. Mpuchane, and B. A. Gasee. 2005. Presence of *Bacillus cereus* in street foods in Gaborone, Botswana. *Journal of Food Protection* 68 (2): 342–46.

Murphy, F. A. 1998. Emerging zoonoses. *Emerging Infectious Diseases* 4 (3): 429–35.

Murray, C. J. L., and A. D. Lopez. 1996. *Global burden of disease.* Cambridge, MA: Harvard University Press.

Murrugarra, E., and M. Valdivia. 2000. The returns to health for Peruvian urban adults by gender, age, and across the wage distribution. In W. D. Savedoff and T. P. Schultz, eds., *Wealth from health: Linking social investments to earnings in Latin America.* Washington, DC: Inter-American Development Bank.

Mushati, P., S. Gregson, M. Mlilo, J. Lewis, and C. Zvidzai. 2003. Adult mortality and the economic sustainability of households in towns, estates, and villages in AIDS-affected eastern Zimbabwe. Paper presented at the Scientific Meeting on Empirical Evidence for the Demographic and Socio-Economic Impact of AIDS, Durban, South Africa, March.

Mutero, C. M., F. Amerasinghe, E. Boelee, F. Konradsen, W. van der Hoek, T. Nevondo, and F. Rijsberman. 2005. Systemwide initiative on malaria and agriculture: An innovative framework for research and capacity building. *EcoHealth* 2 (1): 11–16.

Mwanga, R. 2007. Personal communication. National Agricultural Research Organization.

Mwangangi, J., J. Shililu, E. Muturi, W. Gu, C. Mbogo, E. Kabiru, B. Jacob, J. Githure, and R. Novak. 2006. Dynamics of immature stages of *Anopheles arabiensis* and other mosquito species in relation to rice cropping in a rice agro-ecosystem in Kenya. *Journal of Vector Ecology* 31 (2): 245–51.

Mwaniki, S., G. N. Kibata, S. Pete, J. Kamau, H. Dobson, and J. Cooper. 1998. Pests in peri-urban vegetable systems in Kenya: Spray application rates and distributions in the crop. In G. Farrell and G. N. Kibata, eds., *Crop protection research in Kenya: Proceedings of the 2nd Biennial Crop Protection Conference.* Nairobi: Kenyan Agricultural Research Institute.

Myrdal, G. 1957. *Economic theory and under-developed regions.* London: Duckworth.

Nabhan, G. P. 2009. *Where our food comes from: Retracing Nikolay Vavilov's quest to end famine.* Washington, DC: Island Press.

Nagel, R. 2004. Innate resistance to malaria conferred by red cell genetic defects. In S. H. Abdulla, G. Pasvol, and S. L. Hoffman, eds., *Malaria: A hematological perspective.* London: Imperial College Press.

Nahlen, B. L. 2000. Rolling back malaria in pregnancy. *New England Journal of Medicine* 343 (9): 651–52.

Najera, J. A. 2001. Malaria control: Achievements, problems, and strategies. *Parassitologia* 43 (1–2): 1–89.

Narayan, D., D. Narayan-Parker, and M. Walton, eds. 2000. *Voices of the poor: Can anyone hear us?* Oxford: Oxford University Press for the World Bank.

Narayan, D., R. Chambers, M. K. Shah, and P. Petesch. 2000. *Voices of the poor: Crying out for change.* New York: Oxford University Press for the World Bank.

NEPAD (New Partnership for Africa's Development). 2003. *Health strategy: Executive summary.* Midrand, South Africa.

Nestel, P., H. Bouis, J. V. Meenakshi, and W. Pfeiffer. 2006. Biofortification of staple food crops. *Journal of Nutrition* 136 (4): 1064–1067.

New Scientist. 2008. Parasitic worms may boost African HIV rates. July 27. http://www.newscientist.com/article/mg19926665.600-parasitic-worms-may-boost-african-hiv-rates.html.

Ngoze, S., S. Riha, J. Lehmann, L. Verchot, J. Kinyangi, D. Mbugua, and A. Pell. 2008. Nutrient constraints to tropical agroecosystem productivity in long-term degrading soils. *Global Change Biology* 14 (12): 2810–22.

Ngwira, N., S. Bota, and M. Loevinsohn. 2001. *HIV/AIDS, agriculture, and food security in Malawi: Background to action.* RENEWAL Working Paper No. 1. The Hague: International Service for National Agricultural Research, and Lilongwe: Ministry of Agriculture and Irrigation.

Nosten, F., and N. J. White. 2007. Artemisinin-based combination treatment of *Falciparum* malaria. *American Journal of Tropical Medicine and Hygiene* 77 (6 Supplement): 181–92.

Nurkse, R. 1953. *Problems of capital formation in underdeveloped regions.* Oxford: Oxford University Press.

Nussenblatt, V., and R. D. Semba. 2002. Micronutrient malnutrition and the pathogenesis of malarial anemia. *Acta Tropica* 82 (3): 321–37.

Nyariki, D. M., S. Wiggins, and J. K. Imungi. 2004. Levels and causes of household food and nutrition insecurity in dryland Kenya. *Ecology of Food and Nutrition* 41 (2): 155–76.

Nyindo, M. 2005. Complementary factors contributing to the rapid spread of HIV-I in Sub-Saharan Africa: A review. *East African Medical Journal* 82 (1): 40–46.

Oberhelman, R.A., E. S. Guerrero, M. L. Fernandez, M. Silio, D. Mercado, N. Comiskey, G. Ihenacho, and R. Mera. Correlations between intestinal parasitosis, physical growth, and psychomotor development among infants and children from rural Nicaragua. *American Journal of Tropical Medicine and Hygiene* 58 (4): 470–75.

OECD (Organization for Economic Cooperation and Development). 2009. *OECD health data 2009: Frequently requested data.* http://www.oecd.org/document/16/0,2340,en_2649_34631_2085200_1_1_1,00.html.

Oerke, E.-C. 2006. Crop losses to pests. *Journal of Agricultural Science* 144 (1): 31–43.

Oerke, E.-C., and H.-W. Dehne. 2004. Safeguarding production: Losses in major crops and the role of crop protection. *Crop Protection* 23 (4): 275–85.

Oerke, E.-C., H.-W. Dehne, F. Schönbeck, and A. Weber. 1994. *Crop production and crop protection: Estimated losses in major food and cash crops.* Amsterdam: Elsevier.

Ogle, B. M., P. H. Hung, and H. T. Tuyet. 2001. Significance of wild vegetables in micronutrient intakes of women in Vietnam: An analysis of food variety. *Asia Pacific Journal of Clinical Nutrition* 10 (1): 21–30.

Okoth, J. R., G. Khisa, and J. Thomas. 2002. Towards a holistic Farmer Field School approach for East Africa. *LEISA Magazine* (October): 18–19.

Olsen, S. J., H.-L. Chang, T. Yung-Yan Cheung, et al. 2003. Transmission of the severe acute respiratory syndrome on aircraft. *New England Journal of Medicine* 349 (25): 2416–22.

Omemu, A. M., and S. T. Aderoju. 2008. Food safety knowledge and practices of street food vendors in the city of Abeokuta, Nigeria. *Food Control* 19 (4): 396–402.

Ondieki, J. J. 1996. The current state of pesticide management in Sub-Saharan Africa. *The Science of the Total Environment* 188 (Supplement): S30–S34.

Onsongo, J. 2004. Outbreak of aflatoxin poisoning in Kenya. *EPI/IDS Bulletin* 5 (6): 1.

Orr, A. 2003. Integrated pest management for resource-poor African farmers: Is the emperor naked? *World Development* 31 (5): 831–45.

Orr, A., and J. M. Ritchie. 2004. Learning from failure: Smallholder farming systems and IPM in Malawi. *Agricultural Systems* 79 (1): 31–54.

Oswald, A., and J. K. Ransom. 2001. Striga control and improved farm productivity using crop rotation. *Crop Protection* 20 (2): 113–20.

Oxfam International. 2001. *Global HIV/AIDS and Health Fund: Foundation for action or fig leaf?* Oxford, UK. http://www.oxfam.org.uk/what_we_do/issues/hivaids/downloads/ globalhiv.pdf.

Oxfam International and Save the Children. 2002. *HIV/AIDS and food insecurity in Southern Africa.* http://www.oxfam.org.uk/resources/policy/hivaids/downloads/hiv_food _insecurity.pdf.

Paton, N., S. Sangeetha, A. Earnest, and R. Bellamy. 2006.The impact of malnutrition on survival and the CD4 count response in HIV-infected patients starting antiretroviral therapy. *HIV Medicine* 7 (5): 323–30.

Paxson, C., and N. Schady. 2007. Does money matter? The effects of cash transfers on child health and cognitive development in rural Ecuador. Photocopy, World Bank, Washington, DC.

Pays, E., S. Van Assel, M. Laurent, B. Dero, F. Michiels, P. Kronenberger, G. Matthyssens, N. Van Meirvenne, D. Le Ray, and M. Steinert. 1983. At least two transposed sequences are associated in the expression site of a surface antigen gene in different trypanosome clones. *Cell* 34 (2): 359–69.

Peden, D. G. 1998. Agroecosystem management for improved human health: Applying principles of integrated pest management to people. In R. Blair, R. Rajamahendran, L. S. Stephens, and M. Y. Tang, eds., *New directions in animal production systems.* Proceedings of the Annual Meeting of the Canadian Society of Animal Science, July 5–8, Vancouver, Canada.

Pelletier, D. L., C. M. Olson, and E. A. Frongillo. 2006. Food insecurity, hunger, and undernutrition. In B. Bowman and R. Russell, eds., *Present knowledge in nutrition,* 9th ed. Washington, DC: International Life Sciences Institute Press.

Pelletier, D., E. A. Frongillo, D. G. Schroeder, and J.-P. Habicht. 1995. The effects of malnutrition on child mortality in developing countries. *Bulletin of the World Health Organization* 73 (4): 443–48.

Pepin, J., and J. E. Donelson. 2006. African trypanosomiasis (sleeping sickness). In R. Guerrant, D. Walker, and P. Weller, eds., *Tropical infectious diseases: Principles, pathogens, and practice,* Vol. 2. 2nd ed. Philadelphia: Churchill Livingstone.

Pepin, J., F. Milord, N. Khonde, T. Niyonsenga, L. Loko, and B. Mpia. 1994. Gambiense trypanosomiasis: Frequency of, and risk factors for failure of melarsoprol therapy. *Transactions of the Royal Society of Tropical Medicine and Hygiene* 88 (4): 447–52.

Pereira, P. C. M., D. A. Meira, P. R. Curi, N. de Souza and R. C. Burini. 1995. The malarial impact on the nutritional status of Amazonian adult subjects. *Revista do Instituto de Medicina Tropical de São Paulo* 37 (1): 19–24.

Perkins, D., Jr. 1969. Fauna of Çatal Hüyük: Evidence for early cattle domestication in Anatolia. *Science* 164 (3876): 177–79.

Peters, P., D. Kambewa, and P. Walker. 2007. The effects of increasing rates of HIV/AIDS-related illness and death on rural families in Zomba District, Malawi: A longitudinal study. RENEWAL (Regional Network on AIDS, Livelihoods, and Food Security) Working Paper. Washington, DC: International Food Policy Research Institute. http://www.ifpri.org/renewal/renewalpub.asp.

Philipose, A. 2007. HIV/AIDS, gender, and food security in Sub-Saharan Africa. Case Study #3-1 in P. Pinstrup-Andersen and F. Cheng, eds., *Food policy for developing countries: Case studies.* http://cip.cornell.edu/dns.gfs/1200428152.

Phillips, M., T. Sanghvi, R. Suarez, J. McKigney, and J. Fiedler. 1996. The costs and effectiveness of three vitamin A interventions in Guatemala. *Social Science and Medicine* 42 (12): 1661–68.

Pimentel, D., and A. Greiner. 1997. Environmental and socio-economic costs of pesticide use. In D. Pimentel, ed., *Techniques for reducing pesticide use: Economic and environmental benefits.* West Sussex, UK: John Wiley and Sons.

Pimentel, D., and M. Pimentel. 2003. Sustainability of meat-based and plant-based diets and the environment. *American Journal of Clinical Nutrition* 78 (Supplement): 660S–663S.

Pimentel, D., L. McLaughlin, A. Zepp, B. Lakitan, T. Kraus, P. Kleinman, F. Vancini, W. Roach, E. Graap, W. Keeton, and G. Selig. 1991. Environmental and economic effects of reducing pesticide use. *BioScience* 41 (6): 402–09.

Pimentel, D., H. Acquay, M. Biltonen, P. Rice, M. Silva, J. Nelson, V. Lipner, S. Giordano, A. Horowitz, and M. D'Amore. 1992. Environmental and economic costs of pesticide use. *BioScience* 42 (10): 750–60.

Pingali, P. L., ed. 2001. *CIMMYT 1999–2000 world maize facts and trends: Meeting world maize needs: Technological opportunities and priorities for the public sector.* Mexico City: International Maize and Wheat Improvement Center (CIMMYT).

———. 2006. Westernization of Asian diets and the transformation of food systems: Implications for research and policy. *Food Policy* 32 (3): 281–98.

Pingali, P. L., and M. W. Rosegrant. 1994. Confronting the environmental consequences of the Green Revolution in Asia. Environment and Production Technology Division Discussion Paper No. 2. Washington, DC: International Food Policy Research Institute (IFPRI).

Pingali, P. L., C. B. Marquez, and F. G. Palis. 1994. Pesticides and Philippine rice farmer health: A medical and economic analysis. *American Journal of Agricultural Economics* 76 (3): 587–92.

Pinstrup-Andersen, P. 1980. Incorporating nutritional goals into agricultural sector planning. In W. Santos, J. J. Barbosa, D. Chaves, and J. C. Valente, eds., *Nutrition and food science: Present knowledge and utilization.* New York: Plenum Press.

———. 1981a. Ex ante assessment of consumption and nutrition effects of agricultural research. In *Evaluation of agricultural research: Proceedings of a workshop sponsored by NC-148, Minneapolis, May 12–13, 1980.* Minneapolis: Minnesota Agricultural Experiment Station, University of Minnesota.

———. 1981b. *Nutritional consequences of agricultural projects: Conceptual relationships and assessment approaches.* Washington, DC: World Bank.

———. 1983. Incorporating nutritional goals into the design of international agricultural research. *Food and Nutrition Bulletin* 5 (3): 47–56.

————. 1985. The impact of export crop production on human nutrition. In M. Biswas and P. Pinstrup-Andersen, eds., *Nutrition and development*. Oxford: Oxford University Press.

————. 2006. Agricultural research and policy to achieve nutrition goals. In A. de Janvry and R. Kanbur, eds., *Poverty, inequality and development: Essays in honor of Erik Thorbecke*. New York: Springer.

————, P. 2006a. Agricultural research and policy to achieve nutrition goals. In A. deJanvry and R. Kanbur, eds., *Poverty, inequality, and development: Essays in honor of Erik Thorbecke*. New York: Springer.

————. 2006b. Focus the global food system on health and nutrition goals. *International Journal of Agricultural Sustainability* 4 (1): 2–4.

————. 2007. Agricultural research and policy for better health and nutrition in developing countries: A food systems approach. In K. Otsuka and K. Kalirajan, eds., *Contributions of agricultural economics to critical policy issues*. Malden, MA: Blackwell.

Pinstrup-Andersen, P., and D. Franklin. 1977. A systems approach to agricultural research resource allocation in developing countries. In T. M. Arndt, D. Dalrymple, and V. Ruttan, eds., *Resource allocation and productivity in national and international agricultural research*. Minneapolis: University of Minnesota Press.

Pinstrup-Andersen, P., and A. Herforth. 2008. Food security: Achieving the potential. *Environment* 50 (5): 48–60.

Pinstrup-Andersen, P., and R. Pandya-Lorch. 1994. *Alleviating poverty, intensifying agriculture, and effectively managing natural resources*. 2020 Vision Discussion Paper No. 1. Washington, DC: International Food Policy Research Institute (IFPRI).

Pinstrup-Andersen, P., A. Berg, and M. Forman, eds. 1984. *International agricultural research and human nutrition*. Washington, DC, and Rome: International Food Policy Research Institute and United Nations Administrative Committee on Coordination/Sub-Committee on Nutrition.

Pinstrup-Andersen, P., N. Ruiz de Londoño, and E. Hoover. 1976. The impact of increasing food supply on human nutrition: Implications for commodity priorities in agricultural research and policy. *American Journal of Agricultural Economics* 58 (2): 131–42.

Piot, P., R. Greener, and S. Russell. 2007. Squaring the circle: AIDS, poverty, and human development. *PLoS Med* 4 (10): e314.

Pitt, M. M. 1983. Food preferences and nutrition in rural Bangladesh. *The Review of Economics and Statistics* 65 (1): 105–14.

Pitt, M. M., and M. R. Rosenzweig. 1986. Agricultural prices, food consumption, and the health and productivity of Indonesian farmers. In I. Singh, L. Squire, and J. Strauss, eds., *Agricultural household models: Extensions, applications, and policy*. Baltimore, MD: Johns Hopkins University Press.

Plowright, W. 1982. The effects of rinderpest and rinderpest control on wildlife in Africa. *Symposia of the Zoological Society of London* 50: 1–28.

Polgreen, L., and M. Simons. 2006. Global sludge ends in tragedy for Ivory Coast. *New York Times*, Oct. 2. http://www.nytimes.com/2006/10/02/world/africa/02ivory.html (accessed August 4, 2009).

Pollitt, E. 1993. Iron deficiency and cognitive function. *Annual Review of Nutrition* 13: 521–37.

Pollitt, E., and P. Amante, eds. 1984. *Energy intake and activity*. New York: Alan R. Liss.

Popkin, B. M. 1999a. The nutrition transition and its health implications in lower-income countries. *Public Health Nutrition* 1 (1): 5–21.

————. 1999b. Urbanization, lifestyle changes, and the nutrition transition. *World Development* 27 (11): 1905–16.

———. 2001. The nutrition transition and obesity in the developing world. *Journal of Nutrition* 131 (3): 871–73.

———. 2002. An overview on the nutrition transition and its health implications: The Bellagio meeting. *Public Health Nutrition* 5 (1A): 93–103.

———. 2003. The nutrition transition in the developing world. *Development Policy Review* 21 (5–6): 581–97.

Popkin, B. M., and P. Gordon-Larsen. 2004. The nutrition transition: Worldwide obesity dynamics and their determinants. *International Journal of Obesity* 28 (S3): S2–S9.

Population Council. 2005. *Accelerating girls' education: A priority for governments.* New York. http://www.popcouncil.org/gfd/girlseducation.html.

PRB (Population Reference Bureau). 2004. Transitions in world population. *Population Bulletin* 59 (1): 34.

———. 2007. *World population data sheet.* August. Washington, DC. www.census.gov/ipc/www.

Preston, S. 1980. Causes and consequences of mortality declines in less-developed countries during the twentieth century. In R. A. Easterlin, ed., *Population and economic change in developing countries.* Chicago: University of Chicago Press.

Pretty, J. N., A. S. Ball, T. Lang, and J. I. L. Morison. 2005. Farm costs and food miles: An assessment of the full cost of the UK weekly food basket. *Food Policy* 30 (1): 1–19.

Pretty, J., A. D. Noble, D. Bossio, J. Dixon, R. E. Hine, F. W. T. Penning de Vries, and J. I. L. Morison. 2006. Resource-conserving agriculture increases yields in developing countries. *Environmental Science and Technology* 40 (4): 1114–19.

Quisumbing, A. R., and R. S. Meinzen-Dick. 2001. *Empowering women to achieve food security: Overview.* Washington, DC: International Food Policy Research Institute.

Quisumbing, A., and L. Pandolfelli. 2008. *Promising approaches to address the needs of poor female farmers.* Washington, DC: International Food Policy Research Institute.

Quisumbing, A. R., R. S. Meinzen-Dick, and L. C. Smith. 2004. *Increasing the effective participation of women in food and nutrition security in Africa.* 2020 Africa Conference Brief 4. Washington, DC: International Food Policy Research Institute.

Quisumbing, A. R., L. R. Brown, H. S. Feldstein, L. J. Haddad, and C. Peña. 1995. *Women: The key to food security.* Washington, DC: International Food Policy Research Institute.

Rau, B., and G. Rugalema. 2008. The evolving contexts of AIDS and challenges for food security and rural livelihoods. Photocopy, Food and Agriculture Organization of the United Nations, Rome.

Rau, J. N.d. Interview for the FAO with former Federal President Johannes Rau. Rome: Food and Agriculture Organization of the United Nations. http://www.fao.org/monitoringprogress/docs/Int_former_fedPres_JR_en.pdf.

Ravallion, M., and G. Datt. 1996. How important to India's poor is the sectoral composition of economic growth? *World Bank Economic Review* 10 (1): 1–26.

———. 2002. Why has economic growth been more pro-poor in some states of India than others? *Journal of Development Economics* 68 (2): 381–400.

Ravallion, M., S. Chen, and P. Sangraula. 2007. *New evidence on the urbanization of global poverty.* Policy Research Working Paper 4199. Washington, DC: World Bank.

Reardon, T., C. P. Timmer, C. B. Barrett, and R. Berdegué. 2003. The rise of supermarkets in Africa, Asia, and Latin America. *American Journal Agricultural Economics* 85 (5): 1140–46.

Reddy, S., and A. Heuty. 2005. Achieving the Millennium Development Goals: What's wrong with existing analytical models? Unpublished working paper. Available at http://www.millenniumdevelopmentgoals.org.

Reutlinger, S., and M. Selowsky. 1976. *Malnutrition and poverty: Magnitude and policy options.* Baltimore, MD: Johns Hopkins University Press.

Riches, C. R., L. J. Shaxson, J. W. M. Logan, and D. C. Munthali. 1993. *Insect and parastic weed problems in southern Malawi and the use of farmer knowledge in the design of control measures.* Agricultural Administration Research and Extension Network Paper No. 42. London: Overseas Development Institute.

Rivera, J. A., S. Barquera, T. González-Cossío, G. Olaiz, and J. Sepulveda. 2004. Nutrition transition in Mexico and in other Latin American countries. *Nutrition Reviews* 62 (7): S149–S157.

Rivera, J. A., D. Sotres-Alvarez, J.-P. Habicht, T. Shamah, and S. Villalpando. 2004. Impact of the Mexican Program for Education, Health, and Nutrition (Progresa) on rates of growth and anemia in infants and young children: A randomized effectiveness study. *Journal of the American Medical Association* 291 (21): 2563–70.

Robens, J., and K. Cardwell. 2003. The costs of mycotoxin management to the USA: Management of aflatoxins in the United States. *Journal of Toxicology: Toxin Reviews* 22 (2 and 3): 139–52.

Roberfroid, D., P. Kolsteren, T. Hoerée, and B. Maire. 2005. Do growth monitoring and promotion programs answer the performance criteria of a screening program? A critical analysis based on a systematic review. *Tropical Medicine and International Health* 10 (11): 1121–33.

Roberts, G. 2004. Global obesity epidemic. *New Zealand Herald,* November 1. http://www.globalpolicy.org/component/content/article/217/46130.htmlhttp://www.globalpolicy.org/component/content/article/217/46130.html.

Roche, M. L., H. M. Creed-Kanashiro, I. Tuesta, and H. V. Kuhnlein. 2007. Traditional food system provides dietary quality for the Awajún in the Peruvian Amazon. *Ecology of Food and Nutrition* 46 (5–6): 377–399.

Roll Back Malaria Partnership. 2006. *A guide to gender and malaria resources.* Stockholm. http://www.rollbackmalaria.org/docs/advocacy/gm_guide-en.pdf.

Roll Back Malaria/World Health Organization. 2003. *The Abuja Declaration and the plan of action.* WHO/CDS/RBM/2003.46. Geneva.

Rosegrant, M. W., and S. Meijer. 2002. Appropriate food policies and investments could reduce child malnutrition by 43% in 2020. *Journal of Nutrition* 132 (11): 3437S–40S.

Rosegrant, M. W., S. A. Cline, W. Li, T. B. Sulser, and R. A. Valmonte-Santos. 2005. *Looking ahead: Long-term prospects for Africa's agricultural development and food security.* Washington, DC: International Food Policy Research Institute.

Rosegrant, M. W., C. Ringler, T. Benson, X. Diao, D. Resnick, J. Thurlow, M. Torero, and D. Orden. 2006. *Agriculture and achieving the Millennium Development Goals.* Washington, DC: World Bank.

Rosen, S., and J. L. Simon. 2003. Shifting the burden: The private sector's response to the AIDS epidemic in Africa. *Bulletin of the World Health Organization* 81 (2): 131–37.

Rosenstein-Rodan, P. 1943. Problems of industrialization of Eastern and South-Eastern Europe. *Economic Journal* 53 (210–211): 202–11.

Rosenzweig, M. R., and K. I. Wolpin. 1988. Heterogeneity, intrafamily distribution, and child health. *Journal of Human Resources* 23 (4): 437–61.

Ross, M. L. 1999. Review: The political economy of the resource curse. *World Politics* 51 (2): 297–322.

Rossing, W. A. H., R. A. Daamen, and E. M. T. Hendrix. 1994. Framework to support decisions on chemical pest-control under uncertainty, applied to aphids and brown rust in winter wheat. *Crop Protection* 13 (1): 25–34.

Rubaihayo, E. B. 1994. Indigenous vegetables of Uganda. *African Crop Science Conference Proceedings* 1: 120–24.

Ruel, M. 1995. Growth monitoring as an educational tool, an integration strategy, and a source of information: A review of experience. In P. Pinstrup-Andersen, D. Pelletier, and H. Alderman, eds., *Enhancing child growth and nutrition in developing countries: Priorities for action.* Ithaca, NY: Cornell University Press.

———. 2001. *Can food-based strategies help reduce vitamin A and iron deficiencies? A review of recent evidence.* Food Policy Review 5. Washington, DC: International Food Policy Research Institute.

Ruel, M. T. 2003. Operationalizing dietary diversity: A review of measurement issues and research priorities. *Journal of Nutrition* 133 (11 Supplement): 3911S–26S.

Ruel, M. T., P. Menon, J.-P. Habicht, C. Loechl, G.lles Bergeron, G. Pelto, M. Arimond, J. Maluccio, L. Michaud, and B. Hankebo. 2008. Age-based preventive targetingof food assistance and behaviour change and communication for reduction of childhood undernutrition in Haiti: A cluster randomised trial. *Lancet* 371 (9612): 588–95.

Rugalema, G. 2000. Coping or struggling? A journey into the impact of HIV/AIDS in Southern Africa. *Review of African Political Economy* 28 (86): 537–45.

Rupprecht, C. E., J. Gilbert, K. R. Marshall, and H. Koprowski. 1990. Evaluation of an inactivated rabies virus vaccine in domestic ferrets. *Journal of the American Veterinary Medical Association* 196 (10): 1614–16.

Ryan, M. A., R. S. Christian, and J. Wohlrabe. 2001. Hand washing and respiratory illness among young adults in military training. *American Journal of Preventive Medicine* 21 (2): 150–51.

Sachs, J. 2005. *Investing in development. A practical plan to achieve the Millennium Development Goals.* Millennium Project Report to the Secretary General. London: Earthscan.

Sahn, D. E., and H. Alderman. 1988. The effects of human capital on wages, and the determinants of labor supply in a developing country. *Journal of Development Economics* 29 (2): 157–83.

Sahn, D. E., and A. Gerstle. 2004. Child allowances and allocative decisions in Romania households. *Applied Economics* 36 (14): 1513–21.

Sahn, D. E., and D. C. Stifel. 2003. Urban-rural inequality in Africa. *Journal of African Economies* 12 (4): 564–97.

Sahn, D. E., and S. D. Younger. 2010. Living standards in Africa. In S. Anand, P. Segal, and J. Stiglitz, eds., *Debates in the measurement of global poverty.* Oxford: Oxford University Press.

Said, M., and F. M. Itulya. 2003. Intercropping and nitrogen management effects on diamondback moth damage and yield of collards in the highlands of Kenya. *African Crop Science Journal* 11 (1): 35–42.

Saito, K. A. 1994. *Raising the productivity of women farmers in Sub-Saharan Africa.* World Bank Discussion Paper 230. Washington, DC: World Bank.

Sanchez, P. 2002. Soil fertility and hunger in Africa. *Science* 295 (5562): 2019–20.

Sanders, T. A. 2003. Food safety and risk assessment: Naturally occurring potential toxicants and anti-nutritive compounds in plant foods. *Forum of Nutrition* 56: 407–09.

Santos, P., and C. B. Barrett. 2006. Heterogeneous wealth dynamics: On the roles of risk and ability. Photocopy, Cornell University, Ithaca, NY.

Sauerborn, J. 1991. The economic importance of the phytoparasites Orabanche and Striga. In J. K. Ransom, L. J. Musselman, A. D. Worsham, and C. Parker, eds., *Proceedings of the 5th International Symposium of Parasitic Weeds.* Nairobi: International Maize and Wheat Improvement Center (CIMMYT).

Scherr, S. J., and S. Yadav. 1996. *Land degradation in the developing world: Implications for food, agriculture, and the environment to 2020.* 2020 Vision Discussion Paper 14. Washington, DC: International Food Policy Research Institute (IFPRI).

————. 2001. Land degradation in the developing world: Issues and policy options for 2020. In P. Pinstrup-Andersen and R. Pandya-Lorch, eds., *The unfinished agenda: Perspectives on overcoming hunger, poverty, and environmental degradation.* Washington, DC: International Food Policy Research Institute (IFPRI).

Schoenly, K., J. E. Cohen, K. L. Heong, J. A. Litsinger, G. B. Aquino, A. T. Barrion, and G. Arida. 1996. Food web dynamics of irrigated rice fields at five elevations in Luzon, Philippines. *Bulletin of Entomological Research* 86 (1): 45–66.

Schultz, T. W. 1953. *The economic organization of agriculture.* New York: McGraw-Hill.

Schultz, T. P. 1997. Assessing the productive benefits of nutrition and health: An integrated human capital approach. *Journal of Econometrics* 77 (1): 141–58.

Schultz, T. P., and A. Tansel. 1997. Wage and labor supply effects of illness in Côte d'Ivoire and Ghana: Instrumental variable estimates for days disabled. *Journal of Development Economics* 53 (2): 251–86.

SCN (United Nations Standing Committee on Nutrition). 2004. *5th report on the world nutrition situation: Nutrition for improved development outcomes.* Geneva.

Scott, B., V. Curtis, T. Rabie, and N. Garbrah-Aidoo. 2007. Health in our hands, but not in our heads: Understanding hygiene motivation in Ghana. *Health Policy and Planning* 22 (4): 225–33.

Scrimshaw, N. S., and J. P. Sangiovanni. 1997. Synergism of nutrition, infection, and immunity: An overview. *American Journal of Clinical Nutrition* 66 (2): 464S–77S.

Scrimshaw, N., C. Taylor, and J. Gordon. 1968. *Interactions of nutrition and infection.* Geneva: World Health Organization.

Searchinger, T., R. Heimlich, R. A. Houghton, F. Dong, A. Elobeid, J. Fabiosa, S. Tokgoz, D. Hayes, T.-H. Yu. 2008. Use of U.S. croplands for biofuels increases greenhouse gases through emissions from land use change. *Science* 319 (5867): 1238–40.

Seeley, J. A., and E. H. Allison. 2005. HIV/AIDS in fishing communities: Challenges to delivering antiretroviral therapy to vulnerable groups. *AIDS Care* 17 (6): 688–97.

Semaganda, R., D. Gerling, J. P. Legg, S. Kyamanywa, and E. Adipala. 2003. Augmenting the activity of cassava whitefly parasitoids by intercropping cassava with sweet-potato. Paper presented at Third International Bemisia Workshop, Barcelona, March 17–20.

Semba, R. D., and A. M. Tang. 1999. Micronutrients and the pathogenesis of human immunodeficiency virus infection. *British Journal of Nutrition* 81 (3): 181–89.

Semba, R. D., P. G. Miotti, J. D. Chiphangwi, L. P. Yang, A. Saah, and D. Hoover. 1998. Maternal vitamin A deficiency and infant mortality in Malawi. *Journal of Tropical Pediatrics* 44 (4): 232–34.

Sen, A. 1981a. Ingredients of famine analysis: Availability and entitlements. *Quarterly Journal of Economics* 96 (3):433–64.

————. 1981b. *Poverty and famines.* Oxford: Blackwell.

Shafir, T., R. Angulo-Barroso, Y. Jing, M. L. Angelilli, S. W. Jacobson, and B. Lozoff. 2008. Iron deficiency and infant motor development. *Early Human Development* 84 (7): 479–85.

Shapouri, S., and S. Rosen. 2001. *Toll on agriculture from HIV/AIDS in Sub-Saharan Africa.* Washington, DC: U.S. Department of Agriculture, Economic Research Service.

Shepherd, K. D., and M. J. Soule. 1998. Soil fertility management in west Kenya. *Agriculture, Ecosystems, and Environment* 71 (1–3): 133–47.

Sibanda, L., L. T. Marovatsanga, and J. J. Pestka. 1997. Review of mycotoxin work in Sub-Saharan Africa. *Food Control* 8 (1): 21–29.

Silberner, J. 2008. In highland Peru, a culture confronts blight. NPR (National Public Radio), March 30. www.npr.org/templates/story/story.php?storyId=87811933.

Simonsen, L., A. Kane, J. Lloyd, M. Zaffran, and M. Kane. 1999. Unsafe injections in the developing world and transmission of bloodborne pathogens: a review. *Bulletin of the World Health Organization* 77 (10): 789–800.

Singer, P., and J. Mason. 2006. *The way we eat: Why our food choices matter.* Emmaus, PA: Rodale.

Singh, I., L. Squire, and J. Strauss, eds. 1986. *Agricultural household models: Extensions, applications, and policy.* Washington, DC: World Bank.

Smale, M., and A. D. K. Phiri. 1998. Institutional change and discontinuities in farmers' use of hybrid maize seed and fertilizer in Malawi: Findings from the 1996–97 CIMMYT MoALD survey. CIMMYT Economics Working Paper 98-01. Mexico City: International Maize and Wheat Improvement Center (CIMMYT).

Smith, A. 1960 [1776]. *The wealth of nations.* New York: Modern Library.

Smith, D. H., J. Pepin, and A. Stich. 1998. Human African trypanosomiasis: An emerging public health crisis. *British Medical Bulletin* 54 (2): 341–55.

Smith, K., C. B. Barrett, and P. W. Box. 2001. Not necessarily in the same boat: Heterogeneous risk assessment among East African pastoralists. *Journal of Development Studies* 37 (5): 1–30.

Smith, L. C., H. Alderman, and D. Aduayom. 2006. *Food insecurity in Sub-Saharan Africa: New estimates from household expenditure surveys.* Research Report 146. Washington, DC: International Food Policy Research Institute.

Smith, L. C., U. Ramakrishnan, A. Ndiaye, L. Haddad, and R. Martorell. 2003. The importance of women's status for child nutrition in developing countries. In A. R. Quisumbing, ed., *Household decisions, gender, and development: A synthesis of recent research.* Washington, DC: International Food Policy Research Institute (IFPRI).

Smolinski, M. S., M. A. Hamburg, and J. Lederberg, eds. 2003. *Microbial threats to health: Emergence, detection, and response.* Washington, DC: National Academy Press.

Snapp, S. S., and E. Minja. 2003. Integrated crop management experiences from Malawi. In K. Maredia, D. Dakouo, and D. Mota-Sanchez, eds., *Integrated pest management in the global arena.* Wallingford, UK: CAB International.

Snowden, F. M. 2006. *The conquest of malaria: Italy 1900–1962.* New Haven, CT: Yale University Press.

Solomon, D., J. Lehmann, J. Kinyangi, W. Amelung, I. Lobe, S. Ngoze, S. Riha, A. Pell, L. Verchot, D. Mbugua, J. Skjemstad, and T. Schäfer. 2007. Long-term impacts of anthropogenic perturbations on dynamics and speciation of organic carbon in tropical forest and subtropical grassland ecosystems. *Global Change Biology* 13 (2): 511–30.

Sommer, M. 2009. Where the education system and women's bodies collide: The social and health impact of girls' experiences of menstruation and schooling in Tanzania. *Journal of Adolescence.* doi:10.1016/j.adolescence.2009.03.008.

Spahn, K. 2008. *How to effectively scale up interventions and actions that address malnutrition: Three cases from Helen Keller International.* Beijing Conference Policy Brief. Washington, DC: International Food Policy Research Institute.

Starnes, H. F., R. S. Warren, M. Jeevanandan, J. L. Gabrilove, W. Larchian, H. F. Oettgen, and M. F. Brennan. 1988. Tumor necrosis factor and the acute metabolic response to tissue injury in man. *Journal of Clinical Investigation* 82 (4): 1321–25.

Steele, J. H., and A. F. Ranney. 1958. Animal tuberculosis. *American Review of Tuberculosis and Pulmonary Diseases* 77: 908–22.

Steere, A. C. 2001. Lyme disease. *New England Journal of Medicine* 345 (2): 115–25.

Steinfeld, H., P. Gerber, T. Wassenaar, V. Castel, M. Rosales, and C. de Haan. 2006. *Livestock's long shadow: Environmental issues and options.* Rome: Food and Agriculture Organization of the United Nations (FAO).

Steketee, R. W. 2003. Pregnancy, nutrition, and parasitic diseases. *Journal of Nutrition* 133 (5):1661S–67S.

Steketee, R. W., B. L. Nahlen, M. E. Parise, and C. Menendez. 2001. The burden of malaria in pregnancy in malaria-endemic areas. *American Journal of Tropical Medicine and Hygiene* 64 (Supplement 1–2): 28–35.

Stephenson, L. S. 1987. *Impact of helminth infections on human nutrition.* London: Taylor and Francis.

Stephenson, L. S., M. C. Latham, and E. A. Ottesen. 2000. Global malnutrition. *Parasitology* 121 (S1): S5–S22.

Stillwaggon, E. 2006. The ecology of poverty, nutrition, parasites, and vulnerability to HIV/AIDS. In S. R. Gillespie, ed., *AIDS, poverty, and hunger: Challenges and responses.* Washington DC: International Food Policy Research Institute.

Strauss, J. 1986. Does better nutrition raise farm productivity? *Journal of Political Economy* 94 (2): 297–320.

Strauss, J., and D. Thomas. 1998. Health, nutrition, and economic development. *Journal of Economic Literature* 36 (2): 766–817.

Strong, M. 1998. The effect of adult mortality on infant and child mortality. Paper presented at the Workshop on the Consequences of Pregnancy, Maternal Morbidity and Mortality for Women, Their Families and Society, October 19–20. Available from U.S. Agency for International Development, Nairobi, Kenya.

Stubbs, H. A., J. Harris, and R. C. Spear. 1984. A proportionate mortality analysis of California agricultural workers, 1978–1979. *American Journal of Industrial Medicine* 6 (4): 305–20.

Su, X. Z., V. M. Heatwall, S. P. Wertheimer, F. Guinet, J. A. Herrfeldt, D. S. Peterson, J. A. Ravetch, and T. E. Wellems. 1995. The large diverse gene family *var* encodes proteins involved in cytoadherence and antigenic variation of *Plasmodium falciparum*-infected erythrocytes. *Cell* 82 (1):89–100.

Swift, M. J., A. M. N. Izac, and M. van Noordwijk. 2004. Biodiversity and ecosystem services in agricultural landscapes: Are we asking the right questions? *Agriculture, Ecosystems, and Environment* 104 (1): 113–34.

Swift, M. J., P. D. Seward, P. G. H. Frost, J. N. Qureshi, and F. N. Muchena. 1994. Long-term experiments in Africa: Developing a database for sustainable land use under global change. In R. A. Leigh and A. E. Johnson, eds., *Long-term experiments in agricultural and ecological sciences.* Wallingford, UK: CABI.

Swindale, A., and P. Bilinsky. 2006. *Household dietary diversity score (HDDS) for measurement of household food access: Indicator guide, Version 2.* Washington, DC: Food and Nutrition Technical Assistance Project, Academy for Educational Development.

Tait, A. 1980. Evidence for diploidy and mating in trypanosomes. *Nature* 287 (5782): 536–38.

Talukder, A., L. Kiess, N. Huq, S. de Pee, I. Darnton-Hill, and M. W. Bloem. 2000. Increasing the production and consumption of vitamin A-rich fruits and vegetables: Lessons learned in taking the Bangladesh homestead gardening programme to a national scale. *Food and Nutrition Bulletin* 21 (2): 165–72.

Tang, A. M., J. Foreester, D. Spiegelman, T. A. Knox, E. Tchetgen, and S. L. Gorbach. 2002. Weight loss and survival in HIV-positive patients in the era of highly active antiretroviral therapy. *Journal of Acquired Immune Deficiency Syndromes* 31 (2): 230–36.

Tanzarn, N. 2006. The dynamics of HIV and AIDS among fishing communities in Uganda. Paper presented at the International Workshop on Responding to HIV and AIDS in the Fishery Sector in Africa, February 21–22, Lusaka, Zambia.

Taylor, C. E., and R. L. Parker. 1987. Integrating PHC services: Evidence from Narangwal, India. *Health Policy and Planning* 2 (2): 150–61.

Taylor, L. H., S. M. Latham, and M. E. J. Woolhouse. 2001. Risk factors for human disease emergence. *Philosophical Transactions of the Royal Society of London, Series B* 356 (1411): 983–89.

Taylor-Robinson, D., A. Jones, and P. Garner. 2009. Does deworming improve growth and school performance in children? *PLoS Neglected Tropical Diseases* 3 (1): e358. doi:10.1371/journal.pntd.0000358.

Teitelbaum, M. S. 1975. Relevance of demographic transition theory for developing countries. *Science* 188 (4187): 420–25.

Tendekayi, H. G., B. K. Samende, C. Musuna, and D. Chibanda. 2008. The microbiological quality of informally vended foods in Harare, Zimbabwe. *Food Control* 19 (8): 829–32.

Thomas, D. 1990. Intra-household resource allocation: An inferential approach. *Journal of Human Resources* 25 (4): 635–64.

———. 1993. The distribution of income and expenditure within the household. *Annales de Economie et de Statistiques* 29: 109–36.

———. 1994. Like father, like son, like mother, like daughter: Parental resources and child height. *Journal of Human Resources* 29 (4): 950–88.

Thomas, D., and J. Strauss. 1997. Health and wages: Evidence on men and women in urban Brazil. *Journal of Econometrics* 77 (1): 159–85.

Thomas, D., V. Lavy, and J. Strauss. 1996. Public policy and anthropometric outcomes in the Côte d'Ivoire. *Journal of Public Economics* 61 (2): 155–92.

Thomas, D., E. Frankenberg, J. Friedman, J.-P. Habicht, M. Hakimi, N. Ingwersen, Jaswadi, N. Jones, C. McKelvey, G. Pelto, B. Sikoki, T. Seeman, J. P. Smith, C. Sumantri, W. Suriastini, and S. Wilopo. 2006. Causal effect of health on labor market outcomes: Experimental evidence. California Center for Population Research On-Line Working Paper Series CCPR-070-06. University of California, Los Angeles. http://www.ccpr.ucla.edu/ccprwpseries/ccpr_070_06.pdf.

Thomas, M., and J. K. Waage. 1996. *Integration of biological control and hostplant resistance breeding*. Wageningen, The Netherlands: Technical Centre for Agricultural and Rural Co-operation of the European Union (CTA) and International Institute of Biological Control.

Thresh, M., and R. J. Cooter. 2005. Strategies for controlling cassava mosaic virus disease in Africa. *Plant Pathology* 54 (5): 587–614.

Thurston, H. D. 1992. *Sustainable practices for plant disease management in traditional farming systems*. Boulder, CO: Westview Press.

Timmer, C. P. 2002. Agriculture and economic development. In B. L. Gardner and G. C. Rausser, eds., *Handbook of agricultural economics*. Vol. 2A, *Agriculture and its external linkages*. Amsterdam: Elsevier Science.

Tinbergen, J. 1952. *On the theory of economic policy*. Amsterdam: North-Holland.

Tona, L., K. Kambu, N. Ngimbi, K. Cimanga, and A. J. Vlietinck. 1998. Antiamoebic and phytochemical screening of some Congolese medicinal plants. *Journal of Ethnopharmacology* 61 (1): 57–65.

Tontsirin, K., and P. Winichagoon. 1999. Community-based programmes: Success factors for public nutrition derived from the experience of Thailand. *Food and Nutrition Bulletin* 20 (3): 315–22.

Torlesse, H., L. Kiess, and M. W. Bloem. 2003. Association of household rice expenditure with child nutritional status indicates a role for macroeconomic food policy in combating malnutrition. *Journal of Nutrition* 133 (5): 1320–25.

Torrey, E. F., and R. H. Yolken. 2005. *Beasts of the earth: Animals, humans, and disease.* New Brunswick, NJ: Rutgers University Press.

Tracey, K. J., and A. Cerami. 1990. Metabolic responses to Cachectin/TNF: A brief review. *Annals of the New York Academy of Sciences* 587: 325–31.

Trutmann, P., J. Voss, and J. Fairhead. 1993. Management of common bean diseases by farmers in the central African highlands. *International Journal of Pest Management* 39 (3): 334–42.

Turner, C. M. 1997. Rate of antigenic variation in fly-transmitted and syringe-passaged infections of *Trypanosoma brucei. FEMS Microbiology Letters* 153 (1): 227–31.

Turner, P. C., A. C. Collinson, Y. B. Cheung, Y. Y. Gong, A. J. Hall, A. M. Prentice, and C. P. Wild. 2007. Aflatoxin exposure in utero causes growth faltering in Gambian infants. *International Journal of Epidemiology* 36 (5): 1119–25.

Ulph, D. 1988. A general non-cooperative Nash model of household consumption behavior. Photocopy, Bristol University, Bristol, UK.

UN (United Nations). 2001. Roadmap towards the implementation of the United Nations Millennium Declaration. Resolution A/56/326, September 6. http://www.un.org/documents/ga/docs/56/a56326.pdf (accessed August, 4, 2009).

———. 2004a. *A gender perspective on water resources and sanitation.* Background Paper No. 2. New York: UN Interagency Task Force on Gender and Water, Department of Economic and Social Affairs.

———. 2004b. *The impact of AIDS.* New York: United Nations, Department of Economic and Social Affairs, Population Division.

———. 2005. *The Millennium Development Goals report 2005.* New York.

———. 2006a. Political declaration on HIV/AIDS. Resolution adopted by the General Assembly, June 2. New York.

———. 2006b. *World urbanization prospects: The 2005 revision.* New York: Population Division, Department of Economic and Social Affairs, United Nations.

———. 2007a. Right to food must be a reality for all, urges Ban Ki-moon. Press release, October 16.

———. 2007b. *United Nations world population prospects: The 2006 revision.* New York.

———. 2008. *Millennium Development Goals report 2008.* New York: United Nations Department of Economic and Social Affairs. http://www.un.org/millenniumgoals/pdf/The%20Millennium%20Development%20Goals%20Report%202008.pdf (accessed August 4, 2009).

UNAIDS (Joint United Nations Programme on HIV/AIDS). 2006. *2006 report on the global AIDS epidemic.* Geneva.

———. 2008. *2008 report on the global AIDS epidemic.* Geneva.

UNAIDS/WHO (Joint United Nations Programme on HIV/AIDS/World Health Organization). 2006. *AIDS epidemic update: December 2006.* Geneva.

UNAIDS, WFP (World Food Programme), and WHO (World Health Organization). 2008. *HIV, food security, and nutrition.* Policy Brief. Geneva. http://data.unaids.org/pub/Manual/2008/jc1515a_policybrief_nutrition_en.pdf.

UNCCD (United Nations Convention to Combat Desertification). 2004. UN marks World Day to Combat Desertification: Observances worldwide on June 17, 2004. Press release, June 1. Bonn.

UNDP (United Nations Development Programme). 2006. *Human development report.* New York.

UNEP (United Nations Environment Programme). 2007. *Global environment outlook: Environment for development.* Nairobi.

UNEP/GRID-Arendal. 1998. *Mapping indicators of poverty in West Africa.* Environment Information and Assessment Technical Report 8. Report prepared for the Secretariat of the Technical Advisory Committee to the Consultative Group on International Agricultural Research. Rome: Food and Agriculture Organization of the United Nations (FAO).

UNFPA (United Nations Population Fund). 2007. *State of the world population 2007: Unleashing the potential of urban growth.* New York.

———. 2008a. Calling for an end to female genital mutilation/cutting. New York. http://www.unfpa.org/gender/practices1.htm.

———. 2008b. *UNFPA worldwide: Sub-Saharan Africa.* New York. http://www.unfpa.org/worldwide/africa.html.

———. 2009. Sub-Saharan Africa overview. http://www.unfpa.org/worldwide/africa.html (accessed September 24).

UNICEF (United Nations Children's Fund). 2004. *Vitamin and mineral deficiency: A global progress report.* New York. http://www.micronutrient.org/English/View.asp?x=614.

———. 2006. *The state of the world's children 2006.* New York.

———. 2007a. *The state of the world's children 2007.* New York.

———. 2007b. http://www.childinfo.org/areas/childmortality/infantdata.php

———. 2008a. *The state of the world's children 2008.* New York.

———. 2008b. UNICEF makes plea for additional resources to help stave off malnutrition in Ethiopia. Press release, June 2. http://www.unicef.org/infobycountry/ethiopia_44260.html (accessed July 30).

———. 2009a. Soap, toilets, and taps: A foundation for healthy children: How UNICEF supports water, sanitation and hygiene. http://www.unicef.org/wash/files/FINAL_Soap_Toilets_Taps.pdf (accessed August 4, 2009).

———. 2009b. *The state of the world's children 2009.* New York.

UN News Centre. 2007. Measles deaths in Africa plummet by 91 per cent. http://www.un.org/apps/news/story.asp?NewsID=24838&Cr=measles&Cr1=Africa.

Unwin, N., P. Setel, S. Rashid, F. Mugusi, J.-C. Mbanya, H. Kitange, L. Hayes, R. Edwards, T. Aspray, and K. G. M. M. Alberti. 2001. Noncommunicable diseases in sub-Saharan Africa: Where do they feature in the health research agenda? *Bulletin of the World Health Organization* 79 (10): 947–53.

USAID (U.S. Agency for International Development). 2004. Locust swarms threaten crops in Northwest Africa and the Sahel. *USAID in Africa Newsletter* (Summer): 5.

van de Fliert, E., and A. Braun. 1999. *Farmer field school for integrated crop management of sweetpotato: Field guides and technical manual.* Bogor, Indonesia: International Potato Center.

van den Broek, N. 2001. Anemia in pregnancy in sub-Saharan countries. *European Journal of Obstetrics and Gynecology and Reproductive Biology* 96 (1): 4–6.

van der Geest, S. 1982. The illegal distribution of Western medicines in developing countries. *Medical Anthropology* 6 (4): 197–219.

van der Hoeden, J. 1964. *Zoonoses.* Amsterdam: Elsevier.

van der Hoek, H. W., F. Konradsen, P. H. Amerasinghe, D. Perera, M. K. Plyarath, and F. P. Amerasinghe. 2003. Towards a risk map of malaria for Sri Lanka: The importance of house location relative to vector breeding sites. *International Journal of Epidemiology* 32 (2): 280–85.

Vanderpuye-Orgle, J., and C. B. Barrett. 2009. Risk management and social visibility in Ghana. *African Development Review* 21 (1): 5–35.

Vanhamme, L., F. Baturiaux-Hanocq, P. Poelvoorde, et al. 2003. Apolipoprotein L-I is the trypanosome lytic factor of human serum. *Nature* 422 (6927): 83.

van Stuijvenberg, M. E., C. M. Smuts, C. J. Lombard, and M. A. Dhansay. 1999. Effect of iron-, iodine-, and b-carotene-fortified biscuits on the micronutrient status of primary school children: A randomized controlled trial. *American Journal of Clinical Nutrition* 69 (3): 497–503.

van't Riet, H., A. P. den Hartog, and W. A. van Staveren. 2002. Non-home prepared foods: Contribution to energy and nutrient intake of consumers living in two low-income areas in Nairobi. *Public Health Nutrition* 5 (4): 515–22.

van Weelden, S. W., B. Fast, A. Vogt, P. van der Meer, J. Saas, J. J. van Hellemond, A. G. M. Tielens, and M. Boshart. 2003. Procyclic *Trypanosoma brucei* do not use Krebs cycle activity for energy generation. *Journal of Biological Chemistry* 278 (15): 12854.

Vavilov, N. I., and V. F. Dorofeev. 1992. *Origin and geography of cultivated plants.* New York: Cambridge University Press.

Vickerman, K. 1985. Developmental cycles and biology of pathogenic trypanosomes. *British Medical Bulletin* 41 (2): 105.

Victora, C. G., L. Adair, C. Fall, P. C. Hallal, R. Martorell, L. Richter, and H. S. Sachdev for the Maternal and Child Undernutrition Study Group. 2008. Maternal and child undernutrition: Consequences for adult health and human capital. *Lancet* 371 (9609): 340–57.

Volkman, S. K., P. C. Sabeti, D. DeCaprio, et al. 2007. A genome-wide map of diversity in *Plasmodium falciparum. Nature Genetics* 39 (1): 113–19.

von Braun, J. 2005. The Millennium Development Goals in need of strategy and instruments—Agriculture and rural development matter. *Quarterly Journal of International Agriculture* 44 (2): 95–100.

———. 2007a. *When food makes fuel: The promises and challenges of biofuels.* Keynote address at the Crawford Fund Annual Conference, Australia, August 15.

———. 2007b. *The world food situation: New driving forces and required actions.* Washington, DC: International Food Policy Research Institute (IFPRI).

von Braun, J., M. S. Swaminathan, and M. W. Rosegrant. 2004. *Food, nutrition, agriculture, and the Millennium Development Goals.* 2003–2004 Annual Report Essay. Washington, DC: International Food Policy Research Institute.

von Braun, J., with A. Ahmed, K. Asenso-Okyere, S. Fan, A. Gulati, J. Hoddinott, R. Pandya-Lorch, M. W. Rosegrant, M. Ruel, M. Torero, T. van Rheenen, and K. von Grebmer. 2008. *High food prices: The what, who, and how of proposed policy actions.* Policy Brief. Washington, DC: International Food Policy Research Institute.

von Grebmer, K., B. Nestorova, A. Quisumbing, R. Fertziger, H. Fritschel, R. Pandya-Lorch, Y. Yohannes. 2009. *2009 Global Hunger Index: The challenge of hunger: Focus on financial crisis and gender inequality.* Bonn, Washington, DC, and Dublin: Welthungerhilfe, International Food Policy Research Institute, and Concern Worldwide.

Walker, S. P., T. D. Wachs, J. M. Gardner, B. Lozoff, G. A. Wasserman, E. Pollitt, J. A. Carter, and the International Child Development Steering Group. 2007. Child development: Risk factors for adverse outcomes in developing countries. *Lancet* 369 (9556): 145–57.

Way, M. J., and K. L. Heong. 1994. The role of biodiversity in the dynamics and management of insect pests of tropical irrigated rice: A review. *Bulletin of Entomological Research* 84 (4): 567–87.

Weil, D. N. 2005. Accounting for the effect of health on economic growth. NBER Working Paper No. 11455. National Bureau of Economic Research (NBER), Cambridge, MA.

Weiser, S. D., K. Leiter, D. R. Bangsberg, M. L. Butler, F. Percy-de Korte, Z. Hlanze, N. Phaladze, V. Iacopino, and M. Heisler. 2007. Food insufficiency is associated with high-risk sexual behavior among women in Botswana and Swaziland. *PLoS Medicine* 4 (10): e260.

Whaley, S. E., M. Sigman, C. Neumann, N. Bwibo, D. Guthrie, R. E. Weiss, S. Alber, and S. P. Murphy. 2003. Animal source foods to improve micronutrient nutrition and human functioning in developing countries: The impact of dietary intervention on the cognitive development of Kenyan school children. *Journal of Nutrition* 133 (11) (Supplement): 3965S–71S.

White, J. 2002. *Facing the challenge: NGO experiences of mitigating the impacts of HIV/AIDS in Sub-Saharan Africa.* Chatham, UK: Natural Resources Institute, University of Greenwich.

WHO (World Health Organization). 1983. *Measuring change in nutritional status: Guidelines for assessing the nutritional impact of supplementary feeding programmes for vulnerable groups.* Geneva.

———. 1991. *The impact of development policies on health.* Geneva.

———. 1993. *Macroeconomic environment and health with case studies for countries in greatest need.* Geneva.

———. 1994. *Report of the WHO informal consultation on hookworm infection and anaemia in girls and women.* WHO/CDS/IPI/95.1. Geneva.

———. 1996. *Report of the WHO informal consultation on the use of chemotherapy for the control of morbidity due to soil-transmitted nematodes in humans.* WHO/CTD/SIP/96.2. Geneva.

———. 1997. *Intersectoral action for health: A cornerstone for health-for-all in the twenty-first century.* Report to the International Conference, Halifax, Nova Scotia, Canada, April 20–23. Geneva.

———. 1998. *Report of the WHO informal consultation on schistosomiasis control.* WHO/CDS/CPC/SIP/99.2. Geneva.

———. 1999. *Monitoring helminth control programs.* WHO/CDS/CPC/SIP/99.3. Geneva.

———. 2000. *WHO Expert Committee on Malaria: Twentieth report.* WHO Technical Report Series 892. Geneva.

———. 2001. *Macroeconomics and health: Investing in health for economic development.* Report of the Commission on Macroeconomics and Health. Geneva. http://whqlibdoc.who.int/publications/2001/924154550X.pdf.

———. 2002a. *Health, economic growth, and poverty reduction.* Report of the Working Group 1 of the Commission on Macroeconomics and Health. Geneva. http://www.emro.who.int/cbi/pdf/PovertyReduction.pdf.

———. 2002b. *The world health report 2002: Reducing risks, promoting healthy life.* Geneva.

———. 2003a. *Fruit and vegetable promotion initiative: A meeting report 25-27/08/03.* http://www.who.int/hpr/NPH/fruit_and_vegetables/fruit_and_vegetable_report.pdf (accessed August 4, 2009).

———. 2003b. *Nutrient requirements for people living with HIV/AIDS: Report of a technical consultation.* Geneva.

———. 2004a. *Inheriting the world: The atlas of children's health and the environment.* Geneva.

———. 2004b. *Poverty reduction strategy papers: Their significance for health.* Second Synthesis Report WHO/HDP/PRSP/04.1. Geneva.

———. 2004c. *Prevention and control of schistosomiasis and soil-transmitted helminthiasis: Report of a WHO expert committee.* WHO Technical Report Series No. 912. http://www.who.int/wormcontrol/documents/joint_statements/en/ppc_unicef_finalreport.pdf (accessed August 4, 2009).

———. 2004d. *Water, sanitation, and hygiene links to health.* www.who.int/water_sanitation_health/publications/facts2004/en/index.html (accessed August 4, 2009).

———. 2005a. *The evidence is in: Deworming helps meet the Millennium Development Goals.* WHO/CDS/CPE/PVC/2005.12. http://whqlibdoc.who.int/hq/2005/WHO_CDS_CPE_PVC_2005.12.pdf (accessed August 4, 2009).

———. 2005b. *Fact sheet #292: Indoor air pollution and health.* Geneva. http://www.who .int/mediacentre/factsheets/fs292/en/index.html.

———. 2005c. Participants statement from the WHO consultation on nutrition and HIV/AIDS in Africa, Durban, South Africa, 10–13 April, 2005. http://www.sahims .net/archive/specialfocus/specialcoverage_who_consultation2.htm.

———. 2005d. *WHO Global Salm-Surv Strategic Plan, 2006–2010.* Report of a meeting, Winnipeg, Canada, September 14–15, 2005. http://www.who.int/salmsurv/general/ documents/GSS_STRATEGICPLAN2006_10.pdf (accessed August 4, 2009).

———. 2006a. *The African regional health report: The health of the people.* Geneva. http://www.who.int/bulletin/africanhealth/en/index.html.

———. 2006b. *Constitution of the World Health Organization.* Geneva. http://www.who .int/governance/eb/who_constitution_en.pdf.

———. 2006c. *Five keys to safer food manual.* http://www.who.int/foodsafety/publica tions/consumer/manual_keys.pdf (accessed August 4, 2009).

———. 2006d. A guide to healthy food markets. http://www.afro.who.int/des/fos/publica tions/healthy_food_brochure.pdf (accessed August 4, 2009).

———. 2006e. Mycotoxins in African foods: Implications to food safety and health. *AFRO Food Safety Newsletter,* Issue 2, July. http://www.afro.who.int/des/fos/afro_codex- fact-sheets/newsletter_0706.pdf (accessed August 4, 2009).

———. 2006f. *World health statistics 2006.* Geneva.

———. 2007a. *Assessment of iodine deficiency disorders and monitoring their elimination: A guide for programme managers.* Geneva.

———. 2007b. *Unsafe abortion: Global and regional estimates of the incidence of unsafe abortion and associated mortality in 2003.* Geneva: http://who.int/reproductive- health/publications/ unsafeabortion_2003/ua_estimateso3.pdf.

———. 2007c. *The world health report 2007: A safer future: Global public health security in the 21st century.* http://www.who.int/whr/2007/whr07_en.pdf (accessed August 4, 2009).

———. 2008a. *Foodborne disease outbreaks: Guidelines for investigation and control.* http://www.who.int/foodsafety/publications/foodborne_disease/outbreak_guide lines.pdf (accessed August 4, 2009).

———. 2008b. The informal food trade. http://www.afro.who.int/des/fos/afro_codex- fact-sheets/fact3_street-foods.pdf (accessed August 4, 2009).

———. 2008c. *Initiative to estimate the global burden of foodborne diseases.* http://www.who .int/foodsafety/foodborne_disease/ferg/en/index.html (accessed August 4, 2009).

———. 2008d. *World health statistics 2008.* Geneva. http://www.who.int/whosis/whostat/ 2008/en/index.html.

———. 2008e. *Worldwide prevalence of anaemia 1993–2005.* Geneva. http://www.who.int/ vmnis/anaemia/prevalence/summary/ anaemia_status_summary/ en/index.html.

———. 2009a. The global burden of disease: 2004 update. http://www.who.int/health info/global_burden_disease/2004_report_update/en/index.html (accessed August 4, 2009).

———. 2009b. Member information. http://thor.dfvf.dk/pls/portal/GSS.ALL_GSS_MEM BERS_TEST_REP.show (accessed August 4, 2009).

———. 2009c. *Millennium Development Goals: Goal 1: Food safety.* http://www.who.int/ mdg/goals/goal1/food_safety/en/index.html (accessed August 4, 2009).

———. 2009d. *WHO global Salm-Surv.* http://www.who.int/salmsurv/en/ (accessed August 4, 2009).

———. 2009e. *World health statistics 2009.* Geneva.

WHO Commission on Health and Environment. 1992. *Our planet, our health: Report of the WHO Commission on Health and Environment.* Geneva: World Health Organization.

WHO Commission on Social Determinants of Health. 2005. Action on the social determinants of health: Learning from previous experiences. A background paper prepared for the Commission on Social Determinants of Health. WHO Secretariat of the Commission on Social Determinants of Health, Geneva. www.who.int/social_deter minants/en/.

WHO/FAO (World Health Organization/Food and Agriculture Organization of the United Nations). 1996. *Preparation and use of food-based dietary guidelines: Report of a joint FAO/WHO consultation Nicosia, Cyprus.* Geneva: WHO Nutrition Programme.

———. 2003. *WHO/FAO expert report on diet, nutrition, and the prevention of chronic diseases.* Technical Report Series 916. Geneva: WHO.

WHO/UNAIDS (World Health Organization/Joint United Nations Programme on HIV/AIDS). 2003. *Reconciling antenatal clinic-based surveillance and population-based survey estimates of HIV prevalence in Sub-Saharan Africa.* Geneva.

———. 2006. Progress in scaling up access to HIV treatment in low and middle-income countries. June 2006 Fact Sheet. Geneva.

Wiesmann, D., L. Weingärtner, and I. Schöninger. 2006. *The challenge of hunger: Global Hunger Index: Facts, determinants, and trends.* Bonn and Washington, DC: Deutsche Welthungerhilfe and International Food Policy Research Institute.

Wiesmann, D., I. Schöninger, A. K. Sost, H. Dalzell, S. Collins, L. Kiess, and T. Arnold. 2007. *The challenge of hunger 2007.* Bonn, Washington, DC, and Dublin: Deutsche Welthungerhilfe, International Food Policy Research Institute, and Concern.

Williams, J. H., T. D. Phillips, P. E. Jolly, J. K. Stiles, C. M. Jolly, and D. Aggarwal. 2004. Human aflatoxicosis in developing countries: A review of toxicology, exposure, potential health consequences, and interventions. *American Journal of Clinical Nutrition* 80 (5): 1106–22.

Williamson, S., A. Bal, and J. Pretty. 2008. Trends in pesticide use and drivers for safer pest management in four African countries. *Crop Protection* 27 (10): 1327–34.

Wojciki, J. M. 2005. Socioeconomic status as a risk factor for HIV infection in women in East, Central, and Southern Africa: A systematic review. *Journal of Biosocial Science* 37 (1): 1–36.

Wood, J. W. 1994. *Dynamics of human reproduction, biology, biometry, demography,* Hawthorne, NY: Aldine de Gruyter.

Wood, S. 2008. Personal communication. International Food Policy Research Institute, Washington, DC.

World Bank. 1995. *Development in practice: Toward gender equality.* Washington, DC.

———. 2001. *Engendering development.* Washington, DC: World Bank and Oxford University Press.

———. 2006. *Repositioning nutrition as central to development: A strategy for large-scale action.* Washington, DC.

———. 2007a. *World development indicators.* Washington, DC.

———. 2007b. *World development report 2008: Agriculture for development.* Washington, DC.

———. 2009. *Global economic prospects: Commodities at the crossroads.* Washington, DC.

World Bank/IFPRI (International Food Policy Research Institute). 2007. *From agriculture to nutrition: Pathways, synergies and outcomes.* Report No. 40196-GLB. Washington, DC.

WRI (World Resources Institute). 2009. Demographics: Life expectancy at birth, both sexes, in EarthTrends database. Washington, DC. http://earthtrends.wri.org/text/population-health/variable-379.html.

WRI; Department of Resource Surveys and Remote Sensing, Ministry of Environment and Natural Resources, Kenya; Central Bureau of Statistics, Ministry of Planning and

National Development, Kenya; and International Livestock Research Institute. 2007. *Nature's benefits in Kenya: An atlas of ecosystems and human well-being.* Washington, DC and Nairobi: World Resources Institute.

Yamano, T., and T. S. Jayne. 2004. Measuring the impacts of working-age adult mortality on small-scale farm households in Kenya. *World Development* 32 (1): 91–119.

Yamano, T., H. Alderman, and L. Christiaensen. 2005. Child growth, shocks, and food aid in rural Ethiopia. *American Journal of Agricultural Economics* 87 (2): 273–88.

Yang, J., K. J. Meyers, J. van der Heide, and R. H. Liu. 2004. Varietal differences in phenolic content, and antioxidant and antiproliferative activities of onions. *Journal of Agricultural and Food Chemistry* 52 (21): 6787–93.

Young, A. 2007. In sorrow to bring forth children: Fertility amidst the plague of HIV. *Journal of Economic Growth* 12 (4): 283–327.

Zeddies, J., R. P. Schaab, P. Neuenschwander, and H. R. Herren. 2000. Economics of biological control of cassava mealybug in Africa. *Agricultural Economics* 24 (2): 209–19.

Zeitlin, M. F., J. D. Wray, J. B. Stanbury, N. P. Schlossman, and M. J. Meurer. 1982. *Nutrition and population growth: The delicate balance.* Cambridge, MA: Oelgeschlager, Gunn and Hain.

Zeuner, F. E. 1963. *A history of domesticated animals.* London: Hutchinson and Company.

Zhu, Y., H. Chen, J. Fan, Y. Wang, Y. Li, J. Chen, J. X. Fan, S. Yang, L. Hu, H. Leung, T. W. Mew, P. S. Teng, Z. Wang, and C. C. Mundt. 2000. Genetic diversity and disease control in rice. *Nature* 406 (6797): 718–22.

Zimmer, C. 2001. *Evolution: The triumph of an idea.* New York: HarperCollins.

Zinn, H. 2001. *A people's history of the United States.* New York: HarperCollins.

Zuma, K., E. Gouws, B. Williams, and M. Lurie. 2003. Risk factors for HIV infection among women in Carletonville, South Africa: Migration, demography, and sexually transmitted diseases. *International Journal of STD and AIDS* 14 (12): 814–17.

Zwingle, E. 2002. Cities. *National Geographic* (November): 70–99.

Harold Alderman, with both a master's in nutrition (Cornell) and a Ph.D. in economics (Harvard), has naturally gravitated to research on the economics of nutrition and food policy. After spending 10 years at the International Food Policy Research Institute, he joined the World Bank in 1991. For the past seven years he has worked for the bank in the Africa region, advising on social protection policy.

Christopher B. Barrett is the Stephen B. and Janice G. Ashley Professor of Applied Economics and Management and International Professor of Agriculture at Cornell University. He also serves as the Cornell Center for a Sustainable Future's associate director for economic development programs and the director of the Cornell Institute for International Food, Agriculture, and Development's initiative on stimulating agricultural and rural transformation. Barrett's research program has three basic, interrelated thrusts. The first concerns poverty, hunger, food security, economic policy, and the structural transformation of low-income societies. The second considers issues of individual and market behavior under risk and uncertainty. The third revolves around the interrelationship between poverty, food security, and environmental stress in developing countries.

Kathryn J. Boor is at Cornell University. Boor earned a B.S. in food science from Cornell University and an M.S. in food science from the University of Wisconsin. She conducted research for two years in Kenya as a member of a multidisciplinary team working with small-scale farmers to develop sustainable and safe goat milk production and preservation systems, then earned her Ph.D. in microbiology at the University of California, Davis. She was named the director of the Food Safety Laboratory as an assistant professor in the Department of Food Science at Cornell University in 1994. Boor's research focuses on identifying biological factors that affect transmission of bacteria in food systems and developing effective intervention strategies for improved food protection.

Laura K. Cramer is a program coordinator with the Cornell International Institute for Food, Agriculture, and Development, where she helps bring together students, faculty, and staff with international partners for collaborative learning and knowledge sharing in the field of international development. Previously, she was a master's degree student in the International Agriculture and Rural Development program at Cornell. Cramer worked in the food security and sustainable agriculture division of an international nongovernmental organization based in Washington, DC, before coming to the university. She earned a bachelor's degree in anthropology from Indiana University of Pennsylvania.

Stuart Gillespie is a senior research fellow at the International Food Policy Research Institute (IFPRI); director of the Regional Network on AIDS, Livelihoods, and Food Security (RENEWAL); and coordinator of the Agriculture and Health Research Platform. Recent publications include "Poverty, HIV, and AIDS: Vulnerability and Impact in Southern Africa" (special supplement to the journal *AIDS*, November 2007) and the edited 2006 book *AIDS, Poverty, and Hunger: Challenges and Responses*. Gillespie was conference director of the 2005 International Conference on AIDS, Food, and Nutrition Security in Durban. He has a Ph.D. in human nutrition from the London School of Hygiene and Tropical Medicine (1988) and has worked extensively with several international organizations in Africa and Asia. He is currently based in Geneva.

Anna Herforth received her Ph.D. in international nutrition at Cornell University, working with Per Pinstrup-Andersen. She holds an M.S. in food policy and applied nutrition from Tufts University and a B.S. in plant science from Cornell University. Herforth has worked with universities, nonprofit organizations, agencies of the Consultative Group on International Agricultural Research (CGIAR), and the United Nations, advising on nutrition policy and programs in Africa, South Asia, and Latin America. In each region she has spent considerable time working with agricultural and indigenous communities. The theme of her research is the connection between agriculture, human health, and the environment. Currently she is working on these linkages as a Nutrition Specialist at the World Bank.

Dorothy Nakimbugwe was born in Uganda. She received her bachelor's degree in food science and technology at Makerere University, Kampala, in 1994 and a master of food science degree from Cornell University in 1996. She joined Makerere University's Department of Food Science and Technology and taught food quality assurance and human nutrition. In 2001 she embarked on a Ph.D. at the Katholieke University of Leuven in Belgium and received a doctorate in bioscience engineering in 2006. She returned to Makerere University, where she teaches food microbiology and biotechnology and mentors several graduate and undergraduate students. Her research centers on developing nutrient-dense foods for the nutritionally vulnerable.

Rebecca Nelson is an associate professor of plant pathology and plant-microbe biology, plant breeding and genetics, and international agriculture and rural development at Cornell University. She serves as scientific director for the McKnight

Foundation's Collaborative Crop Research Program. Her laboratory works on the genetic dissection of quantitative disease resistance in maize in collaboration with maize geneticists and breeders at Cornell, in Kenya, and elsewhere. Before moving to Cornell in 2001, she worked at the International Potato Center in Lima, Peru (1996–2001) and at the International Rice Research Institute in the Philippines (1988–96). Nelson holds a B.A. from Swarthmore College and a Ph.D. from the University of Washington. A MacArthur Fellow from 1998 through 2003, she has served on the editorial boards of *Theoretical and Applied Genetics, Phytopathology,* and the *International Journal of Agricultural Sustainability.*

Onesmo K. ole-MoiYoi is the chairman (provost) of Kenyatta University and of the Kenya Agricultural Research Institute (KARI). He recently served as director of research and partnerships at the International Center of Insect Physiology and Ecology, Nairobi, where he is a senior visiting scientist. He was director of the Biochemistry and Molecular Biology Laboratory at the International Livestock Research Institute (ILRAD), where he was leader in the Program on Pathophysiology and Genetics. ole-MoiYoi held an assistant professorship and Capps' Scholar positions at Harvard Medical School and a visiting professorship at the Harvard School of Public Health. He was elected to the Human Genome Organization (HUGO) in 1991. ole-MoiYoi is a graduate of Harvard College (1968), where he was a Harvard Aga Khan Scholar, and Harvard Medical School (1972).

Per Pinstrup-Andersen is the H. E. Babcock Professor of Food, Nutrition, and Public Policy, the J. Thomas Clark Professor of Entrepreneurship, and professor of applied economics at Cornell University, as well as professor of agricultural economics at Copenhagen University. Pinstrup-Andersen has served as the International Food Policy Research Institute's director general; an economist at the International Center for Tropical Agriculture, Colombia; and a distinguished professor at Wageningen University. He is the 2001 World Food Prize laureate and the recipient of several awards for his research and communication of research results. His research includes economic analyses of food and nutrition policy, globalization and poverty, agricultural development and research, and technology policy.

Marie T. Ruel has been director of the Poverty, Health, and Nutrition Division of the International Food Policy Research Institute since 2004. She has worked for more than 20 years on issues related to policies and programs to alleviate poverty and child malnutrition in developing countries. She has published extensively on topics such as maternal and child nutrition, agricultural strategies to improve diet quality and micronutrient nutrition focusing on women's empowerment, urban livelihoods, food security, and nutrition. She has served on various international expert committees. She currently supports the Agriculture and Health

Research Platform, a global initiative aimed at promoting and coordinating policy research on the two-way linkages between agriculture and health. Before joining IFPRI in 1996, she was head of the Nutrition and Health Division at the Institute of Nutrition of Central America and Panama (INCAP)/Pan American Health Organization (PAHO) in Guatemala.

David E. Sahn is a professor of economics at Cornell University. He received his Ph.D. from the Massachusetts Institute of Technology and a master's of public health from the University of Michigan. Before coming to Cornell, he was an economist at the World Bank and a senior research fellow at the International Food Policy Research Institute. He also served as a visiting distinguished scholar at the International Monetary Fund. Sahn has published widely on issues of poverty and inequality and the economics of health and education. Sahn serves as an adviser to several international organizations and has also been actively engaged in advising various government policy makers, working to translate research findings into practical measures to improve the living standards of the poor.

Barbara Boyle Torrey has been a visiting fellow at the Population Reference Bureau. She was previously executive director of the Division of Behavioral and Social Sciences at the National Research Council. She was also chief of the Center for International Research at the Census Bureau and an economist at the Office of Management and Budget. She edited *Population and Land Use Change* for the National Academy Press as well as two other books and has published a number of articles on international population and income trends. She did her undergraduate and graduate work at Stanford University's Food Research Institute. She is a member of the National Research Council's Committee on Population.

E. Fuller Torrey is the executive director of the Stanley Medical Research Institute in Chevy Chase, Maryland, and a professor of psychiatry at the Uniformed Services University of the Health Sciences. He received an A.B. from Princeton University, an M.D. from McGill University, and a master's in anthropology and training in psychiatry at Stanford University. He spent two years as a Peace Corps physician in Ethiopia and has returned there several times. He has published more than 200 professional papers and 20 books, including *Beasts of the Earth: Animals, Humans, and Disease* with Robert Yolken. *The Roots of Treason*, his biography of Ezra Pound, was nominated as one of the five best biographies of 1983 by the National Book Critics Circle. He is married to Barbara Boyle Torrey, an economist.

Joachim von Braun is director of the Center for Development Research and professor of economic and technological change at the University of Bonn, Germany.

Previously he served as director general of the International Food Policy Research Institute (IFPRI), the world's premier research center on food and agriculture policy. Von Braun has published extensively, chiefly on the topics of economic and trade policy; agricultural change; natural resources including water; science and technology; and policy issues relating to food security, health, and nutrition. He was president of the International Association of Agricultural Economists in 2000–2003, is a member of academies in China and Germany, and is a fellow of the American Association for the Advancement of Sciences.

Speciosa K. Wandira is a surgeon with a doctor of science degree in global health and population from the Harvard School of Public Health. She served as executive vice president of Uganda for nearly 10 years, held various cabinet portfolios, and was a member of parliament and a member of the Constituent Assembly that drafted Uganda's 1995 Constitution. As deputy minister for industry and technology, she was instrumental in the revival of the industrial sector and the promotion of small-scale and cottage industries in Uganda. Wandira was cochair of the Inter-Academy Council Panel whose report is the basis for recommendations that have been included in the New Plan for Africa's Development (NEPAD). She was the first president of the African Women's Committee on Peace and Development, which advises the secretary general of the African Union on gender issues and the involvement of women in Africa's development. Currently, Wandira is a special presidential adviser to the president of Uganda on microfinance and chairperson of the Board of Directors of the Microfinance Support Center. She is a poultry farmer, special banana grower, and executive director of Concave International—a research and business management support consultancy firm registered in Uganda.

Derrill D. Watson II is a postdoctoral research associate working with Per Pinstrup-Andersen at Cornell University, where he received his doctorate. His research has focused on the topics of food policy, political will, and rural development. He is cowriting a textbook called *Food Policy for Developing Countries* and writing a book on the changing structure of meatpacking in developed and developing countries. He has also written about hunger in Africa, the environmental Kuznets curve, and food system ethics. Watson is a National Merit Scholar and a member of the American Economic Association and the Agricultural and Applied Economics Association.